The Collective Dimension of Freedom of Religion

The right to freedom of religion or belief, as enshrined in international human rights documents, is unique in its formulation in that it provides protection for the enjoyment of the rights "in community with others". This book explores the notion of the collective dimension of freedom of religion or belief with a view to advance the protection of this right.

The book considers Turkey which provides a useful test case where both the domestic legislation can be assessed against international standards, while at the same time lessons can be drawn for the improvement of the standard of international review of the protection of the collective dimension of freedom of religion or belief. The book asks two main questions: what is the scope and nature of protection afforded to the collective dimension of freedom of religion or belief in international law, and, secondly, how does the protection of the collective dimension of freedom of religion or belief in Turkey compare and contrast to international standards? In doing so it seeks to identify how the standard of international review of the collective dimension of freedom of religion can be improved.

Mine Yıldırım is Head of the Norwegian Helsinki Committee Freedom of Belief Initiative in Turkey, Norway.

Law and Religion

The practice of religion by individuals and groups, the rise of religious diversity, and the fear of religious extremism, raise profound questions for the interaction between law and religion in society. The regulatory systems involved, the religion laws of secular government (national and international) and the religious laws of faith communities, are valuable tools for our understanding of the dynamics of mutual accommodation and the analysis and resolution of issues in such areas as: religious freedom; discrimination; the autonomy of religious organisations; doctrine, worship and religious symbols; the property and finances of religion; religion, education and public institutions; and religion, marriage and children. In this series, scholars at the forefront of law and religion contribute to the debates in this area. The books in the series are analytical with a key target audience of scholars and practitioners, including lawyers, religious leaders, and others with an interest in this rapidly developing discipline.

Titles in this series include:

Religious Expression in the Workplace and the Contested Role of Law
Andrew Hambler

Women's Rights and Religious Law
Domestic and International Perspectives
Fareda Banda and Lisa Fishbayn Joffe

The Collective Dimension of Freedom of Religion

A Case Study on Turkey

Mine Yıldırım

Routledge
Taylor & Francis Group
LONDON AND NEW YORK

First published 2017 by Routledge

2 Park Square, Milton Park, Abingdon, Oxfordshire OX14 4RN
52 Vanderbilt Avenue, New York, NY 10017

Routledge is an imprint of the Taylor & Francis Group, an informa business

First issued in paperback 2020

British Library Cataloguing in Publication Data
A catalogue record for this book is available from the British Library

Library of Congress Cataloging in Publication Data
Names: Yıldırım, Mine, author.
Title: The collective dimension of freedom of religion: a case study on Turkey / Mine Yıldırım.
Description: New York: Routledge, 2016. | Series: Law and religion | Includes bibliographical references and index.
Identifiers: LCCN 2016035254 | ISBN 9781138691223 (hbk) | ISBN 9781315535777 (ebk)
Subjects: LCSH: Freedom of religion–Turkey. | Religious tolerance–Turkey. | Freedom of religion.
Classification: LCC KKX2472 .Y55 2016 | DDC 342.56108/52–dc23
LC record available at https://lccn.loc.gov/2016035254

ISBN: 978-1-138-69122-3 (hbk)
ISBN: 978-0-367-59543-2 (pbk)

Typeset in Galliard
by Taylor & Francis Books

Contents

Acknowledgement

It is a very refreshing feeling to finally have come to the stage of writing the Acknowledgments—the final part of the book. It means that I am almost finished with this immense project that has spun over many years.

In the beginning I had a story—a story of injustice. When I first started my research, I began to learn a language and a cluster of norms that would enable me to translate this story into legal questions so that those who hear and speak the human rights law language would be able to understand the story. It is my hope that the story is not completely lost in the jargon as the human story is the reason for this human rights narrative.

I would like to thank the Åbo Akademi and the Graduate School in Human Rights Research for taking a chance with me. Without their support for my doctoral thesis, the basis of this book, this project could not have been possible. Towards the end of the project the Rector's Scholarship for the Finalization of Doctoral Studies (Åbo Akademi) provided additional support.

The Åbo Akademi Institute for Human Rights staff have always been very welcoming and friendly during my stays in Åbo—for this I am grateful. My first supervisors were Kristian Myntti and Martin Scheinin; Kristian Myntti helped me to shape the first outline of the thesis and gave helpful guidance. Martin Scheinin has continued to support my project even after he was no longer officially my supervisor. His availability, observations and example have been key for me throughout this journey and significant for my development as a human rights researcher. I always got the sense that he thought this project was important and this has been a critical support. When Elina Pirjataniemi became my official supervisor, she brought fresh support to the project with her encouragement and practical approach, especially towards the end of the thesis.

I have benefited greatly from the research seminars held within the framework of the Nordic School in Human Rights Research. In addition, the opportunity to study and research at the European University Institute, Florence, has equipped me in my understanding of international law. A significant part of my research, however, has involved independent and solo work in Turkey: reading cases and interviewing members of various religious or belief communities as well as non-believers. This has been often hard, as I have not had many opportunities to discuss these ideas with colleagues who work in this field. While the thesis perhaps could have been better with such opportunities, I hope that discussions during the defence of the thesis and beyond can help refine ideas further.

Over the years, whilst conducting my research, I had the privilege of meeting with and listening to a wide range of individuals from diverse walks whose paths crossed with the right to freedom of thought, conscience, religion or belief. These conversations have challenged my assumptions, opened new windows helping me to see new dimensions of the question at hand and helped me to be less certain and more open to different points of view. These encounters have helped refine my thoughts through reality checks. This has enriched me tremendously. In particular, the resilience and devotion of many have been inspirational. I would like to mention a few names; Laki Vingas, Fatma Benli, Özge Genç, Dilek Kurban, İştar Gözaydın, Claudio Monge, Otmar Oering, Andras Sajo, Cüneyt Sarıyaşar, Turgut Tarhanlı, Kuryakos Ergün, Erdal Doğan, Sait Susin, Ahmet Yorulmaz, Sahak Maşalyan, Umut Şahin, Nazif Yılmaz, Şemi Levi and Doğan Bermek.

Many have shown support and this has been much appreciated. John Kinahan, Felix Corley, Oya Yavuz, the Stefanus Alliance, Zekai Tanyar, I am grateful for your support along the way. I started working for the Norwegian Helsinki Committee in 2013 heading a project on freedom of religion or belief in Turkey. Special thanks are due to the Norwegian Helsinki Committee for venturing into this project with me and allowing me to continue my research and writing alongside the project management. In particular, Gunnar Ekelove Slydal has been a great support.

The external reviewers Nazila Ghanea and Pamela Slotte have done a very thorough job of reviewing the manuscript. They have helped me in clarifying and nuancing conclusions as well as tidying up the text. Their input has certainly improved the thesis and I am thankful for the input I have received.

I would like to express my thanks to Routledge and the editorial team for their excellent work, professional advice and assistance in the final stages of preparing the manuscript for publication.

I embrace the most important things in my life with my best friend and husband Engin; his support and solidarity shown throughout the project have been immense. For his belief that I can do this, and encouragement to be resilient in the face of obstacles, I am grateful. My son Yeşua Can, a cute boy when I started my research, has become a handsome young man as I come to the end. I am thankful for the joy he has given me, a constant reminder of what is important in life. Finally, I am thankful to my parents whose sacrificial giving has made such a difference to me.

Foreword

Freedom of religion or belief issues are constant items of analysis, debate and discussion in academia, policy making and the media. These issues are discussed at all levels—whether sub-state, national, regional or international—and in relation to a range of issues whether stability, conflict, security, education or non-discrimination. They concern the individual woman, man or child or various groups and religion or belief communities. Collective rights—such as property, charitable work, publishing, and assembly—often prove the main subject of discussion and contention. However, what is the basis of collective claims at the national, regional and international level?

Some claim that freedom of religion or belief is purely an individual right. Others, that this freedom can be captured by the term "freedom of worship". Others still, that the rights that are protected merely concern practice in the private sphere, in the home. All these understandings, however, fall far short of what is captured in both international and European human rights law instruments and case law.

In this monograph, Dr Mine Yıldırım offers the first extended and detailed academic study of precisely this topic—the collective dimensions of freedom of religion or belief in international human rights law. This topic is not without difficulty. The extent to which religious communities are recognized as independent rights-holders and are afforded collective autonomy continues to be a matter of diverse interpretation and controversy at the national level. As Mine Yıldırım shows, this divergence is also reflected at the international level, with the difference that can be observed between the United Nations and European approach, that of the UN Human Rights Committee and the Strasbourg organs.

The author carried out this research as part of her doctoral work at Åbo Akademi, Finland. The novelty of her approach lies in the fact that she develops the collective dimensions of freedom of religion or belief by drawing on international and European standards and case law rather than on minority rights instruments and cases. The rationale for doing so is very clear for pragmatic reasons in relation to her case study, which constitutes the second part of this study and addresses the Turkish context.

This second part of the monograph reflects the detailed empirical work that the author has carried out and legal and other documents from Turkish that are brought into the English language through this research. It reflects a uniquely framed approach, one which is deeply informed by the domestic context and carefully applies the international and regional standards and findings to the Turkish context. The Lausanne Treaty looms particularly large in this regard. In doing so, Dr Yıldırım shows great sensitivity to legal and political constraints as well as the historical rationale for the current legal and policy contexts and understandings in Turkey. These legal and policy understandings create either positive receptivity or an inhospitable terrain for certain human rights approaches. She carefully selects and pursues only those human rights understandings that are likely to resonate with this context for a phased improvement to the protection of the collective dimension of freedom of religion or belief in Turkey.

Whilst the method is purposefully selective, it is also thoroughly informed about policy and legal application and praxis. This concern with implementation and realization constitutes a major strength of Yıldırım's approach. Another of its key strengths is its inclusivity, in giving equal consideration to the collective dimension of the freedom of religion or belief rights of minorities, majorities, Muslims and non-Muslims in Turkey.

The readership of this monograph will include lawyers, academics, historians, students, human rights actors, and regional experts or specialists on freedom of religion or belief and/or Turkey. All will find in this monograph a coherent and well-developed theory of the collective dimension of freedom of religion or belief as well as a detailed understanding of the necessity and application of such an approach to the context of Turkey.

Dr Nazila Ghana
Associate Professor in International Human Rights Law, University of Oxford
June 2016

1 Introduction

1.1 The Significance of the Collective Dimension of Freedom of Religion or Belief

Pertinent domestic and international developments involving issues related to tensions affecting religious or belief communities have been increasingly occupying the international law agenda. As a matter of fact, these issues have *always* been pertinent for suppressed belief communities all over the world; however, together with the challenges of accommodating diverse religious traditions in the West, intensified by a particular security context in which they are perceived, there appears to be greater focus on these issues. Amidst legislation and practices that do not seem to provide adequate solutions to new, and indeed long-standing, demands related to the protection of freedom of religion or belief, international law and adjudicators are ever more given the task of providing answers to how we can live with our differences—in particular those of a religious nature—in peace, while respecting human rights, in particular freedom of religion or belief. Indeed, human rights law, in particular provisions pertaining to the right to freedom of religion or belief, may provide some of the answers. Or, perhaps more accurately, those who generate and, thus, shape international law jurisprudence are in the process of *seeking* some of the answers. Freedom of religion or belief is in need of re-conceptualization, yet again, both as a matter of national and international law.[1] This need for re-conceptualization continues as demands pertaining to the right to freedom of religion or belief challenge the boundaries of religious freedom set in national as well as international law. This book aims to contribute to the process of "re-conceptualization" by exploring the notion of the collective dimension of freedom of religion or belief with a view to advance the protection of the right to freedom of religion or belief. The case of Turkey provides a useful test case where both the domestic legislation can be assessed against international standards, while at the same time lessons can be drawn for the improvement of the standard of international review of the protection of the collective dimension of freedom of religion or belief.

1 Durham, W.C. Jr. (1996) "Perspectives on Religious Liberty: A Comparative Framework". In J.D. van der Vyder and J. Witte Jr. eds., *Religious Human Rights in Global Perspective*, 1st ed., City: Martinus Nijhoff Publishers, p.1.

The right to freedom of religion or belief is a fundamental part of the indivisible and interdependent human rights protection scheme. It is "far-reaching and profound; it encompasses freedom of thought on all matters, personal conviction and the commitment to religion or belief, whether manifested individually or in community with others".[2] It is a multi-faceted right that has bearings on many areas of the lives of individuals and groups of believers. For many individuals, it is the right to *be* as they choose to be—rooted deeply in the autonomy of the individual. For many religious or belief communities, it provides vital guarantees for their survival. The right to freedom of religion or belief, as enshrined in international human rights documents, is unique in its formulation in that it provides protection for the enjoyment of the right "in community with others".[3] It is a human right that cannot be realized in isolation, indeed, it crosses categories of human rights with aspects that are individual, aspects that can be effectively realized only in an organized community of individuals and aspects that belong to the field of economic, social and cultural rights such as those related to religious or moral education.[4] While freedom of religion or belief can be exercised individually it is generally the case that persons sharing the same belief organize themselves in various ways and thus engage in acts they do "together".

Two important assumptions have served as starting points for this book. The first assumption is the recognition of a need to advance the effective international and national protection of the collective dimension of the right to freedom of religion or belief that is firmly grounded on the international provisions protecting the right to freedom of religion or belief.[5] This assumption does not, however, imply that the individual dimension is sufficiently protected, inferior or less important, nor does it assert that there is a greater need to focus on the collective dimension compared to the individual dimension. On the contrary, there is a need to improve the protection of the right to freedom of religion or belief both in its individual and collective dimensions in very many diverse states as it is demonstrated in the annual and thematic reports of the UN Special Rapporteur on

2 General Comment No. 22 of the Human Rights Committee on Article 18 para.1. UN Doc. HRI/GEN/1/Rev.1 at 35 (1994).

3 Found both in the Universal Declaration of Human Rights, G.A. Res. 217A, UN Doc. A/810, p. 71, 1948 (hereafter, "the Universal Declaration"), the International Covenant on Civil and Political Rights, G.A. Res. 2200A (XXI), 21 UN GAOR Supp. (No. 16), p. 52, UN Doc. A/6316 (1966), 999 UNTS 171, 16 December 1966 (entered into force on 23 March 1976) (hereafter the "ICCPR") and the European Convention on Human Rights, Convention for the Protection of Human Rights and Fundamental Freedoms, as amended by Protocol No. 11, Rome, 4 November 1950, UNTS 213:222 (entered into force on 3 September 1953) (hereafter "ECHR"), and the Declaration on the Elimination of Religious Intolerance and Discrimination, GA Res. 36/55, 36 UN GAOR Supp. (No. 51), p. 171, UN Doc. A/36/51, 1981 (hereafter "1981 Declaration").

4 Scheinin, M. (1999) Article 18. In G. Alfredsson and A. Eide eds., *The Universal Declaration of Human Rights, A Common Standard of Achievement,* 1st ed., The Hague: Martinus Nijhoff, p. 392.

5 General Comment 22, *supra* note 2.

Freedom of Religion or Belief.[6] This book, however, chooses to focus and examine the collective dimension. The second assumption pertains to the case of Turkey; a better understanding and implementation of the collective dimension of freedom of religion or belief would greatly advance the protection of freedom of religion or belief in Turkey. It has been assumed that many unresolved issues outstanding in Turkey which are at the core of the right to freedom of religion or belief as well as state–religion relationship could be resolved were applicable international human rights standards implemented.

The important work of Arcot Krishnaswami entitled *Study of Discrimination in the Matter of Religious Rights and Practices* has been an important inspiration for this study.[7] Krishnaswami's study presents a broad view of the manifestations of religion or belief and a realistic description of the various forms of tensions at play in relation to states' ensuing obligations.[8] This broad view was a result of a willingness and readiness to be informed by the diverse manifestations of religion or belief of believers following diverse religious or belief traditions from around the world. He recognized the distinct character of the right to freedom of thought, conscience, religion or belief based on the un-identical demands religions or beliefs make of their followers.[9] In particular, however, his early recognition of the importance of the collective aspect of freedom of religion or belief, precisely because interventions and regulations on the part of states are more frequent when manifestations are performed "in community with others" than when they are performed "alone", has concurred with my own observations in the Middle East and Turkey. This has led me to further explore the scope of the collective dimension of freedom of religion or belief and seek to advance its protection as it appeared to have a key function in advancing the protection of human rights and specifically the right to freedom of religion or belief by way of creating normative demands to correct state practice.

Turkey, at first glance, with its reference to 99% Muslim population may give the impression of a religiously homogenous society.[10] However a slightly closer

6 The reports of the UN Special Rapporteur on Freedom of Religion or Belief are full of vivid examples of restrictions of both individual and collective dimensions of freedom of religion or belief. Thematic reports such as on the right to conversion and issues of recognition of religious communities also present the problems and sensitivities surrounding both dimensions. On the right to conversion see Interim Report of the Special Rapporteur on Freedom of Religion or Belief, UN Doc. A/67/303, 13 August 2012. On freedom of religion or belief and recognition issues see UN Doc. A/HRC/19/60, 22 December 2011.

7 Krishnaswami, A. (1960) *Study of Discrimination in the Matter of Religious Rights and Practices.* UN Doc. E/CN.4/Sub.2/200/Rev.1, UN Sales No. 60. XIV.2.

8 Ibid.

9 Ibid.

10 The reference to 99% Muslim population is widely made by politicians and policy makers, however it has not been possible to confirm this assumption with any public institution. An email inquiry to the General Directorate of Civil Registration and Nationality was answered stating that "statistical information pertaining to the religious affiliation of our public is not kept". Email correspondence with the General Directorate of Civil Registration and Nationality on 25 January 2012.

look reveals that Turkey is a true test case for freedom of religion or belief for individuals and communities with its diverse Islamic traditions and "other" religious or belief groups such as Jews, Christians, the Bahai, the Yezidi, atheists and the unconcerned who exist in a secular state and a predominantly Sunni-Muslim society where both are influenced by the Sunni-Muslim religious tradition. Turkey has undertaken international human rights obligations applicable to the protection of the collective dimension of freedom of religion or belief and has a general constitutional commitment to protect freedom of conscience and worship.[11] Nevertheless, national legislation and practice lag far behind international norms. The paradoxical arrangements ensuing the unique state–religion affair, such as the constitutional institution of the Diyanet and compulsory Religious Knowledge and Ethic lessons, the narrow scope of freedom of conscience, religion or belief and particular understanding of secularism and nationalism are presented as only some of the challenges. In this complex context the collective dimension of freedom of religion or belief is viewed with suspicion and suffers, specifically because of its *collective* nature. The complexity of the Turkish case presents itself as an exceptionally useful case to test national compliance with international norms and the standard of international review.

1.2 Objective, Method and Outline of the Study

This study centers on two primary questions; first, what is the scope and nature of protection afforded to the collective dimension of freedom of religion or belief in international human rights law, and, secondly, how does the protection of the collective dimension of freedom of religion or belief in Turkey compare and contrast to international standards? Thus the study consists of two main parts. The first part of the book explores and examines the notion of the collective dimension of freedom of religion or belief, and the scope of its protection in international law with particular reference to the right to acquire legal personality and autonomy of religious or belief communities. In the second part of the book, the case study on Turkey constitutes the applied part of the study; here, the protection of the collective dimension of freedom of religion or belief is assessed with a view to evaluate the compliance of Turkish legislation and practice with international norms as well as seeking to identify how the standard of international review of the collective dimension of freedom of religion or belief can be improved.

In the first part of the book, the discussion primarily draws from the applicable international human rights instruments, in particular the International Covenant on Civil and Political Rights (ICCPR) and the European Convention on Human

11 For an overview of Turkey's international human rights obligations see Chapter 5 of this study. Article 24 of the 1982 Constitution protects freedom of conscience, religion or belief. The Constitution of the Turkish Republic, entry into force on 7 November 1982, for text in English see the translation of Erhan Yaşar. Available: http://www.anayasa.gen.tr/1982Constitution-EYasar.htm [Accessed 15 May 2015].

Rights (ECHR),[12] and the jurisprudence of the Human Rights Committee (HRCttee) and Strasbourg organs and to a certain extent from the work of the UN Special Rapporteur on Freedom of Religion or Belief. Documents of a soft law nature, such as guidelines are also included in the analysis. Secondary resources, such as books, journal writings as well as reports have also been relied upon. The choice of normative sources—the UN protection scheme and the regional Council of Europe (CoE) protection schemes—has been deliberate in order to benefit from and provide a comparative view that this choice will provide. Throughout the study it has become clear that there are considerable differences in the conceptions of these adjudicators of the respective systems.

The second part of the book employs the case-study method to study the protection of the collective dimension of freedom of religion or belief in Turkey. The case study method is particularly suitable for this project as it gives the opportunity to study a phenomenon in a real life context, as well as allowing for an in depth and nuanced study of a complex situation. The scope of the study is limited to the exercise of the collective dimension outside the Diyanet İşleri Başkanlığı (The Presidency of Religious Affairs, the Diyanet or DİB hereafter) framework. In order to ensure a holistic approach, instead of examining the situation for religious communities individually a thematic approach is adopted. The scope of the investigation is confined to the themes that are explored in the theoretical part of the study, namely, the right to acquire legal entity status and the right to freedom in the internal matters of religious/belief communities.

The choice of the normative framework, the collective dimension of the right to freedom of religion, as opposed to a minority rights framework, has proved to be strategically effective in the Turkish context. In brief, Turkey adopts a narrow approach (recognizing only Greek, Armenian and Jewish communities as minorities based on a restrictive interpretation of the Lausanne Peace Treaty, 1923) for the definition of minorities.[13] On the other hand, so far as legal commitments are concerned the right to freedom of religion or belief is protected through Turkey's international obligations (in particular the ICCPR and the ECHR) as well as through constitutional and other legislative provisions. Thus, while not underestimating the obligation of protection within the Lausanne framework, a fundamental set of legal obligations under Turkey's national and international legal commitments that provide a potentially effective normative protection in its own right as well as being complementary to the Lausanne protection scheme exists. Moreover, in contrast to the Lausanne scheme, the international human right treaties that Turkey is a party to have more comprehensive compliance review mechanisms. This approach has had the added advantage of being inclusive of, not only minority communities, but all belief communities, including the majority

12 Primarily and directly by Article 18 of the ICCPR and Article 9 of the ECHR. For a compilation of UN general provisions relevant to the freedom of religion or belief see the Digest of the Special Rapporteur on freedom of religion or belief. Available: http://www.ohchr.org/EN/Issues/FreedomReligion/Pages/Standards.aspx [Accessed 15 May 2016].

13 For more on Turkey's application of the Lausanne Peace Treaty see Chapter 5.

Sunni-Muslim community in Turkey. Turkey's legal and political commitments in the sphere of freedom of religion or belief offer critical potential for advancing freedom of religion or belief. The scope of protection provided through the collective dimension of freedom of religion or belief provisions lends itself to an effective legal framework for the protection of acts that many religious/belief communities engage in collectively.

In the case of Turkey, the primary normative sources have included the Turkish legislation and case law. In order to assess the compatibility of national legislation and practice with international law pertinent to the key aspects of the collective dimension of freedom for religion or belief, first applicable legal frameworks are described. The case study focuses largely on primary sources such as legal instruments, judgments, administrative body decisions and interview material. Secondary sources, including books, journal articles, reports and newspaper articles have also been used, in particular with reference to historical, political and sociological background. The approach of the Turkish judiciary is submitted through a critical analysis of case law and relevant executive and administrative decisions. Yet, the method employed in this study assumes that analysis based on only written national laws will be inadequate to assess domestic compliance with international standards. This assumption is based on observations made during interviews with various religious community representatives who pointed to important administrative processes and decisions that determine *rules* and outcomes relevant for their internal affairs. Some of these administrative processes have not become the subject of legal disputes but the administrative processes and decisions are indicative of applied rules and practice in the field of freedom of religion or belief. For this reason it has been necessary to determine the content and nature of rules that are applied and patterns established through the decisions of public administrators affecting communities or persons exercising their rights. Finally, it is assumed that the rights holders need to be included in the research on compliance control in order to acquire knowledge on practice and a genuine understanding on trends and current issues that belief communities face in Turkey.

The interviews that were conducted with representatives of religious/belief communities were not concerned with the collection of quantitative data, but rather with gaining insight into relevant issues and the context. Thus an in-depth interview method was employed, which is considered a key tool for hearing and understanding in social science.[14] The interviews guided the identification of practices and patterns, applicable rules or lack of rules and the extent to which these meet the needs of the various religious/belief communities and, thirdly, problem areas. Finally, they were an effective means of including the perspective of religious/belief communities which provided essential information and guidance for the study.[15] On the other hand, some methodological challenges were

14 Seidman I. (2006) *Interviewing as Qualitative Research: A Guide for Researchers in Education and Social Sciences*, New York: Teachers College Press.

15 Mayring P. (2000) *Nitel Sosyal Araştırmaya Giriş* [Introduction to Qualitative Social Research], Adana: Baki Kitapevi, p. 22.

encountered as regards access to information. Interviews that have been conducted and interview requests that have been turned down, demonstrate that confidentiality was a concern for interviewees and potential interviewees. Those who agreed to interviews, at times, showed reluctance to provide specific references (case number, name of institutions etc.) on relevant cases or administrative processes and decisions. The interviews were conducted in Turkish and then the findings were translated as they have been incorporated into this work.

Chapter 2 introduces the notion of the collective dimension of freedom of religion or belief. Key provisions guaranteeing freedom of religion or belief protect the right of individuals, either alone or *in community with others* and in public and private, to manifest their religion or belief, in worship, teaching, practice and observance. It is argued that the collective dimension of freedom of religion or belief is based both on the acts that are protected which are either exercised in community with others and the groups and/or diverse forms of collectivities that exercise this right. The state–religion relations that are deeply contextual are highlighted in this context as being challenged by the normative demands created by obligations ensuing from the provisions protecting the collective dimension of freedom of religion or belief. The attempt to identify these normative demands reveals that the latter are less than clear and that the restraint of international adjudicators has an undermining effect on the protection of freedom of religion or belief for all.

When it comes to individuals coming together in the exercise of their right to freedom of religion, the right to acquire legal personality gains a significant role as an enabling and empowering right. Chapter 3 seeks to explore the protection of the right to acquire legal personality for religious or belief communities. Firstly, the importance and implications of legal personality on the enjoyment of the right to freedom of religion or belief for religious/belief communities are examined. Secondly, grounds for restrictions and other legal problems that arise in the application of restrictions are analyzed with a view to assess and examine the potential of international review to curb repressive legislation and practice.

Chapter 4 explores the notion of autonomy—freedom in the internal matters—of religious or belief communities. Considering that autonomy can have a potentially extensive scope, to a great extent determined by the comprehensiveness of the dogma of the religion or belief in question, a broad approach to autonomy and its manifestations may be employed. So far, autonomy has been generally viewed as restricted to the organizational matters of religious or belief communities and this sphere has been respected. It is argued that if the autonomy perspective is applied as an interpretive tool more rigorous scrutiny of restrictions may be achieved. Where autonomous features of religious or belief communities are not accommodated by states, the latter will have a greater burden to justify the imposed restrictions. In the autonomous sphere many different aspects of the community's manifestations of religion or belief are found, both prescribed and motivated by the belief in question, such as freedom in dogma and teaching, *inter alia*, establishment of places of worship, teaching of religion or belief, freedom in internal organization. In addition, whether the use of religious law in certain matters may be a protected form of manifestation of religion or belief in practice in international law is explored.

The second part of this book aims to present a case study on the protection of the collective dimension of freedom of religion or belief; the case study on Turkey focuses on two key aspects of the collective dimension: the right to acquire legal personality and freedom in the internal affairs of religious/belief groups with particular reference to the right to establish places of worship, the right to teach religion or belief in suitable places, the right to elect and appoint religious leaders and the right to observe days of rest and holidays in accordance with religion or belief.

The Turkish context is introduced in Chapter 5, with a view to provide the demographic and historical background as well as the legal basis for the themes to be examined in the next two chapters. This chapter critically examines the protection of the right to freedom of religion or belief in the domestic legal framework. Here Turkey's international human rights commitments including its minority protections scheme stemming from the Lausanne Peace Treaty and the Constitutional protection of freedom of religion or belief is presented. In addition, the principle of secularism (*laiklik* in Turkish), the Presidency of Religious Affairs (the Diyanet) and the compulsory Religious Culture and Ethics lessons which stand out as paradoxical state–religion arrangements are analyzed. Moreover, the boundaries of the right to freedom of religion or belief, particularly in its individual dimension, are outlined by considering key issues such as coercion to disclose religion or belief, manifestation of religion or belief—religious symbols—in the public sphere and conscientious objection to military service. It will be argued that manifestations of religion or belief are, often, restricted based on aims to protect national security, secularism and to uphold nationalism which, in effect, ultimately protect the interests of the state. Moreover, in order to illustrate the changing paradigm pertaining to state–religion relations in Turkey in the context of freedom of religion or belief a complementary historical overview is presented. It is assumed that these are indispensable for our understanding of the relevant legislative, judicial and administrative rules, interpretation of the law and measures pertaining to the collective dimension of freedom of religion or belief and challenges and opportunities therein.

Chapter 6 focuses on the question of, to what extent, if any, the right to acquire legal personality is protected in the Turkish legislation and practice. Due to the availability of relevant case law it has been possible to engage in extensive analysis of jurisprudence in this part. In Turkey, currently, no religious or belief group may acquire legal personality, as such. The chapter seeks to examine the Turkish legislation and practice pertaining to acquisition of legal personality—to the extent that is applicable for belief communities—and make an assessment of compatibility with international standards determined in Chapter 3. Therefore the available forms of legal entity, namely associations and foundations, are critically assessed, particularly regarding their accessibility, suitability and adequacy for religious or belief groups. It will be demonstrated that the denial of the right to acquire legal personality for belief or religious groups, *per se*, and that the existing alternative formulas lag far behind the standards created by relevant international law provisions.

The legislation and practice pertaining to the right to establish places of worship, the right to teach religion or belief in suitable places, the right to elect and appoint religious leaders and the right to observe days of rest and holidays in accordance with religion or belief are examined in Chapter 7 with a view to critically assess the extent of protection afforded to freedom of religious or belief groups in their internal matters. To this end, in addition to relevant legislation, administrative practices that illustrate the *rules of practice* and outcomes that demonstrate the effectiveness of the domestic protection schemes are included in the discussion. Unfortunately, many issues covered in this chapter have not, yet, been the subject of domestic court cases; therefore, the discussion had to focus on administrative processes. This examination has inevitably included state involvement in religion through the provision of religious services, in particular places of worship and training of religious leaders/clergy/teachers and teaching of religion, and implicitly raised questions concerning the ramification of such involvement in the protection of the right to freedom of religion or belief and the duty on the part of the state to observe the principle of neutrality and ensure pluralism.

Finally, regarding this book's contribution to the accumulated academic research; the issue of religious freedom in Turkey has been the subject of limited academic study. The focus of study has been the principle of *laïcité*, as well as sociology of religion. The right to freedom of religion or belief has been discussed with *laïcité* in the center and in a limited way in relation to minority rights and fundamental rights in general. As far as the study of the right to freedom of religion or belief in academia is concerned the interest has emerged with the study of relevant international norms in this field. The doctoral thesis of Emre Öktem in 2002 provided the first comprehensive study on the right to freedom of religion or belief in international law.[16] The study of Berke Özenç on the European Convention on Human Rights and freedom of belief,[17] and Hande Seher Demir's masters thesis dealt with domestic religious freedom issues in the context of European Court of Human Rights (ECtHR) judgments on Turkey, such as the headscarf issue, the religion section on national identity cards and compulsory Religious Culture and Ethics courses.[18] More recently, a comprehensive overview and analysis of constitutional protection of freedom of religion and the approach taken in judicial assessment has been a valuable contribution to the field.[19] Considering the limited, yet in recent years, increasing academic study on the right to freedom of religion or belief of Turkey's normative field, this book is adding to the knowledge and discussions in this field. There is no study that explicitly

16 Öktem, A.E. (2002) *Uluslararası Hukukta İnanç Özgürlüğü* [Freedom of Religion or Belief in International Law], Ankara: Liberte.

17 Özenç, B. (2006) *Avrupa İnsan Hakları Sözleşmesi ve İnanç Özgürlüğü* [The European Court of Human Rights and Freedom of Religion or Belief], Istanbul: Kitap.

18 Demir, H.S. (2011) *Avrupa İnsan Hakları Mahkemesi Kararları Işığında Türkiye'de Din ve Vicdan Özgürlüğü* [Freedom of Religion and Conscience in Turkey in Light of the Decisions of the European Court of Human Rights], Ankara: Adalet.

19 Vural, H.S. (2013) *Türkiye'de Din Özgürlüğüne İlişkin Anayasal Güvence* [Constitutional Protection of Freedom of Religion in Turkey], Ankara: Seçkin.

focuses on the collective dimension of the right to freedom of religion or belief and aims to discuss domestic issues in light of international law and, *vice versa*, discuss international law issues in light of domestic issues. Therefore this book makes a substantial contribution to the academic knowledge in Turkey.

Since we do not yet have a coherent and well-developed theory of the "collective dimension of freedom of religion or belief" or a comprehensive theory of it in "legal doctrine" the aim of this book has been to promote an understanding of the matter. Thus the study offers original comparative insights pertaining to the understandings of the UN Human Rights Committee and the Strasbourg organs—and, to a lesser extent, that of the Organization for Co-operation and Security in Europe (OSCE)—to the scope and protections relating to the collective dimension of freedom of religion or belief. Moreover, the book offers an introduction to the Turkish system of protection of freedom of religion or belief to an international audience.

2 The Notion of the Collective Dimension of Freedom of Religion or Belief

2.1 Introduction

The right to freedom of religion or belief includes interrelated and interdependent individual and collective aspects; without one or the other the understanding and protection of this right would be incomplete. Indeed, the right to freedom of religion or belief crosses between individual and collective categories of human rights; it comprises of individual aspects, where an individual can enjoy the right to having a thought, religion or belief and manifesting it in worship, teaching, practice and observance as well as collective aspects that can only be enjoyed through organized community activity or acts that are enabled through the establishment of institutions.

The terms *collective dimension of freedom of religion* or *belief* or *religious group rights* are often used in relation to the rights of religious and/or charity institutions,[1] and the possible tensions between a religious group and individuals affiliated with the group in question.[2] Yet, a constricted understanding based on these categories is bound to lead to a narrow or selective understanding of the collective dimension of the right to freedom of religion or belief. The variety of collectivities and the acts that are protected within the scope of the provisions protecting the right to freedom of religion or belief compels a broader and holistic understanding. The legal framework created with the relevant religious freedom provisions has the added advantage of demarcating the boundaries of the collective dimension of the right to freedom of religion or belief considering that the exercise of this right may potentially lead to interferences in the rights of others. It is argued that a better understanding of the collective dimension of the right to freedom of religion or belief will contribute to the improvement of the protection of the right to freedom of religion or belief as a whole.

Amidst legislation and practices that do not seem to provide adequate solutions to new (and indeed long-standing) demands related to the protection of freedom

1 Dijk, P. van, G.J.H. van Hoof, and L. Zwaak (2006) *Theory and Practice of the European Convention on Human Rights*, The Hague: Intersentia, p. 764.

2 For a comprehensive overview of tensions between individual and collective rights see Scolnikov, A. (2011) *The Right to Religious Freedom in International Law: Between Group Rights and Individual Rights*, London: Routledge.

of religion or belief, international law and adjudicators are increasingly given the task of providing answers to how we can live with our religious differences—in particular those of a religious nature—in peace, while respecting human rights—in particular freedom of religion or belief. Indeed human rights law, in particular provisions pertaining to the right to freedom of religion or belief, may provide some of the answers. Or, perhaps more accurately, those who produce and thus shape international law jurisprudence may be in the process of seeking some of the answers. In this context, as will be explained below, the protection of the collective dimension of freedom of religion or belief is particularly relevant in setting forth the standards foreseen in international human rights law that must be upheld in domestic legal systems.

This chapter presents the legal basis of the collective dimension of freedom of religion or belief and explores its substantive scope in terms of the acts it protects, the nature of the rights holders and its boundaries. It is argued that, although firmly grounded in the international provisions protecting the right to freedom of religion or belief, more often than not, the collective dimension of freedom of religion is poorly protected, constitutes a challenge to historically shaped state–religion relations hence having a formative effect on the latter, and that the improvement of the protection of the collective dimension will greatly advance the protection of the right to freedom of religion or belief. This chapter constitutes a key part of the study, since by seeking to clarify the notion of the collective dimension of the right to freedom of religion or belief in international law it attempts to improve our understanding of this right. It is assumed that a better understanding will contribute to advancing its protection.

It is perhaps helpful to flag up in the beginning that it is not assumed or argued that the collective dimension of freedom of religion or belief is more important and should enjoy extra protection than the individual dimension of freedom of religion or belief or is hierarchically superior to the latter. Inevitably, the inter-dependency and inter-connectedness of these complementary dimensions would prove such attempts futile. As it has been underlined in the Introduction, it is believed that the notion of the collective dimension of freedom of religion or belief is a helpful framework for advancing the right to freedom of religion or belief as a whole.

An assumption is that there is reluctance on the part of states to protect the collective dimension, precisely because of the collective nature of the right. This reluctance results in a failure to uphold the standards of international law. Krishnaswami insightfully observed that:

> Intervention by the State to regulate or to limit manifestations of a religion or belief are [sic] more frequent when these manifestations are performed "in community with others" than when they are performed "alone".[3]

3 Krishnaswami, A. (1960) *Study of Discrimination in the Matter of Religious Rights and Practices*, UN Doc. E/CN.4/Sub.2/200/Rev.1, U.N. Sales No. 60. XIV.2.

The collective dimension, however, is intrinsic to the protection of the right to freedom of religion or belief and warrants protection as such.

2.2 The Relevance of the State–Religion Relationship

Since historically and contextually fashioned state–religion relations play a significant role in the nature and degree of protection afforded to the right to freedom of religion or belief, the collective dimension in particular, it is useful to highlight the state–religion relationship as an important overarching theme in this chapter. This brief analysis does not change the essential legal question of the chapter; however, it demonstrates the multi-dimensional (*inter alia*, political, historical, policy) nature of the protection of the collective dimension of freedom of religion or belief. Following a presentation of the implications of state–religion relations for the protection of the collective dimension, the nature of the normative demands made by international law is outlined below.

The position and role of religion or the role of a particular religion in a state or the role it had in the history of a state have strongly influenced existing structures related to and relations between state and religious communities and attitudes towards newly emerging religious groups. In his pivotal study Krishnaswami drew attention to the fact that interference by states in the management of religious affairs varies according to the relations between state and religious communities. He cautioned against discrimination in situations where the state is separated from religion but in its regulatory role prescribes uniform treatment for religions or beliefs which in fact make different demands of their adherents and attach varying degrees of importance to different manifestations.[4] Indeed, the relationships between religious or belief groups and states do not have a standard form but take many different forms in each context.[5] While in some countries there appears to be a somewhat clear separation between religion and state, such as France, according to a world survey, a large number of countries conceive a relationship between the state, its institutions and administration and a current or historically predominant religion or religions of its citizens where this relationship is quite diverse and reflects constant adaptation.[6] Scheduled Caste status and the individual's religious affiliation in the Indian Constitution,[7] the special status given to the Apostolic Autocephalous Orthodox Church in the Georgian Constitution,[8]

4 Ibid.
5 For a survey of different state–religious group relations in the world see, among others, Temperman, J. (2010) *State-Religion Relationships and Human Rights Law*, Dordrecht: Martinus Nijhoff Publishers; Martínez-Torrón, J. and W. Cole Durham (2010) *Religion and the Secular State*, Provo: Bringham Young University; and an earlier study, Boyle, K. and J. Sheen, eds. (1997) *Freedom of Religion and Belief: A World Report*, London: Routledge.
6 Ibid.
7 Report of the UN Special Rapporteur on Freedom of Religion or Belief, A/HRC/10/8/Add.3., 26 January 2009, paras 27–28.
8 Article 9, Constitution of Georgia, 1995 (as amended in 2003).

the recognition of Islam as the state religion in numerous countries,[9] are only a few examples. It is not difficult to imagine that in any country, hardly any belief groups enjoy freedom of religion or belief in a substantively equal manner. The variety of religious demographics and different perceptions of appropriate relationships between religious institutions and state lead some to consider that "it is necessary to consider arguments in favor of freedom of religion or belief that do not rely on strict separation between Church and State".[10] In contrast, however, others have called for a right to religiously neutral government.[11]

International human rights law provisions relevant for the protection of the right to freedom of religion or belief, mindful of the diverse types of state–religion arrangements, refrain from imposing a particular way of association between state and religion. Specific forms of state–religion identification as a condition for compliance with human rights norms are not explicitly described or particular models of state–religion relations are not condemned.[12] Temperman argues that this situation should be considered as "realities of international law and international relations".[13] Nevertheless, they do not provide a *carte blanche* to states in this sphere, either. Normative demands created by international human rights law provisions protecting the collective dimension of freedom of religion or belief as well as others, inevitably have implications for state–religion relations. These legal provisions have significant political consequences,[14] and therefore, often, require adaptation in the established state–religion relations where these give rise to unjustified interferences in the exercise of the right to freedom of religion or belief.[15] It also follows, then, that the effective protection of the collective dimension of freedom of religion will be a factor that may, through normative demands, shape state–religion relations in order to bring them in line with the requirements of human rights law. The fulfillment of the obligation on the part of the state to ensure pluralism, equality and non-discrimination in the protection of the right to freedom of religion or belief, in addition to observing the principles of neutrality and impartiality in the exercise of its regulatory powers,

9 Report of the United States Commission on International Religious Freedom, *The Religion-State Relationship and the Right to Freedom of Religion or Belief: A Comparative Textual Analysis of the Constitutions of Majority Muslim Countries and Other OIC Members*, 2012, p. 8. Available: http://www.uscirf.gov/reports-briefs/special-reports/comparative-study-constitutions-oic-countries-2012-update [Accessed 21 May 2016].
10 Evans, Carolyn (2001) *Freedom of Religion under the European Convention on Human Rights*, Oxford: Oxford University Press, p. 22.
11 Temperman, *supra* note 5.
12 Ibid., p. 1.
13 Ibid., p. 3.
14 Dworkin, Ronald M. (2012) *Is There a Right to Religious Freedom?* Legal Theory Workshop, UCLA Law School, 2 September.
15 See the General Comment 22 of the Human Rights Committee on Article 18 of the ICCPR, UN Doc. HRI/GEN/1Rev.1 at 35 (1994), para. 9. For an analysis of the General Comment 22 see Tahzib, B.G. (1996) *Freedom of Religion or Belief: Ensuring Effective International Legal Protection*, Dordrecht: Martinus Nijhoff. For a comprehensive human rights analysis of relevant state practice see, Temperman, *supra* note 5.

often compel changes in long-standing state–religion relations. On the other hand, this *influence* is not without problems. The substantive content of state obligations may not be clearly set out and/or understood, international review mechanisms may employ a certain restraint. Such restraint may result in the failure to address issues that are at the center of state–religion relations and, yet, result in interferences in human rights, in particular freedom of religion or belief. Political debates and conflicts regarding these issues at both national and international levels can determine the contours of the margin given to states in balancing their relevant human rights obligations and the diverse arrangements of state–religion relations, often to the detriment of human rights and disadvantaging minority religious/belief groups. Indeed, a survey of state practice raises concerns that practices such as the establishment of a religion by the state in fact amount to certain preferences and privileges being given to the followers of that religion and are therefore discriminatory.[16] This tension is hardly sustainable.

As a matter of fact, the nature of normative demands created by international law as well as the approach of international adjudicating bodies to cases raising questions about issues that involve privileged or complex arrangements with various religious groups or institutions remains less than evident.

The HRCttee, in its General Comment on Article 18 maintains that,

> the fact that a religion is recognized as a State religion or that it is established as official or traditional or that its followers comprise the majority of the population, should not result in any impairment of the enjoyment of any rights under the Covenant, including articles 18 and 27, nor in any discrimination against adherents to other religions or non-believers.[17]

It is clear that the HRCttee is not concerned with laying rules or envisaging an arrangement pertaining to the relations between states and religions, religious communities' religious institutions in the context of the right to freedom of religion or belief. However this is realized is up to states. What concerns the Committee is that the enjoyment of the protections for the manifestations that are covered by Article 18 without undue interference is ensured and states are free in their structures or organizations as long as they achieve the former. Undue interference in this context is, *inter alia*, interference that is not prescribed by law, necessary for one of the legitimate grounds for restriction,[18] or that is disproportionate.[19] The HRCttee expressed concern on the paramount role of a given religious institution

16 Benito, E.O. (1989) *Elimination of All Forms of Intolerance and Discrimination Based on Religion or Belief*, Human Rights Study Series No. 2, UN Sales No. E. 89. XIV.3, Geneva: United Nations Centre for Human Rights, para. 88.

17 General Comment 22 of the HRCttee, *supra* note 15, para. 9.

18 *Sister Immaculate Joseph and the 80 Teaching Sisters of the Holy Cross of the Third Order of Saint Francis in Menzingen of Sri Lanka v. Sri Lanka*, 21 October 2005, UN Human Rights Committee, No. 1249/2004, para. 7.3.

19 *Sergei Malakhovsky and Alexander Pikul v. Belarus*, 26 July 2005, UN Human Rights Committee, No. 1207/2003, paras 7.4 and 7.6. In this case, the consequences of the

while considering state reports. For example, in the case of Costa Rica, with respect to Article 18 of the Covenant, the Committee expressed concern over the pre-eminent position accorded to the Roman Catholic Church.[20] Similarly in the case of Iran, where there is a state religion, the Committee emphasized that recognition of a religion as a state religion should not result in any impairment of the enjoyment of any of the rights under the Covenant, including Articles 18 and 27, nor in any discrimination against adherents of other religions or non-believers, since the right to freedom of religion and belief and the prohibition of discrimination do not depend on the recognition as an official religion or belief.[21] Measures restricting eligibility for government service to members of the predominant religion, or giving economic privileges to such persons, or imposing special restrictions on the practice of other faiths were considered incompatible with the prohibition of discrimination based on religion or belief and the guarantee of equal protection under Article 26.[22]

The UN Special Rapporteur on Freedom of Religion or Belief has also challenged the privileged position given to a certain religion; concern over abuses that can happen where there is a state or official religion has been expressed and the unavoidable detrimental effects of "formal or legal" distinctions between religions have been underscored.

> The notion of an official or State religion must never be exploited at the expense of the rights of minorities and the rights linked to citizenship. Formal or legal distinctions between different kinds of religious or faith-based communities carry the seed of discrimination insofar as such a distinction in their status implies a difference in rights or treatment. Consequently, the Special Rapporteur has voiced her concerns that the legalization of such a distinction between different categories of religion is liable to pave the way for future violations of the right to freedom of religion or for discrimination on the basis of religion or belief.[23]

The European Convention on Human Rights (ECHR) and the jurisprudence of the Strasbourg organs shed further light on the nature of normative demands created by international law. Consistent with the International Covenant on Civil

restrictions were the impossibility of carrying out activities such as establishing educational institutions and inviting foreign religious dignitaries to visit the country.

20 UN Human Rights Committee, 50th Session, CCPR/C/79/Add.31 para. 9 (*Concluding Observations: Costa Rica*). The HRCttee expressed concern over certain provisions of Costa Rican legislation (*inter alia*, the Ley de Carrera Docente) that confer on the National Episcopal Conference the power to effectively impede the teaching of religions other than Catholicism in public schools and the power to bar those who are not Catholics from teaching religion in the public school curricula.

21 UN Human Rights Committee, 48th Session, CCPR/C/79/Add.25, para. 22 (*Concluding Observations of the Human Rights Committee: Iran*).

22 Ibid.

23 Report of the UN Special Rapporteur on Freedom of Religion or Belief, UN Doc. A/HRC/6/5, 20 July 2007, p. 13.

and Political Rights (ICCPR) regime, the ECHR does not prescribe a certain state–religion or state-religious institutions paradigm, either. The European Court of Human Rights (ECtHR) has dealt with numerous applications claiming violations of Article 9 that involved issues pertaining to the nature of state–religion relations of the countries concerned. Two, arguably less than consistent, trends appear to be key features of relevant jurisprudence. On the one hand, it is possible to observe a rigorous stance against coercion by the state to adopt a certain religion or to refuse someone to leave a religious institution.[24] On the other hand, an emphasis on the obligation on the part of the state to observe impartiality and neutrality and ensure pluralism, particularly when the interference concerns the involvement of the state in the internal organization of a religious community or institution can be increasingly seen. It has been underscored by the ECtHR that "in exercising its regulatory power in this sphere [religion] and in its relations with the various religions, denominations and beliefs, the State has a duty to remain neutral and impartial".[25]

A certain restraint or reluctance, and as a result reliance on a wide margin of appreciation,[26] continue to raise questions as to the extent and nature of the normative demands created by international law. According to the ECtHR the scope of the margin of appreciation will vary, depending on "the circumstances, the subject-matter and its background",[27] and it always goes hand in hand with European supervision.[28] Where a common European standard exists the international scrutiny will be stricter, the absence of such a common standard would lead to granting a margin of appreciation to states. The latter has been used to justify interferences which would seem to be difficult to reconcile with the obligation to observe the principle of neutrality and the prohibition of non-discrimination; having a state church would not necessarily be contrary to the Convention,[29] privileged state funding for a religious institution does not confer on other religious institutions an entitlement to secure additional funding from the state budget and

24 *Darby v. Sweden*, 23 October 1990, European Court of Human Rights, App. No. 11581/85, paras 45. See also *Kokkinakis v. Greece*, 25 May 1993, European Court of Human Rights, No. 14307/88, paras 46–50; *Manoussakis v. Greece*, 29 August 1996, European Court of Human Rights, No. 18748/91, para. 36.

25 *Hasan and Chaush v. Bulgaria*, 26 October 2000, European Court of Human Rights, No. 30985/96, para. 78.

26 On the doctrine of margin of appreciation see, *inter alia*, Arai-Takahashi, Y. (2002) *The Margin of Appreciation Doctrine and the Principle of Proportionality in the Jurisprudence of the European Court of Human Rights*, Leiden: Intersentia; and Schokkenbroek, J. (1998) "The Basis, Nature and Application of the Margin of Appreciation Doctrine in the Case Law of the ECHR", 19 *Human Rights Law Journal* 1.

27 *Petrovic v. Austria*, 27 March 1998, European Court of Human Rights, No. 20458/92, para. 38.

28 *Lautsi v. Italy*, 18 March 2011, European Court of Human Rights (Grand Chamber), No. 30814/06, para. 70; *Leyla Sahin v. Turkey*, 10 October 2005, European Court of Human Rights (Grand Chamber), No. 44774/98, para. 110.

29 *Darby v. Sweden*, 23 October 1990, European Commission of Human Rights, No. 11581/85.

the refusal to do so would not result in a breach of Article 9,[30] a cross in a classroom of a public school would not necessarily undermine the rights of non-Christians to freedom of religion.[31]

It has been observed that the ECtHR seems to also heavily rely on states' discretion for the differential treatment of religions.[32] Despite diversity of historical and political traditions the ECtHR is appealed to seek "progressively to narrow the margin of appreciation" that is allowed to state parties to enforce different standards that privilege the majority religious groups.[33] Evans and Thomas rightly call for a more searching scrutiny where there is differential treatment between religions when a church–state relations dimension is involved.[34] Where restrictions of manifestations are based on the protection of secularism the ECtHR jurisprudence demonstrates an even broader margin of appreciation for that state concerning its church-state relations in the broad sense.[35]

It follows from the above that the approach of the HRCttee and the UN Special Rapporteur on Freedom of Religion or Belief demonstrate a greater readiness and willingness to tackle freedom of religion or belief claims that also raise issues of state–religion relations in a way to challenge historically conferred privileges given to certain religions or religious institutions. It is important to note that the UN system involves states with much diverse forms of state–religion relations than the Council of Europe. Thus while the UN deals with a wider spectrum of state–religion relations with lack of common standards in the countries concerned, it does not rely on a margin of appreciation.

In contrast, the ECtHR's jurisprudence does not reflect a uniform and predictable standard of review. Where the right to freedom of religion or belief overlaps with other rights such as freedom of expression or freedom of association, to which the Strasbourg system is profoundly committed, the ECtHR holds states up to their international obligations. On the other hand, there appears to be a

30 *Asatruarfelagid v. Iceland*, 7 July 2011, European Court of Human Rights (Dec.), No. 22897/08, para. 31–32.

31 *Lautsi v. Italy*, 18 March 2011, European Court of Human Rights (Grand Chamber), Application No. 30814/06. For a critical appraisal of the *Lautsi* case see, *inter alia*, S. Manchini (2010) "The Crucifix Rage: Supranational Constitutionalism Bumps Against the Counter-Majoritarian Difficulty", 6 *European Constitutional Law Review* 6.

32 Evans, C. and C.A. Thomas (2006) "Church-State Relations in the European Court of Human Rights", *Brigham Young University Law Review*, 699.

33 Danchin, P. and L. Forman (2002) "The Evolving Jurisprudence of the European Court of Human Rights and the Protection of Religious Minorities", in Danchin, P. and E.A. Cole (eds.), *Protecting the Human Rights of Religious Minorities in Eastern Europe*, New York: Colombia University Press, p. 193.

34 Evans and Thomas, *supra* note 32, pp. 723–724.

35 Henrard, K. (2012) "A Critical Appraisal of the Margin of Appreciation Let to States Pertaining to 'Church-State Relations' under the Jurisprudence of the European Court of Human Rights", in M.C. Foblets, K. Alidadi and J. Vrielink (eds.), *A Test of Faith? Religious Diversity and Accommodation in the European Workplace*, Surrey: Routledge, p. 76.

certain restraint or insecurity to firmly hold states up to their international obligations where differential treatment of the traditional religions or religious organizations are concerned. A coherent and continuing systematic approach is indispensable for ensuring that international norms are respected at the domestic level. When international adjudicators emphasize the particular circumstances of the case and the margin of appreciation granted to states, there is a higher risk that national courts will be inclined not to strictly follow international norms. Arguably, we might say that the ECtHR is still in a "searching phase", constantly evolving and being challenged, and has not yet reached the point where it will have a principled and established jurisprudence pertaining to freedom of religion or belief. The unforeseeable standard of international review will, however, not least, reinforce the existing power balance on the axis of privileged and non-privileged religious groups. A greater preparedness to invalidate laws that are discriminatory or are routinely used in a discriminatory manner would be a good step.[36]

In conclusion, it is important to note that while on the one hand international law poses normative demands on state–religion relations, the nature of these obligations remain less than clear.

2.3 The Legal Basis and Scope of the Collective Dimension of Freedom of Religion or Belief

2.3.1 Relevant Notions

The notion of the collective dimension of the right to freedom of religion or belief is firmly founded on the international provisions protecting the right to freedom of religion or belief. This legal basis—protected acts and nature of right holders—and the significance of the collective dimension is presented below.

Conceptions analogous to the "collective dimension of the right to freedom of religion or belief" have historically been part of the normative discourse on religious freedom and the protection of religious minorities. The protection of the collective dimension of freedom of religion or belief is deeply embedded in the historical protection of freedom of religion or belief. In the past, the international protection of the right to freedom of religion or belief has been, to a great extent, protected *via* group rights and minority rights,[37] rather than individual rights. As far as international protection of groups—including religious groups—is concerned Lerner divides these into three major periods; (1) non-systematic protection of groups by way of protective clauses in international treaties,[38] (2) the minority system established within the League of Nations after WW I, (3) the United

36 Evans and Thomas, *supra* note 32, p. 724.
37 Dinstein, Y. (1992) "Freedom of Religion and the Protection of Religious Minorities", in Y. Dinstein and M. Tabory (eds.), *The Protection of Minorities and Human Rights*, Dordrecht: Martinus Nijhoff Publishers, pp. 145–169.
38 For an overview of various treaty protection schemes in Europe see, Evans, M.D. (1997) *Religious Liberty and International Law in Europe*, Cambridge: Cambridge University Press, pp. 42–82.

application to international mechanisms. If a natural belief group does not, at the same time, have a formal representative body, who could make the application? In a case concerning alleged violations of Article 1 and 27 of the ICCPR, the HRCttee recalled that the Optional Protocol allowed only for the submission of complaints by individuals for individual rights.[99] Hence the group, *qua* group, cannot claim the enforcement of a right. On the other hand, individuals can claim the enforcement of a right of a *collective nature*. Within the ECHR protection scheme, natural groups do not have a standing to bring complaints against states parties. Taking into account these limitations, perhaps non-adjudicatory compliance control mechanisms may be the key processes where the collective dimension of freedom of religion or belief may be addressed in the context of the natural belief group.

In the case of the HRCttee, in accordance with the First Optional Protocol to the ICCPR, the Committee can receive and consider communications only from individuals. This is why in a number of cases that have dealt with the rights of religious organizations the claims were brought by a number of individuals who were members of religious organizations. From the perspective of religious or belief organizations, the possibility of application to the ECtHR as an organization rather than individuals is advantageous, whereas a communication to the HRCttee would necessarily mean that individuals take up the responsibility themselves to carry on with the pursuit of the claim, which is likely to cause hesitation where a particular belief group experiences discrimination and persecution.

While an informal group of believers—because they chose not to, or cannot, establish a legal entity—cannot file a complaint in the case of an interference in the enjoyment of rights as a legal entity, they could file a complaint individually—each separately or together, yet without losing their individual standing. This would be possible in cases where there is interference in the individual or the collective exercise of the right.

Whether an established religious organization as a right holder has the right to bring a complaint before Strasbourg organs and the HRCttee varies. The First Optional Protocol of the ICCPR does not foresee standing of a corporate religious group that has a legal entity status.[100] Therefore, in the communication of *Sister Immaculate Joseph and 80 Teaching Sisters et al. v. Sri Lanka*, the religious order as a legal entity could not file a communication with the HRCttee; instead, individuals claimed the enforcement of a collective right, namely the right to establish a corporation for charity purposes.[101]

members of a certain group. Yet, the enforceability of such a right under the ICCPR Article 1 is less than clear.

99 *Lubicon Lake Band v. Canada* (1990) Human Rights Committee, No. 167/1984, UN Doc. Supp. No. 40 (A/45/40) at 1, para. 32.1.

100 Article 1 of the Optional Protocol to the International Covenant on Civil and Political Rights, G.A. res. 2200A (XXI), 21 UN GAOR Supp. (No. 16) at 59, UN Doc. A/6316 (1966), 999 UNTS 302, entry into force 23 March 1976.

101 *Sister Immaculate Joseph and 80 Teaching Sisters of the Holy Cross of the Third Order of Saint Francis in Menzingen of Sri Lanka v. Sri Lanka* (2005) Human Rights Committee, No. 1249/2004, UN Doc. CCPR/C/85/D/1249/2004.

In the ECHR framework the recognition of the standing of a religious organization has been gradual. Initially, the European Commission of Human Rights held that religious organizations had no right to bring claims under Article 9.[102] The rationale was that it was the members of the church and not the church itself that had a right to freedom of religion or belief.[103] The complaint was dismissed because "a corporation being a legal and not a natural person, is incapable of having or exercising the rights mentioned in Article 9, paragraph 1 of the Convention and Article 2 of the First Protocol".[104] This position was however rightly corrected, about a decade later, in the case of *X and the Church of Scientology v. Sweden* relating to the prohibition of advertisements of the "E-meter".[105] The Commission explained the reversal of its position by stating that "the Commission is now of the opinion that the... distinction between the Church and its members under the Article 9(1) is essentially artificial".[106] The Church was perceived as applying "on behalf of its members" with a representative capacity.[107] Evans has noted that the right of a church to bring a claim is derivative, "based on the aggregating of the rights of its members" and that it could not claim a breach of its own rights.[108] Bearing in mind that the entity is established by members, one must take into account the fact that once a legal entity is established by a group of believers, the legal entity has a separate identity, or personhood, from the members that established it. Thus is not necessary to aggregate the rights of individual members. The legal entity, as such, can claim the breach of its own rights under Article 9. Indeed, later, the European Commission has held that religious organizations are rights holders who can bring claims in their own right.[109] In subsequent jurisprudence the Commission held that only organizations analogous to religious organizations may bring claims under Article 9, including "associations with religious and philosophical objects".[110]

The possibility of bringing complaints through a religious organization, instead of an individual or a group of individuals, is essential in certain contexts. In the case of repressed minority religious groups, where it would be very difficult to

102 It may be useful to remember that this was about its own rights under Article 9 of the ECHR; an entity could and can claim its own rights under other Articles, such as Article 6 or Article 1 of Protocol 1.

103 *Church of X v. The U.K.*, 17 December 1968, European Commission of Human Rights, 1968 (Admissibility) No. 3798/68.

104 Ibid., p. 314.

105 *X and the Church of Scientology v. Sweden*, 5 May 1979, European Commission of Human Rights, No. 7805/77.

106 Ibid., p. 70.

107 Ibid.

108 Evans, *supra* note 10, p. 14.

109 *A.R.M. Chappell v. UK*, 14 July 1987, European Commission of Human Rights (Admissibility), No. 12587/86; *Iglesia Bautista El Salvador and Ortega Moratilla v. Spain*, 11 January 1992, European Commission of Human Rights (Admissibility), No. 17522/90.

110 *Omkarananda and the Divine Light Zentrum v. Switzerland*, 16 March 1981, European Commission of Human Rights (Admissibility), No. 8118/77, 25 DR 105, 1981, para. 117.

challenge the state on an individual basis, the standing of a religious organization empowers such vulnerable groups.[111] Equally, the possibility to bring individual complaints concerning a right of a collective nature is also important. This would open the way for challenging, for example, macro public policies that disadvantage a religious group. For example, individuals could seek the enforcement of the right to establish religious schools on a par with other groups, even if they are themselves not victims of an alleged violation. Allowing churches and similar organizations to apply has enabled belief communities to access European supervision and opened the way for the latter in "a whole new *façade* of freedom of religion and belief which otherwise was destined to be dismissed by the ECHR bodies on the basis of being a technical matter".[112]

Standing, however, is not sufficient to bring broad-scale repression on a number of fronts to the Court; there must also be a direct connection between the entity and the acts complained of which would establish the victim status of the said entity. The case of *Scientology Kirche Deutschland v. Germany* illustrates the situation well.[113] The applicants complained exactly of this kind of widespread "administrative practice" of violations against their organization and its members; *inter alia*, strategies adopted by the federal government and the governments of the Länder with the purpose of reducing the influence of the Scientology organization, for example, in Bavaria schools were ordered to inform pupils about the operating procedures of Scientology, a decree was issued in Stuttgart prohibiting the public distribution of printed materials published by Scientology organizations, the Bavarian government announced that Scientologists would be banned from civil service.[114] The applicants complained of these and other administrative practices against which there was no effective remedy. They claimed, in particular, that the administrative practices rendered the remedies which are available in individual cases but were not able to stop the policy or practice, or challenge the fundamental political assessment of the government that lie at the heart of these practices.[115] Finally, the Commission found that domestic remedies were not exhausted and there was no evidence that there were administrative practices in Germany that rendered judicial remedies ineffective, hence the application was found to be inadmissible.[116]

Before arriving at this conclusion, the Commission made some observations that are helpful in identifying problems with applications from religious organizations that deal with broad-scale practices directed against them and their affiliates. The applicants had to show that, as an association, they had been the victim of a violation of the Convention. Firstly, in the Commission's opinion the applicant could claim to be a victim only if there was "sufficiently direct connection"

111 Evans, *supra note* 10, p. 15.
112 Ibid.
113 *Scientology Kirche Deutschland v. Germany*, 7 April 1997, European Commission of Human Rights (Admissibility), No. 34614/97.
114 Ibid.
115 Ibid.
116 Ibid.

between the applicant and the injury he maintains he suffered. In the case in question the Commission held the view that clearly the association was not the victim of alleged violations but members and only the members, as individuals, could claim to be victims. In addition, since the association did not produce the identification of the individuals and instructions from them demonstrating that the association represented them, the association lacked *ratione persone*. Secondly, the Commission observed that the association to a large extent complained of the actions of members of parliament, politicians, commercial companies, other non-governmental organizations and private parties, whereas the Convention could be invoked only when the state party failed to protect the rights of the applicant against interferences by private persons.[117]

In countries where religious minorities are not protected in their own right, protection of the collective dimension of freedom of religion or belief holds strategic importance for religious or belief communities. Individually protected rights and the provision of non-discrimination may not ensure effective protection for the belief groups (informal groups or those which have acquired a legal entity status). In such cases, rights protected through the collective dimension, *inter alia*, the right to establish places of worship, the right to acquire legal personality, the right to train clergy, the right to be free in their internal affairs are crucial for the preservation and sustenance of the religious/belief group. This is not to suggest that in such cases minority rights will be redundant and minority protection is not necessary. In any case, minority rights play a key role. This is so, particularly when in a given country there is a dominant population of a particular religious affiliation or when the state becomes the bearer of a role promoting a majority religion *de jure* or *de facto*. Where both frameworks exist, it may be said that both the collective dimension of freedom or religion or belief and minority rights protection enhance each other. But in the absence of a minority rights protection scheme, the significance of the effective protection of the collective dimension increases. In addition, where minorities are recognized, the collective dimension of freedom of religion or belief may also play a role in terms of protecting minorities within minorities.

In sum, it is important to strive to achieve flexibility about the models of legal personality in order to ensure that claims can be brought to international adjudicators. Lauterpacht had noted that "the range of subject of international law is not rigid and immutable, but capable of modifications and developments in accordance with the will of states and requirements of international intercourse".[118]

While the collective dimension of freedom of religion or belief is intrinsic to this right, there may be situations where in the exercise of rights of a collective nature there may be conflict of interests with individual rights.[119] Surely, states cannot

117 Ibid.

118 Quoted by Lerner, N. (1991) *Group Rights and Discrimination in International Law*, Dordrecht: Martinus Nijhoff, p. 37.

119 Most recently conflicts between religious organizations and employees have been the subject of international legal dispute. See, *Siebenhaar v. Germany*, 3 February 2011, European Court of Human Rights, Application No. 18136/02; *Obst v. Germany*, 23

allow or protect practices that cause violations of human rights. It is true that there are religious practices that lead to interference in the individual rights of others. Though such conflicts do not only arise between a group and an individual; they can also arise between individuals, for example between a parent and a child or among brother and sister or between husband and wife. The possible conflict of interest between a group of believers exercising the collective dimension of freedom of religion or belief and an individual is relevant for the study at hand. The specific conflict may arise between the right of belief groups to be free in their internal affairs and the human rights of individuals that are negatively affected by this freedom. No hierarchy between the collective dimension of freedom of religion or belief and the rights of an individual exist; the interests need to be balanced on a case by case basis.

The question of whether the collective dimension of the right to freedom of religion or belief protects beliefs or religions needs to be considered. Whether existing international human rights provisions have implications for the protection of religions or beliefs and whether new international provisions need to be drafted to create obligations for states to "combat defamation of religions" have been contemporary questions of concern. These considerations may be based on seeking respect for religious diversity and achieving harmony between religions of the world.[120] Such arguments may also be used at the domestic level where such interests may manifest themselves in blasphemy laws that at the outset seek to ensure social harmony, yet, in effect may give rise to human rights violations.[121] International provisions protecting the right to freedom of religion or belief certainly do not refer to religions or beliefs as right holders. Religions, as such, have also not been the subject of international jurisprudence. But do these provisions lay down obligations for states to protect religions or belief? International jurisprudence has been engaged with this issue to the extent it has assessed whether certain "expressions" may be restricted in relation to the obligation of states to prohibit any advocacy of religious hatred that constituted incitement to discrimination, hostility or violence,[122] the obligation to provide legal remedies for unlawful attacks on an individual's honor or reputation, including the connection with his/her religion,[123] and the obligation to ensure peaceful enjoyment of the right to freedom of religion or belief where this may be interfered with because of intensive defamation of a certain religion or religious groups such that believers are

September 2012, European Court of Human Rights, Application No. 425/03; *Schüth v. Germany*, 23 September 2010, European Court of Human Rights, Application No. 1620/03; and *Fernandez and Martinez v. Spain*, 15 May 2014, European Court of Human Rights, No. 56030/07, referred to the Grand Chamber on 25 September 2012.

120 Rivers, J. (2008) *Defamation of Religions and Human Rights*, Aachen: Missio, p. 22.

121 For a representative review of blasphemy laws and their effect on the protection of freedom of religion or belief and other rights see Report by Freedom House, *Policing Belief: The Impact of Blasphemy Laws on Human Rights*, October 2010.

122 ICCPR, Article 20(2).

123 ICCPR, Article 19 and Article 20(2) and ECHR, Article 10.

under the threat of violence from third parties.[124] The latter obligation however does not create a general duty to introduce blasphemy laws, rather it would allow for restrictions on expressions where these constitute actual threat to enjoyment of freedom of religion or belief by others.[125] The HRCttee has noted that,

> Prohibitions of displays of lack of respect for a religion or other belief system, including blasphemy laws, are incompatible with the Covenant, except in the specific circumstances envisaged in article 20, paragraph 2, of the Covenant. Such prohibitions must also comply with the strict requirements of article 19, paragraph 3, as well as such articles as 2, 5, 17, 18 and 26. Thus, for instance, it would be impermissible for any such laws to discriminate in favor of or against one or certain religions or belief systems, or their adherents over another, or religious believers over non-believers. Nor would it be permissible for such prohibitions to be used to prevent or punish criticism of religious leaders or commentary on religious doctrine and tenets of faith.[126]

It is also helpful to point out that the collective dimension of freedom of religion or belief is distinct from a certain constitutional or legal status given to a particular religion. The establishment of religion, with its various forms, cannot be considered a political reflection of the collective dimension. However, legal recognition or legal status given to a particular religion in a given state may have negative implications for the protection of the collective dimension, inhibiting freedom of religion or belief or in a positive manner, facilitating its exercise.

The collective dimension of freedom of religion exists and an improved understanding and willingness to address the collective nature of the right underlying the complaint by adjudicating bodies would significantly improve its protection. Therefore, to ensure better protection in practice, modifications in the accessibility modalities of existing mechanisms and establishment of new mechanisms should be explored. Granting natural religious groups the right to bring cases and appear

124 *97 Members of the Gladani Congregation of Jehovah's Witnesses v. Georgia*, 3 May 2007, European Court of Human Rights, No. 71101/01.

125 This is a highly delicate issue. In *Otto Preminger Institut v. Austria*, the ECtHR found that the state was justified in preventing the distribution of a certain movie that would hurt the feelings of the Catholic majority. *Otto Preminger Institut v. Austria*, 20 September 1994, European Court of Human Right, No. 13470/87. This, arguably objectionable precedent, has been used to justify the existence of laws analogous to blasphemy laws. For example, in the interpretation of Article 216 of the Turkish Criminal Code the public prosecutor has relied on the ECtHR jurisprudence outlined in the Otto Preminger Institut v. Austria in his argument that it is justified to protect the religious feelings of people. This provision has been used against atheist blogs and websites as well as publications critical of Islam. See Mine Yıldırım, "'Denigrating Religious Values' – A Way to Silence Critics of Religion?" 15 February 2012, Forum 18. Available: http://forum18.org/Archive.php?article_id=1667 [Accessed 16 January 2015].

126 Human Rights Committee, General Comment No. 34, UN Doc. CCPR/C/GC/34/CRP.2 (2010), para. 48.

before international monitoring mechanisms in relation to claims of violations of rights of a collective nature may be a step forward. This would, potentially, increase the efficacy of compliance control mechanisms as agents of change.

Following this line of thought, one could envision a greater positive obligation and role of the state; not only as a regulator but as a facilitator of associative life or activities of belief communities. This would include, *inter alia*, making acquisition of legal personality or legal entity status as easy as possible, being meticulous about steering clear of discrimination in drawing legislation and implementing it, providing effective safeguards for legal protection that guarantees legality and excludes excessive arbitrary decisions. In summary, states ought to take steps to free this area of any negative prejudice and repression. Some of the belief communities or groups which have been the subject of this chapter may not qualify as minorities but they are smaller groups of persons who form sub-groups of religious minorities who, thanks to the collective aspect of the right to freedom of religion, can benefit from rights that have been traditionally envisioned for groups that are recognized as minorities. Hence, a conclusion can be made that Article 27 and the 1992 Declaration reinforce the protection of the collective dimension of freedom of religion or belief, but do not replace it, and there are certainly overlapping aspects of both rights. One way to theorize about their correlation would be to view the minority rights framework as the broader sketch of freedom of religion with group/minority as the reference point of protection and the collective aspect of freedom of religion a right with much more flexibility for right holders. On the other hand, if the collective aspect of freedom of belief is not widely interpreted, belief communities might be afforded better and wider protection in making use of provisions that are specifically directed to the protection of religious minorities when dealing with widespread discrimination and repression. Conversely, the right to freedom of religion/belief, unlike minority rights, provides protection also for members of majority groups.

2.4 Compliance Control Mechanisms

Human rights compliance control mechanisms, potentially, may also play an important role in improving the protection of the collective dimension for the many collectivities.[127] Compliance control mechanisms are not confined to the examination of concrete cases, but have the advantage of enabling a review process of domestic legislation and its application in abstract, and provide an assessment of their compatibility with the provisions of domestic legislation and the application of these in light of the relevant international provisions protecting the right to freedom of religion or belief. The flexible nature of these mechanisms makes them more suitable to address broad-scale issues than a court or quasi-judicial body which may be unable to deal with such cases or apply restraint.

127 The improvement of the efficiency of compliance control mechanisms for the protection of the collective dimension of freedom of religion or belief would be a subject worthy of another research project.

Within the UN human rights protection scheme the Universal Periodic Review and the UN Special Rapporteur on Freedom of Religion or Belief and within the Council of Europe system the Commissioner for the Protection of Human Rights and Advisory Committee on the Framework Convention for the Protection of National Minorities are some of the mechanisms to monitor compliance with international human rights law. Due to space limitations, however, our scope will be limited to the HRCttee and the Committee of Ministers of the Council of Europe.

Article 40(1) of the ICCPR requires the states parties "to submit reports on the measures they have adopted which give effect to the rights recognized [in the ICCPR] and on the progress made in the enjoyment of those rights".[128] As a result of the reporting process the HRCttee adopts Concluding Observations which include an assessment of the state's human rights situation in light of the information provided in the state's report, the answers received to the questions posed by the HRCttee members during the examination of the report, and information from other sources, *inter alia*, NGOs, all analyzed in terms of the country's obligations under the Covenant. Buergenthal argues that

> ... given their formal character and the care with which they are increasingly being drafted by the Committee, the findings set out in concluding observations must be viewed as authoritative pronouncements on whether a particular state has or has not complied with its obligations under the Covenant.[129]

This procedure provides the HRCttee with a means to become aware and address broad-scale practices and attitudes toward certain religious or belief groups that may be difficult to make the subject of a complaint. It also gives the representatives of religious groups or their institutions the opportunity to submit reports or even to attend pre-session meetings in order to present their cases directly to the members of the HRCttee. The HRCttee also has a possibility to address laws that are incompatible with obligations of states under Article 18 even in the absence of a complaint from an affected party. In this context the Committee's comment on the treatment of the Bahai in Iran is a case in point. Here the Committee expressed concern about the destruction of places of worship or cemeteries and the systematic persecution, harassment and discrimination of the Bahais, which is in clear contradiction with the provisions of the Covenant.[130] Another example can be found in the comments on the report of the Republic of Moldova where the Committee expressed concern over the "artificial hurdles" for organizations seeking to exercise their religious freedom under Article 18 and commented that the state party should "ensure that its law and policy relating to the registration of

128 Article 40(2) of the ICCPR.

129 Buergenthal, T. (2001) "The U.N. Human Rights Committee", in J.A. Frowein and R. Wolfrum (eds.), *Max Planck Yearbook of United Nations Law*, Vol. 5, Dordrecht: Kluwer, p. 351.

130 Human Rights Committee, 3 August 1993, CCPR/C/79/Add.25, p. 4 (Concluding Observations: Islamic Republic of Iran).

religious organizations fully respects" the rights of persons as required by Article 18.[131] The HRCttee can call states to take certain measures to improve the protection of human rights; for example, in the context of ambiguous registration legislation the Bulgarian authorities were called to "ensure the training of local authorities and law enforcement officials to avoid unnecessary interference with the right to freedom of religion".[132] In response to the problems with registration of religious communities in Mongolia the HRCttee called for the development of "a thorough analysis of the administrative and practical difficulties faced by religious groups to register and therefore conduct their activities, and adopt the modifications that are necessary".[133]

Within the ECHR system, the task of the Committee of Ministers in follow-up of judgments has enormous potential and relevance for eliminating future violations by addressing repressive state legislation and practice related to legal personality, recognition and registration processes. According to Article 46(2) of Protocol No. 11 of the ECHR, once the final judgment of the Court has been transmitted to the Committee of Ministers, the latter invites the state to provide information on the steps taken to pay for just satisfaction and where proper of the individual and general measures taken to prevent new, similar violations.[134] When it is clear that the violation occurred due to a particular domestic legislation, the state party must amend existing laws or draft new appropriate legislation. Similarly, where it is not the legislation *per se* but the case law of domestic courts the change in case law may prevent further violations. Perhaps this is another *fora* that needs to be strengthened and rigorously utilized where the Court's judgments recognize that particular legislation in question is vague or that it has been used against a certain group, particularly when the Court finds violation on the ground that the limitation was not prescribed by law.

Bearing the aforementioned in mind, findings of violations of Article 14 in conjunction with Article 9, 11 or 6 seem all the more important to tackle widespread general repressive legislation and practice. Violations of Article 14 would give the Committee of Ministers the possibility to pursue this thread and follow up with measures to seek corrective action by states. Even in cases where violation is found on other grounds but problems have been noted on the vagueness of legislation or on case law or on its application with reference to particular groups, the Committee of Ministers, having become aware of the wider issues and having more flexible means at its disposal in contrast to the Court, could pursue the

131 Human Rights Committee, 5 August 2002, CCPR/CO/75/MDA, p. 4 (Concluding Observations: Republic of Moldova).

132 Human Rights Committee, 9 August 2011, CCPR/C/BGR/CO/3, p. 7 (Concluding Observations: Bulgaria).

133 Human Rights Committee, 2 May 2011, CCPR/C/MNG/CO/5, p. 6 (Concluding Observations: Mongolia).

134 Protocol 11 to the European Convention for the Protection of Human Rights and Fundamental Freedoms, restructuring the control machinery established thereby, entry into force 1 November 1998. Available: http://conventions.coe.int/Treaty/en/Treaties/Html/155.htm [Accessed 16 January 2015].

introduction of general measures by the state in question in order to bring domestic law and practice in line with Convention commitments.

As noted above, the Committee of Ministers of the ECHR and the reporting mechanism of the ICCPR have the potential to address these issues; however, for this potential to be realized the willingness on the part of these bodies to take up these issues with the governments is indispensable. Doubtless, the HRCttee and Committee of Ministers stand out as key actors, in particular, where broad-scale repressive acts are concerned and where the collectivity in question cannot utilize the ECtHR and Optional Protocol of the ICCPR application mechanisms.

In conclusion, a broad and holistic view of the variety of collectivities as well as the acts that are protected within the scope of collective dimension of freedom of religion or belief would help improve the international and national protection of the right to freedom of religion or belief. In every compliance control process, be it of an adjudicating body or of a body with a mandate of a general review of the domestic protection of human rights, a searching and substantive attention must be given to the collectivities that are the subjects of the right to freedom of religion or belief and the acts that are enjoyed in community with others. The shortcomings of existing processes may be overcome through the willingness of these bodies to take this step. In order to do this, they must consider these aspects as indispensable dimensions of the general protection conferred through the right to freedom of religion or belief. Ultimately, much depends on the conception, status and content attributed to this fundamental right.

The limited recognition of positive obligations in relation to the right to freedom of religion or belief appears to be a factor directly affecting the enjoyment of this right by individuals and various collectivities. The lack of emphasis on positive obligations related to the protected acts strengthens the hand of domestic authorities that remain, not least, unconcerned as to their obligations under the international provisions protecting the right to freedom of religion or belief. The protection of the collective dimension suffers when reluctance by states to protect it precisely because of its collective dimension is compounded with less than firmly and specifically established positive obligations.

Similarly, the Committee of Ministers and the HRCttee in the reporting process may pick up on repressive legislation or recurring repressive practice and seek corrective action with the various means at their disposal.

The normative demands created by international provisions protecting the collective dimension of freedom of religion constitute a challenge to historically shaped state–religion relations. The fulfillment of state obligations in this respect would have a formative effect on these relations. The hesitation in establishing predictable and uniform criteria, particularly by the ECtHR, appears to be a factor that permits the continuation of state legislation and practice that raises serious questions in terms of state neutrality and non-discrimination and equality. Such discord cannot be sustainable in the long-run for international adjudicators if they are to fulfill their key role to advance the protection of human rights, and here the protection of freedom of religion or belief at the domestic level. The jurisprudence of ECtHR should evolve towards an approach that would be willing to substantively tackle freedom of religion or belief claims that challenge long-standing state–religion arrangements based on consistent and predictable interpretive principles. This approach should refrain from relying on the doctrine of margin of appreciation as an easy way out and restraint based on policy considerations.

3 The Right to Acquire Legal Personality

A Substantive Component of the Right to Freedom of Religion or Belief

3.1 Introduction

Acquisition of legal personality plays a key role in the effective protection of the collective dimension of freedom of religion or belief. In spite of the well-established international legal guarantee on freedom of thought, conscience, religion or belief, many religious or belief communities encounter varying degrees of restrictions when exercising the right to acquire legal personality and other forms of recognition. Religious beliefs may be banned entirely, like in the case of Falun Gang in China,[1] making it an offense to profess a certain religion. Theological assessments and lack of observance of the principle of neutrality on the part of state officials and ensuing regulations may trigger violent attacks on specific communities, like in the case of the Ahmaddiya community in Indonesia.[2] Religious activity may be allowed only for registered religious communities and the criteria for registration may be difficult to fulfill, lie in the case of the religion law in Kyrgyzstan.[3] Sadly, it is

1 The UN Special Rapporteur on Freedom of Religion or Belief Reports, E/CN.4/2005/61, paras 37–38; E/CN.4/2006/5/Add.1, para. 109; A/HRC/4/21/Add.1, para. 88; A/HRC/7/10/Add.1, para. 32; A/HRC/10/8/Add.1, para. 22; A/HRC/13/40/Add.1, paras 71–74.

2 The UN Special Rapporteur on Freedom of Religion or belief expressed concern over an impending ban of the Ahmadiyya community in Indonesia and the potential risk of violence in this context. Reportedly, the Government advisory board Bakor Pakem (Coordinating Body for the Monitoring of Mystical Beliefs) on 16 April 2008 asserted that the Ahmadiyya faith was deviant to Islam and issued a recommendation that the organization and its activities be banned by the President. The Special Rapporteur emphasized that an official ban of the Ahmadiyya organization would unduly restrict their believers' religious freedom. In addition, she stressed that a ban might increase the risk of attacks on Ahmadiyya followers by vigilante groups. Report of the UN Special Rapporteur on Freedom of Religion or Belief, UN Doc. A/HRC/10/8/Add.1, 16 February 2009, p. 16.

3 The 2009 Law: requires all religious communities to re-register with the then SARA (now replaced by the SCRA) by 1 January 2010; bars communities not registered by the SCRA and the Justice Ministry from receiving legal status, for which a SCRA certificate is necessary; and bars those with fewer than 200 members from registering with the SCRA. All 200 must be adult Kyrgyz citizens. Even assuming that a community has 200 members willing to act as founders—which many do not—the 200 are to supply their full name, full date of birth, home address, place of work and job title and passport number. See Forum 18, "KYRGYZSTAN: Religious freedom survey,

possible to enumerate too many examples here, ranging from non-accommodation of certain aspects of freedom of religion, such as the right to train clergy for religious groups, to imposition of conditions that are difficult to meet for acquiring religious entity status that is necessary in order to engage in certain activities and enjoy certain legal benefits or privileges.[4] All of these macro level arrangements also have enormous effects on the lives of individuals and doubtless influence their individual enjoyment of the right to freedom of religion or belief.

This chapter examines the right to acquire legal personality in international human rights law, with particular reference to the right to freedom of religion or belief. First, an overview of the legal and practical significance of possessing legal personality for religious or belief communities is presented. Secondly, the chapter sets out to embed the right to acquire legal personality of religious or belief communities in human rights law within the UN and CoE human rights protection schemes and explores its substantive scope and the nature of obligations that have been recognized so far. Thirdly, key central and recurring limitations imposed by states are demonstrated. It is argued that the right to acquire legal personality holds a crucial significance as an *enabling right* and *empowering right* within the scope of the right to freedom of religion or belief and that precisely for this reason it may be the subject of dispute between states and religious or belief groups. It is also argued that while the strict interpretation of the restriction clauses of the provisions protecting the right to freedom of religion or belief may be a guarantee against arbitrary state legislation and practice there is room for improvement of protection against wide-scale repressive practice. Since neutrality and obligation on the part of states to ensure pluralism are traced as overarching themes, in this chapter the role of state religion relations in the enjoyment of religious/belief communities of their right to freedom of religion and belief in the context of acquisition of legal personality will be highlighted.

3.2 The Significance and Function of Legal Personality as an Enabling Right

The collective dimension of freedom of religion or belief is generally exercised in a highly regulated sphere of interaction between states and groups of believers. Although acts carried out in community with others can vary in different belief systems, they can be comprehensively covered under a broad interpretation of worship, observance, practice and teaching. In national laws many of these activities generally require that the communities first have legal personality or a certain formation as a legally recognizable entity.[5] Some examples of such acts may be founding a religious

December 2009", 17 February 2009. Available: http://www.forum18.org/Archive.php?article_id=1388 [Accessed 16 January 2015].

4 The Reports of the UN Special Rapporteur on Freedom of Religion or Belief provide countless examples from across the regions of the world. For documents related to the Special Rapporteur's Mandate, see: http://www.ohchr.org/EN/Issues/FreedomReligion/Pages/FreedomReligionIndex.aspx [Accessed 16 January 2015].

5 Conversely, there are belief groups that reject any kind of official organization and institutional relations with the state.

organization of a certain legal capacity, purchasing buildings for the purpose of worship or other communal activities, maintaining such places, engaging in financial transactions with individuals and institutions, providing education for their followers and others by way of establishing schools. This list is certainly not exhaustive and may differ in accordance with the acts a group of believers seek to engage in based on their dogma and purposes. Since these acts may, generally, necessitate, *inter alia*, accommodation, allocation, regulation, permits, supervision on the part of states, religious or belief communities find themselves in a wide sphere of interaction *vis à vis* the state. This highly regulated and complex sphere of interaction between the state and the religious/belief communities reveals many intricacies that are involved in the international protection of the collective dimension of freedom of religion or belief.

The significance of the right to acquire legal personality is best seen in its *enabling and empowering* function. As an enabling right it empowers belief communities to exercise their rights, including those protected within the scope of the collective dimension of freedom of religion or belief. Legal personality is significant for belief groups because it *enables* religious or belief communities to have a legally recognizable existence and act, not as members, but as one organized body, and engage in religious or other activities as a composite body. A legal person is a legal entity that exists as a body and is so affected by law.[6] Such an entity remains identifiable as the same entity even when its individual membership changes. By acquiring legal personality, a religious/belief community gains a will of its own that expresses it as a community, a capacity that allows the community to directly acquire rights and assume obligations and the right to sue in court as plaintiffs. Hence once the community has gained legal personality, it is no longer individuals who own a place of worship or provide humanitarian assistance or run a faith based school but the *community* as such. It is also crucial that the form of legal entity status that a belief or religious community may acquire be appropriate and adequate for the nature of belief communities; facilitating the exercise of the right to freedom of religion or belief in worship, observance, practice and teaching with certain benefits.

States, more often than not, regulate public activities of religious communities in relation to the state and private actors with a view to facilitate and/or control these acts. In this context, legal personality is, many times, a pre-requisite and thus an element that may function as a form of restriction in national legal systems, in the collective exercise of the right to manifest one's religion or belief in worship, observance, practice and teaching. For religious organizations of a considerable size, legal entity status is vital as a practical matter because otherwise they cannot function effectively and efficiently.[7] Without legal status a belief community cannot directly and in an empowered capacity rent or own property, collect

6 Beale, N. and H. Bateman (2007) *Dictionary of Law: Over 8,000 Words Clearly Defined*, A&C Black.

7 W.C. Durham Jr. (2004) "Religious Association Laws", in T. Lindholm, W.C. Durham and B.G. Tahzib-Lie (eds.), *Facilitating Freedom of Religion or Belief: A Deskbook*, Dordrecht: Martinus Nijhoff, note 7, p. 327.

donations, open a bank account, make contracts with employees. The fact that in many systems legal entity status confers credibility, legitimacy, respectability and prestige may be equally important,[8] and thus may be a motivation to acquire a legal entity status. Legal entity status has also been seen as important for belief groups in the confrontation of opposing groups and media organizations.[9]

In their regulatory role states enjoy a wide discretion in determining how religious or belief communities are to acquire legal capacity and thus establish the means, capacity and form in which belief communities may engage in direct and indirect relations with states and their institutions. In an endeavor to regulate specific collective acts, states may require the acquisition of legal personality and/or establishment of a certain form of an association. These may involve some benefits, such as tax exemptions. Or, states may require registration or a form of legal personality pursuing a legitimate aim of ensuring that religious organizations are acting in accordance with law and do not present any danger for a democratic society.

There may be various ways of acquiring legal personality depending on the arrangement in individual states. In many European countries religious or belief groups have the possibility of acquiring a general form of association or a form of association particularly designed for belief communities.[10] In most European legal systems there are several types of religious organizations all with different criteria that often result in complicated, multi-tiered systems of legal recognition.[11] Most OSCE (Organization for Security and Co-operation in Europe) participating states do not require a religious organization to register, whereas a few require registration as a condition for operating as a religion.[12] There are also situations where a

8 Ibid. p. 333.

9 Lehnhof, L.S. (2002) "Freedom of Religious Association: The Right of Religious Organizations to Obtain Legal Entity Status under the European Convention", *Brigham Young University Law Review*, p. 561.

10 Ferrari, Silvio (2007) "Registration of Religious Organizations in the European Union Member States", February. Available: http://www.statoechiese.it/images/stories/papers/200702/ferraris_oslo.pdf [Accessed 16 January 2015].

11 Uitz, R. (2007) *Freedom of Religion*, Belgium: Council of Europe Publishing, p. 87. Also see, Durham, C., N. Peterson and E. Sewell, (2005) "Introduction to a Comparative Analysis of Religious Association Laws in Post-Communist Europe", in C. Durham and S. Ferrari (eds.), *Laws on Religion and the State in Post-Communist Europe*, Leuven: Peeters.

12 Indeed, several have mechanisms through which a religious group can achieve entity status without going through any formal process with the state. In France, a group can obtain entity status by filing a declaration with the applicable department and publishing it in the Journal Officiel. Not even publication is required for the creation of an entity in Sweden and Switzerland. The Netherlands also recognizes informal associations that can be created by following certain steps. These are simple and can be completed without a notary. Russian law poses some barriers to acquiring entity status, but it is very clear that a group can operate without entity status.

Durham, C. (1999) "Freedom of Religion or Belief: Laws Affecting the Structuring of Religious Communities", OSCE Review Conference (ODIHR Background Paper 1999/4).

state does not have a clear and foreseeable regulation that religious communities can take into consideration when they set out to acquire legal personality or establish a religious association. The latter arrangement, unfortunately, generally results in discriminatory, arbitrary or non-uniform practice. Since legislation in this area can so readily facilitate or restrict religious freedom, it has been observed that it becomes an important barometer of the general climate of freedom of religion in a country.[13] The 2011 Report of the UN Special Rapporteur on Freedom of Religion or Belief provides a comprehensive account of the obstacles that are created to the effective protection of freedom of religion or belief when an adequate legal status framework is not put in place.[14]

Indeed, when it comes to the exercise of associative rights of religious or belief communities state practice generally reflects complex historical and political attitudes toward all or certain religious or belief communities particularly as regards their organized activities. Krishnaswami's remarks in his pivotal "Study of Discrimination in the Matter of Religious Rights and Practices" are helpful in depicting the sphere of contention.

> History and contemporary practice show a remarkable difference in the attitude of public authorities towards these two freedoms [freedom to assembly and associate] when they are applied in the field of religion or belief… In many fields freedom of association and the right to organize have been more readily conceded than freedom of assembly. But in the field of religion, freedom of association and the right to organize have often been, and still are, denied or severely curtailed, whereas freedom of assembly in houses of worship has been recognized first, at least for the dominant religion, and later for a number of recognized—or even all—religions or beliefs. This difference is not accidental; public authorities consider that, in fields other than religion, there is less of a threat to public order and security in the existence of permanent organizations than in the congregation in one place of a large number of people. In the religious field, on the other hand, a meeting held for purposes related purely to matters of religion or belief does not generally present a threat to public order and security, *whereas the establishment of a new and permanent organization may be considered dangerous because of the considerable impact which a religion or belief normally has upon its followers.*[15]

It follows from the above review that legal personality is a crucial enabling right for the enjoyment of both individual and collective rights guaranteed under freedom of religion or belief provisions. Indeed, lack of legal personality eradicates

13 Durham, *supra* note 7, p. 326.

14 Report of the UN Special Rapporteur on Freedom of Religion or Belief, UN Doc. A/HRC/19/60, 22 December 2011, pp. 40–58.

15 Krishnaswami, A. (1960) "Study of Discrimination in the Matter of Religious Rights and Practices", UN Doc. E/CN.4/Sub.2/200/Rev.1, U.N. Sales No. 60. XIV.2, p. 31. Emphasis added.

almost every possible form of collective manifestation.[16] It is equally clear that states, aware of its *enabling* function, regulate this key sphere of state-religious/belief community interaction rather heavily. While recognizing its enabling function, it is important to remember that legal entity status or registration cannot be a pre-condition for manifestations of religion or belief, thus criminalization of non-registered worship is incompatible with states' obligations under international provisions protecting the right to freedom of religion or belief.[17] Its significance and therefore its highly regulated nature compels strict monitoring of its protection in international and national legal systems. Now let us turn to explore the basis of the right to acquire legal entity status within the relevant freedom of religion or belief protection provisions.

3.3 The Legal Basis of the Right to Acquire Legal Personality

While the right of belief communities to acquire legal personality is not explicitly stated in any of the human rights provisions it is deeply embedded primarily and foremost in the right to freedom of religion or belief. It is most directly linked to the right to freedom of religion or belief depending, however, on the context of each case; other interdependent rights become relevant, *inter alia*, the right to association,[18] the right to court,[19] and prohibition of discrimination. Below, based on the protection of the right to freedom of religion or belief and other relevant human rights as they are protected in the ECHR and the ICCPR, a comparative legal analysis of the right to acquire legal personality is presented.

The right of a religious or belief community to obtain legal personality has been progressively recognized as a part of the protection of the collective dimension of freedom of religion or belief. Notwithstanding the lack of explicit reference in the relevant legal provisions, legal personality is theoretically and practically an intrinsic part of the right to freedom of thought, conscience and religion. The reason for this is that acquisition of such an adequate form of legal personality is a pre-condition or a necessary means for the enjoyment of many aspects of the right to freedom of religion or belief. In the case of *Metropolitan Church of Besserabia and Other v. Modova*, the ECtHR held that, because of the absence of recognition, a church could not organize itself or operate, and lacking legal personality, it could not bring legal proceedings to protect its assets, indispensable for worship, while its members could not meet to carry on religious activities without contravening the domestic legislation.[20] Thus providing non-discriminatory procedures and processes for the acquisition of an adequate form of legal personality for belief

16 Taylor, P.M. (2005) *Freedom of Religion: UN and European Human Rights Law and Practice*, Cambridge: Cambridge University Press, p. 291.
17 Human Rights Committee, 7 April 2010, UN Doc. CCPR/C/UZB/CO/3, p. 6 (*Concluding Observations: Uzbekistan*).
18 Article 11 of the ECHR.
19 Article 6 of the ECHR and Article 14 of the ICCPR.
20 *Metropolitan Church of Besserabia and Others v. Moldova*, 13 December 2001, European Court of Human Rights, No. 45701/99, para. 129.

communities for the manifestation of belief or religion should be considered a positive obligation for states.[21] Indeed, the strongest recognition of states' obligations in this sphere came unequivocally in the Hungarian case where the ECtHR held that "there is a positive obligation incumbent on the State to put in place a system of recognition which facilitates the acquisition of legal personality by religious communities".[22]

The UN Special Rapporteur refers to legal personality as a "*necessary* provision by the state" that is needed by religious or belief communities in order to be able to take collective action.[23] In this context the Vienna Concluding Document of 1989 may also be recalled; it stipulates that the participating States "will… grant upon the request to communities of believers, practicing or prepared to practice their faith within the constitutional framework of their States, recognition of the status provided for them in their respective countries".[24]

This commitment is significant not least because it recognizes the need to acquire a certain legal personality in order to practice a religion or belief. It does not prescribe a particular form of legal personality thus leaving it open to states and the possibility of diverse arrangements. States undertake a positive obligation to create a legal status through which religious or belief communities can carry out religious activities.

The core freedom of religion or belief provisions stipulated under Article 18 of the UDHR,[25] Article 18 of the ICCPR,[26] and Article 9 of the ECHR constitute the basis of the right to acquire legal personality. For the purposes of our analysis we will take Article 9(1) of the ECHR:

> Everyone has the right to freedom of thought, conscience and religion; this right includes freedom to change his religion or belief, and freedom, either alone or in community with others and in public and private, to manifest his religion or belief, in worship, teaching, practice and observance.[27]

21 On positive obligations see, *inter alia*, Mowbrai, A.R. (2004) *The Development of Positive Obligations under the European Convention on Human Rights by the European Court of Human Rights*, Oxford: Hart.
22 *Magyar Kereszteny Mennonita Egyhaz and Others v. Hungary*, 8 April 2014, European Court of Human Rights, Nos. 70945/11, 23611/12, 26998/12, 41150/12, 41155/12, 41463/12, 41553/12, 54977/12 and 56581/12, para. 90.
23 Report of the UN Special Rapporteur on Freedom of Religion or Belief, *supra* note 14, para. 23. Emphasis added.
24 Principle 16.3, OSCE, *Concluding Document of the Vienna Meeting of Representatives of the Participating States of the Conference on Security and Cooperation in Europe*, adopted on 17 January 1989.
25 Universal Declaration of Human Rights, GA Res 217A, UN Doc. A/810, 1948, p. 71.
26 International Covenant of Civil and Political Rights, Article 18.
27 ECHR Article 9. The corresponding Article 18 in the ICCPR is substantially the same except for the absence of the word "change his religion". Rather, it uses the phrase "to have or to adopt a religion". See Article 18 of the ICCPR.

It is important to note that "everyone has" the right to freedom of religion or belief.[28] The provisions do not distinguish between citizens of a country and immigrants, residents, stateless persons, refugees and foreign religious personnel, and hence this retains the element of universality.[29] Hence, where a certain legal status or official recognition is required as a precondition to the manifestation of religion or belief, non-citizens also have this right. While states may desire or tend to place restrictions on the involvement of non-citizens by limiting the scope of religious association laws to citizens or permanent residents,[30] these restrictions must be in line with the permissible limitations clause and not be discriminatory. The ECtHR dealt with this issue in the case of *The Moscow Branch of Salvation Army v. Russia* where the "foreign origin" of the applicant was held by authorities as a ground for refusing re-registration.[31] The Russian Religions Act prohibited foreign nationals from being founders of Russian religious organizations.[32] However, the European Court did not find a justification for the difference in treatment of Russian and foreign nationals in regards to their ability to exercise the right to freedom of religion through participation in the life of organized religious communities.[33] A number of other grounds related to its foreign origin did not have their base in domestic law, hence the arguments pertaining to the applicant's foreign origin were found neither "relevant and sufficient" nor "prescribed by law".[34] A restriction based on the foreign origin of an individual would need to be justified by national authorities.

As Durham has duly stressed, it is important to remember the phrase "*has* the right"; this right is not, "something bestowed by the state…but something that individuals and religious groups have simply by virtue of their human nature".[35] Such an understanding also supports the argument that freedom of religion is a right of recognized or registered communities and states have to maintain a facilitative approach to this process in order to guarantee that everyone can enjoy it. The UN Special Rapporteur recalls applicable international obligations:

> Such an administrative decision [on legal personality] should not be misconceived as an act of mercy, however. Under international law, States are obliged to take an active role in facilitating the full enjoyment of human rights, including freedom of religion or belief. By not providing appropriate

28 Evans, M.D. (1997) *Religious Liberty and International Law in Europe*, Cambridge: Cambridge University Press, p. 286. UDHR, Article 18 ICCPR, and Article 18 also contain the word "everyone".

29 Durham, *supra* note 7, p. 351. Also while Article 16 of the ECHR allows states to impose restrictions on the political activity of aliens, no such restrictions are mentioned with regard to the exercise of freedom of religion.

30 Ibid.

31 *The Moscow Branch of Salvation Army v. Russia*, 5 October 2006, European Court of Human Rights, Application No. 72881/01, paras 81–86.

32 Ibid.

33 Ibid. para. 83.

34 Ibid. para. 86.

35 Durham, *supra* note 7, p. 351.

> legal options that, *de jure* and *de facto*, are accessible to all religious or belief groups interested in obtaining a legal personality status, States would fail to honor their obligations under the human right to freedom of religion or belief.[36]

The question of what constitutes a belief or religion in the context of legal personality is a pertinent question for at least two reasons. First, in order to qualify for the protection afforded to manifestation of religion or belief, the belief or religion in question has to be considered a "belief or religion" for the purposes of the respective articles. Secondly, states often tend to make judgments on religions or beliefs in the context of granting legal status to belief groups. Both the HRCttee and the European Court have adopted a broad interpretation of religion or belief so as to cover both theistic and atheistic, traditional and non-traditional beliefs.[37] According to Evans, the lack of a guiding principle utilized by Strasbourg organs in the determination of which religions or belief are protected "made their definition [somewhat] meaningless".[38] Having said that, it is clear that not all ideas or views are regarded as beliefs. Opinions or views are not protected,[39] under freedom of religion or belief. The ECtHR has held that beliefs must have a "certain level of cogency, seriousness, cohesion and importance".[40] The HRCttee, on the other hand, drew the line when it held that a belief consisting primarily or exclusively of the worship and distribution of a narcotic drug cannot be brought under the protection of Article 18.[41]

36 Report of the UN Special Rapporteur, *supra* note 14, para. 43.

37 Van Dijk, P. and G.J.H. Van Hoof (1998) *Theory and Practice of the European Convention of Human Rights*, Dordrecht: Kluwer, pp. 759–760. The HRCttee, in GC 22 on Article 18, elaborated on which beliefs are protected, saying that Article 18

> protects theistic, non-theistic and atheistic beliefs, as well as the right not to profess any religion or belief. The terms "belief" and "religion" are to be broadly construed. Article 18 is not limited in its application to traditional religions or to religions and beliefs with institutional characteristics or practices analogous to those of traditional religions. The Committee therefore views with concern any tendency to discriminate against any religion or belief for any reason, including the fact that they are newly established, or represent religious minorities that may be the subject of hostility on the part of a predominant religious community.

General Comment 22 of the Human Rights Committee on Article 18 of the ICCPR, UN Doc. HRI/GEN/1Rev.1 at 35 (1994), para. 2.

38 For a more detailed coverage, see Evans, *supra* note 28, pp. 386–397 and 392.

39 These would properly be addressed under freedom to hold opinions.

40 *Campbell and Cosans v. UK*, 25 February 1982, European Commission of Human Rights, 7511/76, 7743/76, para. 36.

41 The authors said that they are

> members and "plenipotentiaries" of the "Assembly of the Church of the Universe", whose beliefs and practices, according to the authors, necessarily involve the care, cultivation, possession, distribution, maintenance, integrity and worship of the "Sacrament" of the Church. Whereas the authors also refer to this

The HRCttee, in its General Comment on Article 18, has expressed concern over tendencies to discriminate against any religion or belief for any reason, including the fact that they are newly established, or represent religious minorities that may be subject to hostility on the part of the predominant religious community.[42] The same approach has been rigorously utilized in the review of reports on the implementation of the ICCPR where the HRCttee criticized the differential treatment of traditional and non-traditional religious groups in the process of acquisition of legal personality.[43] The HRCttee has drawn attention to "registration or recognition procedures" that affect the enjoyment of Article 18. With regard to Jordan, the Committee expressed concern about the non-recognition of the Bahai religion.[44] Similarly, in Iran where only three religions are recognized, non-recognized religions, again particularly the circumstances of the Bahai community were viewed with concern and the state practice incompatible with obligations under Article 18.[45] In these cases evidently states are making a judgment on the "legitimacy" of a religion or belief whereas they have no such capacity and this is clearly incompatible with Article 18.

Even though the HRCttee has not produced comprehensive case law on the issue, taken together with its General Comment 22, its deliberations on a case might be helpful in understanding its position on neutrality and impartiality of state in their relations with religious groups. In a case brought before the HRCttee, *Sisters of the Holy Cross of the Third Order of Saint Francis v. Sri Lanka,* where Sister Immaculate Joseph and 80 other sisters applied for incorporation in order to advance their activities in the area of teaching and other charity work, the Committee considered the justifiability of restrictions that resulted in the refusal of incorporation status.[46] The Bill establishing the incorporation was objected to and filed in the jurisdiction of the Supreme Court which upheld the objection taking into account several articles of the Sri Lankan Constitution; the non-recognition of a right to propagate a religion, the special provision giving Buddhism the foremost place and the state's duty to protect and foster *Buddha Sasana*.[47] Hence the Supreme Court held that the propagation and spreading of Christianity as

"Sacrament" as "God's tree of life", it is generally known under the designation cannabis sativa or marijuana.

M.A.B., W.A.T. and J.-A.Y.T. v. Canada, 8 April 1994, Human Rights Committee, No. 570/1993, UN Doc. CCPR/C/50/D/570/1993

42 General Comment 22 of the HRCttee, para. 2.

43 Human Rights Committee, 2 May 2011, UN Doc. CCPR/C/MNG/CO/5, p. 6. (*Concluding Observations: Mongolia*).

44 Human Rights Committee, 10 August 1994, UN Doc. CCPR/C/79/Add.35, para. 10 (*Concluding Observations: Jordan*).

45 Human Rights Committee, 3 August 1993, UN Doc. CCPR/C/79/Add.25, para. 16 (*Concluding Observations: Iran*).

46 *Sister Immaculate Joseph and 80 Teaching Sisters of the Holy Cross of the Third Order of Saint Francis in Menzingen of Sri Lanka v. Sri Lanka*, 3 November 2005, Human Rights Committee, No. 1249/2004, UN Doc. CCPR/C/85/D 1249/2004.

47 Ibid., para. 2.3.

expressed in the terms of clause 3 of the Bill, which listed a number or activities such as humanitarian assistance, teaching and spreading of knowledge of Catholic religion, would not be permissible as these would impair the existence of Buddhism.[48] In the proceedings before the HRCttee, it was recognized that the tenet to spread knowledge, to propagate beliefs and provide assistance to others, is a central part of many religions hence these aspects are part of an individual's manifestation of religion protected under Article 18 paragraph 1. Therefore, the Supreme Court's determination of the unconstitutionality of the Bill establishing the incorporation, needed to be justified under paragraph 3 of Article 18. The justification for the Supreme Court's decision was that the Order's activities would, by means of provision of material and other benefits to vulnerable people, improperly propagate religion. The HRCttee found, however, that the grounds set forth in the case did not form sufficient grounds to show that these restrictions were necessary on the grounds enumerated in the Covenant.

This case is important in that it involves constitutional protection and support of a certain belief, namely *Buddha Sasana*. The HRCttee noted that the decision of the Supreme Court provided no justification for the conclusion that the Bill would impair the very existence of Buddhism and hence the violation of Article 18(1). This finding, however, raises the question of whether the HRCttee's decision would be different if there was evidence indicating that actually the activities of the Sisters' incorporation could impair the existence of Buddhism. Whether, in light of the premise that states should be impartial guarantors of freedom of religion or belief and co-existence of various belief communities, this constitutional clause would have been incompatible with ICCPR calls for further examination and clarification. One belief group may very well, by advancing its teachings and increasing the number of its followers, constitute a threat towards the existence of another belief. This decision of the HRCttee, raises the question of whether at the universal level there is greater respect afforded to "maintaining" religion as opposed to greater protection provided for propagation of religion and possibility of "changing" of religion. Such a difference in approach would be reflective of the debate at the UN level on the "right to change one's religion" and "the right to maintain one's religion" evident in the preparatory work for the drafting of ICCPR Article 18.[49]

On the other hand, the ECtHR unequivocally held that the right to freedom of religion or belief, "excludes any discretion on the part of the State to determine whether religious beliefs or means used to express such beliefs are legitimate".[50] Therefore assessments of legitimacy in the decisions and processes concerning the acquisition of legal personality would not be permissible. The significance of this stance cannot be overestimated for vulnerable groups such as religious minorities or minorities within majorities in the context of decisions concerning associative activities which are questioned by states in light of dominant religious doctrine.

48 Ibid.
49 Evans, *supra* note 28, pp. 201–202.
50 *Manoussakis and others v. Greece*, 26 September 1996, European Court of Human Rights, No. 59/1995/565/651, para. 47.

The ECtHR addressed the issue of legitimacy of belief in the case of *Metropolitan Church of Bessarabia v. Moldova* where the applicants claimed that the authorities' refusal to recognize their church infringed their freedom of religion, since only religions recognized by the government could be practiced in Moldova.[51] While assessing the state's arguments for justifying restrictions, the European Court referred to its established case law which recognizes that in a democratic society where several religions coexist within one and the same population, it may be necessary to place restrictions on this freedom in order to reconcile the interests of the various groups and ensure that everyone's beliefs are respected.[52] Therefore restrictions are viewed as having the purpose of ensuring various groups' coexistence, not of eliminating certain groups so that some groups can exist without experiencing conflict. In ensuring this coexistence the state enjoys a regulatory power in the use of which it has the duty to remain neutral and impartial. The role of states is envisaged as the "neutral and impartial organizer of the exercise of various religions, faiths and beliefs".[53] In addition, this defined role is perceived as "conducive to public order, religious harmony and tolerance in a democratic society".[54] The principle of neutrality requires that any assessment on the part of the state regarding the legitimacy of religious beliefs or ways in which these beliefs are expressed is not acceptable. Consequently, in processes pertaining to acquisition of legal personality or recognition of religious groups states have no room for the assessment of the legitimacy of the religion of the group in question. What is relevant and significant in this context is that "religion or belief" is to be broadly interpreted when states draft and apply rules concerning the acquisition of legal personality, recognition and registration of religious or belief communities and likewise authorities have to be guided not by "whether a religion or belief is legitimate or not", but by whether it is a "religion or belief" as understood under the respective treaty provisions. Unfortunately, so far, neither the Court nor the Committee have provided a definition that can serve as a guide for states.[55]

Bearing in mind the complexities posed by state-religion relations, as it has been underscored in Chapter 2, it may be concluded that the substantive scope given to the respective international provisions so far, considers the assessment of legitimacy of religion or belief incompatible with the ICCPR and the ECHR. On the other hand, while differential treatment of various religious groups may be questioned, as in the case of *Sister Immaculate Joseph v. Sri Lanka*,[56] this does not

51 *Metropolitan Church of Bessarabia and others v. Moldova*, *supra* note 20.

52 Ibid., para. 115.

53 Ibid., para. 116.

54 *Refah Partisi (the Welfare Party) and Others v. Turkey*, 13 February 2003, European Court of Human Rights, Grand Chamber, Nos. 41340/98, 41342/98, 41343/98 and 41344/98, para. 91.

55 See discussion on the definition of religion or belief and how the European Commission of Human Rights has avoided a definition in Evans, C. (2001) *Freedom of Religion under the European Convention on Human Rights*, Oxford: Oxford University Press, pp. 51–62.

56 *Sister Immaculate Joseph and 80 Teaching Sisters of the Holy Cross of the Third Order of Saint Francis in Menzingen of Sri Lanka v. Sri Lanka*, *supra* note 46.

automatically imply a willingness on the part of adjudicators to require that a state observes equal distance to the diverse religions found in the country. A certain restraint seems to withhold a more rigorous scrutiny in this sphere.

An important related question pertains to the types of legal personality that the right to freedom of religion or belief extends to. What is the scope of protection and where is the limit drawn? While a comprehensive examination of the various forms of legal entities belief groups may establish is beyond the scope of this chapter, it is useful to note a number of key guiding principles. Acts that are protected under the right to freedom of religion or belief provisions in the ECHR and the ICCPR extend to manifestations of religion or belief "in *worship, observance, practice and teaching*".[57] The scope of acts protected under these provisions has also implications for the types of legal entity belief groups have a right to establish. Domestic legal entity options must be suitable and adequate for belief groups to engage in acts necessary to manifest religion or belief in worship, observance, practice and teaching. Since it will determine the extent of protection, an accurate understanding of the scope of these categories is crucial. An adequate and appropriate form of legal personality is, more often than not, practically and theoretically, a requirement for exercise of the collective dimension of freedom of religion or belief in virtually all its components. Therefore it is an integral part of the protection. The nexus between legal personality and manifestation of religion or belief lies in the enabling function of the former. The legal question, then, is whether the absence of legal personality or the particular form of it or regulations concerning it, are compatible with the right to manifest one's religion or belief in community with others in its collective dimension. Supervisory bodies assess whether interference in the process of acquisition of legal personality constitutes an unjustified interference in the right to have a belief or religion or to manifest religion or belief. The ECtHR has confirmed that denying legal personality can amount to an interference with the right to freedom of religion as protected in Article 9 of the European Convention on Human Rights,[58] thus the Court first moved toward embracing a right to legal personality, albeit implicitly. However, in 2014, a positive obligation on the part of states to provide a system of recognition which facilitates the acquisition of legal personality by religious communities was recognized explicitly.[59] Further the Court stated that:

> The Court further considers that there is *no right* under Article 11 in conjunction with Article 9 for religious organizations *to have a specific legal status.* Articles 9 and 11 of the Convention only require the State to ensure that religious communities have the possibility of acquiring legal capacity as entities under the civil law; they do not require that a specific public-law status be accorded to them.[60]

57 ECHR, Article 9 and ICCPR, Article 18. Emphasis added.
58 *Metropolitan Church of Bessarabia and others v. Moldova, supra* note 20.
59 *Magyar Kereszteny Mennonita Egyhaz and Others v. Hungary, supra* note 22.
60 Ibid., para. 91. Emphasis added.

The jurisprudence of Strasbourg organs has not provided any description of these categories and what forms of manifestations are protected in each of them. The Commission has said that Article 9 primarily protects personal beliefs and religious creeds and "acts which are intimately linked to these, such as worship and devotion."[61] Here the important criterion has been that the act must be intimately linked to the belief in order to qualify for a form of manifestation in worship. However, in a case involving the wearing of a small cross on a necklace at the workplace, the ECtHR appears to have significantly moved away from this strong link that must be established by individuals.[62]

The European Court has not considered cases pertaining to associative acts of belief groups solely on the basis of Article 9; instead it relied on either Article 9 interpreted in light of Article 11 or on Article 11 interpreted in light of Article 9. This application may be indicative of a certain narrow view of the acts protected under manifestation of religion or belief in worship, teaching, practice and observance. A broader view of manifestations of religion or belief through associative acts would enable the European Court to decide such cases solely under Article 9. On the other hand, the strong protection of associative rights in the ECHR system may be the reason for the strong protection of the associative rights of belief groups found in this system.

In contrast to the narrow view concerning manifestation of the ECHR system—particularly until recently—the HRCttee has held consistently that the freedom to manifest one's religion or belief encompasses "a broad range of acts".[63] The Committee's General Comment on Article 18 underlines that the concept of worship extends to ritual and ceremonial acts giving direct expression to belief and practices integral to such acts, including the building of places of worship, the use of ritual formula and objects, the display of symbols and the observance of holidays and days of rest.[64] As for the observance and practice of religion or belief these may include, in the Committee's view, not only ceremonial acts but also such customs as the observance of dietary regulations, the wearing of distinctive clothing or head coverings, participation in rituals associated with

61 *C. v. United Kingdom*, 15 December 1983, European Commission (Admissibility), No. 10358/83, 37. Accordingly, establishing places of worship, ownership of objects necessary for worship and facilitating religious services in prison have been viewed as included within the right to worship. See among others, *Manoussakis and others v. Greece*, *supra* note 50, *Holy Monasteries v. Greece*, 9 December 1994, European Court of Human Rights, Nos. 13092/87, 13984/88.

62 *Eweida and Others v. United Kingdom*, 15 January 2013, European Court of Human Rights, Nos. 48420/10, 59842/10, 51671/10, 36516/10. The case is also important because "the religious liberty questions were in fact considered by the Court rather than being dismissed as being inapplicable in the workplace.... The Court specifically repudiated both the necessity test and the doctrine of 'voluntary surrender' of Article 9 rights at work". Leigh, I. and A. Hambler (2014) "Religious Symbols, Conscience, and the Rights of Others", *Oxford Journal of Law and Religion*, 3(1), pp. 2–24.

63 General Comment 22, *supra* note 37, para. 4.

64 Ibid.

certain stages of life and the use of a particular language customarily spoken by the group.[65] Practice and teaching may also include acts integral to the conduct by religious groups of their basic affairs, such as the freedom to choose their religious leaders, priests and teachers, the freedom to establish seminaries or religious schools and the freedom to prepare and distribute religious texts and publications.[66] These "broad range of acts" constitute the basis of the types of legal entity status that may be protected; belief groups must be able to acquire the type of legal entity status that will make it possible in their domestic settings to engage in the "broad range of acts".

The HRCttee considered a claim pertaining to associative acts of a belief group solely under Article 18 while noting that the claim also raised issues under Article 22.[67] In this respect the HRCttee and the ECtHR differ in their approach since the latter consistently applies Article 9 in light of Article 11 or Article 11 in light of Article 9. The HRCttee seems to take a broader view of the scope of Article 18 so as to include associative acts of belief groups. In this context it is important to remember that Article 6(b) of the 1981 Declaration protects the right to "establish and maintain appropriate charitable or humanitarian institutions".[68] Traditionally religious or belief groups engage in benevolent acts towards the poor, sick and vulnerable groups and depending on the domestic laws they may need to establish a legal entity to do this. It would be likely that under the ICCPR this would be decided under Article 18 as it has been in the case of *Sister Immaculate Joseph v. Sri Lanka.*[69] On the other hand, the ECtHR may decide such claims under Article 9 or Article 11 viewing them primarily as a matter of the right to association where Article 9 would provide the context where religious purpose is evident. While the right to establish charitable or humanitarian organizations is not unrestricted, given the strong protection of the right to association in the ECHR regime, it would not be wrong to expect that the right of religious or belief groups to establish such institutions would enjoy substantial protection.

Whether based solely on the provision protecting freedom of religion or belief or based on complementary provisions protecting the right to associate, the scope of protection appears to be fairly broad. However, manifestations of religion that seek to establish judicial systems may be where international protection may draw the line. The most relevant case in this respect is the *Refah Partisi v. Turkey*,[70] which dealt with the dissolution of a political party that sought to establish *sharia* and a multi-juridical system. Although the case was decided on the right to

65 Ibid.

66 Ibid.

67 *Sergei Malakhovsky and Alexander Pikul v. Belarus*, 26 July 2005, Human Rights Committee, No. 1207/2003, UN Doc. CCPR/C/84/D/1207/2003.

68 The UN Declaration on the Elimination of All Forms of Discrimination Based on Religion, see UN Doc. *Yearbook of the United Nations 1981*, pp. 880–881.

69 *Sister Immaculate Joseph and 80 Teaching Sisters of the Holy Cross of the Third Order of Saint Francis in Menzingen of Sri Lanka v. Sri Lanka*, *supra* note 45.

70 *Refah Partisi (the Welfare Party) and Others v. Turkey*, *supra* note 54.

freedom of association and not the right to freedom of religion or belief, its significance lies in the fact that it reveals the European Court's reservation about the establishment of religious jurisdiction in the context of the right to associate and implicitly in the context of the right to freedom of religion or belief.

Considering the enabling and empowering function of legal personality, it is reasonable to attribute a positive obligation to states to provide an *adequate* form of legal entity possibility,[71] not only for acquisition of legal personality status but also for the ability to maintain this status. A belief community may need a certain legal entity status in order to engage in acts that manifest their religion or belief. Without legal personality they cannot establish and maintain places of worship,[72] establish charitable or humanitarian institutions,[73] establish and run institutions for the dissemination of relevant publications,[74] establish institutions for teaching religion or belief;[75] thus the collective dimension of freedom of religion or belief may be significantly undermined. There may be situations where, without a proper legal entity, the community may run a risk of interference by the state. Such a risk is also unacceptable; the community must be able to expect to carry on with their affairs without the fear of interference. In *The Moscow Branch of Salvation Army v. Russia* the ECtHR took into consideration that the applicant "continuously ran the risk of having its accounts frozen and its assets seized".[76] The Court held that believers' right to freedom of religion encompasses the expectation that the community will be allowed to function peacefully, free from arbitrary state intervention.[77] Therefore, situations where authorities do not directly interfere but, also, do not provide the necessary legal status or conditions for a religious community as needed for legal protection, do not qualify as ensuring *peaceful enjoyment* of their right. This is particularly so where historical injustices are part of communities' collective memory. Where an organization could continue to profess their faith, hold services of worship and ceremonies and guide their followers, nevertheless where the legal position is affected, the refusal to register may lead to a claim to be a victim even if there was no prejudice and damage.[78]

In the context of states' positive obligation to ensure that an adequate form of legal personality is accessible for belief groups who desire to manifest their religion or belief via a legal entity, guidelines developed to ensure compliance with international law by non-adjudicatory bodies are useful in pointing to good practice. According to the OSCE-Venice Commission guidelines, registration should not be mandatory, although registration for acquiring legal personality is considered as

71 Mowbray, A.R. (2004) *The Development of Positive Obligations under the European Convention on Human Rights by the European Court of Human Rights*, Oxford: Hart.
72 1981 Declaration Article 6(a).
73 1981 Declaration, Article 6(b).
74 1981 Declaration, Article 6(d).
75 1981 Declaration, Article 6(e) and 6(g).
76 *The Moscow Branch of Salvation Army v. Russia, supra* note 31, para. 73.
77 *The Moscow Branch of Salvation Army v. Russia, supra* note 31, para. 71.
78 *The Moscow Branch of Salvation Army v. Russia, supra* note 31.

appropriate.[79] Similarly, lengthy existence in the state before registration is not deemed appropriate, other burdensome constraints or time delays before obtaining legal personality are questioned, caution against excessive governmental discretion in giving approvals is expressed, and requirements for re-registration are called for questioning, in particular provisions operating retroactively or that fail to protect vested interests. It continues:

> out of deference for the values of freedom of religion or belief, laws governing access to legal personality should be structured in ways that are facilitative of freedom of religion or belief; at a minimum, access to the basic rights associated with legal personality—for example, opening a bank account, renting or acquiring property for a place of worship or for other religious uses, entering into contracts, and the right to sue and be sued—should be available without excessive difficulty. In many legal systems, there are additional legal issues that have substantial impact on religious life that are often linked to acquiring legal personality—for example, obtaining land use or other governmental permits; inviting foreign religious leaders, workers, and volunteers into a country; arranging visits and ministries in hospitals, prisons, and the military; eligibility to establish educational institutions (whether for educating children or for training clergy); eligibility to establish separate religiously motivated charitable organizations[80]

Recognition or registration requirements imposed by states may constitute a significant administrative/legal obstacle to the enjoyment of the collective aspects of the right to freedom of religion or belief for belief communities. The detrimental effects of registration requirements on the exercise of freedom of religion have been captured in the reports of the UN Special Rapporteur on Freedom of Religion or Belief with scores of examples of unreasonable registration requirements established by states which amount to a complete denial of the possibility to register and consequently the inability of legal exercise of the collective manifestation of religion or belief.[81] The reports note that these requirements are often used by states as a means to limit the right of freedom of religion or members of certain religious communities.

79 OSCE-Venice Commission, *Guidelines for Review of Legislation Pertaining to Religion or Belief*, OSCE ODIHR, 2004, p. 17. These principles are further reinforced and elaborated in the OSCE-Venice Commission *Guidelines on Legal Personality of Religious or Belief Communities*, 2014.

80 Ibid. p. 18. The UN Special Rapporteur has also promoted these guidelines that point toward an accommodating approach. Report of the UN Special Rapporteur on Freedom of Religion or Belief, UN Doc. A/HRC/6/5, 20 July 2007, p. 8, para.11 and Report of the Special Rapporteur on Freedom of Religion or Belief, UN Doc. A/HRC/19/60.

81 For instance, in Angola current legislation on registration requires 100,000 signatures in order to legalize a religious community. UN Doc. HRC/4/21/Add.1—SR Report on Communications to Governments.

association. Where interference has been found, the assessment has moved on with the test to determine whether restrictions have been prescribed by law, pursued a legitimate aim and were necessary in a democratic society and proportionate to the aim pursued.

The significance of these aforementioned elements that must be taken into account when considering the legitimacy of restrictions cannot be overemphasized for religious groups or belief communities. The latter's right to freedom of religion or belief can be unduly restricted by laws that are drafted vaguely or who suffer as a consequence of a general negative attitudes in society and similarly of administrative authorities. Measures stemming from explicit or implicit negative bias against certain belief groups are evident, *inter alia*, in laws lacking precision paving the way for extensive discretionary powers by public authorities. In spite of the fact that prescription by law and discretion of officials are distinct factors, in terms of their effect they are highly inter-connected. The existence or lack of law and the clarity of its formulation determine the nature of its application by domestic authorities. Where there is lack of legislation or where legislation is too general or vague, conditions conducive for extensive discretion on the part of the officials may be created. In addition, those who are affected by the law in question are left in the dark as to the nature of their rights and obligations.

Related to the "prescribed by law" test is its consequence of extensive discretion that is created for those who apply the law. Conversely, extensive or unfettered discretion can be an indicator that the relevant law does not meet the standard quality of law required. As keenly observed and eloquently depicted by Podoprigora, in actual fact the most typical violations take place not in the form of legislation but in the form of administrative action which prevents believers from engaging in religious activities that are properly protected both by international human rights law and in most cases in domestic constitutions.[90] Religious communities and organizations have to make applications and receive permissions from officials who sit in administrative positions and use their discretion in the determination of numerous issues that have considerable effects on the lives of belief communities; these decisions can range from major issues such as recognition or registration decisions to relatively minor decisions on building permits, licenses for clergy, permits for worship places as well as public worship and gatherings for teaching or celebration purposes.[91] Such decisions may be routine or they can be arenas for discrimination and arbitrary practices depending on the "applicable legal standards that govern approvals, the attitudes of relevant governmental officials, the attitudes of the wider populace, the ability of the populace to exert political pressures on decision makers and a variety of other factors".[92]

90 Podoprigora, Roman (2004) "Freedom of Religion and Belief and Discretionary State Approval of Religious Activity", in Lindholm, Durham and Tahzib-Lie (eds.), *supra* note 7, p. 425.

91 Ibid.

92 Ibid., p. 426.

Since ensuring a fair and non-arbitrary process related to acquisition of legal personality, recognition and registration is important, the quality of *legislation* and its *implementation* by public officials are vital for the question at hand. The requirement that restrictions be *prescribed by law* stands out as a key element for the improvement of review of compliance with international norms and deserves further elaboration. When Article 29 of the UDHR was drafted, the use of the words "prescribed by law" were proposed to underline the need for "legal form"; however in a short while it became evident that it was equally necessary to qualify the nature of laws that states applied.[93] As for Article 18(3) of the ICCPR, the formulation "prescribed by law", according to Nowak, means that interference must be recorded in legislation or an unwritten norm of common law in such a way as to adequately specify provisions for the enforcement organs.[94] The HRCttee outlines its views on the limitations of Article 18 in its General Comment 22, paragraph 8 which calls for a strict interpretation of the limitation clause. The Committee holds that "the limitations imposed must be established by law and must not be applied in a manner that would vitiate the rights guaranteed in Article 18".[95] The nature of the cumulative criteria with regard to permissible restrictions is further emphasized by the Committee's views that the limitations may only be applied for those purposes for which they were prescribed and must be directly related and proportionate to the specific need on which they are predicated.[96] Furthermore, noteworthy is the clarification by the Committee on the meaning of "unlawful" and "arbitrary interference" in relation to the right to privacy.[97] According to the Committee, the term "unlawful" means that no interference can take place except in cases that are envisioned by law; in addition, interference that is authorized by states can only take place on the basis of law and this law must comply with the provisions, aims and objectives of the ICCPR. The concept of "arbitrariness" is used with the intention to guarantee that even interference provided by law should be in accordance with the provisions, aims and objectives of the Covenant and reasonable in the particular circumstances.

The HRCttee adopted a probing approach where conditions related to premises may constitute an obstacle to obtaining legal status. In a communication brought before the HRCttee, *S. Malakhovsky and A. Pikul v. Belarus*,[98] the applicants sought to register as a religious association; however, their application was denied because they did not fulfill one of the conditions for registration, namely, the requirement to have an approved legal address that satisfied certain health and fire safety standards necessary for the purposes of religious ceremonies.[99] In Belarus only religious associations were entitled to establish monasteries, religious congregations, and religious

93 Taylor, *supra* note 16, p. 293.
94 Nowak, *supra* note 86, p. 425.
95 General Comment 22, *supra* note 37, para. 8.
96 Ibid.
97 HRCttee General Comment No. 16 on Article 17 (Right to Privacy), UN Doc. HRI/GEN/1/Rev.1 at 21 (1994), paras 3 and 4.
98 *Sergei Malakhovsky and Alexander Pikul v. Belarus, supra* note 66.
99 Ibid., para. 7.4.

missions or to invite foreign clerics to visit the country for the purpose of preaching or conducting other religious activity.[100] Here, the HRCttee drew a distinction between conditions for the use of premises for religious activities and conditions for a religious association to be registered and have a legal address. The requirement for fulfilling the standards necessary for the administrative seat of the association as well as those that are necessary for premises used for purposes of religious ceremonies, rituals and other group undertakings were found unnecessary. While making this assessment the Committee also considered such a limitation's impact on the applicants, namely the impossibility of establishing educational institutions and inviting foreign clergy to visit the country and found that the restriction on the applicants' right to manifest their religion was disproportionate.[101] Consequently, the HRCttee found that the limitations imposed in the form of unnecessary and disproportionate requirements amounted to a violation of Article 18 of the ICCPR.

The evidentiary or factual basis of restrictions was also questioned by the HRCttee. In *Sister Immaculate Joseph v. Sri Lanka* where a Christian Order applied for incorporation of association and this was found unconstitutional, the grounds for interference were that the Order's activities would, through the provision of material and other benefits to vulnerable people, improperly propagate religion.[102] The Committee did not refer to the *preventive* character of such a restriction but noted that this assessment lacked any evidentiary or factual basis, hence underscoring the necessity for evidence substantiating prevention of activities that *would* or might happen in the future.[103]

Indeed, qualifying the nature of laws has been a matter of focus for Strasbourg organs as well. It has been established by case law that the requirement for the limitations to be prescribed by law does not mean only a literal conformity with national law; instead, it implies a quality of law that has three essential components.[104] First, the law must be adequately accessible; the individual must have an adequate indication as to which legal rules are applicable in a given situation. Secondly, the law must be formulated in a manner that has sufficient precision so that individuals can foresee the consequences of a given act.[105] It follows that laws of an especially general or vague character that do not lay down restrictions in a defined manner may not be able to pass the "prescribed by law" test. Having said that, it has also been noted that legislation that has a somewhat vague character or that is drafted in a broad manner can be given sufficient precision by the interpretation of domestic courts or agencies that apply the legislation.[106]

100 Ibid.

101 Ibid., paras 7.4. and 7.6.

102 *Sister Immaculate Joseph and 80 Teaching Sisters of the Holy Cross of the Third Order of Saint Francis in Menzingen of Sri Lanka v. Sri Lanka*, *supra* note 46.

103 Ibid., para. 7.3.

104 Van Dijk and van Hoof, *supra* note 37, p. 336.

105 *The Sunday Times v. UK*, 26 April 1979, European Court of Human Rights, No. 6538/74, para. 48.

106 Evans, *supra* note 55, p. 138, based on the ECtHR judgment in *Kokkinakis v. Greece*, 25 May 1993, European Court of Human Rights, No. 14307/88.

The third component required for the quality of law is defined as a corollary of the foreseeability test; to be exact, adequate safeguards against abuses must be extended in a manner that would delineate the extent of the authorities' discretion and define the circumstances in which it is to be exercised.[107] The requirement that restrictions be prescribed by law has been employed in numerous cases and is rightly accounted to "provide a potent source of restraint upon abuse of power".[108]

The strategic role of the prescribed by law requirement to potentially improve the protection of freedom of religion or belief in the context of formal processes where religious groups deal with public authorities is seen in the case of *Manoussakis and others v. Greece*. The real change where the potential is realized, however, has been in the case of *Hasan and Chaush v. Bulgaria*.[109] Even though both of these cases do not directly concern the acquisition of legal personality, the findings of the European Court are relevant and informative for the review of processes related to legal personality.

Manoussakis and others v. Greece was initiated with the complaint of three Jehovah's Witnesses who were convicted for unauthorized use of a place of worship.[110] A room was rented to be used for all kinds of meetings of Jehovah's Witnesses and in June 1983 an authorization to use the room as a place of worship from the Minister of Education and Religious Affairs (MERA) was requested.[111] By December 1984 the applicants had received five letters from MERA stating that a decision was not reached on their case as more information was being collected.[112] Finally, in March 1986, criminal proceedings were instituted against the applicants where they were accused of establishing and operating a place of worship for religious meetings and ceremonics of followers of Jehovah's Witnesses without authorization from the recognized ecclesiastical authorities.[113] After establishing that the conviction of the applicants for using the premises without prior authorization was an interference with the exercise of their freedom to manifest their religion in worship and observance, the ECtHR considered whether this interference was prescribed by law.[114] The applicants' complaint was

107 Van Dijk and van Hoof, *supra* note 36, p. 337 See also *Olsson v. Sweden*, 24 March 1988, European Court of Human Rights, No. 10465/83, para. 61; *Silver and others v. UK*, 25 March 1983, European Court of Human Rights, Nos. 5947/72, 6205/73, 7052/75, 7061/75, 7107/75, 7113/75, 7136/75, para. 90; *Malone v. UK*, 2 August 1984, European Court of Human Rights, No. 8691/79, para. 67.

108 Evans, *supra* note 28, p. 326.

109 *Hasan and Chaush v. Bulgaria*, 26 October 2000, European Court of Human Rights, No. 30985/96. See also the case of *Kokkinakis v. Greece* where the applicant complained of vague laws concerning the prohibition of proselytism. Here, while the Court found that the law itself was vague but concluded that the more precise case law established by courts supplemented it so the applicant could regulate his conduct. See *supra* note 106, para. 40.

110 *Manoussakis and others v. Greece*, *supra* note 50.

111 Ibid.

112 Ibid.

113 Ibid., paras 7–12.

114 Ibid.

not less directed towards the treatment they had encountered in the process, but more the "general policy of obstruction" pursued in relation to Jehovah's Witnesses when they wished to set up a place of worship.[115]

In reaching its conclusion the Court made significant observations; the law in question allowed a far-reaching interference by the political, administrative and ecclesiastical authorities with the exercise of religious freedom, numerous formal conditions conferred a very wide discretion to the police, due to the absence of a time limit the Minister of Education and Religious Affairs could defer this reply indefinitely and the decree empowered the Minister to assess whether there was a *real need* for the religious community in question.[116] Thus the nature of this law raised serious issues with regard to the requirement that restrictions must be prescribed by law, particularly the quality of law as it has been examined above. The Court observed from the evidence and cases cited by the applicants that the state has tended to use the possibilities afforded to it to "impose rigid, or indeed punitive, conditions on practice of religious beliefs by certain non-Orthodox movements, in particular Jehovah's Witnesses".[117] This deliberation provides a thorough criticism of general laws that make extensive discretionary authority by public officials possible and may be used against unwanted belief communities. However, exactly where the Court made a very relevant and significant finding, which constituted the crux of the matter, the Court was unable to find a violation. The Court appeared reluctant to deal with this issue under the requirement that limitations imposed had to be "prescribed by law" and moved on with its assessment and found a violation of Article 9 on other grounds. The case was decided on the basis of proportionality; the conviction of the applicants had such a direct effect on the applicants' freedom of religion that it could not be perceived as proportionate to the legitimate aim pursued.[118]

In contrast, in a later case, *Hasan and Chaush v. Bulgaria*, which dealt with interference by the authorities in the organization and leadership of the Muslim community in Bulgaria, the case was decided on the fact that the interference was not prescribed by law.[119] The European Court found a failure by the authorities to remain neutral in the exercise of their powers in relation to the internal organization of the Muslim Community and this failure amounted to interference in the believers' freedom to manifest their religion.[120] The relevant law did not provide for a substantive criteria on the basis of which the domestic authorities register religious denominations and changes of their leadership in the situation of internal divisions and conflicting claims for legitimacy. This taken together with lack of adversarial safeguards led the Court to find that the interference was not

115 Ibid., para. 38.
116 Ibid., para. 37.
117 Ibid., para. 48.
118 Ibid., paras 38–39.
119 *Hasan and Chaush v. Bulgaria*, *supra* note 109.
120 Ibid., para. 78.

prescribed by law, arbitrary and based on legal provisions which allowed unfettered discretion to the executive.[121]

According to Taylor, ECtHR criticism of the legal provisions in *Hasan and Chaush v. Bulgaria* may suggest that there is a willingness on the part of the Court to attack repressive legislation and in the future use the *prescribed by law* condition to condemn state measures that are basically preventive in regulating the practices of religious minorities.[122] Certainly, compared to the European Court's position in *Manoussakis and Others v. Greece*, the Court has come closer to addressing general repressive legislation that is conducive for arbitrary decisions by public authorities through the utilization of the interpretive tools found in Article 9. In this context, Taylor also warns against potential legal problems that may end up at the European Court as a result of recently adopted anti-sect laws in Europe which lack precision and allow excessive discretion to domestic authorities to dissolve religious organizations.[123] Others have also voiced concern about strict restrictions imposed on cults, sects and other allegedly dangerous formations of religious communities in a number of European countries, but they appear less confident that the European Court will be willing to "ward off such governmental intrusions".[124] So far Jehovah's Witnesses have challenged the relevant law in France with an application to the European Court complaining that they would potentially be a victim of the application of the law. But their application was found inadmissible since the law was not invoked against them.[125]

Questioning the evidentiary basis of decisions of public authorities that have not been based on "relevant and sufficient" grounds has also proved to be an important tool to curb arbitrary decisions. In the case of *The Moscow Branch of Salvation Army v. Russia*, the grounds applied by domestic authorities in order to refuse the applicants' application for re-registration were, according to the Court, "lacking evidentiary basis and arbitrary" and those pertaining to its alleged "foreign origin"

121 *Hasan and Chaush v. Bulgaria*, *supra* note 109, paras 85 and 86. Again in *Svyato-Mychalivska Parafiya v. Ukraine* where the change in statute of a religious association constituted the reason for refusing to register the association, the European Court has partially relied on the prescribed by law condition again. In its assessment the Court found it necessary to determine whether the authorities based their decisions on "acceptable assessment of relevant" facts and found that the grounds given for refusing registration were inconsistent and hence arbitrary by the registering authority. In its reasoning the Court considered the "prescribed by law" test and questioned the "forseeability" of the law saying the domestic courts "were clearly prevented from reaching a different finding by the lack of coherence and foreseeability of the legislation". *Svyato-Mychalivska Parafiya v. Ukraine,* 14 June 2007, European Court of Human Rights, No. 77703/01, para. 152.

122 Taylor, *supra* note 16, p. 296.

123 Ibid., pp. 297–298.

124 Uitz, *supra* note 11, p. 178. See Chapter 4 of the same book for a brief survey of constitutional developments and recent legal restrictions imposed on new religious movements in Europe.

125 *The Christian Federation of Jehovah's Witnesses in France v. France*, 6 October 2001, European Court of Human Rights (Admissibility), No. 53430/99 2001.

were not "relevant and sufficient", nor "prescribed by law".[126] The domestic public authorities had held that the applicants did not set out their religious affiliation and practices in a precise manner and omitted to describe all of their decisions, regulations and traditions however the ECtHR found that the Religions Act did not lay down any guidelines on the description of religious affiliation or denomination of an organization.[127] Hence there was no apparent legal basis for the requirement to describe all "decisions, regulations and traditions".[128] Here the Court placed the "task to elucidate the applicable legal requirements and thus give clear notice how to prepare the documents" with the state.[129]

In addition, the ECtHR clearly underscored the unacceptability of "arbitrary and mere speculations" to deny registration. In its assessment, the Court also took into account that "other religious associations professing the faith of The Salvation Army have successfully obtained re-registration".[130] Thus on both of the above accounts the Court found that Moscow authorities neglected their duty to act in "neutrality and impartiality".[131] The District Court inferred from the applicant's articles of association that the members of the applicant branch would "inevitably break Russian law in the process of executing The Salvation Army's Orders and Regulations and the instructions of the Commanding Officer".[132] Referring to its case law from *Refah Partisi* and *Partidul Comunistilor* the ECtHR noted that indeed, an association's program may in certain cases "conceal objectives and intentions different from the ones it proclaims" and in order to verify this the content of the program must be compared with the actions of the association's leaders and the positions they embrace.[133] However in the case at hand there was no such evidence indicating that the members or founders were engaged in other activities than those outlined in the articles of associations, hence the findings of the District Court were found to lack evidentiary basis and were arbitrary.[134] Similarly, in *Metropolitan Church of Besserabia v. Moldova*, the Court dismissed the argument of the government that, once recognized, the Church "might" constitute a danger to national security and territorial integrity as "mere hypothesis", which in absence of evidence could not justify a refusal to recognize it.[135] Indeed, in spite of the fact that "national security" does not constitute one of the permissible grounds for interference in manifestation of religion or belief, issues regarding religious communities that have intricate ties and relations with other countries can be highly sensitive political matters that may cause a broad application of

126 *The Moscow Branch of Salvation Army v. Russia, supra* note 31, para. 85.
127 Ibid., para. 89.
128 Ibid., paras 87–90.
129 Ibid., para. 90. Similarly in *Church of Scientology Moscow v. Russia*, 24 September 2007, European Court of Human Rights, No. 18147/02.
130 *The Moscow Branch of Salvation Army v. Russia, supra* note 31, para. 97.
131 Ibid.
132 Ibid., paras 93 and 94.
133 Ibid., para. 94.
134 Ibid., para. 95.
135 *Metropolitan Church of Bessarabia and others v. Moldova, supra* note 20, para. 125.

restrictions rooted in national security concerns. In *Metropolitan Church of Bessarabia v. Moldova*, the ECtHR considered the government's arguments putting forward the activities of the Church in the political sphere with the aim of achieving reunification with Romania as being a threat to national security and territorial integrity.[136] The European Court observed that the government had not substantiated the alleged political activity.[137] It is interesting that the Court noted, even if the Church were linked to the political activities that allegedly were working towards the reunification of Moldova with Romania, the government had not maintained that these activities were illegal. Therefore political activity, *per se*, would not necessarily constitute a permissible ground for restriction.

It is clear from the above account that both the HRCttee and ECtHR strictly require *evidentiary and factual* basis for preventive interferences. This places the burden on states to substantiate with evidence that their preventive measures were necessary, as opposed to relying on hypothetical possibilities. The result of this requirement for belief communities is that they will not be subjected to practices that are based on perceptions of threat reinforced by particular sensitivities by the authorities, which is often the case for belief groups that are seen as marginal.

Restrictions on the right to acquire legal personality must pursue a legitimate aim to protect "public safety", "order", "health" or "morals" or the "fundamental rights and freedoms of others". Both the United Nations and Strasbourg institutions do not carry out sufficiently rigorous examination when it comes to determining whether a certain restriction is aimed at protecting one of the enlisted grounds.[138] It appears that, for example, states can easily get away with claiming that certain criteria, set out for the acquisition of legal personality, are aimed at protecting one of the permissible legitimate aims, such as public order. It might be difficult to conclusively refute this. Therefore, adjudicating bodies accept that measures "pursued a legitimate aim" and move on with their assessment of the restrictions.[139]

In order to be considered legitimate, any restriction must be necessary in a democratic society.[140] It, moreover, must be *necessary* in order to protect the *aim* the state claims.

While Strasbourg organs have employed the margin of appreciation and thus accommodated states' restrictions in Article 9 cases, applications related to the right to acquire legal personality of belief groups have been exceptions. I suggest that the reason for this has been the strong protection attributed to the right to associate in the ECHR protection scheme by the Convention organs. When the right to acquire legal personality is viewed in the context of Article 9 interpreted in the light of Article 11 or *vice versa*, the threshold for accommodating state

136 Ibid.

137 Ibid.

138 Evans, *supra* note 55.

139 See, *inter alia*, *Buscarini and Others v. San Marino*, 18 February 1999, European Court of Human Rights No. 24645/94, para. 208; *Manoussakis and Others v. Greece*, *supra* note 50, para. 387.

140 See ECHR Article 9(2).

restrictions is high. The exception here is presented in the *Refah Partisi v. Turkey case*, which dealt with the dissolution of a political party that sought, among others, to establish the *sharia* and a multi-juridical system.[141] Although the case is decided on the basis of the right to freedom of association and not the right to freedom of religion or belief, its significance lies in the fact that it reveals the European Court's boundaries in relation to the right to associate, thus demonstrating that when associative rights of religious/belief communities including religious jurisdiction are concerned the margin of appreciation doctrine may apply.

When assessing claims concerning the right to acquire legal personality, a strict application of the respective restriction clauses is necessary in order to heighten the standard of review. In particular, the prescribed by law requirement and necessity of restrictions as well as a rigid scrutiny of the evidentiary basis of restrictive measures and proportionality appear to be key interpretive devices to address relevant violations. When a violation pertaining to recognition or registration of a religious community is found, frequently the violation may be a result of general repression, bias or discrimination against the community in question. Yet, the capacity and the willingness to deal with broad issues that are related, among other reasons, to vague laws creating the possibility for extensive discretion by administrative authorities that may reflect unfavorable attitudes towards certain belief communities may not always be there. While in *Manoussakis v. Greece* the ECtHR clearly demonstrated unwillingness to decide the case on the inclination on the part of the authorities to restrict religious practice of non-orthodox beliefs in general and Jehovah's Witnesses in particular,[142] in *Hasan and Chaush v. Bulgaria*, the ECtHR showed willingness to confront repressive legislation and practice. Finding of a violation based on failure for the restrictions to be prescribed by law could potentially have a better chance to resonate at the domestic level than another ground. Hence the state in question can be challenged to change its law. Surely, for belief communities institutional and attitude problems are of crucial importance and yet more difficult to prove and make a matter of legal proceedings. While improvement in this area would be welcome this may not be without problems even if the Court were willing to take note of wide-scale repressive measures against certain belief communities. As underscored by Evans, since the Court is supposed to be one of the primary organs for protecting human rights in Europe, it should be ready to take a wider view of cases where it is clear that an oppressive pattern of state behavior has been conducted under the law at hand.[143] As it has been demonstrated in Chapter 2, the consideration of state reports on the implementation of the ICCPR and the enforcement of judgments of the ECtHR by the Committee of Ministers may be means of international

141 *Refah Partisi (the Welfare Party) and Others v. Turkey*, Grand Chamber, 13 February 2003, European Court of Human Rights, Nos. 41340/98, 41342/98, 41343/98 and 41344/98.

142 *Manoussakis and Others v. Greece*, *supra* note 50.

143 Evans, *supra* note 55, p. 141.

review conducive to tackle broad-scale repressive and discriminatory legislation and practice in this area. Where violation of Article 18 of the ICCPR or Article 9 of the ECHR is found, extending scrutiny of whether there was a discrimination or not may also be a means of improving standards of international review. This will be briefly examined below.

3.5 The Prohibition of Discrimination

In the process of adjudication, claims concerning discrimination in connection to legal personality, recognition and registration may be potentially a significant tool to identify recurring patterns of discrimination and general repression toward certain groups.[144] It is not the purpose here to provide a comprehensive examination of the concept of non-discrimination and its development in international law—an impossible task considering the limitations of this chapter. Instead here my purpose is to demonstrate that the inclusion of the consideration of the principle of non-discrimination in the assessment of claims concerning the acquisition of legal entity status can strengthen the claims as well as—where violation is found—lead to the formulation of judgments that may potentially point to measures that must be taken to seek corrective action by states. However, as demonstrated below that the non-discrimination clauses have not been utilized to bring about this potential.

Article 26 of the ICCPR is an autonomous provision protecting against discrimination,[145] thereby extending protection of equality and non-discrimination beyond the rights and freedoms enshrined in the Covenant. The HRCttee underscored the importance of observing the principle of non-discrimination in relation to Article 18(3) in its General Comment 22; "in interpreting the scope of permissible limitation clauses, States parties should proceed from the need to protect the rights guaranteed under the Covenant, including the right to equality and non-discrimination on all grounds specified in Articles 2, 3 and 26".[146] In addition, "restrictions may not be imposed for discriminatory purposes or applied in a discriminatory manner".[147] States must ensure that

> the fact that a religion is recognized as a state religion or that it is established as official or traditional or that its followers comprise the majority of the population, shall not result in any impairment of the enjoyment of any of the rights under the Covenant, including articles 18 and 27, nor in any discrimination against adherents to other religions or non-believers.[148]

144 Moon, G. and R. Allen (2000) "Substantive Rights and Equal Treatment in Respect of Religion and Belief: Towards a Better Understanding of the Rights, and Their Implications", 6 *European Human Rights Law Review*, 580: 595–596.

145 Nowak, *supra* note 86, p. 604.

146 General Comment 22, *supra* note 37, para. 8.

147 Ibid.

148 Ibid., para. 9.

In particular,

> certain measures discriminating against the latter, such as measures restricting eligibility for government service to members of the predominant religion or giving economic privileges to them or imposing special restrictions on the practice of other faiths, are not in accordance with the prohibition of discrimination based on religion or belief and the guarantee of equal protection under Article 26.[149]

Indeed, the HRCttee has consistently criticized differentiation in the treatment of "traditional" and other religions, in particular when it comes to the official registration of a church or religious community and the acquisition of "legal personality" and held that these raise issues both under Article 18 and Article 26.[150] Even though there is ample case law regarding Article 14 in the jurisprudence of the HRCttee there have not been cases that have specifically dealt with Article 14 in the context of religious or belief organizations. The HRCttee has expressed that Article 14 is "a key element of human rights protection and serves as a procedural means to safeguard the rule of law".[151]

The ECtHR has not been consistent in its utilization of Article 14 in relation to Article 9 or Article 11 in light of Article 9. In numerous cases where the applicants have raised complaints regarding Article 14 in addition to Article 9, the ECtHR has held that the alleged inequality has been sufficiently taken into account in the assessment that has led to a violation of Article 9 or Article 11 in light of Article 9 and has seen no reason for separate examination of the facts from the standpoint of Article 14.[152] In other cases, the ECtHR has simply not seen it necessary to adjudicate under Article 14 even though there have been indications in the consideration of the case under Article 9 that the interference in question may include a discriminatory pattern.[153]

In a case concerning the refusal by domestic authorities of registration as a religion of an organization of Muslims, the European Court did not find the requirement of presenting the government with a document setting out the fundamental principles of their religion discriminatory.[154] The Court held that, "the State could not establish the authenticity of the organization seeking recognition as a religion and whether the denomination in question presented a danger for democratic society".[155] Interestingly, when considering the admissibility of the

149 Ibid.

150 Concluding Observations of the HRCttee Serbia, UN Doc. CCPR/C/SRB/CO/2, 21 May 2011, p. 6.

151 HRCttee, General Comment No. 32.

152 *The Moscow Branch of Salvation Army v. Russia*, *supra* note 31, para. 101 and *Case of Church of Scientology Moscow v. Russia*, *supra* note 129, para. 101.

153 *Metropolitan Church of Bessarabia and Others v. Moldova*, *supra* note 20, para. 134.

154 *Carmuirea Spirituala A Musulmanilor Din Republica Moldova v. Moldova*, *supra* note 82.

155 Ibid.

application under Article 14, the ECtHR did not find substantiation of this claim since the applicants did not show that the requirements of the Religious Denominations Act were applied more strictly to them in comparison with other organizations.[156] Were the applicants able to demonstrate that other groups were not asked to fulfil the same criteria, the European Court may have been able to view this information as a substantiation of the claim under Article 14. It appears that applicants bringing relevant claims under Article 14 may have a better chance if they can provide statistical information and examples demonstrating their differential treatment.

One way of establishing whether there has been discrimination or not may be through the demonstration of statistical information. The fact that the ECtHR has recently shown willingness to consider statistical evidence will strengthen such claims.[157] However, the fact that the ECtHR requires "undisputed official statistics" in order to take them into account,[158] may be a factor to harden the proof of discrimination for applications. Where there is strong suspicion that there may be discriminatory practice and when there are no relevant official statistics the Court may ask states to demonstrate, perhaps through statistical information, that there is no discrimination. For example, if the case involves restrictions on acquisition of legal personality, where the belief group in question claims to be denied such status through unsuccessful applications, states may be asked concerning similar applications by groups belonging to the same religion or belief, whether their applications have been successful, or the total number of applications and the total of successful applications etc. This type of probing and inquisitive assessment would be a means of determining discriminatory patterns against certain religious or belief groups.

In the case of *Religionsgemeinschft der Zeugen Jehovahs and Others v. Austria*, however, the ECtHR was persuaded that the differential treatment of the applicant, based on the allegedly discriminatory criteria required for the recognition as a religious society, amounted to a violation of Article 14 in conjunction with Article 9.[159] Under Austrian law religious societies enjoyed a privileged treatment, yet, *inter alia*, twenty years' existence of a religious association was one of the requirements for the recognition of a religious society. The Court held that it could accept such a time period in exceptional circumstances as, for example, a newly established religious group, but it was hardly acceptable with regard to religious groups with long international existence. It was held that,

156 Ibid.

157 *DH and Others v. Czech Republic*, 13 November 2007, European Court of Human Rights (Grand Chamber), No. 57325/00, para. 188. For more on this case, see Devroye, J. (2009) "The Case of D.H. and Others v. the Czech Republic", *North Western Journal of International Human Rights*, 7, Spring, pp. 81–101.

158 *Hoogendijk v. The Netherlands*, 6 January 2005 (Admissibility), European Court of Human Rights, No. 58641/00.

159 *Religionsgemeinschaft Der Zeugen Jehovas and Others v. Austria*, 31 July 2008, European Court of Human Rights, No. 40825/98.

> In respect of such a religious group (Jehovah's Witnesses), the authorities should be able to verify whether it fulfills the requirements of the relevant legislation within a considerably shorter period. Further, the example of another religious community cited by the applicants shows that the Austrian State did not consider the application on an equal basis of such a waiting period to be an essential instrument for pursuing its policy in that field.[160]

Hence, the Court found that the difference in treatment was not based on any "objective and reasonable justification".[161]

While the case of *Religionsgemeinschaft der Zeugen Jehovas and Others v. Austria* does not resemble the aforementioned cases concerning registration, they do have commonalities in terms of discriminatory rules. Yet, the ECtHR does not seem to take the route of consistently considering each case substantively under Article 14 in addition to Article 9 or Article 11 in light of Article 9.

Now, let us turn to briefly explore other rights that constitute the basis for the right to acquire legal personality for religious or belief groups. The right to court and the right to association together also establish "a fairly strong right to entity status".[162]

3.6 The Right to Fair Trial—Judicial Protection

The right to fair trial has important implications for ensuring judicial protection of belief communities or organizations and their assets, and in this respect it is closely linked to having legal personality. The absence of legal personality of a belief community may amount to and result in, more often than not, an absence of judicial protection of the community's assets which might be essential for manifesting religion or belief and certain religious activities. Article 14 of the ICCPR and Article 6 of the ECHR, respectively protect the right to fair trial in civil and criminal cases. The HRCttee's General Comment No. 32 on Article 14 of the ICCPR holds that the right to fair trial includes the right to a public hearing before an independent and impartial tribunal within a reasonable time limit, the presumption of innocence, and other minimum rights for those charged in a criminal case.[163] As far as belief groups are concerned it is vital that they have legal personality so that they can have judicial protection. Alternatively, to benefit from judicial protection they need to have legal entity status; this link demonstrates the empowering function of legal personality.

The ECtHR holds that Article 6(1) "secures to everyone the right to have any claim relating to his civil rights and obligations brought before a court", hence it embodies a "right to court", "a right to access a court".[164] While this right may

160 Ibid., paras 98–99.
161 Ibid.
162 Durham, *supra* note 12.
163 HRCttee General Comment 32 on Article 14, UN Doc. CCPR/C/GC/32, 23 August 2007, paras 15 and 25.
164 *Golder v. UK*, 21 February 1975, European Court of Human Rights, No. 4451/70, para. 21.

be restricted, the restriction may not be such that the very essence of the right is impaired.[165] According to established ECtHR case law,

> one of the means of exercising the right to manifest one's religion, especially for a religious community in its collective dimension, is the possibility of ensuring judicial protection of the community, its members and its assets so that Article 9 must be seen not only in the light of Article 11, but also in the light of Article 6.[166]

The link between lack of legal capacity and the resulting restrictions on activities of a church were addressed in *Canea Catholic Church v. Greece* on the basis of Article 6 of the ECHR.[167] The case concerned a very old church community that was never established as a legal entity but nevertheless acquired movable and immovable property, concluded contracts and took part in notarized transactions. The validity of these actions had never been contested, however, the church was denied access to court because it lacked legal personality. In response to the government's argument that the church in one way or another could have sought to carry out formalities in order to acquire some form of legal personality, the Court maintained that this was unacceptable as there was nothing to suggest that one day they would be denied access to court.[168] Hence the burden was not on the church to seek a form of legal personality. This may be significant in establishing that in cases where there is lack of a regulation for procedures related to legal entity of religious communities, or where such regulations are unclear, it is the responsibility of the state to make regulations that are clear and foreseeable so that belief communities can know what is expected of them. Similarly, in the case of *Holy Monasteries v. Greece*, the Court found that depriving the monasteries of the possibility of bringing a complaint in relation to their right to own property impairs the very essence of their "right to court".[169]

3.7 The Right to Freedom of Association

Article 11(1) of the ECHR stipulates: "Everyone has the right to freedom of peaceful assembly and to freedom of association with others".

When belief communities associate for the purposes of manifesting their religion or belief through acts protected under Article 9 of the ECHR and Article 18 of the ICCPR, *inter alia*, establishing places of worship, teaching and training their own clergy, they may establish associations that are also protected respectively by

165 *Canea Catholic Church v. Greece*, 16 December 1997, European Court of Human Rights, No. 25528/94, para. 38.
166 *Metropolitan Church of Besserabia and Others v. Moldova*, *supra* note 20, para. 118.
167 *Canea Catholic Church v. Greece*, *supra* note 165, para. 38.
168 Ibid., para. 42.
169 Having said that, it should be noted that in this case the Court did not find a violation of Article 9 and Article 11 because the monasteries were not deprived of the means necessary for pursuing their religious objectives.

Article 11 (ECHR) and Article 22 (ICCPR). The European Court affirms that "citizens should be able to form a legal entity in order to act collectively in a field of mutual interest", and considers the formation of a legal entity as an important aspect of the right to freedom of association "without which the right would be deprived of any meaning";[170] thus establishing firmly the nexus between the right to association and legal entity status. Groups of believers can also base their claims to acquire legal entity status on the right to freedom of association. Since belief communities also "act collectively in a field of mutual interest", namely their shared beliefs, where this requires the acquisition of a legal entity status, it would reasonably follow that the right to freedom of association would protect this claim. Krishnaswami notes that the generality of the terms of the article protecting freedom of association leaves no doubt that it extends to the sphere of religion or belief.[171] There is no reason for religious associations to be treated less favorably. Also if a religious or belief community were to be denied legal entity status as it is required by the right to association based on their "religious nature", this may give rise to questions on prohibition of discrimination under Article 14 of the ECHR.[172]

When it comes to belief groups, the European Court views Articles 9 and 11 as complementary provisions. Evidently, the fact that the Court feels the need to rely on both Articles implies that it does not view Article 9 solely as a sufficient legal basis for the protection of associative acts of belief groups. In *Hasan and Chaush v. Bulgaria*, the government argued that the organization and leadership of the Muslim community in Bulgaria needed to be analyzed mainly from the angle of Article 11 protecting freedom of association.[173] Here the European Court took a clear stand saying,

> Where the organization of the religious community is at issue, Article 9 of the Convention must be interpreted in the light of Article 11, which safeguards associative life against unjustified State interference… Were the organizational life of the community not protected by Article 9 of the Convention, all other aspects of the individual's freedom of religion would become vulnerable.[174]

The Court was of the opinion that this particular case would not be better dealt with solely under Article 11, as suggested by the government; in its view such an approach would have taken the applicants' complaints out of their context and disregarded their substance.[175] Hence in the Court's view the ideal way to deal

170 *Sidiropoulos v. Greece*, 10 July 1998, European Court of Human Rights, No. 1594/1614, para. 40.

171 Krishnaswami, *supra* note 15.

172 Lehnhof, L.S. (2002) "Freedom of Religious Association: The Right of Religious Organizations to Obtain Legal Entity Status under the European Convention", *Brigham Young University Law Review*, 2(16), 561–609.

173 *Hasan and Chaush v. Bulgaria*, *supra* note 109, para. 61.

174 Ibid., para. 62.

175 Ibid., para. 65.

with the complaint was to examine it under Article 9 of the Convention as interpreted in light of Article 11. The need to bring in Article 11 may indicate that the substantive scope of Article 9, as such, is not viewed as broad enough to include the associative acts as manifestations of belief or religion.

Regarding complaints raised by belief organizations in relation to legal entity status in the context of re-registration procedures, the European Court held that the complaints raised issues both under Article 11 and Article 9.[176] A refusal by domestic authorities to grant legal status to an association of individuals amounts to an interference in the right to association and where an organization of a religious community is at issue, such refusal also constitutes an interference in the right to freedom of religion or belief.[177] In *The Moscow Branch of Salvation Army v. Russia*, it was a violation of Article 11 read in light of Article 9.[178] It seems that where there are complaints regarding an already established organization of a a religious community then the Court looks at whether there is an interference with Article 11 read in light of Article 9. When there is not yet an organization established, then the Court assesses whether there has been an interference with Article 9 read in light of Article 11.

In the communication of *Sisters of the Holy Cross v. Sri Lanka*, the HRCttee addressed complaints under Article 18, and dealt with a claim concerning the establishment of a charity institution. Article 22 was not raised by the applicant, nor by the state. However in *S. Malakhovsky and A. Pikul v. Belarus*, a case about re-registration requirements, the HRCttee dealt with the case solely under Article 18, while noting that it also raised issues under Article 22 so as to merit admissibility.

The associative acts of religious groups that are necessary to carry out their collective acts, however, are not solely protected by Article 9 in the European scheme as there the European Court relies on the protection of Article 9 interpreted in light of Article 11 and the protection of Article 11 in light of Article 9. These acts would be more appropriately dealt with solely under Article 9. Belief groups need not raise their complaints related to their associative rights under freedom of association. Nevertheless, this does not preclude that possibility of the same issues being raised under the right to freedom of association. While the HRCttee observes that associative acts of belief groups raise issues both under Articles 18 and 22 of the ICCPR, it takes a broad view of the scope of Article 18 so as to base its deliberation solely on Article 18. The difference in the approach of the ECHR and HRCttee reflects a difference in the interpretation of the respective religious freedom clauses in how far they extend to associative acts; the HRCttee certainly seems to have a broader view.

In conclusion, for belief groups, the right to acquire an adequate form of legal personality for the enjoyment of the right to manifest religion or belief is a key

176 *Case of Church of Scientology Moscow v. Russia*, *supra* note 125, para. 98 and *The Moscow Branch of Salvation Army v. Russia*, *supra* note 31, para. 98.
177 *The Moscow Branch of Salvation Army v. Russia*, *supra* note 31, para. 71.
178 Ibid., para. 98.

enabling and empowering right without which diversely formed groups of believers generally cannot effectively exercise their right to manifest religion or belief in community with others in worship, teaching, practice and observance. Practically speaking, they cannot own or rent property, including places of worship, establish schools and seminaries, and engage in charity activity which is integral to very many religions. The process of acquiring legal personality, however, remains a highly regulated legal sphere by states where the state-religion relation becomes an important denominator of the nature of this sphere. Conversely, in the exercise of this right, the particular state-religion relationships that have been historically and contextually shaped bring in various privileges or prejudices, cooperation and co-existence between states and religious groups. Normative demands of international obligations constitute a challenge to the ways in which this sphere has been traditionally regulated; the observance of the principles of neutrality and impartiality in the exercise of the regulatory powers of states is given importance by both the ECtHR and the HRCttee. Yet, when international review mechanisms employ self-restraint, in particular the ECtHR, giving substantive content to relevant international provisions will be delayed and lacking.

The right of a religious or belief community to obtain legal personality has been progressively recognized as a part of the protection of the collective dimension of freedom of religion or belief under international law. Considering that positive obligations ensuing from the right to freedom of religion or belief are less than clearly established in international jurisprudence the recognition of the right to acquire legal personality gives the latter a high rank within the constellation of elements making up the scope of the right to freedom of religion or belief, particularly in its collective dimension. Since states are required to ensure the effective protection of human rights, including the right to freedom of religion or belief, there is a positive obligation on the part of states to create an accessible and adequate form of legal personality. While the right to acquire legal personality is first and foremost protected within the scope of the right to freedom of religion or belief, other inter-dependent and complementary rights such as the right to association, the right to fair trial and rights of minorities are also relevant.

The ECHR and the ICCPR have demonstrated similarities and differences in the way they have dealt with claims pertaining to legal personality issues. Conceptually, the most striking difference is the basis of the right to legal personality; for the ECHR such claims may be addressed under Article 9 interpreted in the light of Article 11 or, where the issues concern an already established organization, Article 11 in light of Article 9. It follows that the ECtHR does not view associative acts of belief groups as a matter that is grounded *solely* on Article 9. The HRCttee, on the other hand, while observing that Article 22 may also be applicable, has dealt with similar cases solely under Article 18. Its concluding observations on state reports on the implementation of the ICCPR have also reflected the same approach. The different approaches of the two bodies reflect a narrow view of the scope of manifestations on the part of the Strasbourg organs and a broader view of the HRCttee. On the other hand, as regards the ECtHR, the strong protection afforded to the right to association has lent strong protection, not leaving room for a margin of appreciation to states, to the right to acquire legal personality by believers as long as the latter's activities are compatible with democratic principles.

In the adjudication of cases involving acquisition of legal personality, recognition and registration of religious groups, both the HRCttee and the Strasbourg organs have underscored that states must be strictly guided by restriction clauses enshrined in the provision regulating freedom of religion. Restrictions imposed in the context of the right to acquire legal personality, recognition and registration for religious/belief communities must be "prescribed by law". The latter requirement has immense potential against vague laws and arbitrary actions of domestic authorities at various levels. This is particularly strengthened by the subsequent developments in case law of both the ECHR and the HRCttee and the General Comment on the restrictions clause of Article 18 of the HRCttee where they have elaborated on the quality of law. The role of precise, clear, forseeable legislation in this sphere is crucial in order to avoid arbitrary and discretionary practices.

A more effective utilization of the principle of non-discrimination in the assessment of claims concerning the acquisition of legal personality for belief groups may result in the construction of judgments that may lead to more targeted general measures that must be taken by states in order to prevent similar violations from happening. Hence the judgments will be more impactful.

While the application of permissible restriction clauses has been an important means of blocking arbitrary practice by states, it appears that international compliance review mechanisms may be improved to avert widespread repressive legislation and practice. Where adjudicatory bodies focus on the wider legislative or administrative practices and decide the cases on the basis of these, the effectiveness of international protection may increase. When the cases are decided on broader issues, the enforcement of the judgments and follow-up of opinions may have the potential of seeking corrective action by states on these broader issues. A foreseeable disadvantage of such an approach may be that states may consider the ECtHR and the HRCttee too "active" and show reluctance to enforce judgments and views respectively. However, in the long run such an approach would greatly increase the effect of international review of individual cases on the improvement of national protection. The weakness however lies in the inability or unwillingness to address wider issues related to how the formulation of laws and their applications affects certain religious/belief groups.

4 The Right of Religious or Belief Groups to Freedom in their Internal Affairs

4.1 Introduction

The right to freedom in the internal affairs or autonomy of religious or belief groups constitutes an integral part of the protection of the collective dimension of freedom of religion or belief. Its scope is, however, far from clear. International provisions protecting the right to freedom of religion or belief do not provide an exhaustive list of rights that would provide an all-encompassing list of acts that are protected under the right to autonomy of religious or belief communities. This is rightly so, considering that issues that may arise under the notion of "autonomy of religious/belief communities" are likely to cover a wide range of acts based on the wide range of beliefs and dogma that constitute the basis for what is a matter of autonomy.

This chapter aims to explore the international protection of the right to freedom in the internal matters of religious or belief groups with a view to examining its scope and, possibly, improving the standard of international compliance review. To start with, the notion of autonomy of belief groups and its substantive scope is briefly discussed with reference to the relevant international provisions protecting religious freedom and the jurisprudence developed by the HRCttee and the Strasbourg organs. With a broad approach that conceptualizes autonomy beyond organizational freedom of religious institutions, key aspects of autonomy are analyzed on the basis of the acts listed in Article 6 of the 1981 Declaration on the Elimination of Intolerance and Discrimination Based on Religion or Belief as the legal framework of analysis.[1] Paul Taylor has provided a helpful and comprehensive comparative analysis of UN and European standards based on Article 6 of the 1981 Declaration.[2] The same legal framework will be used here while being mindful that there are innumerable forms of manifestations/acts protected under the religious freedom provisions that may or may not strictly correspond to the categories listed in this framework. Then, the question of whether a right to

1 United Nations Declaration on the Elimination of Intolerance and Discrimination Based on Religion or Belief, G.A. Resolution 36/55, 36 GAOR Supp. (No. 51) at p. 171, UN Doc. A/36/51 (1981).

2 Taylor, P.M. (2005) *Freedom of Religion: UN and European Human Rights Law and Practice*, Cambridge: Cambridge University Press.

religious jurisdiction may also be protected within the scope of the right to freedom in the internal matters is investigated. This overview demonstrates that when positive obligations—thus, often, policy considerations—of states are concerned, international adjudicators tend to adopt a narrow interpretation of the scope of the right to freedom of religion or belief, whereas, where negative obligations are concerned, greater scrutiny is applied. There also appears to be more scrutiny where freedom of religion or belief overlaps with freedom of expression or freedom of association which constitute essential aspects of international human rights protection schemes. Whether or not, and to what extent, viewing rights that also *raise questions under autonomy* can be viewed as an interpretive tool that requires rigorous scrutiny of restrictions is explored as well. With regard to its relation to the whole of the book, this chapter complements the previous chapter on legal personality by exploring other aspects of the collective dimension of freedom of religion or belief in a comprehensive—albeit not exhaustive—manner.

4.2 Autonomy: The Right of a Religious/Belief Community to Freedom in its Internal Matters

Autonomy of religious or belief communities in constructing their own affairs has been considered one of the crucial features of any meaningful system of freedom of religion or belief.[3] The scope and nature of *autonomy* or *internal affairs* is to a great extent determined by the comprehensiveness of the religion or belief in question. Autonomy may be defined in a narrow fashion to include "the right of self-determination of religious bodies" and their ability to decide freely about "the teaching and offices, the range of their activities and the shape of their structures".[4] Religious autonomy has, however, been defined also as a potentially expansive issue.[5] The community life lived as envisioned by a belief constitutes the basis of the right to autonomy and arguably it is a "specialized and heightened form of the right to association".[6] Indeed, taking into account religions that envision and prescribe legal systems, autonomy may be defined broadly to include matters of "personal law" such as marriage and inheritance. Whatever the form and scope of autonomy it will be complex and deeply contextual.[7]

The scope, variety and nature of organizations that are formed by religious or belief groups and their acts are largely governed by the dogma embraced by them.

3 Minnerath, M. (2004) "The Right to Autonomy in Religious Affairs", in T. Lindholm, W.C. Durham and B.G. Tahzib-Lie (eds.), *Facilitating Freedom of Religion or Belief: A Deskbook*, Leiden: Martinus Nijhoff, p. 291.

4 Durham, W.C. (2001) "The Right to Autonomy in Religious Affairs", in G. Robbers (ed.), *Church Autonomy – A Comparative Survey*, Frankfurt: Peter Lang, p. 5.

5 Dane, P. (2001) "The Varieties of Religious Autonomy", in G. Robbers (ed.), *Church Autonomy – A Comparative Survey*, Frankfurt: Peter Lang, p. 117.

6 Durham, W.C. (2004) "Facilitating Freedom of Religion or Belief through Religious Association Laws", in T. Lindholm, W.C. Durham and B.G. Tahzib-Lie (eds.), *Facilitating Freedom of Religion or Belief: A Deskbook*, Leiden: Martinus Nijhoff, p. 355.

7 Durham, *supra* note 4, p. 145.

Religious or belief communities, on the one hand, tend to form their own organized structures for a variety of purposes; these may be, *inter alia*, charities or humanitarian institutions, places of worship, educational institutions, radio or broadcasting institutions. In addition, they often engage in acts, such as to assemble and/or worship, to provide charity/assistance, to teach/train, to publish printed material, to receive or provide financial contributions, to observe days of rest and holidays and ceremonies, in accordance with their religion or belief. The conception of internal affairs as solely "the organizational structure" needs to be challenged as such a narrow conception would fail to sufficiently capture the acts that constitute the "internal affairs" of religious/belief groups and the implications this narrow perception has on manifestations of religion or belief. The adoption of a broad view of autonomy of religious or belief communities would improve the standard of international review. Were it possible for international adjudicators to see the issues raised in terms of autonomy, in addition to manifestation of religion or belief, restrictions by states might be probed and scrutinized more thoroughly.

The right to freedom in internal affairs is not explicitly stated in the core freedom of religion or belief articles, rather it is deduced from the phrase "freedom to manifest religion or belief individually or in community with others in worship, observance, practice or teaching".[8]

The HRCttee states explicitly that freedom to manifest one's religion or belief in worship, observance, practice and teaching encompasses a broad range of activities. The terms "worship, observance, practice and teaching" are understood as providing protection to all possible manifestations of religion or belief.[9] The HRCttee in its General Comment 22 on Article 18 includes a catalog of acts that fall within the sphere of freedom in the management of internal affairs.[10] It is evident that this list is not meant to be exhaustive but illustrative; it was clearly expressed in the drafting discussions that "all ways of manifesting one's religion or belief"[11] are meant to be protected. Views of the Committee also support its position that manifestations listed in paragraph 4 are not meant to be exhaustive. Although the General Comment does not create a general category as "autonomy in internal organization", it contains the phrase "acts integral to the conduct by religious groups of their basic affairs, such as the freedom to choose their religious leaders, priests and teachers".[12] Exactly which acts fall into the category of "integral to the basic affairs" would naturally depend on the teachings and interpretations of

8 Both Article 9 of the ECHR and Article 18 of the ICCPR.

9 Among others, see Krishnaswami, A. (1960) *Study of Discrimination in the Matter of Religious Rights and Practices*, UN Doc. E/CN.4/Sub.2/200/Rev.1, UN Sales No. 60. XIV.2.

10 General Comment 22 of the Human Rights Committee on Article 18 of the ICCPR, UN Doc. HRI/GEN/1Rev.1 at 35 (1994), para. 4.

11 UN Doc. CCPR/C/SR.1166, para. 35. Apparently, it was not possible to list them all. See B.G. Tahzib (1996) *Freedom of Religion or Belief, Ensuring Effective International Legal Protection*, Dordrecht: Martinus Nijhoff, p. 322. For the drafting history and observations of General Comment 22 see same book, pp. 311–375.

12 HRCttee, General Comment 22, *supra* note 10, para. 8.

the religious and belief community in question that avails itself of this freedom. There are, however, two key words to the understanding of the scope of protection afforded here. The first one is the word "integral". The ordinary meaning of this word is "necessary or constituent",[13] emphasizing that these acts have to form an essential part of the conduct by religious groups of their basic affairs. Therefore, not all acts that constitute part of the religious groups' internal affairs are protected under Article 18. As it is often the case, this determination process proves to be problematic as the believer, the state and the HRCttee may have different views on it. During the drafting of the boundaries of admissible acts of religious manifestations it was stated that "the features of a religion or belief are to be ascertained by the adherents of the underlying religion or belief only".[14] Surely, albeit at times problematic for the adjudicator, such an insider's approach[15] would be most welcomed by believers,[16] and informative for the adjudicator.

The second key is the phrase "basic affairs".[17] The practice and teaching of religion or belief includes acts integral to the conduct by religious groups of their basic affairs. The term that qualifies the protected acts is *basic* affairs. A number of acts are listed as illustrations of what these might mean: freedom to choose their religious leaders, priests and teachers and acts that are particularly related to teaching, such as freedom to establish seminaries or religious schools, freedom to establish places of worship, and freedom to prepare and distribute religious texts or publication. It has been suggested that the acts listed in paragraph 4 could have provided states parties with more guidance as to the substantive content of Article 18. Particularly with regard to the organizational matters of religious groups, the following have been proposed for inclusion: freedom to organize and maintain local, regional, national and international associations in connection with one's religion or belief, to participate in their activities.[18]

Whether states take a broad or narrow view of manifestations will always be a crucial determinant of the scope of protected acts and the level of protection. Since domestic authorities will be required to follow international interpretation, the stance taken by international organs authorized to interpret relevant religious freedom provisions is essential. Evans argues that the acts listed in General Comment 22 are limited to "religious rites and customs" and that forms of behavior or

13 Longman Dictionary of Contemporary English. Available: http://www.ldoceonline.com/dictionary/integral [Accessed 16 January 2015].

14 Tahzib, *supra* note 11, p. 321.

15 Brems, E. (2003) "The Approach of the European Court of Human Rights to Religion", in J.C. Mohr (ed.), *Die Rechtsstellung des Menschen im Völkerrecht*, Tübingen: Mohr, p. 8.

16 Similarly, during the elaboration of General Comment 22, Human Rights Committee member Rosalyn Higgins "resolutely opposed the idea that States could have complete latitude to decide what was and what was not a genuine religious belief. The contents of a religion should be defined by the worshippers themselves; as for manifestations, article 18, paragraph 3, existed to prevent them from violating the rights of others". UN Doc. CCPR/C/SR.1166, para. 48.

17 General Comment 22, *supra* note 10, para. 4.

18 Tahzib, *supra* note 11, p. 323.

activities that may flow from religious beliefs are not covered.[19] However, this may not be certain; it may be possible to connect behavior or acts to worship, teaching, practice, or observance, depending on one's conception of these categories. Still, the lists in General Comment 22 and Article 6 of the 1981 Declaration provide a fairly broad construction of manifestations, considering that they are just illustrative. Notwithstanding the nature of the lists, the main criteria is that in order to be protected, an act has to be considered a manifestation of religion or belief in worship, teaching, practice or observance. For example, worship extends to, *inter alia*, assembly for worship and establishing, maintaining and repair of places of worship as well as use of articles necessary in worship. Teaching, practice and observance also have substantive content that extend to cover diverse acts. All of the acts under Article 6 of the 1981 Declaration may be qualified as forms of manifestation in worship or teaching or practice or observance, and some acts may be covered under more than one category. Therefore it is important not to read too extensively into set categories since forms of manifestations of religion or belief are integrated and interrelated acts. The lists are an indication of the extent of these freedoms.[20]

The terms "worship, observance, practice and teaching" are not defined in the ECHR and the preparatory documents do not provide any insight into the components of these categories.[21] Subsequent decisions and judgments of the Strasbourg organs have not provided any description of these categories and the types of manifestations that are protected in each. While worship has been given the highest status of the manifestations listed in Article 9(1),[22] the notion of manifestations has certainly evolved over time. The Commission has said that Article 9 primarily protects personal beliefs and religious creeds and "acts which are intimately linked to these, such as worship and devotion".[23] Here the important criterion has been that the act has to be intimately linked to the belief in order to qualify as a form of manifestation in worship. As for observance, the Commission and the Court have not given this category of manifestation a separate consideration, yet. Evans concludes that "observance" seems to have been conflated into a slightly extended

19 Evans, M.D. (1997) *Religious Liberty and International Law in Europe*, Cambridge: Cambridge University Press, p. 216.

20 Ghanea, N. (2003) "The 1981 UN Declaration", in N. Ghanea (ed.), *The Challenge of Religious Discrimination at the Dawn of the New Millennium*, Leiden: Martinus Nijhoff, p. 22. The list of manifestations enshrined in Article 6 does not seem to have as extensive a scope as hoped by some. For the drafting history and struggles over the content of the 1981 Declaration see Liskofsky, S. (1980) "The United Nations Draft Declaration on the Elimination of All Forms of Religious Intolerance", UNESCO Doc. SS79/CONF.607/10, Annex V.

21 The text of Article 9 was based on Article 18 of the UDHR with a view to avoiding definitions that are inconsistent with those in the UN documents.

22 Evans, C. (2001) *Freedom of Religion under the European Convention on Human Rights*, Oxford: Oxford University Press, p. 107.

23 *C. v. United Kingdom*, 15 December 1983, European Commission of Human Rights (Admissibility) No. 10358/83. Accordingly, establishing places of worship, ownership of objects necessary for worship, facilitating religious services in prison have been viewed as included within the right to worship.

notion of worship and that they are considered together as "worship and observance" without a particular distinction.[24] While "teaching" has not been defined either, it has been subject to more detailed discussion. In a number of cases, acts such as proselytizing, religious teaching in school curriculum and in religious institutions have been considered under the right to manifest religion or belief in teaching.[25]

The term practice has proved to be the most difficult one to define. The ordinary meaning of this term is, "to do or perform often, customarily, or habitually",[26] which would mean, in the context of religion or belief, to act according to the beliefs and customs of a particular religion or belief. It has been pointed out that if one takes a broad view of practice then it would be inevitably understood as covering all acts of "worship, observance and teaching".[27] On the other hand, it can also be construed in a narrow manner, meaning only acts similar to worship. The Commission and the Court had drawn the limits of protection in relation to practice by repeatedly stating that "the term practice...does not cover each act which is motivated and influenced by religion or belief".[28] The approach taken by Strasbourg organs was further narrowed by the "necessary expression" test, whereby it is asked whether a certain act is necessary for the fulfillment of the obligations of believers of a certain religion or belief. However, this position appears to have been abandoned with the finding on *Eweida and Others v. United Kingdom* where the ECtHR repudiated the necessity test and accepted that the applicant had a sense of obligation to wear the cross necklace.[29]

The analysis below will follow the paragraphs of Article 6 of the 1981 Declaration. As noted above, Article 6 does not encapsulate all possible forms of acts in which belief groups engage within the scope of their internal affairs. For example, pilgrimage or membership in a belief or religious community is not included. Article 6 is used, however, since it offers a helpful legal framework for the examination of the right of belief communities to freedom in their internal affairs. It is worth remembering that Article 6 does not refer to "individuals" as right holders, nor does it refer to the right to "manifest individually or in community with others". Instead it refers to "freedoms" that the freedom of thought, conscience, religion or belief includes, which are then listed as "acts". These acts are usually carried out collectively. Moreover, the issue of religious jurisdiction will be examined. The analysis and

24 Evans, *supra* note 22, p. 108.
25 *Inter alia*, *Kokkinakis v. Greece*, 25 May 1993, European Court of Human Rights, No. 14307/88, para. 31; *W. Delgado Paez v. Colombia*, 12 July 1990, Human Rights Committee, No. 195/1985, UN Doc. CCPR/C/39/D/195/1985, para. 5.7.
26 Merriam-Webster Dictionary online. Available: http://www.merriam-webster.com/dictionary/practice [Accessed 16 January 2015].
27 Evans, *supra* 19, p. 305.
28 Among others, *Arrowsmith v. United Kingdom*, 16 May 1977, European Commission of Human Rights, No. 7050/75, para. 71; *Yanasik v. Turkey*, 6 January 1993, European Commission of Human Rights, No. 14524/89; *Karaduman v. Turkey*, 3 May 1993, European Commission of Human Rights, No. 16278/90; *Valsamis v. Greece*, 18 December 1996, European Court of Human Rights, No. 21767/93.
29 *Eweida and Others v. United Kingdom*, 15 January 2013, European Court of Human Rights, Nos. 48420/10, 59842/10, 51671/10, 36516/10.

assessment will be based on the core freedom of religion or belief provisions of the ICCPR and ECHR and the jurisprudence of their respective bodies with interpretive authority. These jurisprudential sources do not provide equally substantive content on each category that is considered below. Therefore in order to gain a better understanding of the relevant legal issues, factual developments, challenges and guidance provided by the UN Special Rapporteur are also included. It should be borne in mind that while there may be differences in the approaches of these respective organs, resulting from their function and context, the standards set by them should not be contradictory.

The OSCE-Venice Commission addressed the issue of autonomy and self-determination of religious or belief communities in its *Guidelines for Review of Legislation Pertaining to Religion or Belief.*[30] It is a helpful tool for understanding the scope of autonomy for religious or belief communities and providing guidance for state action when actions resulting from autonomy conflict with interests of individuals or society. The OSCE-Venice Commission, in line with HRCttee and ECtHR, acknowledge that states can have varying practices regarding autonomy of religious or belief communities.[31] The European Commission, however, places the duty to engage in careful and nuanced weighing of interests where there is a conflict between the interests of religious or belief groups and other societal interest. It elaborates on this weighing of interests by stating that there should be a strong deference towards autonomy except in cases where autonomy is likely to lead to a clear and identifiable harm.[32] The Commission also draws attention to situations where autonomy issues are particularly likely to arise, namely in contexts where religious or belief organizations engage in operating hospitals, schools or businesses and where individuals assert that they discriminate on grounds such as gender, religion or sexual orientation.[33] The competing values of autonomy and non-discrimination are particularly worth paying attention to when the employers receive public financing or tax deductions for their activities. These guidelines are important in that they affirm the autonomous character of religious or belief communities and also offer concrete guidance to states' interference for situations where conflicts with societal interest may arise. In this context they draw particular attention to discrimination.

4.2.1 The Right to Worship or Assemble in Connection with Religion or Belief and to Establish and Maintain Places for these Purposes

The right to manifest religion or belief includes the right to establish places of worship.[34] The rights to worship, assemble for worship and establish and maintain places of worship are widely restricted by near explicit denials to certain belief or

30 OSCE-Venice Commission, *Guidelines for Review of Legislation Pertaining to Religion or Belief*, OSCE Office for Democratic Institutions and Human Rights, 2004, p. 15.

31 Ibid.

32 Ibid.

33 Ibid.

34 Human Rights Committee, General Comment No. 22: The right to freedom of thought, conscience and religion (Art. 18) UN Doc. CCPR/C/21/Rev.1/Add.4,

religious groups and often through restrictions that appear to be imposed through planning regulations, registration requirements and relevant administrative processes.[35] Worship that takes place "in community with others" and "in public" stands out as an essential element of the manifestation of the right to freedom of religion or belief in its collective dimension; the great majority of religious communities or communities of belief need a place of worship where their members can manifest their faith. Unlike other forms of violations of the right to freedom of religion or belief, attacks or other forms of restrictions on places of worship or other religious sites and shrines in many cases violate the right not only of a single individual, but the rights of a group of individuals forming the community that is attached to the place in question.[36] Krishnaswami observed early on that the right to manifest religion or belief in worship is often curtailed through "unreasonable regulations"; by arbitrarily withholding licenses for opening places of worship, or by imposing criteria that are "onerous or difficult", which in effect "negate" the right to worship.[37] Factual developments, globally, show that these challenges remain. Taylor observed that "in recent years registration procedures have taken centre stage in the means by which States constrain the structural aspects of religious practice".[38] Villaroman suggests that the non-compliance results from the "bare and austere" language of international provisions protecting the right to freedom of religion or belief thus leading to a "normative gap".[39] This will be considered below.

The HRCttee has rigorously criticized restrictions on establishing and building places of worship as well as discriminatory treatment of particular religious groups.[40] While considering the implementation of the ICCPR by Iran the HRCttee has expressed concern over a ban on conducting Christian services in Farsi.[41] While considering the Report of Israel, the HRCttee expressed concern

para. 4. *Vergos v. Greece*, 24 June 2004, European Court of Human Rights, No. 65501/01, para. 32.

35 For numerous examples from around the world see the annual reports on the communications received by the UN Special Rapporteur and, among others, the Report of the UN Special Rapporteur Summary of Cases Transmitted to Governments and Replies Received, UN Doc. E/CN.4/2005/61, 15 March 2005, paras 48–52, Report of the Special Rapporteur on Freedom of Religion or Belief Country Visit to Romania, UN Doc. E/CN.4/2004/63/Add.2, 16 December 2003, paras 100–108.

36 The Report of the UN Special Rapporteur Summary of Cases Transmitted to Governments and Replies Received, UN Doc. E/CN.4/2005/61, 15 March 2005, paras 48–52.

37 Krishnaswami, *supra* note 9.

38 Taylor, *supra* note 2, p. 242.

39 Villaroman, N.G. (2012) "The Right to Establish and Maintain Places of Worship: The Development of Its Normative Content under International Human Rights Law", in S. Ferrari and S. Pastorelli (eds.), *Religion in Public Spaces*, Leiden: Ashgate, p. 295.

40 Human Rights Committee, 29 November 2011, UN Doc. CCPR/C/IRN/CO/3, p. 6. (*Concluding Observations: Iran*), Human Rights Committee, 18 November 2011, UN Doc. CCPR/C/KWT/CO/2 (*Concluding Observations: Kuwait*).

41 Human Rights Committee, 29 November 2011, UN Doc. CCPR/C/IRN/CO/3, p. 6 (*Concluding Observations: Iran*).

at frequent disproportionate restrictions on access to places of worship for non-Jews.[42] Similarly, the Egyptian government was asked to respond to the alleged obstruction experienced by the Coptic Church in Egypt "in obtaining permits to repair and build places of worship".[43]

The use of registration or acquisition of legal entity status processes for religious or belief groups to restrict the right to establish places of worship has been underscored by the UN Special Rapporteur.[44] The link between legal entity status and the right to establish places of worship is a vital one. The Special Rapporteur explains:

> Legal status enables religious groups to act as juridical persons in the court system; *it entitles religious communities to build places of worship*, exempts religious communities from customs duties, entitles the community to open bank accounts, secures their standing as officially registered denominations and means that such communities can be fully fledged partners with the Government.[45]

In the case of *S. Malakhovsky and A. Pikul v. Belarus*, which concerned the refusal by the authorities to grant religious association status to the applicants, the HRCttee held that the limitations imposed must be "assessed in the light of the consequences which arise for the authors and their religious association".[46] While the case concerned the registration of a religious association and not the establishment of a place of worship the approach taken by the HRCttee is interesting to note. The HRCttee's questions used in its assessment, namely the consideration of the necessity of the conditions, consequences for the applications and the proportionality of the restrictions on the right of the applications under Article 18(3) are interpretive tools that may also be used in regards to places of worship. Inquisitive assessment of the necessity of restrictions shifts the burden of proof for the justification of the imposed restrictions to states and may be useful in detecting discriminatory patterns.

In a number of cases, the Strasbourg organs have held that the refusal to grant authorization or planning permission for places of worship constituted an interference with the right to manifest their religion.[47] On the other hand, the scrutiny of restrictions has not been strong; in *ISKCON and 8 Others v. United Kingdom*,

42 Human Rights Committee, 3 September 2010, UN Doc. CCPR/C/ISR/CO/3, p. 4 (*Concluding Observations: Israel*).
43 Report of the UN Special Rapporteur on Freedom of Religion or Belief, UN Doc. E/CN.4/1990/46 (1990), para. 40 and E/CN.4/1992/52 (1992), para. 30.
44 Report of the UN Special Rapporteur on Angola, UN Doc. A/HRCTTEE/7/10/Add.4, 6 March 2008, para. 18.
45 Ibid.
46 *Sergei Malakhovsky and Alexander Pikul v. Belarus*, 26 July 2005, Human Rights Committee, No. 1207/2003, UN Doc. CCPR/C/84/D/1207/2003, para. 7.4.
47 *ISKCON and 8 Others v. United Kingdom*, 8 March 1994, European Court of Human Rights (Admissibility) No. 20490/92. *Manoussakis and Others v. Greece*, 26 September 1996, European Court of Human Rights, No. 18748/91.

Johannische Kirche and Peters v. Germany and *Vergos v. Greece* the proportionality of the interference with the applicants' rights to manifest religion or belief was not considered.[48] Planning regulations were considered to be prescribed by law and to pursue a legitimate policy aim; however, they were not considered from the point of view of their suitability for the religious groups in question. The European Commission considered that the restrictions placed on an applicant for a place of worship were necessary for the "protection of the rights and freedoms of others", the residents of a nearby village.[49] It also stressed that "the Commission does not consider that Article 9 of the Convention can be used to circumvent existing planning legislation, provided that in the proceedings under that legislation, adequate weight is given to freedom of religion".[50] In *Vergos v. Greece*, instead of requiring the state to provide a "pressing social need" to justify the interference with the right, the ECtHR held that the applicant had not sufficiently established the "social need" for a "True orthodox Christian" place of worship in his town.[51]

Granting "the wide margin of appreciation of the Contracting States in planning matters" by the Strasbourg organs,[52] without due weight to the consideration of whether restrictions are proportionate to the aim pursued, appears to be a factor making it difficult for belief groups to achieve positive outcomes for their applications. In addition, that Strasbourg organs do not consider whether the planning requirements take into account the specific nature of place of worship requirements of the religious community in question, nor challenge the question asked by states as to whether there really is a need for a particular place of worship, seems to confer wide discretion upon states. This results in underuse of the potential protection provided by the restriction clause. Were states attributed a facilitating role with positive obligations to create conducive conditions for the establishment of places of worship, they would have had a greater burden to justify the restrictions. Likewise, were the rights to worship and establish places of worship viewed as internal matters/autonomy of religious/or belief communities, there would be a greater burden on states to justify restrictions.

The wide margin of appreciation conferred on states in planning matters together with a lack of consideration of proportionality and lack of focus on states' positive obligations to create the conditions for the effective enjoyment of the right to establish places of worship contribute to the non-identification of general repression. Not making the most of the protection offered by the restriction clause allows for the continuation of discriminatory patterns. In the future, the adoption of a more inquisitive review of the proportionality of planning and registration/ recognition processes would help identify systematic discrimination. In order to

48 Berry, S.E. (2012) "A Tale of Two Instruments", *Netherlands Quarterly of Human Rights*, 30(1), p. 23. Through this comparison this article enables us to see the application of law by the ECtHR and the concerns of the Advisory Council on National Minorities in a fresh way so as to reconsider and question the former.

49 *ISKCON and 8 Others v. United Kingdom*, *supra* note 47.

50 Ibid.

51 *Vergos v. Greece*, *supra* note 34, para. 14.

52 Ibid.

Besserabia v. Moldova, in addition to observing the negative outcomes of not having legal personality, the ECtHR noted the refusal of entry of humanitarian goods sent from abroad to the church.[60] Taylor, notes this reference as an "inclusion within Article 9 of humanitarian practices if only by implication".[61] However, if the main legal question raised by the case was interference in the establishment or maintenance of a charity or humanitarian organization, it is likely that such a right would be recognized by the ECtHR. On the other hand, it is possible to envisage situations where this right would be permissibly restricted, for example, where the nature of what is proposed as "charity" or "humanitarian" overlaps with public services or functions of the state, or where funds are raised for funding illegitimate acts or in order to escape from taxes.

4.2.3 The Right to Make, Acquire and Use to an Adequate Extent the Necessary Article and Materials Related to the Rites or Customs of a Religion or Belief

Manifestation of religion or belief in worship, teaching, observance and practice may require the use of various articles and materials ranging from the use of printed materials such as holy books and prayer books to ritual wine.[62] The scope of this provision is difficult to determine; depending on the dogma and practices of the religion or belief in question it can be rather broad. A narrow interpretation of Article 6(c) would limit the application of this provision to materials that are used in the context of a rite, for example, ritual wine may be used in a church building in the act of worship or religious ceremony and thus be strictly related to a ritual that may take place in a worship place. Yet, considering the many different religious traditions of the world, the nature of such articles and materials as well as the context in which they are used can vary. A broad interpretation may, for example, accommodate the use of *halal* meat for Muslims which involves the consumption of it in everyday life, not only in a ritual in a place of worship.

Taylor notes that there may be overlaps between Article 6(c) and other Articles of the 1981 Declaration,[63] or indeed other forms of manifestation of religion or belief. While it may be possible to include, for example, the protection of the use of religious clothing under Article 6(c), the right to manifest one's belief individually or in community with others in "observance and practice" may be better suited to address such claims.[64] Strasbourg organs and the HRCttee have dealt with claims related to religious dress as manifestations in "observance and practice".[65]

60 *Metropolitan Church of Bessarabia and Others v. Moldova*, 13 December 2001, European Court of Human Rights, No. 45701/99, para. 105.
61 Taylor, *supra* note 2, p. 247.
62 Krishnaswami, *supra* note 9.
63 Taylor, *supra* note 2, p. 251.
64 Protected in Article 9 of the ECHR, Article 18 of the ICCPR and Article 1 of the 1981 Declaration.
65 *Inter alia, Eweida and Others v. United Kingdom*, 15 January 2013, European Court of Human Rights, Nos. 48420/10, 59842/10, 51671/10 and 36516/10, and

The right to the use of necessary articles and materials related to the rites or customs of a religion or belief may raise autonomy issues and viewing it as such or not may constitute the thin line between a violation or not.

4.2.4 The Right to Write, Issue and Disseminate Relevant Publications in these Areas

Publications that are used in religious services such as holy books and other literature as well as other material may be used in, *inter alia*, worship and teaching a religion or belief to its followers. From the perspective of the collective dimension of freedom of religion or belief such publications are usually produced taking into account the needs of religious or belief communities and play a significant role in manifesting religion or belief in worship, practice, teaching and observance as well as the preservation and transmission to new generations of a religious group's identity.

The Special Rapporteur on Freedom of Religion or Belief extends the protection to the import of such publications.[66] Similarly, the arrest of persons who have received religious material from oversees has been questioned.[67] Were such cases assessed by the ECtHR and the HRCttee, in the case of importation, perhaps a closer examination would look to whether the production of the publications is possible domestically or not. If the applicants could establish that they need the publications to manifest their religion in worship, teaching, practice or observance, then states would be asked to justify restrictions on import in accordance with Articles 9 of the ECHR and Article 18 of the ICCPR.

The right to freedom of expression may be viewed as the more appropriate legal provision applicable to publications of a religious nature. Indeed, Article 10 of the ECHR and Article 19 of the ICCPR would also protect religious expressions in writing and publications. Having said that, the listing of this right within Article 6 of the 1981 Declaration underscores that to write, issue and disseminate relevant publications in these areas is also protected by freedom of religion or belief. Since relevant publications may be used in worship and teaching, naturally, Article 6(d) is connected to both Article 6(a) and Article 6(e).

Taylor notes that the HRCttee, when reviewing state reports has followed up on the freedom to write, issue and disseminate religious publications.[68] The inclusion of "dissemination of publications" implies that the provision covers promotion or propaganda of religion or belief. For example, the HRCttee has expressed concern over Turkmenistan's implementation of Article 18 due to strict

Karaduman v. Turkey, 1 January 1993, European Commission of Human Rights, No. 16278/90. HRCttee, General Comment 22, Comment No. 22, CCPR/C/21/Rev.1/Add.4 (1993), para. 4.

66 Report of the UN Special Rapporteur on Freedom of Religion or Belief, UN Doc. E/CN.4/1989/44 (1989), para. 31.

67 The Report of the UN Special Rapporteur on Freedom of Religion or Belief Country Visit to Morocco, UN Doc. E/CN.4/1995/91 (1995), p. 60.

68 Taylor, *supra* note 2, pp. 262–263.

regulation of the number of copies of religious texts that religious organizations may import, and called the government to change legislation so that "individuals can import religious texts in quantities they consider appropriate".[69]

As far as the ECtHR jurisprudence is concerned, there has not been consideration of a case where the right of an individual or religious or belief group to write, issue and disseminate publications has been addressed. If that were the case, Strasbourg organs may view this under freedom of expression, but may decide under freedom of religion or belief due to the religious context of expression.[70] Considering the prominent status of freedom of expression in the Convention system, it is likely that the right to write, issue and disseminate publications would be strongly protected as long as it does not amount to religious intolerance, incitement to violence and what the ECtHR would consider improper proselytism.[71]

4.2.5 The Right to Teach a Religion or Belief in Places Suitable for these Purposes

Forms of teaching can vary to a great extent; *inter alia*, teaching/training of religious personnel, teaching of children, youths and adults of the religious or belief community and teaching for proselytism purposes. The teaching of one's congregants, particularly children and youths, is key to preserving and transmiting religious dogma, tradition and identity of a religious or belief community. Therefore teaching needs to be considered as a key component of the autonomous acts of religious or belief groups. State practice regarding religious or philosophical education as well as theological education for training religious personnel can be diverse.

Since both the ICCPR and ECHR protect the right to manifest religion or belief in "teaching",[72] it is an explicitly protected form of manifestation. In addition, both instruments include provisions that create obligations for states to respect the rights of parents and legal guardians to raise their children in line with their religious or philosophical beliefs.[73] Children cannot be required to take instruction in religious or philosophical education against their parents' wishes. Compulsory education *about* religions or world views may be permissible; however, the religious and ideological concerns of parents on behalf of their children must be observed. Where exemptions are put in place these must be non-discriminatory.

69 Human Rights Committee, 19 April 2012, UN Doc. CCPR/C/TKM/CO/1 (*Concluding Observations on Turkmenistan*), p. 5.

70 See the case of *Kuznetsov and Others v. Russia*, 11 January 2007, European Court of Human Rights, No. 184/02. Here the ECtHR considered that the applicants by doing a Bible study "exercised their rights to freedom of expression and to freedom of peaceful assembly under Articles 10 and 11 of the Convention" yet, since the nature of the assembly was primarily religious, the Court first examined this complaint from the standpoint of Article 9: para. 53.

71 For the jurisprudence of the ECtHR on proselytism see in particular *Kokkinakis v. Greece*, 25 May 1993, European Court of Human Rights, Nos. 14307/88; *Larissis v. Greece*, 24 February 1998, European Court of Human Rights, Nos. 23372/94, 26377/95, 26378/94.

72 Article 18 and Article 9 respectively.

73 Article 18(4) of the ICCPR and Article 2 of Protocol 1 of the ECHR.

General Comment 22 on Article 18 refers to "freedom to establish seminaries or religious schools".

In the review of state reports, the HRCttee has expressed concern over reports of prohibition of private religious education at all levels.[74] Although not a straightforward case on the autonomy of religious organizations, in the *W. E. Delgado Paez v. Colombia* case,[75] the HRCttee provides an implication on the autonomy the Church enjoys in theological teaching matters in Colombian public schools. The applicant's teaching of religious education class was allegedly interfered with because of his views on liberation theology which differed from that of the Apostolic Prefect of Leticia. While the case has other dimensions as well, the HRCttee maintained that, without violating Article 18, Colombia can allow the Church authorities to decide who may teach religion and in what manner it should be taught. Although it is not stated as a right of the Church to autonomy in theological matters, in its role as the religion educator in public schools,[76] it is stated as a possibility that would not violate Article 18. When considering teachers' freedom to teach their subjects in accordance with their own views under Article 19, the right to freedom of expression, the Committee was willing to accept that the requirement of the Church to teach religion in a certain way did not violate Article 19. It would have been interesting to see how the Committee would balance the autonomy of the religious organization in theological education and the right to freedom of expression of teachers in delivering this teaching.

The OSCE – Venice Commission Guidelines elaborate on this in relation to establishment of private schools where parents may educate their children, "emphasizing ideological values".[77] States have a sphere of oversight in this context, however. They are permitted to establish neutral criteria for the teaching of standard subjects such as mathematics, history, science, and they can regulate teacher certification.[78] Yet a non-discrimination rule applies and states are not to discriminate between belief groups, including recognized religious or ideological groups.

4.2.6 *The Right to Solicit and Receive Voluntary Financial and Other Contributions from Individuals and Institutions*

Contributions received by religious or belief communities from individuals or institutions are often a sensitive issue for states,[79] particularly when religious

74 Human Rights Committee, 19 April 2012, UN Doc. CCPR/C/TKM/CO/1 (*Concluding Observations on Turkmenistan*), p. 5.
75 *William Eduardo Delgado Paez v. Colombia*, 12 July 1990, Human Rights Committee No. 195/1985, UN Doc. CCPR/C/39/D195/1985 (1990). The applicant complained that he was subjected to persecution by the Colombian authorities because of his progressive ideas in theological and social matters.
76 Due to a special agreement between Colombia and the Church. Ibid., para. 5.8.
77 OSCE-Venice Commission Guidelines, *supra* note 30.
78 Ibid.
79 The Soviet Union opposed the inclusion of this provision during drafting, fearing that contributions from other countries might be used for political purposes to promote

of frequent inquiry when reviewing state reports by the Committee with strong criticism of state interference in the appointment of religious leaders.[87]

The Special Rapporteur on Freedom of Religion and Belief affirms that the right to freedom of thought, conscience, religion or belief also includes the freedom to train, appoint, elect or designate by succession appropriate leaders. "Undue interferences in the training of religious leaders" that can lead to a "shortage of appropriate leaders" have been viewed with concern.[88] The practice of some states to impinge on the appointment procedure of religious leaders or the requirement approval by the authorities for certain promotions within religious groups has also been reported.[89] For example, concern has been expressed over the "grave interference with the Tibetan Buddhists who have the right to determine their clergy in accordance with their own rites" upon allegations that Nyima, then aged 6, had disappeared three days after being recognized as the eleventh reincarnation of the Panchen Lama by the Dalai Lama.[90]

Krishnaswami observed that in some cases public authorities have to adjudicate between rival elements within a religion, where judges must decide between the conflicting claims by interpreting the provisions of the religious law.[91] This necessarily implies some interference in the management of religious affairs; he pointed out, however, that "the line between legitimate interference and undue pressure is in many cases extremely thin".[92]

The ECtHR had the opportunity to address the issue of autonomy in internal structure and selection of leadership in a number of cases brought before it. In this regard, *Serif v. Greece*,[93] *Hasan and Chaush v. Bulgaria*[94] and *Supreme Holy Council of Muslim Community v. Bulgaria*[95] are particularly important in revealing the Court's view toward autonomy of religious communities and the protection given under Article 9. In *Serif v. Greece*, a case which dealt with criminal proceedings brought against Serif who allegedly assumed the role of a minister, *mufti*, of "a known religion", the Court ruled that, in democratic societies, the state need not take measures "to ensure that religious communities remain or are brought under a unified leadership".[96] It should be borne in mind, however, that the Court noted that *Serif* did not attempt to exercise judicial and administrative

87 UN Doc. A/42/40 (1987), p. 36, para. 137.
88 Human Rights Committee, UN Doc. A/HRCTTEE/6/5, para. 16 (*Concluding Observations*).
89 Ibid.
90 Report of the Special Rapporteur on Freedom of Religion or Belief, UN Doc. E/CN.4/2006/5/Add.1, paras 93–95.
91 Krishnaswami, *supra* note 9.
92 Ibid.
93 *Serif v. Greece*, 14 December 1999, European Court of Human Rights, No. 38178/97.
94 *Hasan and Chaush v. Bulgaria*, 30 October 2000, European Court of Human Rights, No. 30985/96.
95 *Supreme Holy Council of Muslim Community v. Bulgaria*, 16 December 2004, European Court of Human Rights, No. 39023/97.
96 *Serif v. Greece*, *supra* note 93, para. 52.

functions of an officially recognized *mufti*.[97] This indicates that measures pursuing a legitimate aim may be taken to protect those whose legal relationships might be affected by acts of ministers from deceit. Clearly, the Court does not provide a *carte blanche* to all activities within the community for the sake of autonomy, but takes into account rights of others. It is also interesting to note, in order to understand the ECtHR's conception of the right to freedom of religion or belief, that these cases have been decided solely on Article 9—not relying on Article 11 in any way—which is indicative of a conception of the right to appoint and select religious leaders that is viewed within the ambit of Article 9.

Where there is room for autonomy, conflict and tension within the community are unavoidable.[98] In fact, in all three of the cases mentioned above there is rivalry in leadership within religious communities and state interference aimed at eliminating competition in leadership and thus securing a unified leadership. But the ECtHR firmly held that "the role of the authorities in such circumstances is not to remove the cause of tension by eliminating pluralism, but to ensure that the competing groups tolerate each other".[99] The attribution of a strong importance to the protection of the right to autonomy in the appointment of leaders stands out as an aspect of freedom of religion or belief that is given priority.

The ECtHR holds that "the internal structure of a religious organization and the regulations governing its membership must be seen as a means by which such organizations are able to express their beliefs and maintain their religious traditions".[100] In *Hasan and Chaush v. Bulgaria*,[101] the applicants complained that the authorities interfered with the organizational life of the Muslim community by replacing the legitimate leadership of the community and refusing recognition of the re-elected leadership.[102] The applicants claimed that the discretionary power of the government to change religious leadership at will in the absence of a clear procedure comprising of a system of *ad hoc* letters, had profound consequences and amounted to replacement of the whole organizational structure of the Muslim community and a complete destruction of normal community life.[103]

In the case of the *Supreme Holy Council of Muslim Community v. Bulgaria*, which dealt with the same conflict, the European Court considered whether the involvement by domestic authorities in the organizational structure and leadership appointment of the applicant organization violated the rights of the applicants under Article 9.[104] Here the rival groups within the organization had asked the Directorate of Religious Denominations for assistance in holding a unification

97 Ibid.
98 *Serif v. Greece*, *supra* note 93, para. 53.
99 Ibid.
100 *Svyato-Mychalivska Parafiya v. Ukraine*, 14 June 2007, European Court of Human Rights, No. 77703/01, para. 150.
101 *Hasan and Chaush v. Bulgaria*, *supra* note 94.
102 Ibid., para. 66.
103 Ibid., paras 66 and 67.
104 *Supreme Holy Council of Muslim Community v. Bulgaria*, *supra* note 95.

conference.[105] The government claimed that this assistance flowed from the authorities' duty under the Constitution to help maintain a climate of tolerance in religious life.[106] While the Court was in agreement with the government on the existence of such a duty, and noted that "neutral mediation between groups of believers would not in principle amount to State interference with believer's rights under Article 9", it cautioned about the sensitivities in this delicate area.[107] Two considerations, however, led to finding a violation. First, domestic law required all believers affiliated with a particular religion to form a single structure, headed by a single leadership even if the community were divided, without the possibility for those supporting other leaders to have an independent organizational life and control over part of the community's assets.[108] State measures seeking to compel the community or part of it to place itself under a single leadership against its will would constitute an infringement of the freedom of religion.[109] Secondly, even though the initial participation of the Directorate was only neutral mediation, the fact that the Directorate insisted on unification, even though the applicant organization's leaders decided to withdraw, was problematic because the state imposed a particular way to resolve the problem.[110]

More recently, in the Grand Chamber judgment concerning the case of *Fernandez and Martinez v. Spain*, instead of balancing between the collective dimension of freedom of religion and individual human rights, the ECtHR accepted the Spanish courts' categorical balancing to the benefit of church autonomy.[111] It will be interesting to see the implications of this evolved position for future cases involving individual rights in relation to employment and rights of religious communities.

Naturally, in such cases, general restriction grounds, public safety, order, health or morals, or the fundamental rights or freedoms of others apply. In addition, the ECtHR acknowledges that a boundary to this autonomy can be drawn with the possible state action when it is necessary to "reconcile the interests of various religions and religious groups that coexist in a democratic society".[112] The basis for this may be the permissible restriction ground, "the protection of the fundamental rights or freedoms of others"; however, in the context of this case it is not expressly stated. However, still the state's role is basically one that is "regulatory" in its relations with religions, denominations and beliefs.[113] At times, provision of autonomy to religious communities and neutrality of the state are closely connected. The state has the positive duty to remain neutral and impartial in the

105 Ibid., para. 69.
106 Ibid., para. 71.
107 Ibid., para. 80.
108 Ibid., para. 81.
109 *Serif v. Greece*, *supra* note 93, paras 49, 52, 53.
110 Ibid., para. 84.
111 *Fernandez and Martinez v. Spain* (Grand Chamber judgment), 12 June 2014, European Court of Human Rights, No. 56030/07.
112 *Supreme Holy Council of Muslim Community v. Bulgaria*, *supra* note 95, para. 93.
113 Ibid.

exercise of its regulatory power which reinforces the protection of the autonomous realm of the religious group.

4.2.8 The Right to Observe Days of Rest and to Celebrate Holidays and Ceremonies in Accordance with the Precepts of One's Religion or Belief

This provision is potentially broad in scope because of the many possible forms of manifestations of worship, practice and observance it can cover; again it is a helpful example of how one should not read too extensively into the set categories since each category may be intimately linked to or extend into other categories. The core religious freedom provisions do not include an explicit reference to the right to observe days of rest and celebrate holidays in accordance with one's religion or belief. Yet, the HRCttee's General Comment 22 explicitly refers to "the observance of holidays and days of rest" as a form of manifestation protected under Article 18.[114] The phrase "to observe ceremonies in accordance with the precepts of one's religion or belief" is potentially an expansive issue depending on the dogma of a religion belief. "Ritual and ceremonial acts giving direct expression to the belief" and "use of ritual formulae and objects" are explicitly mentioned in General Comment 22.[115] Thanks to the rich and diverse examples from all over the world captured by the reports of the UN Special Rapporteur it is possible to gain insight into the extent and nature of these manifestations/ceremonial acts:

> [I]n one country, the religious practice of the circumcision of male children is not permitted; similarly, obstacles are placed in the way of religious traditions such as the celebration of marriage and funeral ceremonies according to the rites of a religion. In another country, certain rites and ceremonies peculiar to tribal religions have been banned. Elsewhere, it is extremely difficult in practice for the followers of a certain religion to bury their dead in accordance with religious ritual.[116]

In addition, Taylor suggests that the use of religious names could be protected under Article 6 of the 1981 Declaration.[117] "The use of a particular language customarily spoken by a group" that is mentioned in paragraph 4 of the General Comment 22 may also be protected under this provision.

Many religions and beliefs have special days when believers take time off for rest or engage in acts of worship in community with others; often, on these days they perform, or abstain from performing, certain activities according to the requirements of their religion or belief. Community life is generally arranged around observing these days that are significant based on the dogma and traditions of a

114 Ibid., para. 4.
115 Ibid.
116 E/CN.4/1987/35, para. 57
117 Taylor, *supra* note 2, p. 279. So far the HRCttee has dealt with such a case under Article 17 (right to privacy) in *A.R. Coeriel and M.A.R. Aurik v. The Netherlands*, Human Rights Committee, No. 453/1991, UN Doc. A/50/40 vol.2 (1999), p. 21.

did not work on two Muslim holidays, wanted to benefit from the exemption permitting the observance of Muslim holidays, based on his conversion to Islam.[132] Since he was not able to substantiate his "sincerity" through objective facts at the national courts, the case was taken to the ECtHR. The European Court held that where "the employee seeks to rely on a particular exemption, it is not oppressive or in fundamental conflict with freedom of conscience to require some level of substantiation".[133] He needed to substantiate his Islamic faith in order to be able to benefit from the exemption.

Clearly, a positive obligation on states and private employers to take necessary measures for accommodating requests for observance of religious holidays or days of rest is not foreseen in the Council of Europe context. There seems to be an emphasis on the choice employees have when making their contracts.[134] Where such accommodation is already made available in a given state, the European Court may supervise this process assessing whether it gives rise to questions concerning Article 9 and prohibition of discrimination.

In conclusion, the right to observe religious holidays and special days of rest seems to have gained greater support under the UN human rights protection scheme, whereas under the ECHR it has not reached the level of recognition as a right that would require states to take positive steps for accommodation. Nevertheless, states have the obligation to facilitate the full enjoyment of the right to freedom of religion or belief in all of its components, including the right to observe days of rest and holidays in accordance with religion or belief. Mere policy considerations cannot account for negation of this right. It should be remembered that the designation of the existing days of rest or holidays also had policy consequences in the past. Naturally, it is not an absolute right and restrictions may be considered as in the case of other components of the right to freedom of religion or belief. Relevant international standard setting must recognize this right and perhaps seek modalities of how it can be effectively protected in domestic settings.[135] Reasonable accommodation may be a way of moving forward. Also, whilst monitoring the right to freedom of religion or belief, a closer and rigorous assessment of this right as an aspect of the right to freedom of religion or belief in its collective dimension would bring international review closer to advancing its protection. Where conditions are created for the right to observe special days of rest and holidays in accordance with the precepts of one's religion or belief, this will also have the effect of advancing support of religious diversity within a society.

132 *Kosteski v. Former Yugoslav Republic of Macedonia*, 13 April 2006, European Court of Human Rights, No. 55170/00.

133 Ibid., para. 39.

134 Uitz, R. (2007) *Freedom of Religion*, Strasbourg: Council of Europe Publications, p. 48.

135 In fact in numerous countries measures are taken for the realization of this right and to eliminate the inequalities between majority/dominant religious groups and others.

4.2.9 The Right to Establish and Maintain Communications with Individuals and Communities in Matters of Religion or Belief at the National and International Levels

This freedom accommodates the need and tendency of belief communities to cooperate and interact with akin communities within the religious sphere both nationally and internationally.[136] Acts such as "inviting foreign clergy to visit the country or establish monasteries" have been regarded by the HRCttee as activities that are intrinsic to the right to manifest one's belief.[137] The reports of the UN Special Rapporteur are filled with examples of restrictions on such communications, particularly at the international level.[138] International communication or cooperation is of particular importance for minority religious groups whose existence might be dependent on support from co-religionists abroad in a variety of ways. There may be situations where there is an organic relationship with groups outside the country because of the trans-border nature of religious organization, hence international communication would be indispensable. In most cases, when communication is denied, more fundamental rights are denied as a result.[139]

The "seemingly weak recognition"[140] of this right, particularly at the international level, may be explained by its likely competition with national security concerns or national interests. Foreign "interference" through communication with domestic religious groups, in particular minorities, is generally viewed with suspicion. However, this is an essential right, such as the right to worship, and restrictions need to be subject to rigorous tests based on the relevant human rights provisions.

4.3 Freedom of Religious Communities to Apply Religious Law in Spheres Analogous to Civil/Criminal Law and Dispute Settlement

Norms derived from religion in a broad sense govern many aspects of life for religious or belief communities and individual believers. Depending on the scope of precepts of the religion or belief in question, rules or laws and conceptions may influence the food that can and cannot be consumed, the clothes that can and cannot be worn, the manner in which religious authority is structured and appointed as well as the manner in which finances are handled within a religious community. The education of children, community and religious teachers and clergy are also determined by religion based norms. Religious norms and values may also shape the conception of the roles of women and men in marriage and society and leadership, the methods of conflict resolution and arbitration, how evils in the form of illnesses, natural disasters or misfortune are dealt with as well as

136 For drafting history see Taylor, *supra* note 2, p. 287.
137 *Malakhovsky and A. Pikul v. Belarus*, *supra* note 46, para. 7.2.
138 See, *inter alia*, the restrictions on the Ahmadi community in Pakistan, UN Doc. E/CN.4/1996/95/Add.1, paras 23–24, 45 and 85 and on charges against a Czech priest for his contacts with religious orders E/CN.4/1988/45, para. 48.
139 For an overview see Taylor, *supra* note 2, pp. 288–289.
140 Ibid., p. 289.

the attitudes towards relations with the state. In addition, explanations provided by religions on fundamental issues of life form cultures' understandings of many issues which in turn play a role in shaping the common law amongst a community. These may be rules and mechanisms governing the activity of communal life, and are sometimes referred to as customary law as opposed to formal law.[141] In some cases religions provide highly complex and detailed rules, analogous to civil and criminal law, concerning regulation of marriage, divorce and inheritance, and rules related to conduct in trials and methods of punishment. There are also rules that may not be directly derived from religion, but religion can form a basis for legitimizing certain rules and forms of behavior.

Clearly, implications of laws and rules derived and condoned by religion or law are highly divergent, complex and comprehensive. The dynamics of the establishment, development, modification and elimination of such practices in a given community, society or country vary significantly in each situation and are deeply contextual. Sometimes traditional religion cannot be separated from custom, which makes it difficult to determine what is derived from religion and what is derived from tradition.[142] Another complicating factor is that believers, indeed, do not have a monolithic view when it comes to the place of religious law in the perception of their belief. The complexity is further increased by issues that arise when normative rules derived directly or indirectly from religious precepts or value systems have an impact on human rights of individuals. The religious law itself, interpretations of it and social custom that is derived from it or justified by reference to the religious law may conflict with human rights.[143] These are some of the forms of illustrative interactions that can be observed when attempting to put use of religious law into a legal framework for inquiry.

Before moving any further, it is necessary to determine the scope of discussion in this section. As illustrated above, religious law may be applied in various spheres of life and hence there can be a countless variety of implications that this notion may have for human rights. However, here the assessment is limited to the use of religious laws or laws derived or condoned by religion, in situations analogous to civil/criminal law and in dispute settlement by religious or belief communities as a form of manifestation of religion or belief as understood in its individual and collective dimensions. Hence the term religious law in this section means unwritten and written norms that regulate issues similar to those regulated by private law as well as those used in alternative dispute settlements which are derived from the dogma of a religion or belief. The interest of this book in the use of religious law by religious or belief communities is derived from the general theme of the study, the collective dimension of freedom of religion and in the autonomy of religious

141 Care, J.C. (2006) "Between a Rock and a Hard Place", in A. Whiting and C. Evans (eds.), *Mixed Blessings: Laws, Religions and Women's Rights in the Asia-Pacific Region*, Leiden: Martinus Nijhoff, p. 105.

142 Ibid., p. 107.

143 Sullivan, D.J. (1991) "Gender Equality and Religious Freedom: Toward a Framework for Conflict Resolution", *New York University Journal of International Law and Politics*, 24, p. 795.

communities.[144] It is observed that when religions are as comprehensive as to include religious law as described above, the use of it by individuals and religious or belief groups becomes a way of manifestation of religion or belief and preservation and development of their religion and/or culture.

Plural legal orders are, more often than not, viewed in the context of indigenous populations, cultural rights and accommodation of minority cultures and identities.[145] This is understandable since, traditionally, non-state legal orders may rarely be based solely on religious law, instead they tend to have diverse sources. This does not, however, eliminate the freedom of religion or belief dimension which this part seeks to highlight.

Then the question is whether a right to use religious law by individual believers in community with others can be deduced from the international norms protecting the right to freedom of religion or belief. To the extent that religious law provides for rules that regulate relations within families and dispute settlement, for the individual believers the application of this law qualifies as "practice" of religion or belief. This is true when the term is understood not closely linked to worship but in a broader fashion.

Both the ICCPR and the ECHR stipulate, in their respective articles, that the right to freedom of religion or belief includes "the freedom, either individually or in community with others and in public or in private, to manifest his religion or belief in worship, observance, *practice* and teaching".[146] While these four categories are exhaustive, the specific acts that constitute protected forms of manifestation under each heading are doubtless a subject of unending debate, particularly as unusual or non-traditional forms of manifestations and traditional manifestations in new settings confront the HRCttee and the European Court.

The discussions on the drafting of General Comment 22 disclose a strikingly different approach from the one held by Strasbourg organs. The discussions indicate that there seems to be a general agreement that only believers themselves can decide what is and is not a genuine religious belief and, as for manifestations,

144 It should be noted that situations where religious law is the state law are excluded since in my view this does not qualify as a manifestation of religion because it is enforced and not freely chosen and my research specifically focuses on autonomy of religious/belief communities. The writer takes a very critical view on enforcement of religious law by states because it does not pass the "consent test" for manifestation of religion. When a state argues that its law, based on religion, is a form of manifestation of religion or belief, the inevitable question is whose manifestation of religion is it? The lack of "voluntariness" or consent disqualifies these systems from being forms of manifestation of religion or belief. Obviously, there are numerous forms of application of religious laws and I am not proposing that religious law is never a manifestation of religion, but neither am I unhesitatingly accepting that religious law is always a manifestation of religion.

145 For a comprehensive overview of the variety issues related to cultural/religious jurisdictions see Report of the International Council on Human Rights Policy, *When Legal Worlds Overlap: Human Rights, State and Non-State Law*, 2009.

146 ECHR, Article 9 and ICCPR Article 18. Emphasis added.

Article 18(3) existed to prevent these from violating rights of others.[147] The approach of the HRCttee is to leave the determination of whether an act is a manifestation of religion or belief to the believers and, only when there is a need to restrict the manifestation in question, then to employ the use of restrictions clause. Krishnaswami also affirms this approach,

> Bearing in mind that on the one hand the Declaration [Universal Declaration on Human Rights (UDHR)] was prepared with a view to bringing all religions or beliefs within its compass, and on the other hand that the forms of manifestation, and the weight attached to each of them, vary considerably from one religion or belief to another, it may safely be assumed that the intention was to embrace *all* possible manifestations of religion or belief within the terms "teaching, practice, worship and observance".[148]

There is no explicit or direct reference to whether the use of religion based law is a form of manifestation that is protected under the right to manifest religion or belief in community with others. So far the most comprehensive list of manifestations has been compiled in the study prepared by Krishnaswami where, in addition to many manifestations linked to worship, observance and teaching, explicit reference to celebration and dissolution of marriage was made.[149] However, the latter were not included in the core freedom of religion or belief clauses[150] and General Comment 22 of the HRCttee.[151] The reason might be the lack of a uniform practice among states as to whether these are viewed in the realm of regulatory acts of the modern state or in the realm of the religious or belief community, or the inequalities that these might cause. For instance, even though not explicitly articulated, disciplinary acts within religious communities may be seen as protected acts under the autonomy of religious or belief communities. An example of this could be "excommunication or shunning" of Jewish courts.[152]

147 For discussions during the drafting of paragraph 4 of General Comment 22 which deals with manifestations of religion or belief, see UN Doc. CCPR/C/SR. 1162 and CCPR/C/SR. 1162.

148 Krishnaswami, *supra* note 9. Emphasis added.

149 Krishnaswami, *supra* note 9. He notes that a particularly fertile ground for conflicts between the prescriptions of religious law and those of secular law is to be found in questions pertaining to the celebration and dissolution of marriage. These conflicts occur because most religions or beliefs consider these questions to be within their competence, whereas the modern state assumes the right to regulate family relationships on the ground that the family is the basic unit of society.

150 Article 23 of the ICCPR stipulates the right to marry and does not specifically refer to national law as contrasted to ECHR, Article 12. Article 23 lays down the requirement of "free consent" and "equal rights and responsibilities" of spouses as to marriage.

151 Paragraph 4 mentions "ceremonies" without further detail.

152 Broyde, M.J. (1996) "Forming Religious Communities and Respecting Dissenter's Rights", in J. Witte, Jr. and Johan D. van der Vyver (eds.), *Religious Human Rights in Global Perspective: Religious Perspectives*, Leiden: Martinus Nijhoff, pp. 203–233.

In spite of the absence of explicit allusion to religious law which governs issues similar to family law and dispute settlement, these can be best categorized as practices in the ordinary sense of the word; "to act according to the beliefs and customs of a particular religion". Obviously, this depends on the nature of religion or belief and whether and to what extent such religious law is an integral part of the religion or belief in question. Individual believers may wish, in community with others, to act in accordance with their own beliefs in a sphere that may overlap with family law, private law or dispute settlement. Quite apart from the question of potential problems in relation to human rights law to influence judgment, manifesting religion in practice would cover such acts.

As for the ECHR, the terms "worship, observance, practice and teaching" are not defined in the Convention and the preparatory documents do not provide any insight into the content of these categories.[153] Subsequent decisions and judgments of the Strasbourg organs have not provided any description of these categories and what forms of manifestations are protected in each. Worship has been given the highest status of the manifestations listed in Article 9(1).[154] The Commission has said that Article 9 primarily protects personal beliefs and religious creeds and "acts which are intimately linked to these, such as worship and devotion".[155] As for observance, the Commission and the Court have not given this category of manifestation a separate consideration, yet. Evans concludes that "observance" seems to have been conflated into a slightly extended notion of worship and that they are considered together as "worship and observance" without a particular distinction.[156] While "teaching" has not been defined either, it has been subject to more detailed discussion.

The term practice has proved to be the most difficult one to define. The ordinary meaning of this term in the context of religion is, "to act according to the beliefs and customs of a particular religion".[157] It has been pointed out that if one takes a broad view of practice then it would be inevitably understood as covering all acts of "worship, observance and teaching".[158] On the other hand, it can also be construed in a narrow manner, meaning only acts similar to, but beyond, worship. The Commission and the Court have drawn the limits of protection in relation to practice by repeatedly stating that "the term practice…does not cover each act which is motivated and influenced by religion or belief."[159] Similarly

153 The text of Article 9 was based on Article 18 of the UDHR with a view to avoiding definitions that are inconsistent with those in the UN documents.

154 Evans, *supra* note 22, p. 107.

155 *C. v. United Kingdom*, 15 December 1983, European Court of Human Rights, No. 10358/83. Accordingly, establishing places of worship, ownership of objects necessary for worship, and facilitating religious services in prison have been viewed as included within the right to worship.

156 Evans, *supra* note 22, p. 108.

157 *Encarta Webster's Dictionary of the English Language* (2004) Soukhanov, A. (ed.), Bloomsbury Publishing.

158 Evans, *supra* note 19, p. 305.

159 Among others *Arrowsmith v. United Kingdom*, 16 May 1977, European Commission on Human Rights, No. 7050/75.

many times, the act in question was not specified as belonging to a particular category of manifestation but, rather, was viewed as manifestation of religion or belief. This approach has led to focus on whether an act constitutes manifestation of religion or not rather than development of a detailed understanding of what each category includes.[160] The approach taken by Strasbourg organs has been further narrowed by the "necessary expression" test, whereby it is asked whether a certain act is necessary for the fulfillment of the obligations of believers of a certain religion or belief. Obviously, the question is who determines what is necessary; the individual believer, the Court or even an expert opinion may differ on what exact acts are necessary for the precepts of a certain religion or belief. This position appears to have changed in the case of the *Eweida and Others v. United Kingdom*; however, it will be necessary to see future cases in order to ascertain if there has been a permanent change toward adopting a broader approach to manifestations.[161] Where religious communities are granted rights in national systems to act according to their religious law on certain matters, there is nothing in the Convention and its Protocols to prevent one from viewing these acts as a manifestation of religion or belief. For instance, as regards marriage, Article 12, regulating the right to marry and found a family, states that "Men and women of marriageable age have the right to marry and found a family, according to the national laws governing the exercise of this right". Hence, the Convention here takes note of the possibility that legal systems vary among states parties where for instance in some states religious marriage ceremony is attached the legal consequence of matrimony, while in others it is not.[162]

While the approach taken by the European Court may not at first sight look very promising, due to the narrow view it has taken of manifestation of religion or belief as outlined above, this may not necessarily mean a categorically negative answer to our question. The ECHR has taken a very open and inclusive approach to the collective dimension of freedom of religion particularly in terms of associative rights of religious or belief communities,[163] recognizing their autonomous existence of religious communities and their protection as such, as a prerequisite of pluralistic democracy. Legal pluralism may be a suitable way of furthering freedom of religion of communities belonging to different religions,[164] as well as cultural rights. As far

160 Evans, *supra* note 19, see discussion on pp. 304–314.

161 *Eweida and Others v. United Kingdom*, *supra* note 29.

162 Van Dijk, P. and G.J.H. Van Hoof (1998) *Theory and Practice of the European Convention of Human Rights*, Leiden: Kluwer, p. 844.

163 This is analyzed extensively in Chapter 3, where I examine legal status and recognition of religions/belief communities. The ECHR has adopted a strong approach to acknowledge that believers traditionally exist in autonomous communities.

164 Indeed, it is proposed that legal pluralism is a more acceptable model for secularism in a liberal state. For a discussion on legal pluralism as an appropriate implementation of freedom of religion, see Javid Gadirov (2007) "Freedom of Religion and Legal Pluralism", in M.L.P. Loenen and J.E. Goldschimidt (eds.), *Religious Pluralism and Human Rights in Europe: Where to Draw the Line?*, Cambridge: Intersentia, pp. 81–93. And from a political theory perspective see Shachar, A. (2001) *Multicultural Jurisdictions: Cultural Differences and Women's Rights*, Cambridge: Cambridge University Press. On legal

as religious or belief communities are concerned, the use or application of religious law in matters such as family law or dispute settlement is just another sphere where norms of a religion or belief are implemented. All are derived from their respective dogma, are considered authoritative, and individual believers, in community with others, either informally or formally put them into practice in their internal matters.[165]

One possible reason that the European Court may not be willing to conclude that there exists under Article 9 a right to use religious law would be that such an interpretation may be considered by states parties as an undue intervention into their domestic affairs, in particular state-religion relations. Another reason might be that they may not view such manifestation as "closely linked to worship". It may be that the European Court does not view the use of religious law by individual believers as protected under Article 9 but within the ambit of Article 9; similar to its long-standing, however recently changed, approach toward conscientious objection to military service.[166] This would not be without any benefit to religious communities. Where a state facilitates the use of religious law by a group of believers, other groups claiming the same right may be protected by the prohibition of discrimination. It is also highly likely that the European Court could, without making a decision on whether or not it is a manifestation of religion or belief, move to assessment under the restrictions clause. The latter might lead the Court to find that the state would be justified in its measures or apply the notion of margin of appreciation by relying on national authorities.

The most explicit claim on matters relating to religious jurisdiction came with the *Refah Partisi v. Turkey* case,[167] where the applicants alleged, in particular, that the dissolution of *Refah* by the Turkish Constitutional Court and the suspension of certain political rights of the other applicants, who were leaders of *Refah* at the time, had breached, *inter alia*, Articles 9, 10, 11, 14. The case is interesting in that it provides some insight into the European Court's view on plural legal

pluralism see Warwick, T. (2003) *Legal Pluralism: Towards a Multicultural Conception of Law*, Aldershot: Ashgate.

165 This is analogous to application of religious rules in, for example, the organizational and hierarchical structure of a religious organization, only in a different sphere of relations.

166 The ECHR does not recognize that Article 9 protects the rights to conscientious objection to military service. However it views it within the ambit of Article 9 and where the right to conscientious objection is recognized by a state the European Court assumes its supervision by employing prohibition of discrimination. It may be that the Court views some forms of manifestation as within an "outer circle" of Article 9, suggesting that the protection of these by a member state would be an extra right granted by the latter and not necessarily a requirement of Article 9.

167 *Case of Refah Partisi (Welfare Party) and Others v. Turkey*, 13 February 2003, European Court of Human Rights (Grand Chamber), Nos. 41340/98, 41342/98, 41343/98 and 41344/98. It should be noted this claim came from a political party and not a religious community. See Boyle, K. (2004) "Human Rights, Religion and Democracy: The Refah Party Case", *Essex Human Rights Review*, 1(1), pp. 1–16; Cumper, P. (2003/2004) "Europe, Islam and Democracy: Balancing Religious and Secular Values", in *European Yearbook of Minority Issues*, Volume 3, pp. 166–175.

systems and private law rules of religious inspiration. Although the Court noted that it will not express an opinion in the abstract on the advantages and disadvantages of a plurality of legal systems, in the Court's view, a plural legal system, *as proposed by Refah*, was clearly incompatible with the Convention system because *Refah*'s policy was to apply some of sharia's private law rules to a large part of the population, namely Muslims, within the framework of plurality of legal systems.[168] One crucial factor in the Court's view was that such a policy went beyond the private sphere to which Turkish law confines religion. This approach once again indicated that the Court was taking the national accommodation of religious freedom as a reference point. In response to the applicants' argument that prohibition of a plurality of private-law systems amounted to discrimination against Muslims who wished to live their private lives in accordance with the precepts of their religion, the Court emphasized that manifestation of religion was primarily a matter of individual conscience which is quite different from the field of private law.[169]

While the Court's approach in the *Refah Partisi v. Turkey* case is not one that wholeheartedly welcomes legal pluralism with the introduction of sharia, it cannot be definitely concluded that the Court could not envision within the framework of the Convention, a pluralist legal system where religious laws would be implemented. It seems it would be subject to the content of the religious law proposed, to what extent national legal systems allow it, and whether it will be imposed on individuals based on their religious affiliation. Malcolm Evans points out that according to the Court if religious communities are to be welcomed as participants in the public life of the state, it is on the condition that they respect the principles of democracy and human rights; of tolerance and pluralism.[170] And if they threaten either, then the state may be obliged to take steps. This, in his view, gives the state an interventionist and regulatory role rather than a restricted one which is that of facilitation in accordance with Article 9 itself.[171] It also has been suggested that the ECHR has been all too sweeping in order to strike a proper balance in the issue of accepting the exercise of certain regulatory powers of religious entities in relation to their members.[172] Scheinin views this judgment as an indication of exclusion by the ECtHR, as a matter of principle, the diversification of rights and obligations in a multicultural society according to religious affiliation and through the delegation of certain regulatory authority to religious entities.[173] In my view this is not so certain; the ECtHR seems to reject this possibility *as it is proposed by*

168 *Refah Partisi (Welfare Party) and Others v. Turkey*, *supra* note 167, para. 119.
169 Ibid., para. 128.
170 Evans, M.D. (2004) "Believing in Communities, European Style", in N. Ghanea (ed.), *The Challenge of Religious Discrimination at the Dawn of the New Millennium*, Leiden: Martinus Nijhoff, pp. 152–154.
171 Ibid.
172 Scheinin, M. (2004) "How to Resolve Conflicts Between Individual and Collective Rights?", in M. Scheinin and R. Toivanen (eds.), *Rethinking Non-Discrimination and Minority Rights, Institute for Human Rights*, Åbo: Åbo Akademi University Publications, p. 230.
173 Instead he proposes a human rights approach that would look at the concrete modalities and safeguards of such a delegation. Ibid., p. 230.

Refah,[174] and therefore may be open to other propositions. Also, the national legislative arrangements concerning an acceptance of legal plurality may play a role in rejection or openness of the ECtHR.

There are a number of conclusions that one can draw about the position of the European Court in regards to manifestation of religion or belief through the use of religious law, or "private law rules of religious inspiration" as the Court phrases it. The first one is that the Court views manifestation of freedom of religion or belief as primarily a matter of individual conscience and is cautious about manifestation in the field of private law. Secondly, the Court sees this aspect of manifestation of religion or belief as a matter of national law and up to the state in question. Where the application of religious laws in matters such as family law are facilitated by a state then the Court would not be opposed to this, as such, but would engage in its regular supervisory role. Thirdly, the Court has a certain view of the sharia as static and prejudicial to public order and the values of democracy. Fourthly, it is important not to lose sight of the fact that it is not a religious community but a political party that is propagating this idea. This may also play a role, as a political party may have the possibility of changing the legal system in a manner that can impose the religious law on individuals without their consent.

By way of summary on the question of whether the use of religious law, in areas such as family law and dispute resolution, is a form of manifestation that is protected by the right to manifest religion or belief in community with others, it follows from the above examination that, as regards the European Court, it would depend on whether the Court would adopt a narrow or wide approach to practice of religion or belief. If the Court views practice in a broad manner, the use of religious law may be seen within the ambit of Article 9. The second important factor for the Court would be the way in which the state party has regulated this sphere. It is highly likely that the Court would see this within the discretion of the state, hence not necessarily within the protection of Article 9, regardless of how it is viewed by the state in question. The major challenge may be that religious law endeavors to regulate the same sphere as the state itself, namely family law and dispute settlement. Still the closest the European Court comes to protecting religious law is in the religious celebration of marriage that has the effect of official marriage.[175]

As regards the universal level, there is not an explicit recognition of the right to apply religious law by believers among themselves and, in spite of the fact that the General Comment is silent and there is no jurisprudence, as of yet, to support it, it is likely that the HRCttee, in principle, will consider a claim by a religious community to use religious law within the ambit of protection of Article 18 due to its broad approach to manifestations and reliance on believers' views on these matters and the various legal traditions found at the global level.

174 *Refah Partisi (Welfare Party) and Others v. Turkey*, *supra* note 167.

175 The necessary structure and processes would be highly contextual and it is not my purpose here to propose a complete institutional model. The point is that the state has to be willing to make necessary adjustments.

If one assumes that the right to manifest religion or belief in practice protects the use of religious law, the realization of this right would certainly require significant obligations on the part of the state. Broadly speaking, it is possible to envision states' role as one of facilitation and supervision with an emphasis on legal safeguards. Facilitation would require that the state assists with the necessary processes and institutional structures[176] and negotiation with the community in question. The second area of engagement by the state would be in its supervisory role as guarantor of human rights. This sphere necessitates that the state takes positive measures with regard to safeguards that would protect individuals against human rights abuses by fellow group members while at the same time balancing the interests of the collective dimension.

While Krishnaswami provided a very comprehensive catalog of manifestations, he also recognized that some of these, such as human sacrifice, self-immolation, mutilation, slavery, prostitution, subversive activities, polygamy and other practices that may clash with the requirements found in Article 29 of UDHR, could be subject to permissible limitations. Where traditional religious practices come into conflict with the basic rights of the individual, it is the former that have to give way. These limitations by the state on religious practices, for example, have increased freedom for Indian society as a whole.[177]

In conclusion, notwithstanding its limitation, the right to freedom of religion or belief in its collective dimension offers substantive protection to the right of belief groups to freedom in their internal affairs—autonomy. Where problems remain, this may not be so much a result of a "normative gap" in the international protection of human rights, but of a lack of a holistic understanding of and willingness to enforce the implications of the existing norms. A great deal can be learnt from the approaches of the UN HRCttee and the UN Special Rapporteur about the proactive steps that may need to be taken by states, and the positive obligations that arise under Article 18 of the ICCPR and Article 9 of the ECHR. Some obligations are more clearly defined than others. The differing approaches of the HRCttee and the Strasbourg organs to the various elements of this right, including the nature of obligations, creates inconsistencies and disparities in international standard setting. The account above indicates that some aspects of the collective dimension of freedom of religion or belief are given more attention, while others do not receive as much attention in international review. This inconsistency may be attributable to policy considerations, but also to the evolving nature of obligations as our understanding of issues and their implications on the right to freedom of religion or belief becomes more clear.

Autonomy of religious or belief communities appears as an area of the collective dimension that needs to be re-interpreted as an interpretive tool in adjudication. It has been suggested that such re-interpretation should seek to employ the term

176 Scheinin emphasizes the importance of negotiations with the group and obtaining its consent in the process of drawing the borderline of jurisdictional spheres. Scheinin, *supra* note 172, p. 231.

177 Krishnaswami, *supra* note 9.

beyond organizational matters. This would then have the effect of changing positive obligations on the part of the states to accommodate the autonomous acts of belief groups. A greater burden to justify restrictions on the part of the states would also be required.

There is a tremendous variety among the legal traditions of the countries of the world on whether to allow or provide space for religious communities to apply their religious law and to what extent. An important factor seems to be whether, historically or traditionally, a certain sphere is viewed as a sphere regulated by the state which sees an interest in it or as a sphere of religious tradition or manifestation. In some countries marriage, divorce, custody and guardianship issues have become codified and institutionalized and regulated by the state and therefore are no longer a matter of private concern.[178] Whereas in others, where customary law has a wide influence, these matters are viewed within the framework of religious affiliation and religious jurisdiction.

It is clear that there is great concern that religiously motivated laws violate individual rights, in particular women's human rights.[179] While these concerns may be valid, this should not lead to a categorical rejection of the use of religion based laws by religious or belief communities. These concerns are better addressed in the process of finding a resolution between competing interests.

It is very important not to lose sight of the fact that religious communities, like individuals, are not static and that they are highly divergent. When they find themselves in new circumstances they also feel the need to re-evaluate their practices, and religious laws are not an exception.[180] Indeed, human rights are a

178 Shaheen, S.A. (2007) "Religious Pluralism, Human Rights and Muslim Citizenship in Europe: Some Preliminary Reflections on an Evolving Methodology for Consensus", in M.L.P. Loenen and J.E. Goldschmidt (eds.), *Religious Pluralism and Human Rights in Europe: Where to Draw the Line?*, Cambridge: Intersentia, p. 75.

179 Chinkin, C. (2001) "Cultural Relativism and International Law", in C. Howland, *Religious Fundamentalisms and the Human Rights of Women*, New York: Palgrave Macmillan, p. 56.

180 For instance Donald Brown relays the example of the *Fiqh* Council of North America, which is a group working on the development of *fiqh* that is culturally relevant in North America. He argues that since there is no *ulema* in North America, the development of *fiqh* is unimpeded and this means that an opportunity that has not been presented to Muslims in nearly 1,000 years, at least in the area of family law, is at stake. He further argues that in Canada this opportunity was missed since Premier McGuinty announced rejection of all religious arbitration within Ontario's legal system. See, Brown, D. (2007) "A Destruction of Muslim Identity: Ontario's Decision to Stop Shari'a Based Arbitration", *North Carolina Journal of International Law and Commercial Regulation*, Spring, pp. 495 and 519. Also see An-Na'im, A.A. (2000) "Islam and Human Rights: Beyond the Universality Debate", ASIL Annual Meeting Proceedings, ASIL Washington, p. 361. Another example is the Jewish community, which for too many years has lived under laws of different states and responds to new circumstances. The Jewish law, *halakhah*, which means entire body of Jewish law, from scripture to the latest rabbinical rulings, at least in its application has undergone changes throughout history and different approaches have developed in different wings of the Jewish community with regard to major *halakhic* problems. For a survey of divergent approaches and their development see Novak, D. (2005) "Halakhah:

valuable framework for the development of religious traditions.[181] Where there are domestic laws that are in serious contradiction with religious laws, the community in questions may be able to find a modified version of the precept in question. But for this to take place the community first and foremost has to have the capacity, means and forum to engage in the development of its laws and interaction with the state.

In brief, as shown above, the right to autonomy of religious or belief communities needs to be understood as an issue beyond organizational freedom in the internal affairs religious organizations. Depending on the content of the dogma, doctrine and traditions of religious or belief groups, it can be a significantly expansive issue presenting itself in diverse—sometimes unexpected—spheres. Adjudicators need to be willing to see and use the notion of autonomy of religious or belief communities as an interpretive tool in cases where the collective dimension of freedom of religion or belief can be identified. The discussion above suggests that adjudicators have not applied the notion of autonomy consistently—in particular they have been unwilling to see the collective dimension and implications for the autonomous existence of communities outside the framework of organizational matters. Consistent application would mean that adjudicators attribute to states positive obligations to accommodate and ensure that third parties accommodate, for example, time off from work for religious rituals or celebrations. The cases on worship places, however, revealed that burdensome positive obligations are not the only reason for preference to overlook issues that seem on the periphery of the right to freedom of religion or belief. The reason might be simply not seeing the autonomy issues involved because of a certain conception of the nature of the right to freedom of religion or belief.

Structure of Halakhah" in L. Jones (ed.), *Encyclopedia of Religion*, Vol. 6. 2nd ed., Detroit: Macmillan Reference USA, pp. 3747–3755.

181 Charlesworth, H. (1999) "The Challenges of Human Rights Law for Religious Traditions", in M.W. Janis and C. Evans (eds.), *Religion and International Law*, Leiden: Martinus Nijhoff, pp. 410–412.

5 Introduction to the Case Study on Turkey and the General Turkish Legal Framework Pertaining to the Right to Freedom of Religion or Belief

5.1 Introduction

This section examines and assesses the protection of the collective dimension of the right to freedom of religion or belief in Turkey in light of applicable international law standards. Mirroring the structure of the two preceding chapters, the case study reviews the protection of the collective dimension of freedom of religion or belief, in particular the right to acquire legal personality and the right to freedom in the internal affairs of belief groups as it is exercised in the right to establish and maintain places of worship, the right to teach religion or belief in suitable places, the right to train, appoint and elect clergy and the right to observe days of rest and holidays. Indeed, the enjoyment of the right to freedom of religion or belief is closely related to the national legal structures available to individuals and religious communities to exercise the right to freedom of religion or belief without any discrimination.[1]

State-religion relations evolve over the course of history and are shaped by the unique political experiences of nations. This highly contextual relationship plays a significant role in the evolved legal framework pertaining to the protection of the right to freedom of thought, conscience, religion or belief, particularly in its collective dimension. Bearing this in mind, this chapter seeks to briefly present the historical evolution of the state-religion relation in Turkey in order to present a complementary background that is necessary to provide the relevant context for the legal questions that will be discussed in the following chapters. The reason for adopting this somewhat broader framework for the case study is to situate the treatment of the questions of the book in the overall climate created with the arrangement pertaining to religion and protection of freedom of religion or belief, rather than studying them as isolated legal questions. Key aspects of the arrangement of religion in the Ottoman Empire and in the period of the establishment of the Turkish Republic and a brief account of current trends are presented below. Tracing this progression is critical to understanding the state-religion arrangement that evolved

1 Durham, W.C. (1999) *Freedom of Religion or Belief: Laws Affecting the Structuring of Religious Communities*, ODIHR Background Paper 1999/4 Published by the Office for Democratic Institutions and Human Rights of the Organization for Security and Cooperation in Europe.

in Turkey. This account may be useful in *explaining* the current practice, sensitivities and particular interpretations of the Turkish judiciary—though it may not necessarily *justify* them. A presentation of a comprehensive account and critical analysis of the historical formation of state-religion relations in Turkey is, however, beyond the scope of this study. The following account aims to follow the thread of the general legal paradigm of state-religion relationship, including neutrality of the state, protection of freedom of religion or belief and principle of equality through the Ottoman Empire and the period of the establishment of the Turkish Republic.

Following the brief review of state-religion relations in Turkey, an analytical and critical overview of the general Turkish legal framework for the protection of the right to freedom of religion or belief is presented. The discussion will touch upon key issues, *inter alia*, the Diyanet, compulsory Religious Culture and Knowledge of Ethics (Din Kültürü Ahlak Bilgisi—DKAB) courses, coercion to declare one's religious affiliation, manifestations of religious symbols in the public sphere and conscientious objection to military service. Since issues concerning the collective dimension of freedom of religion or belief will be considered in detail in Chapters 6 and 7 this chapter will focus on general matters. Analysis will be based on the relevant legal resources of applicable international instruments that create legal obligations for Turkey, including the Lausanne Peace Treaty,[2] which creates a special legal regime for non-Muslim minorities, relevant principles and provisions of 1982 Constitution and pertinent legislation.

5.2 Turkey's Religious Demographics

In contrast to the generally presented picture of Turkey as a country with a 99 percent Muslim population,[3] alternative sources provide additional information that can contribute toward drawing a more complete picture concerning the religious make-up of the population in Turkey, including diversity within the Muslim population. Turkey has an estimated population of 77.6 million people.[4] According to the General Directorate of Civil Registration and Nationality, official statistics on religious demographics are not kept.[5] As a result we are dependent on other

2 Lausanne Peace Treaty, 24 July 1923. Available http://www.mfa.gov.tr/lausanne-peace-treaty.en.mfa [Accessed 18 April 2014].

3 It has not been possible to confirm this information with the General Directorate of Civil Registration and Nationality.

4 As of 2014, according to the statistics provided by the Turkish Statistics Institution. Available: http://www.tuik.gov.tr/HbGetirHTML.do?id=18616 [Accessed 29 January 2015].

5 Email correspondence with the General Directorate of Civil Registration and Nationality on 25 January 2012. The kind of religious demographics that are used by states are important. Public policies that have implications for the right to freedom of religion or belief will be different for a country where 99 percent of the population are assumed to belong to the same belief and where the state recognizes the considerable religious diversity within the society. In very many fields—*inter alia*, the content of the curricula of the Religious Culture and Ethics classes, activities of the Diyanet, city planning for places of worship—one can foresee a high risk of not being able to

sources. According to the International Religious Freedom Report of 2014 released by the US Department of State there are approximately 15–20 million Alevi; 90,000 Armenian Orthodox Christians; 25,000 Roman Catholics (including a large number of recent immigrants from Africa and the Philippines); 18,000 Jews; 20,000 Syriac Orthodox Christians; 10,000 Bahais; 22,000 Yezidis (17,000 of whom are refugees who arrived in 2014); 5,000 Jehovah's Witnesses; 7,000 members of Protestant denominations; 3,000 Chaldean Christians; and up to 2,000 Greek Orthodox Christians; and a small, undetermined number of Bulgarian, Chaldean, Nestorian, Georgian, Roman Catholics, and Maronite Christians present in Turkey.[6] Among these minority religious communities there is a significant number of Russian Christian immigrants.[7]

While the official position is that Turkey does not keep statistics of the religious demographics of the country, in practice, Turkey exerts tremendous control over how religious identity is recorded. The population register records religious affiliation;[8] the options available for the religion field in the register are determined by the Ministry of Interior on the basis of, "views of Institutions that provide religious services and Universities and decisions of the Court of Cassation, the Court of Appeals and the Constitutional Court".[9] The believers' views on their religion or belief, as such, are not part of the basis on which decisions are made.[10]

accommodate for the needs of believers affiliated with the various Islamic denominations and non-Muslims and potential discrimination as a result of that. Similarly, information on the number of persons affiliated with various religious denominations is absent in the official statistics concerning Turkey's religious demographics. It may be argued that the lack of denominational information reinforces a unified Muslim identity by disregarding diversity within Islam.

6 Turkey, International Religious Freedom Report 2015, US Department of State. Available: http://www.state.gov/j/drl/rls/irf/religiousfreedom/index.htm#wrapper [Accessed 1 May 2016].

7 Ibid. 15,000 Russian citizens.

8 The reason for this is that everyone in Turkey up until 2006 was obliged to indicate the religious affiliation of a child when registering a newly born child in the public register. The Law on Population Services indicates religion as one of the required fields of information that must be registered in the family register: Article 7 of Nüfus Hizmetleri Kanunu (Law on Population Services), No. 5490, 25 April 2006. Official Gazette, No. 26153, 29 April 2006. It is possible to request to change the information in this field or to leave it blank through a personal declaration: Article 25(b). In addition, it is important to note that the recording of religious affiliation in national register and ID cards constitutes a basis for potential discrimination. The fact that there is a limited list of religions one can chose from with the exclusion of particular religions embraced by some Turkish citizens in itself is a discriminatory practice that must be justified.

9 Email correspondence with the General Directorate of Civil Registration and Nationality on 29 July 2011.

10 Considering that the institutions that provide religious services must be related to the Diyanet, which is the only institution providing public religious services, and that there are only Islamic theological faculties in Turkey and that High Courts in Turkey make requests from the Diyanet concerning other religions, it may be argued that the decision concerning the options on religion will be heavily influence by the Sunni-Islamic tradition.

The Bahai faith, Jehovah's Witnesses or the Alevi faith, for example, are not on the list of possible options. While it is not the main focus of this study to examine why and how Turkey keeps records on the religious affiliation of its citizens, it is important to note that Turkey adopts a selective practice about recording religious affiliation. Turkey disregards denominational differences and does not recognize certain religions, as such.[11] This deliberate practice is an indication of the nature of the state-religion relation in Turkey. One result of this practice is that a perception is created that Turkey has a 99 percent homogenous Muslim society and religious diversity is ignored. This is naturally inter-related to the fact that the state determines what constitutes a religion or belief in Turkey.

5.3 Turkey's International and National Obligations in the Area of Human Rights with a Special Focus on Freedom of Religion or Belief

5.3.1 International Human Rights Treaties

Turkey is party to a significant number of universal and regional human rights treaties.[12] Turkey has placed reservations or made interpretive declarations on some of these treaties thus restricting certain rights to a significant degree. Within the UN human rights protection scheme, Turkey has ratified the ICCPR thereby undertaking the obligation to protect the right to freedom of thought, conscience, religion or belief in line with Article 18 of the Covenant. Yet, Turkey placed an interpretative declaration on Article 27 of the Covenant, reserving the right to interpret and apply the provision on the protection of ethnic, religious or linguistic minorities in accordance with the related provisions and rules of the Turkish Constitution and the Treaty of Lausanne.[13] Turkey is also party to the International Covenant on Economic, Social and Cultural Rights (ICESCR) with reservations to Article 13(3), right to education, thus refusing to undertake to respect the liberty of parents to choose schools for their children, other than those established by

11 For example the Bahai faith is not recognized as a religion and thus is not an option one can choose.

12 Convention Against Torture (CAT), International Covenant on Civil and Political Rights (ICCPR), Convention on Discrimination Against Women (CEDAW), International Convention on the Elimination of All Forms of Racial Discrimination (ICERD), International Covenant on Economic, Social and Cultural Rights (ICESCR), Convention on the Rights of All Migrant Workers and Members of their Families, Convention on the Rights of the Child (CRC). Turkey has also ratified the Optional Protocol to CEDAW, the Optional Protocol to ICCPR, the Optional Protocol to the CRC on the involvement of children in armed conflict and the Optional Protocol to the CRC on the Sale of Children, Child Prostitution and Child Pornography.

13 Ratified on 23 September 2003. Turkey does not accept inter-state complaint under Article 41. On November 2006 Turkey also ratified Optional Protocol I to the ICCPR but placed a reservation on Article 5(2)(a) thus restricting the receipt of communications of alleged violations that result from acts or omissions that occur within the national boundaries of the Republic of Turkey. The latter reservation must be a precaution against extra-territorial applicability, such as Cyprus and Northern Iraq.

public authorities and to ensure the religious or moral education of their children in conformity with their own convictions and Article 13(4).[14] Turkey has ratified the CRC with reservations to Article 17, 29 and 30,[15] again reserving the right to interpret and apply the provisions of the said articles according to the letter and spirit of the Turkish Constitution and the Treaty of Lausanne.[16]

Turkey is a founding member of the Council of Europe (CoE),[17] as well as a party to two of its fundamental human rights treaties, the European Convention on Human Rights (ECHR),[18] and the European Social Charter,[19] and other treaties within the human rights protection scheme of the CoE. Turkey has ratified Protocol 1 of the ECHR; however, it has placed a reservation on Article 2 that protects the right to education and at the same time creates an obligation on the part of the states to "respect the rights of parents to ensure such education and teaching in conformity with their own religious and philosophical convictions" on account of Law No. 6366 on the unification of education.[20] Not surprisingly, in line with Turkey's detached stance on minority rights, Turkey is not party to the European Charter for Regional or Minority Languages and the Framework Convention for the Protection of Minorities.

Turkey's reservations or interpretive declarations point to two areas of rights that seem to have a certain "sensitivity" domestically. Firstly, in the spheres of religious education and, secondly, the recognition of minority rights, international obligations are avoided. These will be explored further in relevant sections below.

Legally, not only do Turkey's international human rights commitments constitute the principal standard, but they are also recognized as such, explicitly as having precedence over domestic standards that are found in the Turkish Constitution and other legislation. In 2004, Article 90 of the Turkish Constitution was amended so as to recognize the supremacy of ratified international treaties over domestic legislation in the sphere of human rights. Article 90 reads:

> In the case of a conflict between international agreements in the area of fundamental rights and freedoms duly put into effect and the domestic laws due to differences in provisions on the same matter, the provisions of international agreements shall prevail.[21]

14 Ratified on 23 September 2003.
15 Provisions, respectively, dealing with the right to access to information, the right to education and the protection of minorities.
16 Ratified on 4 April 1995.
17 Turkey acceded to the Council of Europe on 9 August 1949.
18 Ratified on 18 May 1954.
19 Ratified on 24 November 1989.
20 Ratified on 18 May 1954, see Turkey's declaration. Available: http://conventions.coe.int/Treaty/Commun/ListeDeclarations.asp?NT=009&CM=7&DF=18/04/2012&CL=ENG&VL=1 [Accessed 28 January 2015].
21 Article 90 of the 1982 Turkish Constitution. On the application of this provision see Başlar, Kemal (2004) "Uluslararası Antlaşmaların Onaylanması, Üstünlüğü ve Anayasal Denetimi Üzerine" [On the Ratification and Superiority of International Treaties], *Milletlerarası Hukuk ve Milletlerarası Özel Hukuk Bülteni*, Prof. Dr. Sevin Toluner'e

The application of this provision by the domestic courts has been, however, limited and subject to a wide sphere of discretion granted to the judiciary without much guidance as to the application of this norm.[22]

It is important to note here that numerous ECtHR judgments that have found Turkey in violation of Article 9 or Protocol 1, Article 2 have not been enforced. The weak enforcement is also illustrative of how Turkey is reluctant to make changes when needed changes resonate deeply on domestically sensitive issues. Some of the key issues that have been decided upon and, yet, remain unenforced concern the Compulsory Religious Culture and Ethics lessons, *Hasan and Eylem Zengin v. Turkey and Mansur Yalçın and Others v. Turkey*,[23] on the coercion to disclose religious affiliation in national identity cards, *Sinan Işık v Turkey*,[24] on conscientious objection to military service, *Ercep v.Turkey*, *Feti Demirtas v. Turkey*, *Mehmet Tarhan v. Turkey*, *Halil Savda v. Turkey* and *Osman Murat Ülke v. Turkey*.[25]

In addition to international legal commitments, Turkey has undertaken political commitments to protect human rights in general, and freedom of religion or belief in particular, within the Organization of Security and Cooperation in Europe structure.[26] Since 1975 starting with the Helsinki Final Act the participating members of the OSCE have affirmed their commitment to "respect human rights and fundamental freedoms, including the freedom of thought, conscience, religion or belief" as well as non-discrimination and tolerance as key matters within a comprehensive security approach in the region.[27] Most of all, the 1989 Concluding Document of Vienna, Principle 16 entails detailed, explicit and comprehensive principles for the protection of religious communities, *inter alia*, the right to establish places of worship, to freedom in internal organizational matters, to receive

Armağan, 24, pp. 1–2; Gülmez, Mesut (2004) "Anayasa Değişikliği Sonrasında İnsan Hakları Sözleşmelerinin İç Hukuktaki Yeri ve Değeri" [The Place and Value of Human Rights Treaties After the Constitutional Amendment], Türkiye Barolar Birliği Dergisi, Eylül-Ekim, p. 54.

22 Şahbaz, İbrahim (2004) "Avrupa İnsan Hakları Sözleşmesi'nin Türk Yargı Sistemindeki Yeri" [The Place of the European Convention on Human Rights in the Turkish Judicial System], *Türkiye Barolar Birliği Dergisi*, Eylül/Ekim 54, p. 216.

23 Respectively, *Hasan and Eylem Zengin v. Turkey*, 9 October 2007, European Court of Human Rights, No. 1448/04 and *Mansur Yalçın and Others*, 16 September 2014, European Court of Human Rights, No. 21163/11.

24 *Sinan Isik v. Turkey*, 2 February 2010, European Court of Human Rights, No. 21924/05.

25 Respectively, *Ercep v. Turkey*, 22 February 2012, European Court of Human Rights, No. 5260/07, *Feti Demirtas v. Turkey*, 17 January 2012, European Court of Human Rights, No. 5260/07, *Mehmet Tarhan v. Turkey*, 12 July 2012, European Court of Human Rights, No. 9078/06, *Halil Savda v. Turkey*, 12 June 2012, European Court of Human Rights, *Osman Murat Ülke v. Turkey*, 24 April 2006, European Court of Human Rights, No. 43965/04.

26 Available: http://www.mfa.gov.tr/turkiye-ve-avrupa-guvenli-ve-isbirligi-teskilati-_agit_.tr.mfa [Accessed 16 April 2012].

27 OSCE Human Dimension Commitments, Vol. 1, Thematic Compilation, 2nd ed., OSCE, 2005, Poland, pp. xxv–xxvi, 106–110.

financial aid, to religious education, and to training of religious personnel.[28] Hence the general statement of respect for freedom of religion or belief is expanded upon with specific references to the scope of the right. As an OSCE participating state, Turkey is committed to upholding the political commitment to the protection of these rights and others that are crucial for the protection of freedom of religion or belief in all of its dimensions. Through these commitments Turkey has also taken upon itself the obligation to implement them with goodwill thus reinforcing the expectation that international standards, legal and political, in the field of freedom of religion or belief, will be adhered to in Turkey.

For Turkey, a candidate for European Union accession, the Copenhagen political criteria,[29] including human rights, also has significant implications for the protection of freedom of religion or belief. Over the years the European Commission's Turkey progress reports have highlighted a wide range of issues pertaining to the right to freedom of religion or belief in Turkey.[30] The European Commission 2014 Progress Report on Turkey, captures the state of affairs concerning freedom of religion or belief in Turkey, observing "there is a need for comprehensive reform of legislation on freedom of thought, conscience and religion and application of this legislation, in line with ECtHR rulings, Council of Europe recommendations and EU standards".[31]

5.3.2 Lausanne Peace Treaty

The Lausanne Peace Treaty, besides being the founding document of modern Turkey,[32] is a key Treaty that establishes the minority protection regime for Turkey's non-Muslim communities.[33]

28 Ibid., p. 107.

29 "Membership requires that the candidate country has achieved stability of institutions guaranteeing democracy, the rule of law, human rights and respect for and protection of minorities, the existence of a functioning market economy as well as the capacity to cope with competitive pressure and market forces within the Union." Declaration of the European Council in June 1993 of rules that define whether a country is eligible for European Union membership or not. Available: http://europa.eu/legislation_summaries/glossary/accession_criteria_copenhague_en.htm [Accessed 18 January 2015].

30 See the European Commission's Turkey Progress Reports published in 2011, 2012, 2013, 2014, available on the European Commission's website.

31 European Commission (2014) *Turkey Progress Report*, p. 16. Available: http://ec.europa.eu/enlargement/pdf/key_documents/2014/20141008-turkey-progress-report_en.pdf [Accessed 28 January 2015].

32 The Lausanne Peace Treaty was ratified in domestic law by Law No. 340 and is thus part of national law.

33 While the minority protection scheme in the Lausanne Treaty pertains primarily to non-Muslims, there are certain provisions that give rise to obligations to protect linguistic rights (Article 39/5) for those of Turkish descent who speak a language other than Turkish, equality of all before law (Article 39/2) and prohibition of discrimination based on religion (Article 39/3) for all Turks. Yet, Turkey does not accept these obligations.

The *problem* of the protection of minorities in Turkey was one of the most sensitive issues in the Lausanne Peace Conference negotiations because there was reluctance on the part of the Turkish government to commit to any obligations for the protection of minorities.[34] Bozkurt observes two paramount concerns underlying Turkey's position. Firstly, the minority protection may be only reciprocal and secondly, minority protection may not be used to attack Turkey's existence and integrity.[35] The reason for this was the century-old "East Question", concerning the Western scheme to dismantle the Ottoman Empire.[36] The perception that in the Ottoman Empire non-Muslim minorities, particularly the Christian minority, were instrumental in the interference by the Western Powers in the internal affairs of the Empire is a crucial point for understanding the spirit and philosophy of the implementation of provisions enshrined in the Lausanne Treaty pertaining to the protection of minorities. The new Turkish government was determined not to give any "privileges" to non-Muslims.

It is important to understand this historical context and competing interests that were at play in relation to the Lausanne Treaty since these have produced and continue to keep alive at least four factors that have shaped the interpretation and implementation of the minority protection scheme in the Lausanne Treaty to this day. First, the protection of minorities, in particular Christian minorities, has been largely congested into the foreign relations sphere, rather than being essentially a human and minority rights issue. Secondly, the Turkish state, based on historical experiences, has viewed the claims for minority protection in Turkey as a functional tool for foreign powers to interfere in its sovereignty.[37] Thirdly, minority rights have been understood as privileges or exceptions that were conceded unwillingly, instead of legitimate fundamental rights. Finally, the principle of reciprocity has been strictly observed and this has led to a conditional approach based on the expectation that there would be reciprocal protection for Muslims particularly in Western Thrace.

34 The Congress records prior to the Independence War specifically emphasized that political sovereignty and privileges for Christian peoples may not be accepted. Gülnihal Bozkurt refers to this: (1998) Bozkurt, G. *Azınlık İmtiyazları Kapitülasyonlardan Tek Hukuk Sistemine Geçiş* [The Transition from Minority Privileges Capitulations to a Unified Legal System] Ankara: Atatürk Kültür, Dil ve Tarih Yüksek Kurumu, pp. 44–45.

35 Ibid., p. 45.

36 Şimşir, Bilal N. (2003) "Lozan'a Göre Azınlıklar", in *80. Yılında 2003 Penceresinden Lozan Sempozyumu* [Symposium on 80th Anniversary of Lausanne—from the Window of 2003] Ankara: Türk Tarih Kurumu Yayınları XVI. Series No. 100, p. 171. Also, see Adıvar, H.E. (2009) *Türkiye'de Şark-Garp ve Amerikan Tesirleri* [East-West and American Influences in Turkey], Istanbul: Can Publications.

37 This can be clearly observed in the correspondence between the Turkish Chief negotiator in Lausanne and the government in Ankara as well as the minutes of the Lausanne Peace Conference. See generally, Şimşir, B.N. (1990) *Lozan Telgrafları (1922–1923)* [Lausanne Telegrams (1922–1923)], Ankara: Türk Tarih Kurumu Publications. Meray, S.L. (translator) (2003) *Lozan Barış Konferansı Tutanaklar Belgeler* [Lausanne Peace Conference Records Documents], Series 1, Vol. 1, Book 2, 2nd ed., Istanbul: Yapı Kredi Yayınları. Kaptan, E. (2002) *Lozan Konferansı'nda Azınlıklar Sorunu* [The Question of Minorities in the Lausanne Conference], Istanbul: Harp Akademileri Basım Evi.

Articles 37–45 of the Lausanne Treaty cover the protection of non-Muslim minorities. The principle place that must be given to the Lausanne protection scheme within the Turkish legal system is explicitly mandated through Article 37 that obliges Turkey to recognize Articles 38–44 as basic law. It also stipulates that there shall not be any laws or regulations or official acts that are contrary to, nor take priority over, the said Lausanne provisions. This explicit prohibition, however, has not stopped Turkey from restricting or preventing non-Muslim minorities from fully enjoying their rights through the creation of incompatible laws, bureaucratic obstacles, and arbitrary decisions of public authorities in relevant official processes.[38]

In contrast to its contemporary minority protection schemes that protected racial, linguistic and religious minorities, the Lausanne Treaty identifies solely non-Muslim minorities as minority right holders.[39] There has been much debate during the negotiations and drafting of the document as to which categories of people will have the protection afforded in the minority protection scheme.[40] The Turkish government denied that there were any ethnic groups in Turkey other than Turks and Kurds and underlined that no group except for the Greeks demanded "these kind of rights".[41] Since Turkish authorities regarded the efforts to include protection of ethnic minorities as a scheme to incite division through the Kurdish population by foreign powers, Muslim minorities of different ethnic backgrounds were not granted specific rights. However, there are certain provisions that are applicable to all Turkish citizens.[42]

The category of groups that the term "non-Muslim minorities" identified was not specified.[43] Indeed, there appears to be a lack of coherency in this respect

38 For numerous examples see, among others, Kurban, D. and K. Hatemi (2009) *Bir Yabancılaştırma Hikayesi: Türkiye'de Gayrimüslim Cemaatlerin Vakıf ve Taşınmaz Mülkiyet Sorunu* [A Story of Alienations: The Foundation and Property Problems of Non-Muslim Communities in Turkey], Istanbul: TESEV. Kurban, D. and K. Tsitselikis (2010) *Bir Mütekabiliyet Hikayesi: Yunanistan ve Türkiye'de Azınlık Vakıfları* [A Story of Reciprocity: Minority Foundations in Greece and Turkey], Istanbul: TESEV.

39 Baskın Oran attributes this "victory" on the part of Turkish authorities to the fact that they represented Turkey as the victor of the National Independence War. Oran, B. (2004) *Türkiye'de Azınlıklar: Kavramlar, Teori, Lozan, İç Mevzuat, İçtihat, Uygulama* [Minorities in Turkey: Concepts, Theory, Lausanne, National Legislation, Caselaw, Practice], Istanbul: İletişim, p. 64.

40 Meray, *supra* note 37.

41 Ibid., p. 153.

42 Article 39(3) protects all from discrimination based on religion, denomination and belief, and paragraph 2 of the same article recognizes equality of all before the law regardless of religious affiliation. Article 39(4) protects freedom to use any language in private or commercial activities as well as public meetings and publications, and Article 39(5) provides for ensuring facilitation by Turkey for Turkish citizens who speak a language other than Turkish in the use of their own language in courts. Article 38 protects the right of everyone residing in Turkey to enjoy their right to observe the requirements of their religion or denomination in public or private.

43 During the negotiations the words "Christians and Jews" were used and references were made to churches and church law. Meray, *supra* note 37. However, there was no reference to Bahai, Assyrian Orthodox community, or any other non-Muslim community. It is important to note that the minority communities were not represented in

throughout the time of drafting. In practice, the Turkish government extended the protection only to the Armenian Orthodox, Greek Orthodox and Jewish communities, in spite of the fact that these are not mentioned in the Lausanne Treaty. The rights of other, then existing, non-Muslim groups, such as the Syriac Orthodox and Syriac Chaldean, Latin Catholic, and those of the Bahai faith are not viewed by Turkey as subject to the Lausanne protection scheme. For example, until very recently, Syriac and Chaldean Christians were not able to establish their own schools in accordance with Article 40 of the Lausanne Treaty. The explanation given by the state for this anomaly has been that Syriacs had given up these rights after the establishment of the Turkish Republic.[44] Yet, even if there had been any declarations made by religious leaders of this community at the time, certainly they were in no position to make such a decision for the members of the Syriac community. Following repeated denials to demands for opening a school, it was only in 2013, through a court decision that also reflected the political will at the time, that Syriacs were allowed to open schools as a protected group under the Lausanne Treaty.[45] In addition, currently, newer non-Muslim groups like Jehovah's Witnesses or Protestants of Turkish ethnic origin are not recognized as non-Muslim minorities protected under the Lausanne Treaty. Hence in practice the Turkish government has been interpreting the term "non-Muslim minorities" restrictively and arbitrarily. While it may be argued that Turkey's restrictive practice counts as subsequent practice for the application of the Lausanne Treaty, this argument is not sustainable since subsequent practice must first and foremost be in line with the word of the treaty.[46] This restrictive interpretation has, however, not been a matter of any national or international legal dispute so far.

Specific rights protected for non-Muslims are listed below:

- Article 38(3) guarantees the right of non-Muslims to movement and migration on a par with Turkish nationals.
- Article 39(1) ensures that non-Muslims will benefit from all civil and political rights that are granted to Muslims.

the negotiations. Instead their case was defended by Allied Powers; however, Greece argued mostly for the rights of the Greek Orthodox community and the US mostly for the rights of Armenians, in particular for the creation of an Armenian homeland in Turkey. Thus negotiations were not striving for a generally applicable minority rights framework for all non-Muslim minorities. And it was understood by the Turkish government as such.

44 Oran suggests that there may be a secret Ministry of Interior Declaration about limiting the application of the Lausanne Treaty to Greeks, Armenians and Jews, and because Syriacs were dispersed in the South Eastern part of Turkey they may not have been able to defend their rights. Oran, *supra* note 39, p. 70.

45 *Aksiyon*, Rahime Sezgin and Murat Uçar, "Syriacs", 2 March 2002. *Agos*, "Utandıran yasak bitti Süryaniler anadilde eğitime başlıyor" [End of Embarrassing Prohibition – Syriacs to Begin Education in Mother Tongue], 10 August 2013.

46 Vienna Convention on the Law of Treaties, Article 31. Available: https://treaties.un.org/doc/Publication/UNTS/Volume%201155/volume-1155-I-18232-English.pdf [Accessed 28 January 2015].

- Article 40 protects the rights to establish, manage and control charity institutions, religious social institutions, schools, teaching and education institutions and use their own language in these freely, and freely conduct religious worship services.
- Article 41 protects the right to education in the mother tongue in primary schools where they are intensely populated and to receive funding from the national budget.
- Article 42(1) protects the right to settlement of disputes in accordance with traditions and customs in family and private matters.
- Article 42(2) sets forth facilitation for the establishment of religious institutions.
- Article 43 stipulates that they cannot be forced to act *a contrari* to their beliefs and religious precepts and to engage in official acts during their holidays.[47]

Turkey has a positive obligation to put in place the necessary normative framework in order to make these rights available and accessible to non-Muslim minorities. Beyond negative obligations that require states to avoid interference in the enjoyment of rights, positive obligations require states to take necessary steps in order to make full and effective equality a reality. In particular, Articles 41, 42 and 43 obligate Turkey to take relevant measures in order to ensure effective protection of the rights in questions. However, this has not been the case; for example, the support mentioned in Article 41(1) has not been given, special commissions mentioned in Article 42(2) have not been applied, and the obligations derived from Article 42(3) have not been carried out.[48]

Article 42(1) maintains a provision that envisages, in general terms, the continuation of the plural legal system that existed in the Ottoman Empire. While the Turkish government accepted this provision for the time being, there was a strong determination to eventually eliminate any "privileges" pertaining to the jurisdictional sphere of personal and family law of religious minorities. The new Turkish government had plans to adopt a Civil Code that would be applicable to all without any differentiation based on religious affiliation. Later, when the Civil Code was adopted it was said that the non-Muslim minorities renounced their rights to resolve family law matters according to their own traditions and agreed to be subject to the Civil Code that was applicable to all.[49] The reluctance to observe obligations in the sphere of religious jurisdictions may be explained by the perceived tension between neutral law that was applicable to all and special minority arrangements that were seen as incompatible with the principle of equality and the sovereignty of the state. There have not been claims by non-Muslim minorities to exercise their rights in this sphere.

47 Lausanne Treaty, Articles 39–43.
48 Oran, *supra* note 39, p. 72.
49 Ibid.

It is important to consider the interpretation and utilization of the principle of reciprocity,[50] since it constitutes the basis of Turkey's conditional approach to the protection of minority rights. Here, again one has to turn to the underlying spirit that has shaped the approach of the Turkish Republic to the issue of minority protection. A decree related to the minorities issued by the *Misak-i Milli* (National Pact of 1920) demarcates the extent of protection to be granted to minorities:

> minority rights will be embraced by us and secured, with the hope that Muslim people in the neighboring states would benefit from same rights, within the framework of principles enshrined in treaties concluded between the members of the Alliance and their enemies or partners.[51]

The conditional approach based on the expectation that there will be reciprocal protection for Muslims, particularly those in Western Thrace, has been an integral part of the constrictive application of the general minority rights protection scheme. While the Lausanne Treaty establishes a special legal regime for the protection of the Muslim minority in Greece and non-Muslim minorities in Turkey,[52] it was clearly stated in the negotiations by some representatives that the obligations were *parallel obligations* and were not based on realization of obligations by the other country.[53] The reciprocity condition continues to constitute a problem up to this day.[54] Since under international law subjects of the reciprocity principle are foreigners, it is perceived by some as an indicator that non-Muslim minorities are seen as foreigners instead of citizens.[55] On the other hand, even if the principle of reciprocity were accepted, it could only affect the rights of the Greek Orthodox minority in Turkey in relation to the rights of the Muslim population in Greece. Armenian Apostolic and Jewish communities would not be subject to the

50 Article 45 reads "The rights conferred by the provisions of the present Section on the non-Moslem minorities of Turkey will be similarly conferred by Greece on the Moslem minority in her territory."

51 Şimşir, *supra* note 36, p. 172. The Allies objected to the principle of reciprocity. In practice, reciprocity was only possible between Greece and Turkey since in other Balkan countries such as Romania and Serbia there were no Turkish minorities. Meray, *supra* note 37, pp. 194–196.

52 *Radikal*, Turgut Tarhanlı, 29 November 2005, "Sorun Lozan Değil" [Lausanne is not a Problem].

53 Meray, *supra* note 37.

54 For example the 2008 Law on Foundations includes the principle of reciprocity in its Article 2.

55 Çetin, F. (2002) "Yerli Yabancılar" [Indigenous Aliens] in *Ulusal, Ulusalüstü ve Uluslararası Hukukta Azınlık Hakları* [Minority Rights in National, Supranational and International Law], Istanbul: İstanbul Barosu Publications, p. 78. The author supports her argument with a judgment of the Court of Appeals related to legal personality of foundations established by non-Muslim minorities, where the court specifically refers to the applicants' foundations as "legal entities of non-Turks are prohibited from new ownership of property". Judgment of the Court of Appeals, Second Chamber, 4449E, 4399K, 6 July 1971. Hence the law on provisions applicable to foreign legal entities applies to them.

reciprocity principle since there is not a country that is party to the Lausanne Treaty that undertakes the commitment to protect the rights of a Muslim population reciprocally.

In conclusion, the Lausanne Treaty creates crucial obligations for Turkey toward its non-Muslim citizens and thus continues to be a significant legal instrument for the protection of the right to freedom of religion or belief, particularly in its collective dimension. Yet, the restrictive interpretation and application of the rights remain as serious obstacles to effective protection for non-Muslim minorities.

5.4 Turkish Constitution and the Protection of Freedom of Religion or Belief

The 1982 Turkish Constitution embodies key elements that reflect Turkey's approach toward religion and manifestations of religion. On the one hand, the Turkish state confers the principle of secularism, defined as separation of state and religion, a central and supreme position while at the same time permanently instituting state's involvement in religion through, *inter alia*, the Presidency of Religious Affairs and compulsory religion lessons in schools, and interpreting secularism so as to create blanket restrictions on many forms of manifestation of religion or belief, or to provide for state facilitation of Islamic religious services. It is important to note that, in addition, a certain form of Turkish nationalism constitutes an overarching and pervasive spirit of interpretation and practice in the above construction both in society and state administration.[56]

*5.4.1 Turkish Secularism—*Laiklik[57]

The concept of Turkish secularism, *laiklik,* in the Turkish Constitution as a legal principle must be explored and understood for the overall purpose of the study because of its conceptual significance and its powerful functional effect in jurisprudence. The term *laiklik* formally entered the Turkish legal system through its inclusion in the Constitution in 1937.[58] The paramount place and particular

56 This was also observed by the Special Rapporteur on Freedom of Religion or Belief: "This particular form of nationalism pervades not only State institutions but society as a whole, and generally conveys a message that leaves no room for the Christian minorities." Interim report of the Special Rapporteur of the Commission on Human Rights on the elimination of all forms of intolerance and of discrimination based on religion or belief: The Situation in Turkey, A/55/280/Add.1, 11 August 2000, p. 26.

57 I will use the term "*laiklik*" in order to preserve the autonomous meaning of secularism in Turkey. While this principle was adopted from the French term *laïcité* it has a unique meaning in Turkey.

58 It must be noted that secularism had been part of public discussion since II. Tanzimat. And many measures had been taken to eliminate the influence of religion from state affairs before this principle was explicitly acknowledged in the Constitution. For a relatively recent evaluation see Kalaycıoğlu, E. (2009) "Democracy, Islam and Secularism in Turkey", in Nathan J. Brown and Emad Shahin (eds.), *The Struggle Over*

meaning given to the principle of secularism in the Turkish Constitution and its application by the high courts—in particular the Turkish Constitutional Court[59] and the Council of State[60]—create the general legal framework and the spirit of interpretation concerning cases pertaining to freedom of religion or belief in Turkey. Çağlar observes that the meaning of ***laiklik*** in Turkey does not include the impartiality of the state; instead, it means "active or militant secularism and the control of the state over religion".[61]

In the 1982 Turkish Constitution,[62] ***laiklik*** is directly or indirectly protected through a number of provisions. It is one of the attributes of the Republic,[63] that cannot be changed,[64] and no activity that is contrary to Atatürk's nationalism, principles and reforms that are based on *laiklik* can find protection.[65] The state's fundamental social, economic, political, and legal order cannot be based on religious tenets.[66] Reform laws,[67] most of which are directly or indirectly linked to secularism, are under Constitutional protection and cannot be understood as

Democracy in the Middle East: Regional Politics and External Policies, Abingdon, Oxon, UK and New York, NY, USA: Routledge, pp. 153–186.

59 According to Article 148 of the Turkish Constitution, the Constitutional Court examines the constitutionality, in respect of both form and substance, of laws, decrees having the force of law, and the Rules of Procedure of the Turkish Grand National Assembly. Constitutional amendments are examined and verified only with regard to their form. The judgments of the Constitutional Court are final.

60 Administrative courts deal with cases which are brought against the administrative organs because of the implementation of the administrative legislation. The administrative decisions and judgments of courts can be appealed to the Council of State. The Council of State is the last instance for reviewing decisions and judgments given by administrative courts and cases which are not referred by law to other administrative courts.

61 Çağlar, B. (1994) "Türkiye'de Laikliğin Büyük Problemi" [The Great Problem of Secularism in Turkey], *Cogito* No.1, p. 115.

62 Article 24(5) of the 1982 Turkish Constitution. Available: www.anayasa.gen.tr/1982constitution.htm [Accessed 16 January 2015.]

63 Article 2.

64 Article 4.

65 Preamble, para. 5

66 Article 24(5).

67 Reform Laws include revolutionary laws adopted in the early years of the Turkish Republic. These are: Tevhid-i Tedrisat Kanunu [Law on the Unification of the Educational System] Law No. 430 of 3 March 1340 (1924); Şapka Kanunu [Law on Wearing Hats] Law No. 671 of 25 November 1341 (1925); Tekke ve Zaviyelerin Kapatılmasına İlişkin Kanun [Closure of Dervish Monasteries and Tombs, the Abolition of the Office of Keeper of Tombs and the Abolition and Prohibition of Certain Titles] Law No. 677 of 30 November 1341 (1925); Article 110 of Medeni Kanun [Civil Code] No. 743 of 17 February 1926; Yeni Türk Harflerinin Kabulü ve Tatbiki Hakkında Kanun [Law on the Adoption and Application of the Turkish Alphabet] Law No. 1353 of 1 November 1928; Efendi, Bey, Paşa gibi Lakap ve Ünvanların Kaldırılmasına Dair Kanun [Law on the Abolition of Titles and Appellations such as Efendi, Bey or Pasa] Law No. 2590 of 26 November 1934; Bazı Kisvelerin Giyilemeyeceğine Dair Kanun [Law on the Prohibition of the Wearing of Certain Garments] Law No. 2596 of 3 December 1934.

contradictory to the Constitution.[68] Political parties also have to abide by the principle of *laiklik* or risk closure.[69] Secularism also finds its reflection in the restriction of fundamental rights that cannot be used to establish a state order, or any part of this order, based on religion.[70]

The principle of non-interference in the affairs of religious communities that follows from the notion of separation of state and religion is not envisioned in the Turkish legal framework.[71] This has significant implications for freedom of religion or belief, particularly in its collective dimension for religious or belief groups—as regards their associative rights. This is particularly evident in the substantial restrictions on the autonomy of religious communities as well as the state monopoly on certain religious services/activities, such as those provided by the Presidency of Religious Affairs (Diyanet or DİB hereafter) and religious education provided by the Ministry of Education and universities. The implications of the failure to observe non-interference in the affairs of religious communities for the collective dimension of freedom of religion or belief are critically analyzed in Chapter 7.

The Turkish Constitutional Court (Anayasa Mahkemesi, hereafter AYM) has understood the principle of *laiklik* to mean, firstly, that religion cannot in any way interfere in state affairs and secondly, taking into account historical realities, that the state will reflect an interventionist, restrictive, supervisory, controlling approach toward religious manifestation.[72] The Turkish position is explained by the AYM with reference to the unique circumstances in Turkey, observing that the circumstances and the conditions of each religion necessitate differences in the overall understanding of secularism in different countries.[73] It is explained that the difference lies in the conditions of Christianity and Islam and in particular the existence of a hierarchical clergy structure found in the former in contrast to a lack of clergy class in the latter.[74] This particular situation in Islam makes it impossible to grant independence in internal affairs to those involved in places of worship and religious affairs.[75] Since Islam regulates not only religious belief in the conscience of individuals but also social relations, state affairs and law, it is argued that an

68 Article 174.

69 Article 68.

70 Article 14/1.

71 Tanör, B. and N. Yüzbaşıoğlu (2005) *1982 Anayasasına Göre Türk Anayasa Hukuku* [Turkish Constitutional Law According to the 1982 Constitution], Istanbul: Yapı Kredi Publications, p. 89.

72 Dinçkol, B. (1992) *1982 Anayasası Çerçevesinde ve Anayasa Mahkemesi Kararlarında Laiklik* [Secularism within the Framework of the 1982 Constitution and the Judgments of the Constitutional Court], Istanbul: Kazancı Kitap, p. 182.

73 Constitutional Court, E1970/53 and K1971/76, 21 October 1971, *Anayasa Mahkemesi Kararları Dergisi* [Journal of Judgments of the Constitutional Court] (AMKD) No. 10, 52–79.

74 Such a definition can of course easily be refuted with not least, the various traditions in Christianity, including free churches which are not part of a hierarchical structure.

75 Ibid., pp. 61–62.

The Diyanet is a multi-dimensional and massive organization,[91] with far reaching activities both at the national and international level.[92] It was established in 1924 as an institution under the Office of the Prime Minister.[93] The 1961 Turkish Constitution instituted the Presidency of Religious Affairs as a constitutional organization within the state administration,[94] with the purpose of fulfilling the tasks that are enumerated in a special law concerning the organization. The 1982 Constitution preserves the Presidency of Religious Affairs in Article 136:

> The Department of Religious Affairs, which is within the general administration, shall exercise its duties prescribed in its particular law, in accordance with the principles of secularism, removed from all political views and ideas, and aiming at national solidarity and integrity.

91 In its activity report for 2013 the Diyanet declared its personnel number as 119,845 and its spending as 4.604.649.000 TL (approx. 1,705,425,555 Eur), "2013 Faaliyet Raporu" [Activity Report], *Diyanet İşleri Başkanlığı*, Ankara, 2013.

92 As of 1971 the Diyanet began providing religious services to nationals and cognates abroad. The Law 1982 on Some Amendment to Law No. 633 on the Establishment and Duties of the Presidency of Religious Affairs and the Addition of Four Temporary Provisions to This Law in 26 April 1976, in Article 1 made it possible to establish offices abroad and appoint religious workers in order to provide religious services. These services developed in the following years and currently the organization of the Diyanet outside of Turkey is established in countries where Turkish citizens and cognates reside at Turkish Embassies and Consulates with a very broad mandate including: enlightening Turkish citizens living abroad on religious matters; planning religious education; providing follow-up of courses on the Quran and religious knowledge in mosques abroad working towards efficiency; engaging in inter-religious dialogue; the following-up of destructive and divisive missionary activities and assimilation activities directed toward Turkish citizens collecting relevant documents and conducting evaluation and acting as necessary in this respect; the following-up of religious activity outside of Islam in Turkey; and analyzing and preparing reports. According to Ruşen Çakır and İrfan Bozdağ, the Diyanet operates through activities that can be defined as "missionary activity" also in countries where there are no Turkish citizens but a large Muslim population, such as Balkans, Caucasus, Middle Asia and the Baltics. See, Çakır, R. and İ. Bozan (2005) Sivil, Şeffaf ve Demokratik bir Diyanet İşleri Başkanlığı Mümkün mü? [A Civil, Transparent and Democratic Presidency of Religious Affairs—Possible?], Istanbul: TESEV, pp. 93–99.

93 Law No. 429 Şerriye ve Evkaf ve Erkan-ı Harbiye Vekaletlerinin İlgasına Dair Kanun [Law on the Abolishment of the Ministries of Sharia, Foundations and War], 2 March 1924.

94 Debates surrounding the establishment of a religious institution within a secular state present two main views, one relying on a strict separation of state and religion and principle of neutrality of state and thus also envisioning more autonomy for religious groups and less state intervention, and the other relying on Turkey's unique circumstances, seeing as a necessity that the Presidency of Religious Affairs was established as a state organization regulating and controlling religious affairs. See Gözaydın, İ. (2009) *Diyanet: Türkiye'de Dinin Tanzimi* [The Diyanet: Arrangement of Religion in Turkey], Istanbul: İletişim, pp. 38–39.

Consistent with the efforts to protect *laiklik* and to try to reconcile religion with it, the Diyanet is to work in line with the principle of *laiklik* removed from all political views and ideas, and aiming to ensure national solidarity and unity.[95] The purpose of the Diyanet is stipulated in its own law, "Carrying out activities related to the beliefs, worship and ethics of the Islamic religion, enlightening the society about religion and administrating worship places".[96]

Ensuring the neutral character of "public service" seems difficult considering that the Diyanet has been criticized for being involved only with service to the Sunni-Muslims.[97] In addition, on the one hand, the Diyanet is the only religious institution that receives financial state support for all of its activities and personnel, on the other hand it is under the control of the state—enjoying limited autonomy.[98] Through this arrangement the Turkish state is involved in and through the religious affairs of a particular Islamic tradition at the expense of significantly undermining the principle of impartiality. The constitutional principle of equality must be upheld in public services by state organs. The massive state support in terms of funding and privileges creates significant inequality for those of other beliefs. As for members of non-Muslim communities, the Lausanne Treaty of 1923 prescribes that their communities will provide religious services with their own resources. In addition, Muslim groups that object to the Diyanet's claims of providing services for all Muslims without embracing any particular denomination within Islam, point out that the Diyanet is unconcerned with their needs and does not provide services for them. According to Kara, the Diyanet has engaged in a struggle against popular religiosity and the religious communities and *tarikats*,[99] that nurture this religiosity and thus weaken the popular religiosity and the embodiment of religion in this region.[100] Thus the question of observing the principle of equality extends beyond making funds available to adopting an inclusive theology. The Diyanet has a mission that is both theoretical and practical. While on the one hand it manages certain religious affairs, on the other hand, it is tasked with the enlightenment of the society on religion. As rightly pointed out,

> The mission to enlighten people on religion makes it necessary to understand religion and enlighten people in accordance with what one understands. For this reason the Diyanet develops an understanding of religion (jurisprudence) enlightens the people in accordance with this understanding (convey) and provides religious services accordingly.[101]

95 Article 136.
96 Law No. 633, Article 1. Official Gazette No. 12038, 2 July 1965.
97 Çakır and Bozan, *supra* note 92, p. 38.
98 For discussion on various proposals for the transformation of the Diyanet to become an autonomous institution within the state administration see Gözaydın, *supra* note 94, pp. 279–283.
99 Religious paths, orders.
100 Kara, İsmail (2008) *Cumhuriyet Türkiyesi'nde bir Mesele olarak Islam* [Islam as an Issue in the Turkish Republic] Istanbul: Dergah, p. 79.
101 Quoted by Gözaydın, *supra* note 94, p. 119.

The understanding of religion according to Diyanet is based on the foundational resources of the Islamic religion.[102] Gözaydın notes that the emphasis on "true religion" has been ever present as a narrative throughout the Republic though there have been changes in state-religion relations.[103] This claim of true interpretation functions also as a point of differentiation from other interpretations of Islam. The Diyanet is criticized for "closing its doors to different interpretations of Islam",[104] and representing solely the Sunni interpretation of Islam.

Yet, in a controversial decision, the AYM found that the Diyanet and the civil servant status of its personnel are compatible with *laiklik*.[105] The decision was based on the consideration of firstly, the country's experience that an understanding of "uncontrolled religious freedom and independent religious association" is loaded with heavy dangers and, secondly, the nature of Islam which regulates social relations, state affairs and law.[106] Hence the AYM held that there is no doubt that the regulation of the Diyanet in the Constitution and the "civil servant" status of its personnel is a requirement in light of historical reasons, facts and circumstances of the country.[107] This decision has been criticized both for its contradiction with the principle of *laiklik* as well as its inconsistency with legal logic by basing normative results on sociological and historical observations.[108]

Another dimension of this complex issue concerns the exclusive nature of the Diyanet framework which results in the Diyanet being the sole means of the enjoyment of key freedom of religion or belief rights. On the one hand, Muslims may be the receivers of this "public service", on the other hand, they do not have the legal possibility of engaging in the exercise of certain rights protected in the right to freedom of religion or belief, such as the right to establish places of worship outside of the Diyanet structure. Thus this arrangement results in a system where all Muslims, in practice, are compelled to enjoy certain rights through the Diyanet. Formal religious associative activities for Muslims are quite limited outside of the Diyanet organization and the latter holds monopoly, in law and fact, over key areas of manifestation of religion or belief. Only the Diyanet can open and establish places of worship and mosques, and administer them.[109] Similarly, staff for religious services are provided and supervised and trained by this institution.[110] The Diyanet is also tasked with assuring that the Quran is printed accurately,

102 http://diyanet.gov.tr/.
103 Gözaydın, *supra* note 94, p. 172.
104 Çakır and Bozan, *supra* note 92, pp. 114–117.
105 Constitutional Court, E1970/53, K1971/76, 21 October 1971 AYMD, No. 10, pp. 67–68.
106 Ibid.
107 Ibid., pp. 60–70.
108 Gözler, Kemal (2000) *Türk Anayasa Hukuku* [Turkish Constitutional Law] Ekin Kitapevi, pp. 137–153.
109 Law No. 633 Diyanet İşleri Başkanlığı'nın Kuruluşu ve Görevleri Hakkında Kanun [Law on the Establishment and Duties of the Presidency of Religious Affairs and the Addition of Four Temporary Provisions to This Law], 26 April 1976, *inter alia*, Article 35.
110 Ibid., Article 16.

scrutinizing relevant publications and making decisions on whether such publications may be imported from abroad. The only organization that can provide Quran courses legally and formally is the Diyanet. The Diyanet's mandate and the impossibility of enjoyment of key freedom of religion or belief rights outside the Diyanet framework create a rather restricted system for Muslims in Turkey.

The Diyanet assumes a role for countering religious propaganda that comes from other sources: "Follow-up of publications on religion in and outside of Turkey and decide on what they necessitate and prepare counter publication in line with scientific contestation".[111] Such counter publications include books on Jehovah's Witnesses and Christian missionary activity.[112] Clearly, the Diyanet has assumed an active role in propagating its *scientific* Islam understanding and engaging in counter-propaganda against other movements that find their sources in other religions, philosophies and Islamic understanding. Such a position might be compatible with an independent religious organization as a manifestation of freedom in dogma and internal matters; however it is hard to reconcile it with a publicly funded provider of religious public services within a secular state structure.

On the other hand, there are a number of issues raising questions about the autonomy of the Diyanet. It should be noted that the expectation that the Diyanet complies with criteria concerning the principle of equality required of public institutions providing public services creates tension between theological autonomy of the Diyanet as an institution with a religious nature, and its role as a public service provider. Similarly, the fact that the Diyanet must "exercise its duties prescribed in its particular law, in accordance with the principles of secularism",[113] creates a restrictive general framework in which the Diyanet can produce its dogma and exercise its duties. In terms of appointment of leadership, neither the Muslim community in Turkey nor the Diyanet organization is involved in this decision; instead the president of the Diyanet is appointed by the Prime Minister. Diyanet personnel belong to the special category of Religious Services Class comprised of public servants who have received religious education at various levels.[114]

111 Ibid., Article 5/e.

112 The book on Jehovah's Witnesses points out that Jehovah's Witnesses have had the opportunity to develop in Turkey as a result of certain weaknesses in national spiritual education and lack of knowledge. It makes a list of measures to be taken against Jehovah's Witnesses and Christian missionaries. These include sending religious personnel who are equipped to preach and talk on these issues to foreign countries, as well as measures to be taken by the police, legislation and courts, education system and the media. Tanyu, H. (2006) *Yehova Şahitleri*, Elips Kitab, pp. 143–144. Gözaydın quotes from a document sent by the Diyanet to the Higher Education Council warning against "divisive and destructive activities such as Jehovah's Witnesses, Missionary activities, Babism, Bahais, Satanism, Hizbuttahlil, Hizbullah etc." Gözaydın, *supra* note 94, p. 169.

113 1982 Turkish Constitution, Article 136.

114 Law No. 1327 Article 9 of 1970 Amending Law No. 657 on Public Servants Article 36. For the differing views among the High Courts on whether all personnel of the Diyanet can be considered public servants see Gözaydın, *supra* note 94, pp. 177–184.

It follows from the above that this institution raises numerous questions pertaining to the obligation on the part of the states to observe neutrality as well as to uphold the right to freedom of religion or belief. While the existence of an organization providing religious services within a state structure may not be incompatible with international standards protecting freedom of religion or belief,[115] the Diyanet, as such, certainly must go through a reform process in order to comply with relevant human rights standards.

5.4.3 The Protection of Freedom of Religion or Belief—Its Scope and Limits

The general protection of freedom of religion or belief in Turkey is reviewed below. This examination will be based on constitutional and legislative rules and relevant jurisprudence.

The right to freedom of religion or belief is enshrined in Article 24 of the Constitution:

1 Everyone has the right to freedom of conscience, religious belief and conviction. Acts of worship, religious services, and ceremonies shall be conducted freely, provided that they do not violate the provisions of Article 14.
2 No one shall be compelled to worship, or to participate in religious ceremonies and rites, to reveal religious beliefs and convictions, or be blamed or accused because of his religious beliefs and convictions.
3 Education and instruction in religion and ethics shall be conducted under state supervision and control. Instruction in religious culture and moral education shall be compulsory in the curricula of primary and secondary schools. Other religious education and instruction shall be subject to the individual's own desire, and in the case of minors, to the request of their legal representatives.
4 No one shall be allowed to exploit or abuse religion or religious feelings, or things held sacred by religion, in any manner whatsoever, for the purpose of personal or political influence, or for even partially basing the fundamental, social, economic, political, and legal order of the state on religious tenets.

The provision guaranteeing the right to freedom of religion or belief in the Turkish Constitution comprises of three key components, apart from its limitation clause.[116]

115 An institution like the Diyanet providing services for the people of the majority must not lead to any impairment of the enjoyment of any rights, including freedom of religion or belief, for members of any religion or belief. General Comment 22 of the HRC on Article 18 of the ICCPR, para.9 is applicable.

The fact that a religion is recognized as a state religion or that it is established as official or traditional or that its followers comprise the majority of the population, shall not result in any impairment of the enjoyment of any of the rights under the Covenant, including articles 18 and 27, nor in any discrimination against adherents to other religions or non-believers.

116 The paragraph stipulating the limitation is dealt with under the section on limitations.

The first paragraph constitutes the inviolable part of the right to freedom of religion or belief, namely the right to freedom of conscience, religion, belief and convictions. This right includes the right not to believe and change one's religion or belief. While the notion of conscience has not been invoked as a separate component, it is usually referred to together with religion as "freedom of religion and conscience" which seems to point to the individual's inner sphere made up of deep convictions that may not necessarily be religious. However, it is not interpreted as broad as to include the protection against being compelled to act against one's conscience.[117]

The second paragraph is evocative of the understanding of the scope of the protection conferred to manifestations—even though this term is absent in the provision—which is limited to "worship, religious services and ceremonies" in contrast to the protection afforded to the non-exhaustive list of manifestations of religion or belief in "worship, observance, practice and teaching" stipulated in Article 9 of the ECHR. This narrow scope envisioned by the drafters of the 1982 Constitution, somewhat restricting manifestations into places of worship, is in line with restrictions on manifestations of religion in the public sphere, religious symbols, and teaching of religion. Sezer, agreeing with the narrow scope of protection, observes that one has to differentiate between "worship" and "practice"; it is only the right to worship that the Constitution guarantees; "practice" that is not worship is not protected.[118] The narrow view of freedom of religion or belief enshrined in this provision is difficult to reconcile with the non-exclusive list of manifestations enshrined in international provisions protecting the right to manifest one's religion or belief, in particular Article 9 of the ECHR and Article 18 of the ICCPR.[119]

Teaching, as a form of manifestation, of religion is not expressed as a right; instead, it is referred to in the context of the institution of strict state control in Article 24(3) through the *regulation* concerning compulsory Religious Culture and Knowledge of Ethics classes and other religious instruction which can only be carried out under state control. Through this provision the state takes upon itself the role of teaching religion,[120] giving it direction, content and function. In addition, all "other" religious teaching or instruction that may be carried out by private individuals or religious groups must take place under state control. This construction exposes the domestic conception of the right to freedom of religion

117 For example, the right to conscientious objection to compulsory military service is not recognized. Yıldırım, Mine (2010) "Conscientious Objection to Military Service: International Human Rights Law and the Case of Turkey", *Religion and Human Rights* 5, pp. 65–91.

118 Sezer, Abdullah (2004) "Türkiye'de Din-Vicdan Özgürlüğü ve Din-Devlet İlişkisi" [Freedom of Religion and Conscience and Religion and State Relation in Turkey], *Bülent TANÖR Armağanı*, 1. Bs. (Legal 2004), pp. 561–609.

119 Article 9 of the European Convention on Human Rights, Article 18 of the International Covenant on Civil and Political Rights.

120 The content of DKAB classes are not specified in the Constitution. This was later defined by jurisprudence; see the decision of the Council of State, 8th Chamber, E/2006/4107, K/2007/481, 28 December 2007, E/2007/679, K/2008/1461, 29 February 2008.

or belief and the regulatory role foreseen for the state; the right to manifest religion or belief in teaching is an area where state control is deemed strictly necessary. It is not recognized as a right, instead it is expressed in the form of a regulation.

As captured succinctly by Çağlar, the case law on the right to freedom of religion or belief of the AYM and Council of State in Turkey is constructed in an effort to reconcile *laiklik* and freedom of religion or belief.[121] This reconciliation has been achieved, more often than not, at the expense of the latter. There are several constitutional provisions that function as restriction clauses for the right to freedom of thought, conscience and religion as recognized under Article 24.

The limitation enshrined in Article 24(5) stating that "no one shall be allowed to exploit or abuse religion or religious feelings or things held sacred by religion" is a special constitutional limitation that is intrinsic to the provision. It is clear from the latter part of the paragraph that the purpose of this provision is to restrict the use of religion to gain personal or political influence as well as to prohibit the "abuse" of religion in order to base the order of the state on religious tenets. The particular position of this restriction clause is interesting. It seems to express caution against actions that may appear like the exercise of the right to manifest one's religion or belief, but in effect may be religious activity that causes personal gain or exerts political influence. It must be noted, however, that "abuse of religious feelings" and "things held sacred by religion" are vague terms that may be difficult to reconcile with precision and foreseeability criteria that are required for permissible restrictions.

The general restrictions clause that is applicable to all fundamental rights is found under Article 13. It stipulates that fundamental rights may be restricted "only by law", without "infringing upon their essence" and restrictions may not be "in conflict with the letter and spirit of the Constitution and the requirements of the democratic order of society and the secular Republic and the principle of proportionality".[122] The "essence of rights" is a somewhat vague notion which has not been defined by the AYM in terms of the right to freedom of thought, conscience and religion. Article 13 does not include other "general" restriction grounds thus making Article 24 subject to its own special constitutional restriction clause. Gözler argues that without a general restrictions clause, Article 24 cannot be restricted based on, for example, the protection of health or public order.[123] Yet, considering the many potential and explicit restriction clauses, including the Preamble, it has not been difficult to find a suitable general restriction clause that can be applied to restrict the right to freedom of thought, conscience and religion.[124]

121 Çağlar, *supra* note 61, p. 113.

122 As amended on 17 October 2001.

123 Gözler, K. (2001) "Anayasa Değişikliğinin Temel Hak ve Hürriyetler Bakımından Getirdikleri ve Götürdükleri" [Pros and Cons of the Constitutional Amendments on Fundamental Rights and Freedoms], *Ankara Barosu Dergisi*, Year 59, No. 4, pp. 53–67.

124 See also Aslan, A. (2002) "Temel Hak ve Özgürlüklerin Sınırlanması: Anayasa'nın 13. Maddesi Üzerine Bazı Düşünceler" [The Restriction of Fundamental Rights and Freedoms: Some Thoughts on Article 13 of the Constitution], *Anayasa Yargısı*, No. 19, p. 143.

An additional and somewhat vague restriction clause is found in Article 14 stating that:

> None of the rights and freedoms embodied in the Constitution shall be exercised with the aim of violating the indivisible integrity of the state with its territory and nation, and endangering the existence of the democratic and secular order of the Turkish Republic based upon human rights.[125]

The requirement of democratic order of society has been used to restrict the state, whereas the requirement of secular Republic has been used to restrict fundamental freedoms.[126] Interestingly, the same provision goes on to create a restriction on the state and on individuals to destroy fundamental rights and freedoms embodied in the Constitution, thus creating an obligation both for the state and the individual.

As far as suspension of fundamental rights are concerned even in times of war, mobilization, martial law or in times of emergency, "no one may be compelled to reveal his/her religion, conscience, thought and convictions or be accused because of them".[127]

The nature of the Reform Laws that are protected under Article 174 of the Constitution may also be viewed as an additional limitation clause with implications for the restriction of the right to manifest one's religion or belief. Reform Laws protected under this provision relate to a number of issues,[128] with direct or indirect connection to the protection of *laiklik*. As a result of this clause, for example, the prohibition on wearing religious garments for clergy of any religion or the prohibition of the use of certain religious leadership titles and the closure of certain places of worship, such as dervish lodges, may not be challenged on grounds of their unconstitutionality. Thus the laws in question enjoy an absolute protection in the Turkish domestic legal system, since they cannot be interpreted as incompatible with the constitution.

It is clear from the review above that the right to freedom of thought, religion or belief is subject to a number of restriction clauses with varying themes and degrees of precision and importance. It will not be difficult to predict, then, that the interpretation and balancing of high courts plays an important role in the determination of permissible restrictions.

(a) Compulsory Religious Culture and Ethics Lessons

The issue of compulsory religion classes continues to be an unresolved domestic issue despite numerous concurring national and international court decisions that

125 As amended on 17 October 2001.

126 Can, O. (2002) "Anayasa Değişiklikleri ve Düşünceyi Açıklama Özgürlüğü" [Constitutional Amendments and the Freedom to Express Thoughts], *Anayasa Yargısı*, No. 19, pp. 503–532.

127 Article 15.

128 *Supra* note 67.

regard current practice in Turkey as incompatible with Turkey's human rights commitments under the ECHR. The National Security Council (MGK),[129] seeing religion as a unifying factor in society, advised the drafters of the Constitution that compulsory religious education under state control was appropriate; however, it needed to be in the form of religious culture.[130] Not surprisingly, the compulsory nature of this education has been viewed by many as a practice that is irreconcilable with the *laik* nature of the state.[131] The Constitutional provision on religious education stipulates:

> Education and instruction in religion and ethics shall be conducted under state supervision and control. Instruction in religious culture and moral education shall be compulsory in the curricula of primary and secondary schools. Other religious education and instruction shall be subject to the individual's own desire, and in the case of minors, to the request of their legal representatives.[132]

As it is clear from the text above, the Turkish Constitution foresees two different kinds of religious instruction and education, and creates different legal regimes for each. Firstly, there is a reference to the "Religious Culture and Knowledge of Ethics" (DKAB) course that is compulsory in primary and secondary schools. Secondly, the third sentence refers to "other religious education and instruction" and makes these subject to the individual's own desire and in the case of children, the request of their legal representatives. However, both kinds of religious instruction and education have one common element in that they are both subject to state supervision and control.

The lack of a definition for the DKAB classes in the Constitution leaves it to the Ministry of Education and the judiciary to interpret what kind of lessons these ought to be. It has been observed that the key phrase here is "culture" which seems to indicate that DKAB lessons must provide content that is relevant for all and not only for members of a particular religion.[133] Thus it would follow from the text firstly, that the "religious culture" lessons would be compulsory for all—without any exemption—and that they would be compulsory in all primary and secondary schools. In practice, however, the DKAB lessons extend beyond Culture of Religion to instruction in *Sunni* Islam. This is demonstrated by the Ministry of Education curricula,[134] the objections of atheist and Alevi

129 According to Article 187 of the Constitution the MGK comprises of the Chief of Staff, select members of the Council of Ministers, and the President of the Republic (who is also the Commander-in-chief). The MGK develops the national security policy.
130 *Cumhuriyet* Daily, 27 June 1987.
131 Dinçkol, *supra* note 72, p. 64.
132 Article 24 of the Turkish Constitution.
133 Gözler, K. (2010) "1982 Anayasası'na Göre Din Eğitim ve Öğretimi" [Religious Instruction and Teaching Under the 1982 Constitution], Prof. Dr. Tunçer Karamustafaoğlu'na Armağan, Ankara: Adalet Yayınevi, pp. 317–334.
134 Course program available in Turkish at www.dkab.org [Accessed 1 May 2015].

parents,[135] as well as the possibility of exemption for Christian and Jewish students.[136] On the other hand, the majority of the people in Turkey consider the DKAB as a religion course, yet, wish it to continue as a compulsory course.[137]

The ECtHR ruled that the compulsory DKAB lessons in Turkey amount to religious instruction in the case of *Hasan and Eylem Zengin v. Turkey.*[138] The case concerned the request of an Alevi parent for the exemption of his daughter from the compulsory DKAB lessons and the rejection of the Provincial National Education Directorate. The ECtHR held that these classes cannot be considered to meet the criteria of objectivity and pluralism, and found a violation of the right to education protected under Article 2 of Protocol 1.[139]

In Turkey, the Council of State (*Danıştay*) has given conflicting messages about the nature of these courses. First, it has ruled that the books taught in DKAB classes are based on teaching a particular religion and that practices such as doing the *namaz* and memorization of Arabic prayers are part of these lessons.[140] Thus, in light of the course content the Council of State held that these constituted not teaching on Religious Culture and Knowledge of Ethics but "religious instruction".[141] The Council of State held that under Article 24(4) of the Constitution this type of religious instruction may only be given subject to the desire of the individual and that rules that make it compulsory without a request from parents for such instruction were in violation of the Constitution as well as the ECHR.[142] Sezer asks the bidding question, "What can be the reason for a secular state to desire to give all of its citizens religious information in a compulsory manner?" and proposes that "compulsory religion" lies behind this practice.[143]

At the time of writing, the DKAB lessons remain compulsory, yet certain changes have been made in the program and content. According to a report by

135 *Bianet*, "Aile Çocuğun Dışlanmaması için Dava Açmak İstemiyor" [Parents Do Not Want to Sue because they Do Not Want their Children to Be Excluded], 22 June 2011 Available: http://bianet.org/bianet/insan-haklari/130932-aile-cocugun-dislanmamasi-icin-dava-acmak-istemiyor [Accessed 15 January 2015].

136 On 9 July 1990, the Education and Teaching High Council took a decision regarding Religious Culture and Knowledge of Ethics courses and the right of Christian and Jewish students to be exempted from these classes.

137 According to a survey 82.1 percent of the people in Turkey think that compulsory religious education should be given in public schools. 85.5 percent think that worship Diyanet practices such as ritual ablution and *namaz* should be taught as part of general teaching about Islam. Çarkoğlu, A. and B. Toprak (2007) *Religion, Society and Politics in a Changing Turkey*, Istanbul: TESEV, p. 60.

138 *Hasan and Eylem Zengin v. Turkey*, *supra* note 23. A more recent judgment concurs with this finding, this time also finding that even the revised curricula does not meet the ECHR standard. *Mansur Yalçın and Others*, 16 September 2014, European Court of Human Rights, No. 21163/11.

139 Ibid.

140 Council of State, 8th Chamber, 28 December 2007, E/2006/4107, K/2007/481, 29 February 2008, E2007/679 K2008/1461.

141 Ibid.

142 Ibid.

143 Sezer, *supra* note 118.

the ERG (Eğitim Reformu Girişimi—Reform in Education Initiative) changes in the curricula, which amount to interjecting information on Alevi and Caferi traditions, do not change the nature of the lessons as "instruction in a certain religion", thus the compulsory nature of the lessons continues to raise issues with the protection of the right to freedom of religion or belief of the child and the right of parents and legal guardians to bring up their children in line with their religious or philosophical views.[144] Unfortunately, however not unexpectedly given the political climate, following the changes in the curricula the Court of Cassation has changed its jurisprudence on the compulsory DKAB lessons, stating that the lessons are no longer "religious instruction on a particular religion" but "religious culture".[145]

The second kind of religious education is allowed by the Constitution, however, subject to individuals' wishes and must be carried out under state supervision and control. A separate regulation concerning "other religious education" also reinforces the interpretation that the "Religious Culture" classes ought not to amount to "instruction in a certain religion". There is no constitutional restriction concerning the content of "other religious education" nor a regulation on the nature of state supervision and control. If such education is provided by public institutions one may assume that state supervision and control is present; however, there is no constitutional rule concerning how the state supervision and control can be exercised if such education is provided in the family, in informal arrangements or in religious establishments. Legal regulation exists concerning "Quran courses", which may be carried out only under the Diyanet.[146] On the other hand, it is not possible for children to receive religious education in an institutional framework, apart from the summer Quran courses that are organized by the Diyanet without cost. For non-Muslims an option similar to the summer Quran courses does not exist; usually families or religious communities provide religious education in an informal manner and without state support.

(b) Coercion to Disclose Religion or Belief

The prohibition of coercion to declare one's religion or belief is a fundamental component of the right to have a thought, religion or belief.[147] The AYM had the opportunity to address this issue for the first time in an appeal case that concerned the request of three individuals to change the religion that was indicated in their

144 Yıldırım, M. (2012) "2011–2012 Öğretim Yılında Uygulanan Din Kültürü ve Ahlak Bilgisi Dersi Programına İlişkin bir Değerlendirme" [An Assessment of the 2011–2012 Religious Culture and Knowledge of Ethics Course Program], Istanbul: Eğitim Reformu Girişimi, p. 12.

145 *Milliyet*, "Danıştay'dan Din Dersi Kararı" [Council of State's Decision on Religion Course], 31 August 2012.

146 Diyanet İşleri Başkanlığı Kur'an Kursları ile Öğrenci Yurt ve Pansiyonlarına ilişkin Yönetmelik [Regulation on the Presidency of Religious Affairs Quran Courses and Dormitories and Hostels], R.G. 23982, 3 March 2000. Upon completion of Grade 5 children can take part in these courses: Article 4(k).

147 General Comment 22 of the Human Rights Committee on Article 18, UN Doc. HRI/GEN/1/Rev.1 at 35 (1994), para. 5.

national identity cards.[148] The case was taken to the Constitutional Court with the claim that the relevant provisions of the Public Registration Law violate the Constitution, in particular the provisions protecting the right to freedom of religion or belief, the right to freedom of expression, the principle of secularism and the principle of equality. The fundamental question was whether the requirement to register one's religion constitutes coercion to disclose one's convictions and opinions. The AYM did not find a violation and held that the said provisions of the Public Registration Law do not include any elements that constitute coercion to disclose one's belief. The decisive factor for the AYM was that the said provisions did not require the disclosure of religious convictions and opinions, instead "just religion". The difference between "religious convictions and opinions" on the one hand, and "just religion" on the other, was not clarified by the AYM. In contrast, the dissenting judges drew attention to the fine that is due for the non-disclosure of religion or belief for population register and identity cards purposes. Thus they held that "there is no doubt that there is coercion".[149] They also found the requirement to register one's religion or belief incompatible with the principle of secularism, saying, "for whatever reason and regardless of the level of coercion, the coercion of citizens to disclose religious convictions and opinions means nothing short of an infringement of secularism".[150]

In a relatively more recent case dating from 1995, the Constitutional Court maintained its previously held position on the constitutionality of the requirement in Public Registration Law to register religion in public register.[151] This time the court elaborated on the difference between "religion" and "religious conviction and opinion", noting that religious conviction and opinion is a broader term including one's religious views on a variety of issues, whereas religion amounts only to demographic or personal information. Hence the court maintained that what was prohibited in Article 24 of the Constitution protecting the right to freedom of religion or belief, was not the "noting of one's religion", but instead "the disclosure of one's religious convictions and opinions in a coercive manner". Taking account of the possibilities of changing the religion recorded in the religion section or erasing it through administrative action the court found that a coercive element was non-existent.[152]

The problem of coercion that results from the registration of religious affiliation in identity cards or the population register is a problem that could have been solved in the domestic legal system. Nevertheless, the narrow interpretation of the

148 Constitutional Court, E1979/9, K1979/44, 27 November 1979.
149 Ibid.
150 Ibid.
151 Constitutional Court, E1995/17, K1995/16, 21 June 1995. The case involved the referral of a case by the Council of State arguing that the requirement to register "religion" in the population register is contrary to the Constitution. The case considered by the Council of State involved a Bahai citizen requesting a change in the religion section of his ID case from Islam to "Bahai".
152 The dissenting judges held that there was a clear coercive element in the requirement to register one's religion.

Turkish judiciary caused one such case to be taken to the ECtHR. The Turkish practice concerning the registration of religious affiliation in public register and ID cards was the subject of the *Sinan Işık v. Turkey* case considered by the ECtHR.[153] Here, the European Court found that

> when identity cards have a religion box, leaving that box blank inevitably has a specific connotation. Bearers of identity cards which do not contain information concerning religion would stand out, against their will and as a result of interference by the authorities, from those who have an identity card indicating their religious beliefs. Accordingly, the Court considers that the issue of disclosure of one of an individual's most intimate aspects still arises.[154]

Yet, the ECtHR did not hesitate to touch upon the real issue, namely that the breach did not arise from the refusal to indicate the applicant's Alevi faith, rather, the indication of religion on the identity card, as such.[155] Even though over a decade has passed since the delivery of this judgment, the needed legislative changes in order to prevent similar violations have not been made.

Individuals are under an obligation to take an oath on "God and honor" in the Turkish courts.[156] This provision makes it compulsory for everyone, including non-believers to take an oath by reference to "one's God". This is incompatible with the right to freedom of religion or belief, the secular nature of the state which should be impartial towards believers and non-believers. This provision has thus far not been the subject of consideration by the AYM on its constitutionality.

(c) Manifestation of Religion—Religious Symbols—in the Public Sphere

PUBLIC WORK PLACE—CIVIL SERVANTS AND DRESS CODE[157]

The manifestation of religious symbols in the public work place has been an issue polarizing society and politics. Finally with the consolidation of power of the Justice and Development Party (Adalet ve Kalkınma Partisi—AKP), fundamental change has become possible; this change is also an indication of a power and mentality shift in the context of politics of religion. The Turkish Constitution recognizes the right of all Turkish citizens to enter public service and stipulates that no criteria other than the qualifications for the office concerned may be taken into consideration

153 *Sinan Işık v. Turkey*, *supra* note 23.
154 Ibid., para. 51.
155 Ibid., para. 52.
156 Article 339 of the Law No. 1086. Hukuk Usulü Muhakemeleri Kanunu [Law on Legal Procedures], 18 June 1927, R.G. No. 622, 623, 624, 02./03./04./07.1927.
157 This part is based on an article by Yıldırım, M. (2012) "Religion in the Public and Private Turkish Workplace: the Approach of the Turkish Judiciary", in K. Alidadi, M.C. Foblets and J. Vrielink (eds.), *A Test of Faith? Religious Diversity and Accommodation in the European Workplace*, Surrey: Routledge.

for recruitment into public service.[158] The general provisions of the Law on Public Servants, however, have implications for the restriction of manifestations of religion or belief.[159] As far as public servants working in schools connected to the Ministry of Education are concerned, they are subject to a regulation requiring the head to be uncovered.[160]

The dress code of public servants is regulated by the Framework Regulation of October 1982 (the Regulation of October 1982).[161] The purpose of the Regulation of October 1982 is to ensure that public servants have uniformity in terms of clothing and wear modest and contemporary clothes that are in line with the reforms and principles of Atatürk.[162] It is not possible to find a definition in any positive law document of what these terms mean or imply for clothing. This was later determined by jurisprudence.

The Turkish judiciary has interpreted *laiklik* functionally so as to exclude not only the headscarf, but also "persons with certain religious affiliations" (the word "*dinci*" has a special negative connotation in Turkish meaning a pious person who is religious at the expense of being modern), in general, from the public workplace.[163] This was done by attributing manifestations of religion, in particular the headscarf, a meaning and significance that is ideologically incompatible with *laiklik* and by the imposition of heavy sanctions upon persons who use these symbols. The judiciary equated the act of wearing the headscarf in a public workplace with disrupting the order of an institution for ideological or political purposes, thus warranting dismissal from work, and thus transforming the action of wearing the headscarf to a different category.[164] As a result, the effect and strength of the prohibition and its sanction has been aggravated.

158 Article 70 of the Turkish Constitution.

159 Devlet Memurları Kanunu [Law on Public Servants] No. 657, 14 July 1965, R.G., 23 July 1965, No. 12056, Article 6.

160 Milli Eğitim Bakanlığına ve Diğer Bakanlıklara Bağlı Okullardaki Memurların ve Öğrencilerin Kılık Kıyafetine İlişkin Yönetmelik [Regulation on Attire and Clothing for Officials and Students in Schools under the Ministry of Education and Other Ministries], No. 8/3349, December 1981, R.G. No. 17537, 7 December 1981.

161 Kamu Kurum ve Kuruluşlarında Çalışan Personelin Kılık ve Kıyafetine Dair Yönetmelik [Regulation Pertaining to the Attire of Personnel Employed at Public Institutions] (October 1982 Regulation), R.G. 25 October 1982, 17849.

162 Article 16 of the October 1982 Regulation. Article 5 regulates many aspects of appearance, *inter alia*, the length and form of hair, moustache, beard, shirts, ties, how much a shirt or blouse can reveal, how loose or tight trousers can be, heels of shoes, nails, make-up, etc.

163 It has been observed that the Turkish judiciary has a strong tendency to protect the state and sanction severely what it perceives as a threat to the state. Sancar, M. and E. Ü. Atılgan (2009) *Adalet Biraz Es Geçiliyor* [Justice is Somewhat Overlooked], TESEV, pp. 124–150.

164 The case of Züheyla Zeybel set the precedent for this interpretation, 25 January 2001, E2000/1244, K2001/474, Council of State, General Council of Chambers of Administrative Cases. A report by AK-DER claims that during 1998–2002 approximately 5,000 public servants were dismissed and another 10,000 were forced to resign. A Report by AK-DER (2008) *İstatistiki Verilere Göre Türkiye'de Kadınların Genel Konumu ve Başörtüsü Yasağının Cinsiyet Endekslerine Etkileri* [A Statistical

The broad approach taken by the judiciary has raised questions about the predictability and clarity of the application of relevant laws. In the Turkish context, in the assessment of compatibility of a civil servant's actions with the dress code and the principle of secularism, dress outside the public workplace,[165] "sincerity" in abiding by the relevant regulations,[166] manifestations of religion or belief outside the workplace and affiliations with certain groups and religious worldview,[167] have also been taken into account. It is not possible to find a detailed set of reasons as to exactly how the nexus between, on the one hand, manifestations of religion, such as religious garb and practice outside the workplace and, on the other hand, the threat to secularism is established. The assumed connection seems to be based on general perceptions and presuppositions rather than concrete acts of individuals that pose an immediate and material threat to the secular nature of public service they are delivering.

The Turkish judiciary has not taken into account the right to freedom of religion or belief in its assessment of the permissibility of religious symbols in the public workplace. The right to freedom of religion or belief is protected in the Turkish Constitution, as well as through Turkey's international human rights commitments. The interest of protecting the secular system may be ultimately based on the legitimate aims of protecting public order and the rights of freedoms of others. However, the balancing of competing interests and proportionality are absent in the reasonings.

Interestingly, the relationship of religious symbols and state neutrality or impartiality and the possible problems in this respect find limited reflection in the jurisprudence. Yet, Demir argues that the ban on religious symbols for public servants is a requirement of the principle of secularism since the neutrality of the public servant will become concrete with her/his outlook and behavior.[168] Hence

Analysis of the Situation of Women in Turkey and the Effect of the Headscarf Ban on Gender Index], AK-DER, p. 7.

165 The judgment of the Council of State demonstrates that the headscarf, even though it was worn outside the workplace, is viewed by the judiciary as a religious manifestation that undermines certain qualities that are expected from teachers, *inter alia*, "being a good example" and the secular character of public education. It was specifically mentioned that she did not wear the headscarf at her workplace. *The Case of Aytaç Altındağ*, Council of State Judgment, 8th Chamber, E2004/4051, K2005/3366, 26 October 2005.

166 The wearing of a wig over the headscarf by a teacher was considered as a sign that the applicant was not really sincere in abiding by the applicable dress code. *The Case of Kevser Sönmez*, Sakarya Second Administrative Court, E2001/14, K2001/2854, 26 December 2001.

167 The judgment of an administrative court upholding the decision of the Ministry of Education for the transfer of an educational administrator, Mr. Mustafa Ünsal, was based on manifestations of religion or belief such as his religious affiliations or practices outside the workplace. The Case of Mustafa Ünsal, Council of State, 5th Chamber, E1999/4212, K1999/4325.

168 Demir, H.S. (2011) *Avrupa İnsan Hakları Mahkemesi Kararları Işığında Türkiye'de Din ve Vicdan Özgürlüğü* [Freedom of Religion and Conscience in Turkey in Light of the Decisions of the European Court of Human Rights], Ankara: Adalet, p. 127.

the protection of *laiklik* as the paramount interest functions as a trump card or hierarchically superior interest against which other competing interests cannot even be regarded as legitimate interests that require balancing. Religious symbols and/or practices are not assessed as legally protected manifestations of religion or belief, but as indicators of certain religious affiliations that are viewed as threats to *laiklik*.

In 2013 a fundamental change took place and the Regulation was amended so as to allow the headscarf for public servants with the exception of those working in the security class, those working as judges, prosecutors and those working in the military.[169] The relaxation of the ban on religious symbols has been selective as it did not extend to other religious symbols such as the cross or the *kippa*.

MANIFESTATIONS OF RELIGION OR BELIEF IN TURKISH SCHOOLS—THE HEADSCARF

The extent of protection afforded to the right to manifest one's religion or belief in Turkish schools needs to be analyzed in relation to the rights of teachers, minor and adult students, the state and parents. Due to the constraints of this chapter, I will try to evaluate the Turkish legislation and practice in these areas focusing on their common feature, namely the decisive factor which has been the understanding of *laiklik* by the Turkish high courts. Dress code for teachers, be it public or private, or primary or high education, prohibits the use of the headscarf.[170] Until 2014 students in primary or high school were not allowed to enter schools wearing a headscarf,[171] and only recently are university students allowed to enter university wearing the headscarf.[172] Schools where religious vocational training takes place have accommodated the wearing of the headscarf since they were founded.[173] School administrations may not display any religious symbols in both public or private schools; however this is also changing in practice through elaborate celebrations of the Prophet Mohammed's birthday. The state's obligation to respect parents' religious or philosophical beliefs in education becomes increasingly an issue.

The common element in all religious symbol cases has related to the privileged protection and particular understanding of *laiklik* which finds it difficult to reconcile the use of the headscarf with *laiklik*. The jurisprudence of the Council of State in a case concerning disciplinary measures against a university student who wore the

169 Şimşek, Y. (2013) "Kamuda Başörtüsü Artık Serbest" [Headscarf Free in Public Workplace], *Radikal*, 9 October 2013.
170 *Supra* note 156.
171 Gürsoy, S. (2014) "Ortaokul ve lisede başörtüsü serbest" [Headscarf is free in Middle and High Schools], *Sabah*, 27 September 2014.
172 The Head of the Higher Education Council (YÖK) Prof. Y.Z. Özcan announced that instructors in universities may no longer take action against students wearing the headscarf. Head, J. (2014) "Quiet End to Turkey's Headscarf Ban", *BBC News*. Available: http://www.bbc.co.uk/news/world-europe-11880622 [Accessed 15 January 2015].
173 *Supra* note 159. Article 12 stipulates that during courses on the Quran, female students may cover their hair with an Islamic veil.

headscarf at university was striking.[174] The Council of State considered the wearing of the headscarf as a symbol that shows a strong objection to the *laik* Republic and demonstrates that the students embrace a state order that is based on religion.[175] The nexus between the act of wearing the headscarf and thus being a threat to the *laik* state appears to have been drawn with certain assumptions or perceptions that cannot be regarded as legal facts. Also, other possible "means" of expressing an ideology, whether it has been a badge or long beard etc., are not treated the same way, thus undermining equality by singling out the headscarf as the only prohibited ideological symbol.[176]

Constitutional amendments initiated by the National Assembly to overcome the restriction on wearing the headscarf by university students were also made ineffective by the relevant AYM judgments. The adoption of Law No. 3511 in 1989,[177] and after its annulment,[178] the adoption of the Law No. 5735 in 2008,[179] also did not lead to a solution. The AYM held that the proposed constitutional amendments had the main aim of un-restricting religious symbols in higher education institutions without eliminating public fears, foreseeing safeguards against abuses and inputting measures necessary for the protection of third party rights.[180] According to the Court, the unlimited use of the religious symbols would create pressure on non-believers and on Muslim females and would also damage state neutrality by opening a pathway for religion to be used for political purposes.[181]

Turkey has put the ban on headscarf in the past; however, the ongoing challenge remains the accommodation of *all* religious symbols in the public work place which has now opened to religious symbols.

(d) Conscientious Objection to Military Service

The right to conscientious objection to military service is a highly contested right and an indicator that, contrary to common belief, problems pertaining to *laiklik* do not sufficiently explain failures of Turkey's protection of freedom of religion or

174 Council of State 8th Chamber, E1983/207, K1984/330, 23 December 1984.
175 Ibid.
176 Ulusoy, A. (2004) *Kamu Hizmeti İncelemeleri* [Study on Public Service], Ülke Kitapları, p. 239.
177 This Law included an additional Article 16 to Law No. 2547 on Higher Education. Article 16 stipulated that "[w]ithin higher education establishments, classrooms, laboratories, clinics, and policlinics and in corridors it is obligatory to be in modern clothing and looks. The closing of the neck and hair with a cloth or with a turban due to religious reasons is unrestricted."
178 The Turkish Constitutional Court annulled the Law on grounds that it was contrary to the Preamble and Articles 2, 10, 24, and 174 of the Constitution. Constitutional Court, E1989/1, K1989/12, 7 March 1989.
179 It read, "No one can be denied, for any reason at all, the right to higher education in cases not openly stipulated by law".
180 Constitutional Court, E/1989/1, K/1989/12, 7 March 1989; Constitutional Court, E1990/36, K1991/8, 9 April 1991.
181 Ibid.

belief. Interestingly, the right to conscientious objection has been the subject of numerous applications to the ECtHR and judgments on Turkey; however, none has been effectively enforced.[182]

Article 72 of the Constitution regulates military service. Article 72 reads: "National service is the right and duty of every Turk. The manner in which this service shall be performed, or considered as performed, either in the Armed Forces or in public service shall be regulated by law."

The fact that military service is enumerated as *only one of the alternatives* of national service has important implications. It allows the possibility for national service to be performed within the Armed Forces *or* through public service. Alternatively, it can be considered performed under certain circumstances that are prescribed by law.

According to Article 1 of the Military Code, military service is obligatory for every male citizen of the Turkish Republic.[183] The Military Criminal Code requires that those who have the obligation to perform military service report to their military unit as soon as they are called up for recruitment.[184] Since there is no legal provision that addresses conscientious objection to military service, the only relevant provisions applied to objectors are those dealing with disobeying orders and desertion. When a person is summoned to perform military service and does not present himself to his unit, in accordance with Article 63 of the Military Criminal Code, criminal responsibility occurs. Each act of disobedience following the first one is reckoned as insistence on disobeying orders.[185] Military duties have a strong precedence over acts motivated by belief; Article 45 of the Military Criminal Code stipulates that the fact that a person has considered an act as necessary according to his conscience or religion does not exempt him from punishment.[186]

Since military service becomes compulsory through national law it is possible to observe a conflict with the provision in the Constitution where it appears to be deemed optional. According to Can, since military service is not an obligatory form of national service and freedom of conviction is protected as a right that cannot even be suspended under a state of emergency, within the constitutional framework there is not a conflict or potential restriction on the recognition of the right to conscientious objection to military service.[187] Furthermore, according to High Court of Appeals Prosecutor Eminağaoğlu, exemption from military service

182 See *supra* note 25. Also, the part on conscientious objection to military services is partly based on a previously published article, Yıldırım, M. (2010) "Conscientious Objection to Military Service: International Human Rights Law and the Case of Turkey", *Religion and Human Rights*, 5, pp. 65–91.

183 Askerlik Kanunu [Law on Military Service] No. 1111, 21 June 1927.

184 Askeri Ceza Kanunu [Military Criminal Code], No. 1632, 22 May 1930.

185 Ibid.

186 Ibid.

187 Can, O. (2014) "Vicdani Red ve Anayasa" [Consciencious Objection and the Constitution], in Ö. Çınar and C. Üsterci (eds.), Çarklardaki Kum: Vicdani Red [Sand in the Wheels: Conscientious Objection], Istanbul: İletişim, pp. 291–312.

for conscientious objectors is not in contradiction with the principle of equality since according to Article 14(2) none of the provisions set forth in the Constitution can be interpreted in a way as to provide broader restrictions of rights than those prescribed by the Constitution itself.[188]

Consequently, in light of Articles 13, 14, 24, 25 and 72 of the Constitution, a right to conscientious objection to military service is compatible with the Turkish Constitution and in fact Article 1 of the Turkish Military Code, and Article 45 of the Military Criminal Code 61 can be considered incompatible with the Constitution's aforementioned provisions.

Conscientious objection to military service is a critical issue bringing the interest of the individual and the interest of the state into conflict. The Turkish judiciary has at its disposal key international human rights treaties that Turkey has ratified,[189] and the human rights obligations and a flexible regulation regarding military service found within the Turkish Constitution; however, the judiciary has been unable to draw from these legal sources in order to deal with conscientious objection cases where national security, the principle of equality and the right to freedom of religion or belief and other substantive human rights are interpreted in a harmonizing manner that would be in conformity with existing international human rights jurisprudence. Exploring factors influencing judges in the process of reaching a judgment, a study points to *preconceptions* that are shaped by state ideology and perception of the law system as a means of protection of the state rather than a neutral adjudicator of justice.[190] Naturally, the claim to conscientious objection to military service is a key point where notions of national security, survival of state and the position of the individual versus the state are reference points. Therefore in cases dealing with conscientious objectors, preconceptions of prosecutors and judges certainly play a crucial role and constitute an obstacle to assessing these claims as a human rights issue.

Nevertheless, two Turkish military court decisions concerning conscientious objection claims have shown a partial recognition of the right to conscientious objection to military service as a human right.[191] One concerns a Jehovah's Witness conscientious objector, Baris Görmez, the other a Muslim conscientious objector, Muhammed Serdar Delice. In both cases military courts to some degree relied on the changed jurisprudence of the ECtHR on conscientious objection following the *Bayatyan v. Armenia* case. However, in both cases a key factor was the declared religions of the conscientious objectors.

188 Eminağaoğlu, Ö.F. (2005) "Özgürlük ve Vatan Hizmeti" [Freedom and Service to Homeland], *Radikal*, 22 August 2005.

189 *Inter alia*, the European Convention on Human Rights and the UN International Covenant on Civil and Political Rights.

190 Sancar, M. and E.Ü. Atılgan (2009) *Adalet biraz es geçiliyor: Demokratikleşme Sürecinde Hakimler ve Savcılar* [Justice is Somewhat Overlooked: Judges and Prosecutors in the Democratization Process], Istanbul: TESEV, p. 111.

191 For detailed review of these cases see Yıldırım, M. (2012) "Selective Progress on Conscientious Objection", Forum 18. Available: http://forum18.org/Archive.php?article_id=1696 [Accessed 1 May 2016].

It will be remembered that Article 90 of the Turkish Constitution states that in cases of conflict between international agreements in the area of fundamental rights and domestic laws, the provisions of international agreements will prevail.[192] This provision was applied in both military court judgments.

Malatya Military Court's Delice decision outlines the Turkish military judiciary's interpretation of the right to conscientious objection to military service.[193] Delice declared his conscientious objection approximately five months after he had been conscripted based on his Islamic and nationalist beliefs.[194] The Malatya Military Court interpreted the ECtHR's approach to the right to conscientious objection as one based on the theological position of a religious group, and excluded the beliefs of the individual. It ruled out an individual rejecting military service according to his own views. Instead, the Military Court relied on the rejection of military service by an intellectual, religious or political group, as such. It referred to the example of Jehovah's Witnesses, stating: "persons who are members of the Jehovah's Witnesses reject military service, because they are part of this group or institution which fundamentally rejects military service".[195]

Based on this understanding, an individual claiming conscientious objection to military service would have to be a member of a religious group considered by a court to be categorically opposed to military service. In the Malatya Military Court's view, Delice belonged to "Islam which is not a belief or ideological movement that rejects the performance of military service".[196]

This view of Islam was a theological statement by the court. But when Delice wanted to bring in the mufti of Malatya as an expert witness, the court rejected his request. In excluding the mufti, the court cited Law No. 5271 on Criminal Procedure.[197] Article 62 of the latter law states that experts must take an oath saying that they will perform their tasks based on science. The court stated that "the religious sphere is intrinsically related to beliefs and is dogmatic, hence any view expressed from this field cannot be based on science and includes subjective elements".[198]

This explanation seems to contradict the court's view that Islam does not reject the performance of military service. On the one hand, the court maintains that religious views cannot be presented in proceedings by experts, as they are not scientific and include subjective elements. Yet on the other, it bases its decision on its own theological assessment.

According to the Military Court, Delice had Islamic and nationalist views when he was conscripted and he only declared his conscientious objection to military service after he "saw wrongs and deficient aspects of military service for himself and thus declared his conscientious objection".[199] The court also argued that

192 *Supra* note 21.
193 Malatya Military Court, E/2012/98, K/2012/40, 24 February 2012.
194 Ibid.
195 Ibid.
196 Ibid.
197 Ibid.
198 Ibid.
199 Ibid.

Delice did not from the beginning of his military service have a "one and undivided purpose" of conscientious objection.[200] The court thus ignored in relation to conscientious objection a key part of international law's understanding of freedom of religion or belief, which is also found in ECH, Article 9—the right to change beliefs.[201] Under this ruling, a conscientious objector must demonstrate that his objection existed before conscription, and that it is his "one and undivided purpose"—i.e. that he has no other reasons for wanting to leave military service.[202]

Isparta Military Court recognized the right to conscientious objection to military service when it acquitted Jehovah's Witness Baris Görmez on 13 March 2012.[203] He had spent a total of four years in prison from November 2007 and had been charged with "rejecting wearing of the uniform" and "rejecting orders".[204] As in the Delice case, the court relied on the changed jurisprudence of the ECtHR.

In the assessment of conscientious objection claims by public authorities, assessments based on theological views must be avoided. Otherwise—as in the Delice case—there is a grave risk of making decisions based on a court's or public authority's purely subjective views, and not based on the evidence of a particular case.

In conclusion, the above review of the legal guarantees, issues and, at times, paradoxical practices found in the domestic legal system and context present the complexities surrounding the state-religion relationship paradigm and the state of protection of the right to freedom of religion or belief in Turkey. The asymmetrical arrangements and disproportionate restrictions imposed on the right to freedom of thought, conscience, religion or belief stand in sharp contrast to the normative demands of international standards for the protection of the right to freedom of religion or belief. This is also evident in the numerous ECtHR decisions pertaining to Article 9 that remain not enforced. Manifestations of religion or belief are, often, viewed incompatible with the interests of the state, concretized in protecting national security, *laiklik* and upholding nationalism. This tension is seldom resolved by a rigorous application of relevant provisions protecting freedom of religion or belief including the limitation clauses. Instead, the right to manifest religion or belief is given scarce and limited consideration in judicial assessments in contrast to the strong protection of *laiklik*, national security and nationalism.

Following the consolidation of power by the AKP in the 2011 elections, a new era has begun in the state-religion relationship where the public sphere has been opened up to Islamic religious symbols. This development, seen together with the mechanisms that are already built into the system for the state to control religious

200 Ibid.

201 Ibid.

202 Delice has appealed against the ruling, and the High Court of Appeals decision and its reasoning will be awaited with great interest by many in and outside Turkey.

203 Isparta Military Court, 13 March 2012; Karaca, E. (2012) "Yehova Şahidine Vicdani Ret Hakkı" [JW has the Right to Conscience Objection]. Available: http://www.bianet.org/bianet/ifade-ozgurlugu/136899-yehova-sahidi-ne-vicdani-ret-hakki, *Bianet* [Accessed 16 January 2015.]

204 Ibid.

services, points to new religious freedom challenges; ensuring pluralism and the principles of neutrality and equality as well as the obligation to protect everyone's freedom of thought, conscience and religion or belief.

The recognition of the religiously pluralistic nature of the society in Turkey, recognition of the right to manifest one's religion or belief in worship, practice, teaching and observance as well as a new conception of *laiklik* that creates a conducive framework for the protection of freedom of religion or belief may be steps to move forward.

In the following chapters specific components of the collective dimension of freedom of religion or belief will be closely examined.

6 The Right of Religious or Belief Communities to Acquire Legal Personality in Turkey

6.1 Introduction

In Turkey no religious or belief community can acquire legal personality, *per se*. Yet, as it has been explained in Chapter 3, in the enjoyment of the right to freedom of religion or belief in its collective dimension, whether a belief community can or cannot acquire legal personality becomes a significant factor affecting the enjoyment of this right.[1] The reason for this is that legal personality functions as a crucial *enabling* element and, at times, a precondition for the enjoyment of rights that make up the right to freedom of religion or belief or related rights, *inter alia*, the right to own property, the right to establish a place of worship and representation of a belief community. Conversely, proper enjoyment of the right to freedom of religion or belief in its collective dimension requires an adequate form of legal personality that is suitable to the nature of belief communities. This key function also constitutes the reason for the contention over this right.

This chapter presents an overview of the legislation and legal and administrative practice on legal personality in the context of freedom of religion or belief in Turkey. It will be argued that the existing forms of legal personality fall short of providing an adequate form of legal entity status for belief groups to exercise their right to manifest religion or belief in its collective dimension. It will be further demonstrated that the absence of an adequate legal personality framework for belief communities is incompatible with Turkey's international human rights obligations. For this purpose, first, an overview of key elements of legal personality and the practice in the Ottoman era and Turkish Republic is presented. Turkish legislation and practice on the available forms of legal personality, namely, *vakıfs* (foundations) and associations will be critically examined. These options will be assessed on their adequacy as legal personality options for belief communities in the exercise of their right to freedom of religion or belief in line with international human rights law without unjustified state interference. Finally, some observations are made on the elements that an adequate form of legal personality—one that can facilitate the exercise of the collective dimension of freedom of religion or belief in Turkey—should entail.

1 See Chapter 3.

An effective basic form of legal personality for belief communities must include certain elements, such as an entity status that allows a group of believers to act as a single composite body for certain purposes. It must allow religious or belief communities to exist—if they wish to do so—not as individual members, but as one organized body. Hence, once the community has gained legal personality, it is no longer individuals who, for example, own a place of worship or provide humanitarian assistance or run a faith-based school but the community as such. While international human rights law provisions do not include an explicit reference to the right to acquire a certain form of legal entity status, the right to legal personality has gained gradual international recognition in international jurisprudence,[2] as well as being acknowledged in documents of a soft law nature. The OSCE and the Venice Commission have published a specific document including guidelines for states to follow while creating legislation pertaining to legal personality.[3]

6.2 Legal Personality in the Ottoman and Republic Era

6.2.1 Ottoman Era

While it is not the primary goal of this study to provide an in depth account and analysis of associative life of belief communities in the Ottoman era, basic insight into its nature makes a valuable contribution to the understanding of relevant current legal issues. The question of whether there was a provision for legal personality in Islamic Law and during the Ottoman period becomes a pertinent one because of its particular relevance for the exercise of rights for belief communities that have existed in the Turkish geography before the Turkish Republic was founded. The atypical character of the arrangement in this sphere in the Ottoman era may have provided ample room for arbitrary administrative and, not least, unpredictable judicial decisions that disadvantaged belief communities in the Republic era.

The nature of the notion of legal personality in the Ottoman Empire stands out in its distinctness from the idea of legal personality in Roman Law. Hatemi argues that although it is less clear cut when compared to Roman Law, it is possible to talk about certain clues indicating that the notion of legal personality was recognized in the Ottoman Empire.[4] Reyna and Zonana, on the other hand, state clearly that there was no legal personality in the Ottoman State.[5] Karaman, argues that while the term "legal personality" may be absent in Islamic Law, the concept is not. He observes that the notion of legal entity is an assumption that Islamic

2 See Chapter 3.

3 OSCE-Venice Commission *Guidelines on Legal Personality of Religious or Belief Communities*, 2014.

4 Hatemi, H. (1979) *Medeni Hukuk Tüzelkişileri* I [Civil Law Legal Entities I], Istanbul: Istanbul University Publications, p. 47.

5 Reyna, Y. and E. Zonana (2003) *Son Yasal Düzenlemelere Göre Cemaat Vakıfları* [Community Foundations under the Latest Legal Regulations], Istanbul: Gözlem Publications, p. 41.

Law accepts, however, in the Ottoman era, there was no need for it to be recognized.[6] The Ottoman *Mecelle* (Civil Code) refers to a village and certain professional institutions of a religious character, as entities with responsibilities and certain rights.[7]

For the study at hand, it is important to note a key difference between legal personality in Roman Law and the notion of legal personality in Islamic Law. Roman Law tends to recognize a group of persons as a legal entity and considers property acquired by such a group as owned by the legal entity, whereas Islamic Law, through the *vakıf* (foundation or endowment) institutions, views the collection of property as having legal entity status and the group of persons as "those benefiting" from the property.[8] Beneficiaries of the revenues generated by the property, however, do not have any legal personality. The Ottoman *vakıf* formula, therefore, does not provide a form of legal personality that would allow a group of believers to act as a composite entity. It is important to note this key conceptual distinction as the *vakıf* institution is still one of the legal personality options available to members of religious communities.

Despite a lack of a legal personality—as understood in Roman Law—in the Ottoman state,[9] the factual situation of religious communities compelled the development of certain improvised formulas. For example, religious communities registered their property under the name of real people, who only appeared on paper as owners but did not claim ownership, or under the names of persons who no longer lived, such as saints or respected religious figures.[10] Only in 1912, with

6 Karaman, K. (1974) *Mukayeseli Islam Hukuku* [Comparative Islamic Law], Istanbul: Iz Yayıncılık, pp. 206–220.

7 Hatemi, *supra* note 4, pp. 46–47.

8 Ibid., p. 51.

9 The former was referred to as *nam-müstear* (pseudo name) and the latter as *nam-ı mevhum* (name of a historical or religious figure). Within the Ottoman context, two factors may possibly explain the absence of legal personality for belief communities. First, in the Ottoman society, generally speaking, association, as distinct from the state, was not foreseen and encouraged by the state. Second, the *ummah* (Islamic nation) nature of the dominant religious community and its relation with the state created a framework that may have rendered the need for legal personality on the part of belief communities unnecessary. As far as the development of general legal personality is concerned, Mardin argues that the Ottoman state was unwilling to allow differentiation in society—through the establishment of associations—and thus acquiring autonomy. Mardin, S. (2007) *Türkiye'de Din ve Siyaset* [Religion and Politics in Turkey], 13th ed., Istanbul: İletişim, p. 93. Together with Westernization and Reorganization in the latter part of the 19th century, however, the beginnings of public legal entity status started to emerge within the *vakıf* institution structure. The establishment of the Turkish Republic and fundamental changes in law and state structure provided the legal basis for the establishment of public and private legal entities. However Mardin does not examine the suitability of these institutions for religious/belief communities. For an overview of the establishment of various institutions such as universities, public legal entities such as the Radio Television Institution, economic, social and political institutions see Hatemi, *supra* note 4, pp. 120–130.

10 Reyna and Zonana, *supra* note 5, p. 41.

the passing of an *interim* law, did it become possible to register these properties under the name of the respective communities, thus, according to Reyna and Zonana, recognizing their legal entity status.[11] Still, the *interim* law, does not go as far as formulating a legal entity status. It refers to registering the non-movables that belonged to various Ottoman *millets* in the name of the "corporation" (*müessese*), yet, there was not a clear and complete description of the elements of this "corporation" and its legal nature. Nevertheless, it is possible to observe a certain "limited notion of legal personality". The fact that there were religious communities who *in fact* owned property was recognized for a *certain purpose* and *certain period of time*, namely the registration of property in their name within a certain time frame.[12] Indeed, after the specified time it was no longer possible to register property in the name of the religious communities. While this arrangement is a move towards embracing the notion of legal personality, its nature is far from complete, lacking elements that would create an adequate form of legal personality with a clear and foreseeable legal basis.

As far as belief communities are concerned, the legal framework of legal personality, or the lack of it, may suggest that there was an assumption of a customary way of organizing, one that does not function through legal personality. On the one hand, belief communities existed in their traditional ways yet without a legal entity status. On the other hand, their members had the possibility of donating property to establish *vakıf* institutions and/or professional organizations with religious character and thus to support their communities or engage in actions similar to contemporary civil society organizations. It may be argued that this situation is a natural result of the *ummah* understanding; all Muslims form the Muslim people, and the state—as an Islamic state—is the ultimate legal entity representing the Muslim people. Secondary institutions that have been formed in the West between the state and the individual did not exist in Islamic societies. Mardin argues that the connection of *ummah*, the Islamic millet or community, corresponds to the secondary institutions found in the West.[13] For non-Muslim communities the *millet* system may have functioned as a substitute, similar to the *ummah*, each religious community may have been "assumed" to be a composite, represented by their respective religious leaders.

In conclusion, it may be observed that the legal framework for the associative life of belief communities was one that did not include the notion of legal personality found in contemporary legal systems. The theocratic state constituted the ultimate legal personality for the Muslim *millet*. As for non-Muslim communities, through the recognition of religio-ethnic communities, the *millet*, and

11 An interim law, entitled Eşhas-ı Hükmiyenin Emvali Gayrimenkuleye Tasarruflarına Mahsus Kanunu Muvakkat [Temporary Law on the Possession of Non-Movables by Legal Persons], was adopted in 1912.

12 First for six months, then it was extended for another six months.

13 Mardin, *supra* note 9, p. 58.

the creation of special legal regimes,[14] belief communities were recognized as composite entities. It may be argued that this legal structure resembled a minority protection scheme rather than the granting of a legal entity status to a belief community. In the Ottoman practice, the *vakıf* stands out as the legal entity, a collection of assets, from which the various belief communities benefited as assumed communities which did not have a *direct legal link* to them. It is important to bear in mind this Ottoman arrangement, which partly accounts for irregularities, when considering the transition to the modern legal system of the Turkish Republic.

6.2.2 The Republic of Turkey

The Turkish legal system does not provide a clear, consistent and coherent law and practice on the legal status of belief communities. It is not possible for belief communities, as such, to acquire legal personality in Turkey.[15] Yet, it is important to note that there are certain court decisions recognizing that certain belief communities have legal capacity to exercise the right to property or have access to court. Despite a lack of special legal entity status for belief communities, in the current Turkish legal system, *members* of belief communities may establish associations, foundations or, possibly, commercial companies in order to gain a certain legal entity status.[16] None of these options, however, provides the possibility of acquisition of legal personality for belief communities, *per se*.

Before examining the legislation and practice on legal personality, it is worthwhile considering briefly some of the possible interests that lie behind the pre-emptive legal framework that is designed to bar the very possibility of acquiring a direct legal entity status for belief groups. As it has been demonstrated above, while no belief community in the Ottoman Empire had legal personality, the Islamic nature of the state and the *millet* system have allowed certain belief communities to exist as *de facto* composite, organized bodies under their respective religious leaderships. Yet, with the secular modern Republic, this *quasi*-legal entity status, the *millet* categories were abolished. The modern Republic also barred members of belief communities to establish *vakıfs* or any other associations with the purpose of supporting any, including their own, religious community.[17] Hence not only did belief communities not have the possibility of being recognized as quasi-legal entities (*millet* or *ummah*), the possibility of establishing *vakıfs* for the benefit of their communities was also no longer possible.

14 In the latter part of the 19th century, efforts to regulate the status and internal organization of religious communities resulted in the adoption of several Regulations for a number of *millet*.
15 The Council of Europe Venice Commission (2010) *Opinion on the Legal Status of Religious Communities in Turkey*, para. 32.
16 This list excludes political parties and unions.
17 Türk Medeni Kanunu [Turkish Civil Code] No. 743, 17 February 1926, Article 74(2) explicitly prohibited the establishment of foundations that pursued the aim of supporting a certain race or community (*cemaat*, meaning religious community).

The underlying conceptions and reasons for this are critical to understanding legal interpretation pertaining to relevant restrictions and the critical assessment of their justification. An essential reason for these restrictions may be found in the paradigmatic shift that occurred together with the establishment of the modern Turkish Republic. Firstly, in contrast to the *millet* system of the Ottoman Empire, the Turkish Republic set out to establish a system of a nation state based on the principle of a formal equality of citizens with an emphasis on the relationship of the individual and state rather than the *millet*, religious community and the *sultan*. Secondly, the secular ideal of the Turkish Republic and the revolutionary measures taken for the realization of this ideal, were perceived intrinsically in contradiction to the notion of a society based on or organized as a collection of religious communities.

The third major reason underlying the restrictions of religious association may be found in the national security interest of the Turkish Republic in decreasing the power of religious communities—both Muslim and non-Muslim—in state affairs. Since the secular Republic strove to eliminate the role and influence of religion, in particular Islam, in state affairs it was crucial to drive them out of the state sphere. Oran argues that the clearance of *vakıf* institutions and their transfer to the various ministries of the state sought to diminish the economic power of Muslim *vakıfs*.[18] As far as non-Muslim communities were concerned, it was equally crucial to eliminate their influence in state affairs through other states. The memories of interference of foreign powers in the Ottoman affairs and the role attributed to the cooperation of foreign powers and non-Muslim minorities, in particular the Greek and Armenian minorities, in the decline and occupation of the Empire were still vivid and the founders of the Republic were determined to prevent this from happening again.[19] Thus, it is not surprising that legal personality formula for belief communities was not created and the weakening of associative abilities of all belief communities was actively sought.

Bearing in mind the above, it is possible to understand the reasons for the lack of legal entity status to belief communities, *per se*. As noted in the Venice Commission opinion, "to the outside legal observer, there is nothing in the constitutional provisions that would explicitly prohibit a legislative reform providing legal personality to religious communities".[20] Yet, it is the context which has been briefly described above that determines the interpretation of the constitutional and other provisions. Turkish particularism in the interpretation of the principle of secularism and the determining factor of national security/public order interests have deemed necessary a strict control over religious activity and restriction of autonomy of belief communities.

18 Oran, B. (2004) *Türkiye'de Azınlıklar: Kavramlar, Lozan, İç Mevzuat, İçtihat, Uygulama* [Minorities in Turkey: Concepts, Lausanne, Domestic Law, Case-Law, Practice], Istanbul: İletişim, p. 100.

19 Meray, S. (translator) (2001) Lozan Barış Konferansı/Tutanaklar: Belgeler [Lausanne Peace Conference/Records: Documents], Istanbul: Yapı Kredi Publications.

20 The Council of Europe Venice Commission, *supra* note 15, para. 33.

6.3 Current Practice on Legal Personality of Belief Communities

A look at the issue of legal personality of belief communities in modern Turkey reveals an apparent lack of adequate legislative provisions and vagueness as a result of inconsistent and incoherent case law and administrative practice. The lack of legislation pertaining to legal personality of belief communities rules out the possibility of acquiring legal personality as a religious or belief community. Yet, case law and administrative practice demonstrate a lack of clarity in respect to whether some belief communities, as such, or in some cases their leadership, e.g. Patriarchates or Chief Rabbinate, have legal entity status—that which they may have acquired before the Republic—and if so, what is the nature of such legal capacity?

Legal personality is an important issue for all belief communities in Turkey, including Muslims and non-Muslims. Muslim communities, *per se*, do not own mosques in Turkey. Mosques are administered by the Diyanet İşleri Başkanlığı (Presidency of Religious Affairs, the Diyanet hereafter) but their ownership varies, such as private persons, associations, foundations, General Directorate of Foundations, village corporate entities, and municipalities. The Diyanet provides religious public services for Muslims based on the *Hanefi* school, thus it may be argued that these public services make it unnecessary for some Muslim belief communities to seek to organize themselves in a way that non-Muslim communities strive to do.[21] However, it is important to bear in mind that regardless of the services provided by the Diyanet, there are Muslims from various Islamic traditions, including the Hanefi school, who wish to manifest their religion or belief in community with others, for example by establishing a mosque or a *cem* house.[22]

Case law and administrative practice demonstrate, albeit constantly in an unclear and incomplete manner, the existence of a certain form of legal personality for some non-Muslim belief communities that have existed in the Turkish geography before the establishment of the Republic. The cases below present legal disputes arising from a lack of adequate legislation pertaining to the structure of various religious formations which manifest themselves in issues related to the right to property in relation to places of worship or properties that provide revenues for the management of their internal affairs. These cases also serve as illuminating examples of how legal personality is directly affecting the right to manifest religion or belief in community with others and the right to property.

The lack of clarity on the matter of legal personality of belief communities or their leadership is apparent in legal and administrative practices. An administrative notification[23] on property serves as an example: "it is observed that the status of legal personality of the owner of the non-moveable, the Chief Rabbinate of

21 For more on the Diyanet see Chapter 5.

22 Kaya, A. and Ö. Genç (2011) *Türkiye'de İnanç Grupları: Sorunlara ve Taleplere Yönelik Yeni bir Çerçeve* [Belief Groups in Turkey: A New Framework for Problems and Demands], Istanbul: Alevi Vakıfları Federasyonu.

23 Given by the General Directorate of Land Titles and Cadastral Records.

Istanbul and its subjects [*tevabii*], is unclear and that it is not a *vakıf*".[24] For the authorities it is obvious that the Chief Rabbinate and its subjects, the Jewish community, are not a *vakıf* or an association. But it is not possible to categorize them legally because there is not a suitable legal category. Interestingly, while the communication refers to the lack of clarity on the legal entity status of the Rabbinate it refers to it as the *owner*. It is also noteworthy that the communication refers to the "Rabbinate of Istanbul and its subjects" or those who are bound to it, as the owner, thus implying that the whole Jewish community under and through the Chief Rabbi exercise the right to property.

The decisions in court cases brought by governmental bodies against the Chief Rabbinate imply the recognition of a certain legal and representative capacity of the Chief Rabbinate and are significant for the facilitative *factual* approach they adopt.[25] Some court decisions recognize the legal entity status of the Office of the Chief Rabbi. A first instance court referred to the existence of the Rabbinate as a matter of *fact* and observed that, "its existence cannot be denied".[26] Another court decision concerned the rejection of a claim by the Treasury and the registration of a land title in the name of the Edirne Jewish Community.[27] The decision recognized the representative status of the Turkish Rabbinate—albeit without reference to any particular Regulation or Lausanne Treaty—by saying: "the Jewish community is one of the known communities in Turkey and is represented by the Rabbinate of Turkey. The Turkish Jewish communities are subject to the Rabbinate of Turkey".[28]

In some cases the pre-Republic legal instruments have served as a basis of recognition of legal personality. The Court of Appeals reasoned thus:

> It has been established by the testimonies of the witnesses that the *synagogue* which is not registered in the land register, is under the *de facto* possession of [*zilliyet*, as distinct from lawful ownership] the Jewish Community. According to the Interim Law on the Possession of Non-Movables by Legal Persons, *communities whose existence is recognized by the state* are permitted to possess non-movables within villages and provinces. The Rabbinate was established through the Regulation of Rabbinate and this Regulation was approved and adopted on 23 *Şevval* 1281 [19 March 1865] and thus the community title of the plaintiff is recognized. Therefore the appeal objection is not justified.[29]

24 Communication of the General Directorate of Land Registry and Cadastral Records, No. 698, 4 June 1998.
25 Edirne Provincial Administration sued the Rabbinate of Turkey for a cancellation of a land title.
26 Edirne 2nd Peace Court E2000/277, K2002/304, 30 May 2002.
27 Edirne 1st Peace Court E1998/469, K1998/715, 22 December 1998. The decision became final by the approval of the Court of Appeals, E2002/4282, K2002/5693, 17 December 2002. The title of the land was obtained by the said community. Reyna and Zonana, *supra* note 5, p. 233.
28 Ibid.
29 Reyna and Zonana, *supra* note 5, pp. 232–233. Emphasis added.

It has been argued that the approach taken by the Court of Appeals, that is to view the Rabbinate as a position rather than a person and recognize its legal capacity to represent the Jewish community, would be a fair solution.[30] While this proposal may solve certain problems of the Jewish community concerning legal recognition of the Rabbinate as a representative body that can act on behalf of the Jewish community, it falls short of providing a general solution to the problem of legal status of belief communities. This is because, first, there is no common agreement on the binding nature of the Ottoman Regulations pertaining to the Rabbinate and Patriarchates. Also, if the sole justification of the legal entity status of an "office" representing a belief community is based on the recognition of the belief community in an Ottoman Regulation or the recognition derived from the Lausanne Treaty, again this would have limited application. This would not be applicable to communities for whom these legal sources are not applicable. Pre-Republic or Lausanne recognition would not be applicable to non-Muslim communities that did not exist before the Republic, or that were not recognized by way of a Regulation or *millet* system, such as Muslim and Bahai communities. Lausanne justification would exclude non-Muslim communities that are not recognized as protected under the Lausanne Treaty even though they are non-Muslim.[31] Such a formula might also have the disadvantage of forcing belief communities to emulate the Jewish community's organizational structure and unite under one leadership.

A relatively recent judgment by the Court of Appeals directly addressed the question of whether the Rabbinate has legal personality and capacity to open a court case.[32] The case concerned the request of the Jewish Community to have the *synagogue*, which they had been using for centuries, registered in the land registry in the name of the Jewish community. The State Treasury argued that the Jewish community did not have legal personality and requested the rejection of the case.[33] The court, on the one hand, contended that the community did not have legal personality and that it was not a community *vakıf* (*cemaat vakfı*).[34] On

30 Reyna and Zonana, *supra* note 5, p. 233.

31 On the narrow interpretation of the Lausanne Treaty see Chapter 5.

32 Court of Appeals 8th Chamber, E/2008/3743, K/2009/773, 12 February 2009. Despite positive recognition of capacity to own and open a court case, the said synagogue could not be registered in the name of the Jewish community. The synagogue building was a 1st group cultural heritage property; according to Article 11 of the Law on the Protection of Cultural and Natural Heritage No. 2863 (Changed by Law No. 5663 Article 1) 1st group cultural heritage property may not be acquired through possession. Therefore if the building were not in this category the Jewish community could have acquired the building through its possession of the building over many years, even though the title on the deed was blank. 1st group cultural heritage property may not be acquired through possession. If the building were not in this category the Jewish community could have acquired the building through its possession of the building over many years, even though the title on the deed was blank. This provision must be re-evaluated in light of its implications for the right to freedom of religion or belief, in particular to owning places of worship.

33 Ibid.

34 "Cemaat vakfı" meaning community foundation is a *sui generis* foundation type that only certain non-Muslim minorities have a right to administer. This is a new category of foundations that existed under the Ottoman Empire and has been transferred to the

the other hand, it was observed that since the capacity to acquire property of the applicant community was recognized through the 1912 temporary Law on the Possession of Non-Movables by Legal Persons,[35] and the Regulation of the Rabbinate, and by the will of the Sultan, there was no question that the applicant community had competence to acquire non-movables and thus has active legal capacity to open a court case.[36] The Court of Appeals explicitly recognized the capacity to acquire property and open a court case and thus in effect recognized that the Rabbinate possessed a number of key elements of a legal entity status. This, however, does not indicate that the Rabbinate or the community has a defined legal personality that is sufficiently clear to both the community itself and state authorities.

In contrast, certain decisions pertaining to the Greek Orthodox Patriarchate present a harsh rejection of any representative status or legal capacity. In 1964, the print house in the Patriarchate was closed on grounds that it violated the Lausanne Treaty; the explanation given to the Patriarchate was that "only legal institutions and legal persons can own publishing houses".[37] In a court case concerning a dispute between the Ecumenical Patriarch of the Greek Orthodox Church and a priest of the Bulgarian Church, the Patriarch had to appear before the court as a private person even though an action of the Patriarchate was the subject of the case. The case concerned the removal of the priest of the Bulgarian Church by the Patriarchate for theological reasons.[38] The Court of Appeals rejected the ecclesiastical authority of the Patriarch over the Bulgarian Church and found that the disciplinary measures exceeded the authority of the Patriarch which was restricted to attending to the religious affairs of Turkish citizens of Greek origin and not Bulgarian or other.[39] In this case the court explicitly rejected the argument that the Patriarchate is an entity and relied on the Lausanne *travaux préparatoires* to conclude that the Patriarchate is a "religious institution" that has lost all its privileges that it enjoyed in the Ottoman Empire.[40] Accordingly, this religious institution had to be considered in light of the Lausanne Treaty Articles 35–45.[41] Yet, the court failed to draw from Lausanne Article 40, which protects associative rights of non-Muslims in Turkey, that the Patriarchate is protected as a religious institution. In contrast to the cases concerning the Jewish Rabbinate that drew from the recognition in the Ottoman Empire, the Court of Appeals did not take into account any status given to the Patriarchate during the Ottoman period—not even mentioning the Regulation Pertaining to the Greek

modern law system as community foundations following the establishment of the Republic.

35 *Supra* note 11.

36 *Supra* note 32.

37 Macar, E. (2003) *Cumhuriyet Döneminde İstanbul Rum Patrikhanesi* [Istanbul Greek Patriarchate in the Republic], İstanbul: İletişim, p. 202.

38 Court of Appeals 4th Chamber, E/2005/10694, K/2007/5603. The priest was not naming the Patriarch in his prayers although he was supposed to in the liturgy used in church.

39 Ibid.

40 Ibid.

41 Ibid.

Patriarchate.[42] Therefore, the differential treatment of the Chief Rabbinate and the Ecumenical Patriarchate by the judiciary regarding recognition of belief communities and their leadership organizations, demonstrates vagueness of the rules that result in unforeseeable law and discriminatory application by the judiciary.

The case of a Latin Catholic order also demonstrates the exiting problems clearly. A large number of properties of the Latin Catholic Church across Turkey have been seized by the state and since these orders do not have legal personality of any kind—they cannot establish community foundations[43]—property cannot be registered in the name of orders or churches.[44] For example, the Dominican Order have been using their church building and adjacent property since the 15th century.[45] The Dominican Priests owned their monastery building, but a *vakıf*, not their own, owned the land.[46] The property documents of their various properties show the title either blank or say "Dominican Priests".[47] In a decision concerning a dispute over the annulment of the title, the Istanbul Cadastral Court saw no legal provision or reason for the annulment of the title of property that has the name "Dominican Priests" in the owner section.[48] This decision was based on the acceptance of the title by the Ottoman *Devlet Şura* (High Court of Administration) and the Ottoman *Irade-i Seniye* (Financial Audit Committee).[49] The court based its decision on the recognition of the title by the Ottoman state.

While the Cadastral Court decision described above is a positive and significant decision, the Dominican Priests experience great difficulty in "convincing" other public authorities of their legal status.[50] Routine procedures, which should be conducted easily, are made burdensome as a result of the non-recognition of the, court recognized, legal personality of "Dominican Priests". For example, the municipality officials do not recognize this legal entity status and ask the question,

42 A Regulation pertaining to the Greek Patriarchate was adopted in 1862 under the Ottoman Empire. For the text of this Regulation see Bebiroğlu, M. (2008) *Osmanlı Devletinde Gayrimüslim Nizamnameleri* [Regulations of non-Muslim Communities under the Ottoman State] Istanbul: Adam, p. 83.

43 They cannot establish community foundations because they did not have *vakıfs* in the Ottoman era and are not subject to protection under the Lausanne Treaty which enables the Armenian Apostolic, Jewish and Greek Orthodox communities to have community foundations.

44 The Head of the Bishops Conference in Turkey made a statement saying that the acquisition of legal personality is the most important problem for Latin Catholics in Turkey when he met with the Sub-Commission of the Constitutional Reconciliation Commission. See *Milliyet Daily* "Yeni Anayasa Çalışmaları Devam Ediyor" [Work on the New Constitution Goes on], 16 April 2012.

45 Interview with Fr. Claudio Monge, Dominican Priest, 9 June 2011, Galata, Istanbul. The order has existed in Turkish geography since the 13th century.

46 Ibid. The reason for this is that under the Ottoman Empire the land and the building upon it were separately owned. Land was owned by God—in practice by the state and *vakıf* institutions.

47 *Supra* note 45.

48 Istanbul Cadastral Court, E944:74, K944:66, 1974.

49 Ibid.

50 *Supra* note 45, interview with Claudio Monge.

"Who are the Dominican Priests?".[51] Interestingly, the same authorities recognize the "Dominican Priests" when they claim taxes: "We exist when we need to pay, but we do not exist when we want to exercise our rights", observes Fr. Claudio Monge.[52]

As a result of the vagueness that results from the absence of a well-defined legal basis, the recognition of their legal status is tied closely to the attitude of the governing party towards their community.[53] Hence the Dominican Priests are confronted with a situation where they will have to engage in a legal battle for each administrative procedure in order to prove their legal entity status. Another alternative might be to break away from the "weak" legal entity status they seem to have recognized through case law and try to fit into a legal status that may be recognized by all, such as a foundation or association, or claim their ties with the Italian Dominican Priests and assert a foreign legal entity status. The association or foundation status will not fit their nature and needs, as will be discussed later, yet, the foreign legal entity status, which Turkey might have to recognize due to bilateral agreements with Italy, may be a solution. As a result of these complexities, the Dominican priests are required to pay property tax even though their building is a church, thus a worship place, normally qualifying for exemption from property tax.[54]

In the case above, the legal basis for the recognition of certain key elements of legal personality resulted from, first, taking a factual approach, and secondly, relying on pre-Republic instruments. The factual approach, which considers the actual facts about the belief community and its connection to property and its use of places of worship, appears to be the one that has the potential of solving relevant legal questions in the absence of an appropriate and adequate legal framework of reference. It has the added advantage of being facilitative. The disadvantage of the factual approach is its dependency on the adjudicating judge and its inadequacy to afford a solution for daily business of belief communities where legal personality is a requisite.

The second approach involves relying on legal instruments adopted in the Ottoman Empire that predate the Turkish Republic. This requires the assumption that these instruments are still in force even though they may not be acknowledged, as such, by public authorities. Yet, the question remains whether all provisions of these instruments are still valid, or only those that seem compatible with current legislation. For instance, the Rabbinate Regulation sets forth the formation of a temporal council, dealing with issues such as education and care of elderly community members, assuming the responsibility of running the community's worldly

51 Ibid.

52 Ibid.

53 The lack of clarity and predictability creates vulnerability according to Fr. Cladio Monge. *Supra* note 45.

54 The practice has been inconsistent also in terms of claiming property tax. There were times when they were exempted and times when they were required to pay property tax. *Supra* note 45.

affairs.[55] Yet, these communities had to abolish their temporal assemblies,[56] even though under the Regulation this was a right.

The judgments concerning non-Muslim religious communities demonstrate the fact that despite a lack of clear and adequate legal framework, in some cases, there is judicial recognition of certain legal personality for certain belief communities and certain religious leadership. This judicial recognition seems to be based on, on the one hand, Ottoman laws, regulations and documents *when* the judiciary chooses to rely on them. On the other hand, the cases where the judiciary relied on the *de facto* existence and possession and use of the belief communities go toward embracing a right to legal personality as a matter of *fact*. Contrasting decisions concerning the Jewish and Greek Orthodox communities are difficult to reconcile with the principle of equality and prohibition of non-discrimination resulting from ambiguity of law that provides public authorities with unfettered discretion. This situation stands in strong contrast to grounding the protection of freedom of religion or belief in the rule of law, instead of making it subject to state interests in a constantly changing political climate, in particular international political developments. Inconsistencies concerning the recognition of legal personality by various public authorities appear to be common. Vagueness and inconsistencies in practice create unpredictability about the law and insecurity and vulnerability for belief communities in the exercise of their rights. A significant consequence of non-recognition of legal personality is that religious or belief communities, then, are not entitled to pursue judicial protection of their assets and activities. Finally, it is striking that the right to freedom of religion or belief is not taken into account in any of these cases; instead, the issues are treated exclusively within the sphere of the right to property.

The lack of an adequate form of legal personality stands in contrast to empowered and enabled belief groups that can enjoy the collective dimension of freedom of religion or belief, including the right to association, to own property and to seek judicial protection for these.

Now, let us consider the *vakıf* (foundations) and assess their adequacy as a legal entity formula.

6.4 *Vakıf* (Foundation) Institutions

Vakıf institutions are one of the available forms of legal entity status in Turkey. There are two questions that need to be answered in order to assess their adequacy for the exercise of the collective dimension of the right to freedom of religion or belief. The first question relates to their availability to belief communities: Can belief communities establish *vakıf* institutions? The second, and equally important, question is whether *vakıf* institutions create a suitable legal entity status for belief communities in the exercise of the collective dimension of the right to freedom of

55 Bebiroğlu, *supra* note 42, p. 169.

56 Bali, R. (2004) *Devletin Yahudileri ve "Öteki Yahudiler"* [State's Jews and "Other Jews"], Istanbul: İletişim, p. 92.

religion or belief. Considering that volumes may be written on *vakıfs*, it is necessary to circumscribe the focus of this part. Here, I will try to explain the legal nature of *vakıf* institutions—in the Ottoman era—with a view to understanding their function and limits in relation to providing legal entity status in the context of religious activity. The Ottoman practice on *vakıfs* is important today because firstly, the *vakıfs* belonging to non-Muslims (community foundations)[57] were established in the Ottoman era and secondly, many facilities designated for Muslim religious activity were created and supported through the Ottoman *vakıf* institutions. The description of changes pertaining to *vakıfs* that took place in the modern Republic era will not be exhaustive; however, they will focus on key legal changes and actions that had significant impact on the exercise of the collective dimension of freedom of religion or belief. In this view, attention will be given to the clearance of Muslim *vakıf* institutions, the unique position of community foundations (*cemaat vakfı*) and the legal and administrative practice on new *vakıfs*. Current legal frameworks on the *vakıf*, inherent legal restrictions on the establishment of *vakıfs* and practice as well as the suitability of *vakıf* institutions for belief communities will be discussed.

6.4.1 The Origin and Rational of the Vakıf *Institutions*

Foundations have a long history in Turkish geography with a unique heritage and function throughout Ottoman history and a legacy in the Turkish Republic.[58] In the Islamic tradition the *vakıf*, property set aside for pious endowment, was dedicated to the cause of God and it became the property of God.[59] Thus the *vakıf* is a privately owned property endowed *permanently* for a charitable purpose and its revenue is spent for this purpose—many consider the *vakıf* as one of the greatest

57 Not all non-Muslims, these include Jewish, Armenian Orthodox, Armenian Protestant, some Syriac Foundations, Greek Orthodox foundations.

58 Whether the tradition of *vakıf* institutions can be based on any precepts in the Quran or the *Hadith* (words attributed to the Prophet Mohammed that are considered general rules) seems indeterminate. Hatemi concludes that it is not possible to find an explicit basis for *vakıf* institutions in the Quran; however, the concept of "*sadaka*" found in the Hadis has been a more specific basis for the later development of the institution. See Hatemi, H. (1969) *Önceki ve Bugünkü Türk Hukuku'nda Vakıf Kurma Muamelesi* [Establishment of Foundations in the Old and Contemporary Turkish Law], Istanbul: Istanbul University Publications, p. 37. Hatemi notes rightly that although the same term, *vakıf*, has been used throughout the ages there are differences and even conflicts associated with the term in different legal systems, cultures and times. Thus one has to always be mindful that what is called *vakıf* in a given time may have or may have had different characteristics in another time.

59 Lev, Y. (2005) *Charity, Endowments and Charitable Institutions in the Medieval Islam*, University Press of Florida, p. 53. Generally on foundations see Baer, G. (1997) "The Waqf as a Prop for the Social System (Sixteenth–Twentieth Centuries)", *Islamic Law and Society*, 4, pp. 264–297. Gerber, H. (1984) "The Waqf Institution in Early Ottoman Edirne", in G.R. Warburg and G.G. Gilbar (eds), *Islamic Studies in Islamic Society: Contributions in Memory of Gabriel Baer*, Haifa, Haifa University Press, pp. 29–47.

achievements of the Islamic civilization.[60] It has never been the rationale of the *vakıf* institution to provide a legal entity status for belief communities.

In the Ottoman period, until the period of *Tanzimat* (Reorganization), there was a lack of legal regulation on *vakıf* institutions.[61] Instead, the practice pertaining to *vakıf* institutions was left to the discretion of judges.[62] Some key components of *vakıf* institutions, however, may be discerned for a proper understanding of these institutions for the purposes of the study. Persons affiliated with every *millet* could establish *vakıf* institutions. According to Islamic law, the purpose of *vakıf* institutions had to be one that would be a means of fulfilling charity or worship, which was called the requirement of *kurbet*.[63] Both Muslims and non-Muslims could establish *vakıf* institutions to support Islamic institutions.[64]

The non-Muslim community foundations, even in the Ottoman era, maintained a *sui generis* nature. Since neither Muslims nor non-Muslims were allowed to establish *vakıf* institutions to support the building or repair of churches or synagogues, or to publish and distribute the New Testament or the Jewish Holy Book with the purpose of propagating non-Islamic belief,[65] the non-Muslim community *vakıfs* that exist today have all been established by Sultan's decree. They were not *vakıfs* in a strict sense since they were anonymous institutions that lacked a person that endowed property and a *vakıf* deed.[66] The reason for this was that the

60 Çizakça, M. (2000) *A History of Philanthropic Foundations*, Istanbul: Boğaziçi University Press, p. 1. According to Çizakça, the *vakıf* system has made numerous contributions to the public welfare, as well as having certain aspects that constitute challenges to its proper functioning. On the one hand, the *vakıf* institutions provided scores of services which a modern social state is expected to provide in areas such as health, education, culture, maintenance of worship places and cultural heritage sites, welfare, etc. On the other hand, it has been observed that the success of *vakıf* systems has been closely linked to the state under which they operated and that corruption of *vakıf* officials has been widespread throughout history.

61 Akgündüz, A. (1996) *Islam Hukukunda ve Osmanlı Tatbikatında Vakıf Müessesesi* [The Institution of Foundations in Islamic Law and Ottoman Practice], Istanbul: OSAV, p. 92. In the latter period of the Empire a draft code on *vakıf* institutions was formulated, p. 94

62 Judges were to follow the doctrine of jurists whom they preferred but they would be required to decide in a way that would benefit the *vakıf* institution. Ibid., p. 167.

63 Ibid., p. 234. There have been exceptions in practice. The development of *vakıf* institutions with the purpose of supporting one's children surely did not comply with the *kurbet* purpose. Nevertheless, these kind of *vakıf* institutions existed until they were abolished in the Republican period.

64 The state also established *vakıf* institutions (*irşad vakıfları*) for the provision of general public services permanently. Akgündüz, *supra* note 61, pp. 525–561.

65 Kurban, D. and K. Hatemi (2009) *Bir 'Yabancı'laştırma Hikayesi: Türkiye'de Gayrimüslim Cemaatlerin Vakıf ve Taşınmaz Mülkiyet Sorunu* [A Story of Alienation: The Problem of non-Muslim Minorities' Problems Pertaining to Foundations and Unmoveable Property], Istanbul: TESEV, p. 14.

66 Bakar, D. (2002) "Uygulamadan Ayrımcılık Örnekleri" [Practical Examples of Discrimination], in *Ulusal, Ulusalüstü ve Uluslararası Hukukta Azınlık Hakları* [Minority Rights under National, Supra-National and International Law], Istanbul, Istanbul Bar Association Publications, p. 263. Also note that in the Eşhas-ı Hükmiyenin Emvali Gayrimenkuleye Tasarruflarına Mahsus Kanunu Muvakkat [Temporary Law on the

propagation of a religion other than Islam could not be justified under Islamic law, thus this was not compatible with the *kurbet* requirement.[67] The exceptions to this rule would be special non-Muslim *vakıf* institutions established with a Sultan *ferman* (decree).[68]

It is important to note that the state always maintained a tight control over *vakıf* institutions, yet the control was to be carried out by courts.[69] The size of *vakıf* property, substantial amounts of land that had been endowed for charitable purposes, made tight supervision necessary.[70] Alleged irregularities in the use of their revenues have led to increased state supervision. The autonomous *vakıf* institutions were centralized through the establishment of a Ministry of *Vakıfs* (*Evkaf*), thus paving the way for state supervision and interference in the *vakıf* affairs.[71] The move was justified on the grounds that the *vakıf* revenues were let to the discretion of dubious trustees.[72] The rationale of state "interest" in *vakıf* affairs has been based also on the protection of the (*vakıf*) endowment; supervision was needed to ensure that the initial donor's endowment would be duly administered.

It is important to note that the *vakıf* institutions of the Ottoman period were not institutional solutions for the collective exercise of the right to freedom of religion, yet they were a crucial means of maintaining community life through, *inter alia*, educational, charity and health services provided for the benefit of a belief community. The purpose of *vakıfs* was not to create legal personality for religious communities, nor were they primarily a kind of religious organization—even though they

Possession of Non-Movables by Legal Persons], the term used for these non-Muslim institutions is "Ottoman Charity Institutions" (*Osmanlı Müessesat-ı Hayriyesi*), not *vakıf*. In an index book titled *Evkaf-ı Hristiyan* [Christian Foundations] of the General Directorate of Foundations only 31 non-Muslim *vakıf* institutions are recorded according to Öztürk: Öztürk, N. (2003), *Azınlık Vakıfları* [Minority Foundations], Istanbul: Altınküre, pp. 120–123.

67 Hatemi, H. (2004) "Cemaat Vakıfları Konusunda Düşünceler" [Thoughts About Community Foundations], in *Özsunay Armağanı*, Istanbul: Istanbul University Press, p. 804.

68 According to Öztürk vakıf establishments that are founded without permission or a license were extraordinary acts influenced by national or foreign political developments. Öztürk, *supra* note 66, p. 118.

69 Akgündüz, *supra* note 61, p. 167. Accordingly, the approval of the *vakıf* deed by the courts guaranteed immunity for the *vakıf* property unless it was used for purposes contrary to the deed. Nevertheless, there were exceptions to this rule, for example, the property would lose immunity if it were beyond repair, or the *vakıf* institution would be dissolved by a judge if the property no longer provided any benefit.

70 Çizakça, *supra* note 60, p. 79.

71 Barnes, R.J. (1987) *An Introduction to Religious Foundations in the Ottoman Empire*, Leiden: Brill, pp. 68–73.

72 Çizakça, *supra* note 60, p. 82. However, the centralization process had its own problems, too: the cost involved and not calculated when the original endowment was made, interference in *vakıf* affairs and the dubious practices of the new *vakıf* bureaucrats. Consequently, the *vakıf* were left at the hands of the central authority. Çizakçı concludes that the harm caused by an individual trustee is minimal compared to what a corrupt high level official can do to the entire centralized system. Çizakça, pp. 81–85.

may be established for religious purposes. The requirement of the *kurbet* purpose[73] constituted a serious challenge before equality because it allowed all religious communities to engage in charitable actions; however, it permitted only Muslim communities to establish and maintain worship places or support activities that would propagate their religion. Legally speaking, non-Muslim belief communities could not establish *vakıf* institutions to support the building of their worship places.[74] Also, both Muslim and non-Muslim *vakıfs* could not acquire new property.[75] The increasing regulation of and supervision over *vakıfs* had serious implications for the autonomy of belief communities. On the other hand, notwithstanding their limitations, their function as subsidiary institutions for the support of a limited range of activities of belief communities has been of vital importance for the sustainability of the latter.

6.4.2 Legal Developments Pertaining to Vakıf *Institutions in the Turkish Republic*

The developments regarding *vakıfs* throughout the Republic era are important because of the impact they had on the associative rights of members of belief communities, including Muslims and non-Muslims. These significantly deprived these communities of sources that had been used for the benefit of their members and communities, in particular for the maintenance and use of their worship places, charitable organizations, schools etc. The Turkish Republic continued the process of regulation and supervision of the *vakıf* system that was started by the Ottoman state administration. It is not possible to provide a thorough description and analysis of all legal and administrative developments on *vakıfs* spreading over nearly a century in this chapter.[76] In this section I will examine key developments that continue to impact religious communities today: Muslim foundations that were established before the 1926 Civil Code, non-Muslim community foundations and new foundations.

Regardless of their aim,[77] measures aimed at clearance of pre-Republic *vakıfs* had the effect of depriving Muslim *vakıfs* endowed with the support of Muslim religious, educational and charitable institutions and activities and therefore had significant impact on freedom of religion or belief. These were eliminated and

73 Kurban and Hatemi, *supra* note 65.
74 This was overcome by the special *ferman* of the Sultan. See Bakar, *supra* note 66.
75 Kurban and Hatemi, *supra* note 65, p. 10, quoting Murat Bebiroğlu's article on "Cemaat Vakıfları" [Community Foundations].
76 For a detailed overview of *vakıfs* before and after the 1926 Turkish Civil Code see İşeri, A. (1964) "Vakıflar" [Foundations] in *Ankara Üniversitesi Hukuk Fakültesi Dergisi*, Volume 21, No. 1–4, pp. 199–250.
77 Some argue that the clearance of pre-Republic *vakıfs* was aimed at depriving Muslim communities of their economic power. Others, on the other hand, argue that it was the government's duty to take over *vakıfs* that were to a great extent governed poorly and failed to fulfill their purposes, see İşeri, *supra* note 76, p. 242. Here I will not focus on this debate, rather on the effects on Muslim communities' associative abilities as well as their resources.

transferred to the state, thus drastically depriving many Muslim communities of resources and capacity utilized for the realization of religious activity and support and sustenance of their community.[78] For example, the religiously based schools, *medrese* and related *vakıf* and property were transferred to the Ministry of Education.[79] Some of the other actions aimed at the clearance of *vakıf* institutions include, *inter alia*, the abolition of financial autonomy of *vakıfs* through the declaration of collection of *vakıf* revenues by the Ministry of Finance; the establishment of a Committee for the Abolishment of the *vakıf*; and finally the abolishment of all cash *vakıfs* and the establishment of the Bank of Avakıf (*Vakıflar Bankası*) with the confiscated capital.[80] It has been argued that the interest in the clearance of *vakıfs* was based on a determination to control Islamic brotherhoods that were financed by *vakıfs*.[81] Religious buildings with historical or architectural significance that had been owned by foundations were registered in the name of public entities.[82] Foundations established by Muslims with religious intent were susceptible to changes in political climate. For example, the closure of *tekke* (dervish lodges) and *zaviye*[83] led to the inability to use these buildings for their purposes; hence the "inability to fulfill their purpose" allowed the transfer of these assets to the Ministry of Education and City Private Administration.[84]

As far as non-Muslims were concerned, *community foundations*, as they are called today, are non-Muslim minority institutions that were established by the Ottoman Sultan decrees and that have a *sui generis* legal status in the Turkish Republic.[85] The religious basis of community *vakıf* was, on the one hand, considered incompatible with the secular nature of the Republic, yet, on the other hand, obligations arising from the Lausanne Treaty forced the Republic to maintain, albeit imperfectly, the community foundations as an exceptional institution within the general *vakıf* framework. The challenge was to create a legal framework that could ensure the circumstances for the compatible co-existence of the autonomous community *vakıf* regime within the modern legal regime. A solution to this fundamental problem is, yet, to be reached. Their *sui generis* nature that

78 Hatemi, *supra* note 4.
79 Öztürk, *supra* note 66, pp. 88 89.
80 Ibid., pp. 45–48 and Çizakça, *supra* note 60, pp. 88–89.
81 Ibid., p. 86.
82 These were transferred to the General Directorate of Foundations in 1957 under a special law, Aslında Vakıf Olan Tarihi ve Mimari Kıymeti Haiz Eski Eserlerin Vakıflar Umum Müdürlüğüne Devrine Dair Kanun [Law on the Transfer of Works that Have Historical and Architectural Value that are Actually Vakıfs to the General Directorate of Foundations], No. 7044, 10 September 1957.
83 Tekke ve Zaviyelerle Türbelerin Seddine ve Türbedarlıklar ile Bir Takım Unvanların Men ve İlgasına Dair Kanun [Law on the Closure of Dervish Lodges, Hospices and Shrines and on Abolition and Prohibition of the Use of Certain Titles], No. 677, 13 December 1925.
84 İşeri, *supra* note 76, p. 245.
85 Under Article 40 of the Lausanne Peace Treaty, Turkey is under the obligation to protect the rights to establish, manage and control charity institutions, religious social institutions, schools, teaching and education institutions and use their own language in these freely, and freely conduct religious worship services.

does not include all components of *vakıfs* may explain the difficulties these institutions were subjected to when they found themselves in a position where they were obliged to fit the *vakıf* framework in the modern Republic.

Community foundations own the buildings and properties of, for example, the Greek Orthodox Church, the Armenian Church and the Jewish Rabbinate and are run by independent *vakıf* managers.[86] In accordance with the Ottoman Regulations, spiritual and temporal assemblies would be elected in order to administer the affairs of these communities and the *vakıfs* dedicated to their benefit.[87] These institutions—which are called *vakıf*—are atypical *vakıfs* because they did not have any person who endowed certain estate for a certain purpose. Thus their anonymous quality sets them apart from regular foundations even today, for example they do not have any founding deeds.[88] Their atypical status has also provided the basis for arbitrary administrative and judicial decisions.

Key features of legal and administrative action or inaction pertaining to community foundations are considered below under four headings; new legal status for community foundations, extensive powers of the Directorate General of Foundations (Vakıflar Genel Müdürülüğü—VGM) and restrictive and discriminatory administrative and judicial practice which fed off of each other leading to the deterioration of the capacities of community foundations. The reader should bear in mind that the legal entity of *vakıf*, as opposed to a direct ownership of property by a belief community (if they were to have a legal entity status of their own) creates vulnerability of religious communities to interferences by the state.

It will be seen that, often, legal, and regulations of other kinds, and administrative practice impacting community foundations have been primarily viewed and constructed with national security perceptions. These have been highly prone to changes in the political climate, in particular international politics. For example, during the period of transition from a single-party system to a pluralist democracy in the 1950s some developments in favor of the *vakıf* system took place.[89]

86 Non-Muslim religious communities more recently established in Turkey (Protestant churches, Jehovah's Witnesses, and others) do not have any community *vakıf* in this status. Members of these communities may, under certain circumstances, establish new foundations, yet these would not have the community foundation status.

87 These regulations would require various commissions to be established, which in turn would manage institutions that were owned by these minorities, e.g. education commission, monastery commission, law commission etc. Until the end of the Ottoman Empire charity institutions belonging to the *millet* were administered and audited by various commissions established by temporal and spiritual assemblies. Bakar, *supra* note 66, p. 265.

88 Ibid., p. 263.

89 The adoption of Law No. 903 in 1967 aimed to modernize the *vakıf* system. Some key provisions opened the way for breathing life into the heritage of the Ottoman *vakıf* system, such as the possibility for persons, associations and companies to establish *vakıf* institutions, the possibility for *vakıf* institutions to establish companies, a simpler process to establish *vakıf*, the introduction of possibile tax exemptions. Law No. 903 (Türk Kanunu Medenisinin Birinci Kitabının İkinci Babı Üçüncü Faslının Değiştirilmesi, Bu Kanuna Bazı Madde ve Fıkralar Eklenmesi, Bazı Vakıfların Vergi Muafiyetinden Faydalandırılması Hakkında Kanun) was adopted on 13 July 1967,

Community foundations acquired property through purchasing, donations or inheritance.[90] On the other hand, a change in the international political climate, namely the Cyprus crises between Turkey and Greece, changed the practice for Turkey's non-Muslim minorities. In this context, Kurban and Hatemi argue that Turkey has used the Greek minority in Turkey in order to gain an advantage over Greece.[91]

(a) New Legal Status

When provisions on new foundations were made in the 1926 Civil Code, regulations concerning *vakıfs* that were established before the adoption of the Civil Code were postponed to a later date with a view to draft a special law on foundations.[92] The special law on foundations had significant implications for both old (pre-1926) and new foundations. The Law on Foundations adopted in 1935 standardized the status of *vakıfs* established before the 1926 Civil Code.[93] The community *vakıfs* were categorized as *mülhak vakıf* (*vakıfs* that have been added later) thus gaining a new legal status. *Mülhak vakıfs* were administered by their own governing bodies however under the *supervision* and control of the VGM.[94] Hence this new status opened the way for interference, and in numerous cases the seizure of *vakıf* management, by the VGM. This new legal entity status, under the legal representation of the VGM, resulted in a limited or restricted legal personality.[95]

(b) The Extensive Powers of the VGM and Restrictive Administrative Practice

The VGM replaced the Ottoman ministry that administered the *vakıfs* (*Şer'iyye ve Evkaf Vekaleti*) taking the name General Directorate of Foundations in 1924 as the supervisory institution over all foundations.[96] The extensive powers—beyond inspection—conferred to this institution compromised the autonomous nature of *vakıf* administrations. As far as community foundations were concerned, it created conditions that were in stark contrast to the rights protecting the autonomous

R.G. No. 12655, 24 July 1967. For an account of the process leading up to the adoption of this law and the implications of changes for financial wellbeing of *vakıf* institutions see Çizakça, *supra* note 60, pp. 91–107. The new term "tesis" (establishment) in the Turkish Civil Code was replaced with the term "vakıf" under Article 3 of Law No. 903.

90 Kurban and Hatemi, *supra* note 65.

91 Ibid.

92 Article 88(2).

93 Vakıflar Kanunu [Law on Foundations] No. 2762, 5 June 1935, R.G. No. 3027, 13 June 1935.

94 Öztürk, *supra* note 66, p. 45.

95 Kurban and Hatemi, *supra* note 65, p. 13.

96 Law No. 429 on Şer'iye ve Evkaf ve Erkanı harbiye-i Umumiye Vekaletlerinin İlgasına Dair Kanun [The Abolishment of the Ministry on Sharia and Foundations], 3 March 1924.

administration of non-Muslim minority institutions under Article 40 of the Lausanne Treaty. In addition, the restrictive regulations and practices directed to the community *vakıfs* may be considered as efforts to cut the life source of these institutions in order to cause them to die out slowly—somewhat parallel to the diminishing non-Muslim population.[97] The lack of a Regulation specifying the application of the Law on Foundations has been identified as a key factor in the lack of clarity and predictability of the Law and leading to conditions that were conducive for discretionary decisions of administrative bodies, in particular the VGM.[98]

The VGM's capacity to take over management and properties of community foundations has been gradually increased. In cases where it has not been possible to appoint managers or establish a governing body for ten years these *vakıfs* are administered and represented by the VGM by a court decision.[99] Similarly, *vakıfs* that were not able to fulfill their charitable purpose were seized by the VGM and turned into *mazbut vakıf*.[100] This practice gave the *mülhak vakıf* a new status called *mazbut vakıf* (seized *vakıfs*).[101] Seized *vakıfs* were permanently represented and administered directly by the VGM, and the management and seizure of property would be permanent.[102] The diminishing non-Muslim population in Anatolia meant that many *vakıfs* and their properties were seized by the VGM.[103]

The enormous loss of property of the community *vakıfs*, and non-Muslim communities benefiting from them, caused by the administrative and legal practice related to the 1936 Declaration needs to be highlighted. The use of this Declaration is demonstrative of the administrative and judicial cooperation guided by political climate/will to diminish the capacity of non-Muslim minorities through measures taken in relation to *vakıfs*. In 1936 all foundations were served notifications requesting them to provide the VGM with a list of their non-movables. The list was necessary in order to regularize the land registry of the Republic. The community foundations, like other foundations, provided a list of their property.[104] The VGM requested the community foundations to submit their founding deeds in order to prove their ownership of non-movables in their disposal, fully aware that they were founded by Sultan decrees, and thus they did not have any founding deeds.[105] The innovative solution the VGM found to this problem was to consider

97 For some examples see Bakar, *supra* note 66.
98 Ibid.
99 Kurban and Hatemi, *supra* note 65.
100 Ibid.
101 *Mazbut vakıf* stands for *vakıfs* that are seized by the VGM.
102 Kurban and Hatemi, *supra* note 65, p. 17. The Greek Orthodox community is a community that has been damaged by the practice of seizure. As of October 2007, 24 Greek Orthodox community *vakıfs* had been seized by the VGM. The number of properties seized through this process is 990. As of February 2008, 24 community *vakıfs* dedicated to the benefit of the Jewish community had been seized by the VGM.
103 For example, as of 2009, 24 *vakıfs* of the Greek Orthodox community and 990 properties belonging to these *vakıfs* had been seized by the VGM. Kurban and Hatemi, *supra* note 65, p. 17.
104 This list was later used as their founding document; see below.
105 Bakar, *supra* note 66, p. 263.

the declarations—really only a list of non-movables— as the community foundations' founding deed. In the 1960s, together with changes in the international political climate, due to the Cyprus crisis, these 1936 Declarations were used against the community foundations. The rationale was the following: since these lists did not mention that the respective foundations had the legal capacity to acquire property, the VGM deduced from this that they did not have the legal capacity to acquire ownership—the legal effect of all acquisition of property since 1936 was declared null and void.[106] Clearly, a list of non-movables could not contain a provision stating that the respective *vakıfs* had the right to acquire property. They had been asked to provide a list of their property not a description of their purpose and activities. Consequently, property they had acquired through purchase, inheritance or donation throughout the period 1936 through to the 1970s was seized by the VGM, the Treasury or National Real Estate.[107] It is interesting to note that these properties were registered in the land register in the name of the community *vakıfs* with a document provided by the respective governorships.[108]

The inadequacy of legal regulations, largely caused by the lack of a Regulation that should have accompanied the Law on Foundations, stipulating the specifics of its application, constituted the basis of various unpredictable and discretionary rules that were applied and these diminished the control of the management of community foundations, sometimes to the point of losing the foundations and their assets permanently.[109] The lack of legal certainty made it possible for the *de facto rule-makers*[110] to make rules that increased their sphere of influence at the expense of community foundations. For example, over the years there have been times when the rules concerning the election of the governing bodies of community foundations were not prescribed by law. Instead for many years a police order of 1972 constituted the manner in which elections were conducted.[111] These rules led to the loss of control over some community foundations and their property. According to this police order, every church parish was considered an election district and community foundation administrators had to reside in the election district where they were elected. In many districts or cities where non-Muslims did not reside any more, for various reasons, including insecurity, discrimination and pressure, elections could not be held. Hence the VGM seized the management of these community foundations—effectively taking away resources belonging to community foundations dedicated to the benefit of non-Muslim communities.[112]

106 Kurban and Hatemi, *supra* note 65, p. 14.
107 Ibid.
108 Diran Bakar observed that the governorships would issue a document stating that "there is no problem regarding the acquisition of property of the X foundation since it has legal personality". Bakar, *supra* note 66, p. 270.
109 Ibid., p. 267.
110 Rule-maker here refers to public authorities who had the discretionary powers to interpret legislation.
111 Regulations and Principles on the Elections Concerning Foundations, 1972.
112 Bakar, *supra* note 66, p. 270.

Another example illustrating the lack of legal certainty and its detrimental consequences concerns the coordination of various *vakıfs* dedicated to the benefit of the Armenian Apostolic community. In 1954 a committee was established to administer the various properties belonging to all of these *vakıfs*; in 1960, after the military coup the military Governor Refik Tulga ordered the dissolution of this committee.[113] Since then all community foundations have been administered independently, thus decreasing the capacity to manage and coordinate foundations for the benefit of the respective ethno-religious communities.

Lastly, a secret rule, thus completely unforeseeable, concerns the payment of a contribution fee for the auditing task of the VGM. In 1967 the Law on Foundations No. 903 stipulated that all foundations had to contribute 5% of their income as a contribution towards the "inspection and auditing" expenses.[114] In 1979 a decree ruled that foundations that were established before the entry into force of the Turkish Civil Code would not be liable to pay this contribution.[115] In 1981, Article 1 of the Law on Foundations was changed and this time the community foundations were to pay the contribution; however, the provision said that this contribution could be paid by the general state budget by a Decision of the Committee of Ministers.[116] Bakar relates that in the proceedings of a case in 1986 it was disclosed that according to a secret decision of the Committee of Ministers, the Greek Orthodox community foundations listed in the Decision were not to pay the contribution, based on a reciprocity principle taking into account the practice in Greece.[117] The objection to this Decree on the basis of the principle of equality was rejected and the case dismissed on grounds saying: "It is not against the principle of equality. The Decree was kept confidential in order to avoid polemic".[118]

(c) Restrictive Judicial Practice

As will be seen below, the treatment of non-Muslims as "foreigners" has been an innovative and instrumental legal category that facilitated and legitimized the discriminatory treatment of community foundations.[119]

The right of the community *vakıfs* to acquire property was first crippled by administrative practice in the late 1960s and then permanently thwarted by the judgment of the General Council of the Court of Appeals (General Council, hereafter), setting a precedent and establishing subsequent jurisprudence.

113 Ibid., p. 271.
114 Ibid., p. 273.
115 Ibid.
116 Ibid.
117 Ibid.
118 Ibid. Eventually in a decree of 1999 all community foundations were exempt from paying the contribution fee.
119 The term "foreigner" has been used by the Court of Appeals in its decision concerning the legality of the seizure of property belonging to community foundations by the General Directorate of Foundations in accordance with the 1936 Declaration.

Documents provided in accordance with the Land Register Law for the registration of non-movables were denied on grounds that the community foundations lacked legal personality.[120] Finally, the Court of Appeals developed a jurisprudence, which was later embraced by the General Council, reasoning that unless a *vakıf*'s founding deed permits the acquisition of property it cannot acquire new property.[121] The highly criticized landmark decision by the Court of Appeals in 1971 was based on the complaint by the *Balıklı Rum Hastanesi Vakfı* (Balikli Greek Hospital Foundation) challenging the legality of the seizure of their property by the Treasury, and requesting the restoration of the said property.[122] The Court of Appeals unanimously decided that, "The legal entities formed by those who are not Turks are prohibited from acquiring property".[123] Hence an innovative, yet explicitly discriminatory legal categorization was created by case law. Those who had formed non-Muslim community foundations were considered non-Turks and thus subject to laws that were applicable to foreigners in the sphere of property rights. It was not until 2002 that the application of this discriminatory jurisprudence was made ineffective by the adoption of Law No. 4771, recognizing explicitly the right of community foundations to acquire new property, albeit with a highly burdensome bureaucratic process.[124]

(d) New Foundations

The Republic's legal arrangement pertaining to new foundations over the years may be characterized as *shifting* depending on the governing party, yet always closed to the possibility of establishing foundations for the support of religious communities. Here we will focus briefly on permissible grounds for the establishment of foundations.[125] The Turkish Civil Code which was adopted in 1926[126] used the term *tesis*[127] and not *vakıf* in order to create a sharp distinction between *vakıfs* that existed before the Republic and new *vakıfs*. Article 74(2) of the Civil Code allowed the establishment of new foundations; however, these could not be contrary to law or national interests, neither could they support a certain political

120 Bakar, *supra* note 66, Article 2, p. 269.
121 Judgment of the General Council of the Court of Appeals, 8 May 1974, E971/2-8420 and K974/505.
122 The Court of Appeals 2nd Chamber, 6 July 1971, E4449, K4399.
123 Ibid.
124 Çeşitli Kanunlarda Değişiklik Yapılmasına İlişkin Kanun [Law on the Amendment on Various Laws] No. 4771, 3 August 2002, R.G. No. 24841, 9 August 2002.
125 Here we will not focus on the difficulties of management of foundations and the extensive powers of the VGM. The reason for this is that the latter issues will be addressed in the "current practice" section below.
126 Türk Medeni Kanunu [The Turkish Civil Code] No. 743, 17 February 1926.
127 *Tesis* means institution. The term "tesis" was replaced with "vakıf" on 13 July 1967 with the adoption of Law No. 903 Türk Kanunu Medenisi'nin Birinci Kitabının İkinci Babı Üçüncü Faslının Değiştirilmesi, Bu Kanuna Bazı Madde ve Fıkralar Eklenmesi, Bazı Vakıfların Vergi Muafiyetinden Faydalandırılması Hakkında Kanun (Amendment to the Turkish Civil Code).

thought, a certain race or community (*cemaat*—religious community).[128] This neutral provision was applicable to both Muslims and non-Muslims. Yet, as far as non-Muslims were concerned, the explicit prohibition on establishing new foundations "to support a certain religious community" was incompatible specifically with Article 40 of the Lausanne Treaty guaranteeing the rights to establish, manage and control charity institutions, religious social institutions, schools, teaching and education institutions.[129]

Practice concerning new foundations that were established with a religious intent demonstrates the permissible boundaries of *vakıf* purpose as far as they concerned religious activity. Interestingly, the new foundations (*tesis*) that were established during this time included many that were dedicated to the maintenance of property used for religious purposes or support of religious activity. These are viewed as having the intent of providing for the possibility of worship. Hence, *vakıfs* with the purpose of building *mesjids*, mosques, maintenance of churches and *synagogues*, the maintenance of these and the provision for the needs of persons who would work in these places of worship, building of religious schools, and providing for the needs of students who would study in these institutions were permissible in the application of the law. Many religious *tesis* were established as new foundations.[130] The only non-Muslim example is the Walter Wiley Foundation which was established in 1962 with the purpose of dedicating the revenues of *tesis* property to the costs of personnel of a Protestant Church adjacent to the Dutch Consulate, the maintenance of the building and other related costs.[131] It is important to note that the revenues of these foundations are allocated to certain church buildings and costs related to the building and not the benefit of the church community as such.[132] Establishing foundations for the benefit of a community was and is, still, prohibited.

6.4.3 Current Legislation and Practice

Bearing in mind the complex past of the community foundations, it is not surprising that the legal/administrative realm of rules applicable to community foundations is "chaotic",[133] and that every new regulation pertaining to them

128 Article 74(2) prohibits the establishment of foundations having the aim of supporting members of a certain race or community (original *cemaat*, this word implies "religious community" in Turkish).

129 Article 40 of the Lausanne Treaty. See Chapter 5 on Turkey's obligations under the Lausanne Treaty.

130 A study indicated that 106 religious institutions (*tesis*) were established during 1926–1967. Şenel, Ş. and Z. Tuyan (2009) "1926–1967 Yılları Arasında Türkiye Cumhuriyeti'nde Kurulan Tesisler (Vakıflar)" [Institutions (Foundations) Established in the Turkish Republic Between the Years 1926–1967], in *Akademik Bakış* (IBT), Vol. 3, No. 5, Winter.

131 Ibid.

132 For example the revenues cannot be used to support the elderly of only members of that community or open an orphanage only for those affiliated with their religion.

133 Hatemi and Kurban conclude that the legal rules pertaining to foundations, with many different categories developed over the years without a holistic arrangement, do reflect an appearance of chaos. Kurban and Hatemi, *supra* note 65, p. 35.

involves multi-dimensional sensitivities. Following the failure to adopt Law No. 5555 as a result of the veto of the then President Ahmet Necdet Sezer,[134] the new Foundations Law No. 5737 that was adopted in 2008 is significant in what it does and does not accomplish.[135] The new Foundations Law was adopted, amidst strong opposition, within the Third Harmonization Package for the European Union accession, and has significant implications for both community foundations and new foundations.

It is worthwhile briefly considering the case brought to the Turkish Constitutional Court (Anayasa Mahkemesi, hereafter AYM) by the main opposition party, the Republican People's Party (Cumhuriyet Halk Partisi—CHP) challenging the constitutionality of the new Law on Foundations; it was claimed that it was in contradiction with the secular nature of the Republic and the indivisibility of the state with its people as well as other constitutional provisions, such as the principle of equality.[136] The arguments put forth for and against improving the conditions of community foundations help our understanding of the many dimensions of the bar before the legal personality of belief communities in Turkey. The approach taken by the Constitutional Court might be indicative of the way forward; this approach overcomes the blanket restrictions on religiously based associations that Turkish secularism and national interests have been so far interpreted to justify.

134 Vakıflar Kanunu [The Law on Foundations] No. 5555, containing similar provisions to the new Law on Foundations, was partly vetoed and sent back to the Parliament by President Ahmet Necdet Sezer on 29 November 2006. The vetoed provisions mainly concerned the right of foreigners to establish foundations, the right to acquire property for foundations and provisions regulating their international relations and economic activities (Articles 12, 14, 16, 25, 26 and 41) on the basis of their contradiction with the Preamble and Articles 2, 3 and 5 of the Turkish Constitution. The crux of the rejection of these provisions was based on the elimination of the exceptional nature and limited capacity of community foundations (*cemaat vakıfları*), claiming that the rigorous supervision established over community foundations and their limited capacity aimed the eradication of the "old foundations established within the Sharia Law order" that was eliminated by the Turkish revolution. He reiterated that Turkey embraced the contemporary secular rule of law that was based on a citizen-state relationship, rather than on the organization of people according to their religious affiliation, each with its respective religious leader. Veto reasoning of President Ahmet Necdet Sezer, Document sent from the Presidency to the Turkish Grand National Assembly, Doc. No. B.01.0.KKB.01–18/A-10-2006-830 29 November 2006 http://hyetert.blogspot.com/2006/12/vakflar-kanunu-veto-gerekcesi.html [Accessed 16 January 2015]. The exceptional structure of the community foundations, which allows associative activity based on religious affiliation, and the contrasting Republican tendency to abandon the religion based societal organization demonstrates that the community foundations are viewed as an anomaly within the Republican legal framework. In fact, one explanation of the restrictive practices against the community foundations might be that there has been a will to abolish this anomaly and exception which was accepted reluctantly in the first place, within the Lausanne regime, and was always seen as a concession.

135 Vakıflar Kanunu [The Law on Foundations] No. 5737, adopted on 20 February 2008, R.G. No. 26800, 27 February 2008.

136 Constitutional Court, 11 January 2011, E/22/2008, K/82/2010, 17 June 2010, R. G. No. 27812.

The objections of the main opposition party centered around provisions that brought the community foundations to the same category as ordinary foundations in relation to their capacity to enjoy certain rights that were previously denied. These include, establishing branch offices (Article 25), election of the executive board of community foundations from among the community (Article 6), acquisition of new property (Article 12(1)), possibility of altering "purpose and function" (Article 14), international activities, receiving donations from foreign countries (Article 25), establishing economic corporations and companies (Article 26).[137] The opposition Party's case emulated the veto reasoning of President Sezer to the previous Law on Foundations, in which he had stressed that granting community foundations capacity that had been denied previously would undermine their exceptional status—remnants of the multi-jurisdictional Ottoman regime—and counter the process of their slow elimination from the secular modern rule of law which is based on equal citizenship as opposed to a society organized on the basis of religious affiliation.[138]

The AYM's assessment of the case stands out most in the way in which it refuses to deal with the objections in relation to national interests and the indivisibility of the state with its nation, secularism and the frequently used principle of reciprocity in relation to the Lausanne Treaty, instead focusing on fundamental rights and their wide interpretation. By adopting such an approach the Turkish Civil Code (TCC) marks an important progress in jurisprudence concerning religious minorities in Turkey.[139] Some important examples may illustrate this point. It was argued that the election of the executive board for community foundations needed to be rejected on the basis of the principle of reciprocity found in Article 45 of the Lausanne Peace Treaty,[140] in light of the fact that in Greece non-Muslim communities were not allowed to elect the administration of their foundations. Therefore, according to Article 90 of the Constitution, international law (Lausanne Treaty) had to prevail. The evaluation of the AYM is interesting because it finds that Article 90 is relevant for situations where there is an incompatibility among norms pertaining to human rights and in this situation there was no incompatibility. Thus, without dealing with the principle of reciprocity the AYM regarded it as a clear fundamental rights issue that did not require reference to the Lausanne Treaty.

Another vital provision concerned the right of community foundations to acquire new property.[141] The opposition to this right centered on this being a concession to minorities in Turkey and that there was no "public interest" in granting community foundations the right to acquire new property. Strikingly, basing the reasoning on provisions found in Article 35 of the Turkish Constitution and Article 1 of Protocol 1 of the ECHR, protecting the right to property for legal entities, the AYM found that the right to property is a human right and

137 Ibid.

138 Ibid.

139 It is difficult to draw conclusions from its approach in this case on how it would deal with associative rights of other religious communities.

140 *Supra* note 136.

141 Law on Foundations, Article 12(1).

hence that there was "public interest" in correcting the infringement suffered by community foundations over decades.[142] It is highly important that the AYM views the practice of recognizing the 1936 Declaration as a "founding deed" and deducing from this that community foundations do not have a capacity to acquire new property because it is not stated in their founding deed, as "no longer relevant". Thus the AYM has rejected decades' long judicial practice that resulted in significant loss of property for community foundations, depriving these communities of vital resources needed for their survival as well as their religious acts.[143] When dealing with the objection to the possibility for community foundations to alter their "purpose and function", because this would give them the chance to survive and adopt to changing circumstances and thus bring them to the same status as ordinary foundations and that this would constitute a *privilege*, the AYM decided that on the contrary it would be compatible with the principle of equality.[144]

The adoption of Turkey's current Law on Foundations has been a move toward bringing in line the protection of the rights of non-Muslim minorities with the protection afforded in international human rights treaties, the Treaty of Lausanne and the Turkish Constitution.[145] The Law on Foundations protects the right of community foundations to acquire property, enjoy the right to manage, to exchange property that they have acquired with more beneficial ones and to turn these into cash under certain circumstances. An important gain for community foundations has been that they are able to register non-movables that they had declared in the 1936 Declaration in the name of their community foundations. In addition, it has provided a limited solution for the property purchased by or donated to community foundations and then transferred to the ownership of the State Treasury or VGM. The return of these properties to community foundations has become possible. Also, provided that it is stated in their deed and they notify the VGM, foundations can receive donations from institutions in Turkey and abroad. Foundations may establish commercial companies and be shareholders of companies. No doubt, these rights have breathed life into community foundations and established that community foundations also enjoy the rights that new foundations have.

Despite its improvements, the 2008 Law on Foundations fails to address past injustices and retroactive actions that have resulted in significant loss for community foundations. The status of community foundations as *mülhak vakıf*[146] has not been changed.[147] The regulation pertaining to seized (*mazbut*) foundations stands out in this respect. The VGM, in the past, had seized and placed under its administration foundations that did not have any administrator and that did not

142 *Supra* note 136.
143 Ibid.
144 Ibid.
145 Ibid.
146 Öztürk, *supra* note 68, p. 45.
147 Hatemi views such change as necessary for substantial change. The added (*mülhak) vakıf* status of both Muslim and community foundations must change and a regulation that observes equality and advances freedom must be instituted. Hatemi, *supra* note 67, p. 806.

have members of community living in its region based on the Law on Foundations No. 2672.[148] The 2008 Law on Foundations closes the door to the recovery of these foundations and the return of their non-movables permanently by stating that "election and appointment of new administrators for these foundations may not be made". For example, 24 synagogue foundations endowed for the benefit of the Jewish community in Turkey and 24 community foundations endowed for the benefit of the Greek Orthodox community were seized by the VGM, thus transferring the management or control of these foundations as well as the property belonging to these foundations to the VGM.[149] Kurban and Hatemi argue that this provision not only does not provide for the restitution of administration and property of seized foundations, but also opens the way for the continuation of unlawful and arbitrary bureaucratic practice.[150]

The inclusion of the principle of reciprocity in the 2008 Law on Foundations has caused substantial reaction from the non-Muslim community. The principle of reciprocity constitutes the basis of Turkey's conditional approach to the protection of minority rights. It is based on the expectation that there will be reciprocal protection for Muslims, particularly those in Western Thrace. This has been an integral part of the constrictive application of the general minority rights protection scheme. Article 2 preserves the principle of reciprocity, thus continuing and reinforcing the practice of the Turkish state to treat its citizens as foreign citizens.

In the assessment of the associative rights of non-Muslim minorities in Turkey it is important to note that it is not possible to establish new community foundations. This practice is contrary to Turkey's obligations under Lausanne 40 which provides guarantees for the associative rights of non-Muslims. It is only possible to establish new foundations which are subject to the TCC. Yet, Article 101(4) of the TCC stipulates that one cannot establish foundations that aim to support a certain race or community (religious community).[151]

Following the significant, but nevertheless inadequate, domestic legal improvements that were adopted within the context of reforms for Turkey's accession to the European Union, community foundations have taken their complaints regarding the right of community foundations to the protection of property to Strasbourg. Their success in cases concerning the seizure of property belonging to community foundations by the Turkish state has led to numerous applications. In the case of *Fener Rum Erkek Lisesi Vakfi v. Turkey*, the ECtHR decided that the manner in which the 1936 Declaration was used to restrict the right of the community foundations to property violated Article 1 of Protocol 1.[152] The case of *Yedikule Surp Pırgiç Ermeni Hastanesi Vakfi v. Turkey*, dealing with the seizure of property that belonged to the foundation, resulted in a finding of violation by

148 Kurban and Hatemi, *supra* note 65.
149 Ibid., pp. 38–40.
150 Ibid.
151 Türk Medeni Kanunu [Turkish Civil Code] No. 4721, 22 November 2001, R.G. No. 24607, 8 December 2001.
152 *Fener Rum Lisesi Vakfi v. Turkey*, 9 January 2007, European Court of Human Rights, No. 34478/97.

Turkey, which was followed by a friendly settlement between the parties.[153] This case is significant in being the first case where Turkey returned seized property to a community foundation.

In an effort to take further steps to solve the property problems of the Lausanne minorities, the Legislative Decree ("the Decree" hereafter) was adopted on 28 August to allow community foundations to apply to regain property confiscated from them by the state since 1936. It has been applauded by many as a "revolution"; however, it is best seen as a further step in the process of trying to solve the property problems of non-Muslim community foundations.[154] The Decree amends the current Law on Foundations (No. 5737) by adding the temporary Article 11. Basically, the Decree aims to provide for the restitution of some of the property that was wrongfully taken from non-Muslim community foundations.[155] On the other hand, it is important to note that it is far from creating an overall solution to all the property problems of community foundations. A number of exceptions foreseen in the Decree weaken the restitution process. One of the exceptions in the Decree concerns property that was "nationalized" and property confiscated by the state from community foundations and handed back to previous owners from whom the foundations had legally acquired it. In addition, the Decree does not address the property of community foundations seized by the VGM.

Regardless of their reason,[156] reforms pertaining to community foundations have brought the protection afforded to some non-Muslim communities in Turkey closer to the protection ensured in international human rights provisions, the Lausanne Treaty and the Turkish Constitution. On the other hand, it is difficult to say that legal issues concerning associative abilities of non-Muslim communities have been freed from national security concerns subject to the national and international political climate. There has certainly not been a firm shift to view the associative abilities of non-Muslim communities as a right protected under the collective dimension of freedom of religion or belief.

153 *Yedikule Sırp Pırgiç Ermeni Hastanesi Vakfı v. Turkey*, 16 December 2008, European Court of Human Rights, No. 50147/99, 16.

154 Provisional Article 11 of the Law on Foundations No. 5737, 20 February 2008, adopted through Legislative Decree (KHK) No. 651, 22 August 2011.

155 According to the Decree, to qualify for restitution, non-movable property must be registered in the 1936 Declaration of the community foundations of the VGM and the name of the owner recorded in the Land Registry must be blank; or the non-moveable property must be registered in the 1936 Declaration and registered in the name of the State Treasury, the VGM, a municipality or city special administration for reasons other than nationalization, sale, or exchange.

156 Hatemi and Kurban argue that the fundamental reason for the AKP government to demonstrate a political will to start the reform process for *vakıfs* was that this was a precondition for the European Union membership process and to take a preventive measure against the applications pending at the ECtHR. Kurban and Hatemi, *supra* note 65, p. 24. On the other hand, the AK Party government's approach to non-Muslim minorities (albeit strictly toward those who are remnants of the Ottoman millets) demonstrates signs of being based on tolerance, somewhat inspired by the Ottoman practice, and this might also explain the reforms or their justification.

(a) New Foundations

Legislation pertaining to the establishment and administration of new foundations is relevant for our assessment of the adequacy of new foundations as a form of legal personality in the exercise of the collective dimension of freedom of religion or belief. The new Law on Foundations[157] does not include an explicit prohibition of the establishment of foundations with a religious intent. Yet, Article 101(4) of the Civil Code prohibits the establishment of a foundation "contrary to the characteristics of the Republic as defined by the Constitution, Constitutional rules, laws, morals, national integrity and national interest, or with the aim of supporting a distinctive race or *community*".[158] The prohibition of the establishment of foundations dedicated to the support of a belief community is potentially problematic because it may be interpreted in a way to prohibit the establishment of foundations with a religious purpose or dedicated to support the activities of a certain religious community, especially if the purpose of the foundation goes beyond support for a specific building or institution set aside for religious purposes.[159]

There appears to be an inconsistency in the way the administrative authorities and high courts have dealt with the compatibility of the establishment of foundations dedicated to supporting religious and other activities of members of certain belief communities and Article 101(4) of the Civil Code. The cases of the Istanbul Protestant Church Foundation (Istanbul Protestan Kilisesi Vakfi—IPKV), Kurtuluş Churches Foundation (Kurtuluş Kiliseleri Vakfi—KKV) and the Seventh Day Adventists Foundation (Yedinci Gün Adventistleri Vakfi—YGAV) illustrate the ambiguity in law and practice and their restriction on the associative abilities of belief communities perfectly. The IPKV[160] was established by a court decision and its aim, as stated in its founding deed, is "to meet the religious needs of citizens affiliated with the Protestant faith and foreigners residing in Turkey who are affiliated with the same religion".[161] In the case of the IPKV the VGM appealed the first instance court decision establishing it as a foundation and took the case to the Court of Appeals, yet the latter upheld the decision concerning the establishment of the foundation.[162] It is not clear from the case report on what basis the VGM opposed the establishment of the foundation.[163] The application of the KKV, on

157 *Supra* note 135.

158 Emphasis added; community, *cemaat* in Turkish, signifies a religious community.

159 It will be remembered that this provision is not evoked to close the community foundations established before the Republic since they enjoy a special protection based on Turkey's obligations under the Lausanne Treaty.

160 Original name, Istanbul Protestan Kilisesi Vakfi. Beyoğlu 4th Court of Civil Law, E646/1999, K530/1999, 10 November 1999.

161 IPKV statute.

162 Court of Appeals, 18th Chamber, E/3402/2000, K/5989/2000, 29 May 2000.

163 However, the legal counsel of the IPKV submits that it was Article 74 that was invoked by the VGM in court proceedings. Interview with Murat Cano on 5 November 2011.

the other hand, was not successful.[164] The founding deed of the KKV stated in Article 3,

> The main aim of the foundation is to meet the religious needs of citizens affiliated with the Protestant faith and residents in Turkey and those living in Turkey affiliated with the same faith, to ensure their educational, social and cultural development within the framework of freedom of religion or belief, and by providing every kind of material and moral support and to provide supportive services to people in need and those affected by natural disasters.[165]

The application was rejected on the basis of the prohibition of Turkish Civil Code, Article 74[166] that prohibited the establishment of a foundation with the purpose of supporting a certain denomination or religious community.[167] The court referred in its reasoning to an Opinion of the VGM, which underscores that the said foundation's aim was to "meet the religious needs of persons affiliated with the Protestant faith" and that this was prohibited under Article 74 of the Civil Code.[168] The court recognized that the freedom of religion or belief is protected by international treaties; however, these must be exercised in accordance with "legal norms related to public order that reflect the basic philosophy of the state".[169] Interestingly, the court pointed out that while it is possible to critique Article 74(2) of the Turkish Civil Code in the context of abstract human rights and related regulations, because of the explicit prohibition in law, bearing in mind that the foundation deed states clearly in its Article 3 that its purpose is to meet all kinds of need of persons affiliated to the Protestant faith, it is not possible to approve the establishment of the foundation in light of national legislation.[170] While the court observes the incompatibility of domestic law with international law, it does not go so far as to invoke Article 90 of the Turkish Constitution,[171] and give primacy to Article 9 or Article 11 of the ECHR and Article 18 or Article 22 of the ICCPR. The Court of Appeals upheld this decision, observing that while it is possible for members of the Protestant belief who live in Turkey to establish foundations to exercise their rights to freedom of belief and religion, as protected by the Turkish Constitution, by building places of worship, carrying out necessary educational, social and cultural activities within the framework of freedom of religion or belief,

164 Ankara 31st Peace Court, E/819/2000, K/370/2001, 12 June 2000. The decision of the first instance court was upheld by the Court of Appeals, 18th Chamber, E/9599/2001, K/10706/2001, 4 January 2002.
165 Ibid. Decision of the Court of Appeals.
166 At the time of the case, Article 74 of the Turkish Civil Code was the equivalent of Article 104 of the new Turkish Civil Code enshrining the prohibition of establishment of foundations with the purpose of supporting a certain race or religious community.
167 *Supra* note 164.
168 Opinion of the VGM, No. 688, 14 March 2001.
169 *Supra* note 164, the decision of the First Instance Court.
170 Ibid.
171 Article 90 upholds the primacy of international treaties where there is an incompatibility with national law in relation to human rights. See more in Chapter 5.

the purpose of the KKV was different, in that "it especially supports members of the Protestant community".[172] The Court of Appeal's perception of exercise of freedom of religion or belief presents a focus on facilities which may be used by religious groups. A link or focus on the religious group that may use such facilities appears to be not compatible with Turkish legislation. Also, the restriction is not evaluated in relation to its aim, its necessity in a democratic society and the proportionality of the consequences it has on religious groups to the aims pursued.

An application by the YGAV was also rejected by the court based on the same justification as in the case of KKV. It has been observed that the primary concern of the High Courts in KKV and YGAV has been the protection of public order and security.[173] In the Turkish judicial practice, there have been situations where non-judiciary actors have tried to influence the decisions of courts.[174] In the cases of KKV and YGAV, their missionary activities and Turkey's identification of them as a national threat[175] may have constituted the decisive element. However, since the judgment does not include a discussion of these issues as a basis for restrictions, it is not possible here to discuss substantively the validity of this argument. Although the YGAV used an almost identical deed to that of IPKV—which was successfully established—its attempt to establish a foundation was thwarted. This raises the question of whether the decision of the court is based on conjecture.[176] It will be very interesting to see the proceedings on the case of the YGAV which is now pending with the ECtHR.[177]

A more recent application to set up a foundation which aimed to carry out some religious and educational activities for Armenians was also rejected by the 5th Court of First Instance in Istanbul. The court relied on Article 101/4 of the Civil Code, which forbids setting up foundations that aim to support members of a specific race or community.[178]

172 *Supra* note 164, the decision of the Court of Appeals.

173 Interview with Murat Cano, legal counsel for the YGAV, 5 November 2011. In the case of YGAV, the VGM and legal counsels from the Prime Minister's Office presented the argument that the establishment of this foundation would be detrimental to public order and public security because of the missionary activities of this group.

174 Some examples concern briefings given by military personnel to judges in the 28 February process in 1997.

175 Turkey has identified missionary activities as a national threat in a National Security Memorandum adopted by the National Security Council in December 2001 session.

176 Macar and Gökçatı also argue that in Turkey, freedom of religion or belief issues are never seen solely as such, but are highly political issues. In particular, in the study about the Future of the Heybeliada Theological Seminary, they argue that the demands for opening the Seminary are always seen steps to divide the integrity of Turkey and a threat to the country's future. See Macar, E. and M.A. Gökaçtı (2005) *Heybeliada Ruhban Okulu'nun Geleceği Üzerine Tartışmalar ve Öneriler* [Discussions and Recommendations on the Future of the Halki Theological School], Istanbul: TESEV.

177 *Altınkaynak and Others v. Turkey*, 22 March 2006 (communicated), European Court of Human Rights, No. 12541/06.

178 *Batman Çağdaş Daily* (2011) "Sasonlu Ermeniler AİHM'e gidiyor" [Armenians from Sason are Going to the EctHR], 9 March 2011. Available: http://www.batmancagdas.com/sasonlu-ermeniler-aihme-gidiyor-h12830.html [Accessed 16 January 2015].

A case dealing with the restriction of the establishment of foundations aimed at supporting a religious community in the context of an Alevi foundation demonstrates how the Court of Appeals chose to resolve competing interests. The case deals with an objection to the establishment of the Anatolian Science Culture and Cem Foundation (Anadolu Bilim Kültür ve Cem Vakfi—ABKCV) where the VGM objected to the words "Alevism", "Cem",[179] "Halk semahları" in its statute,[180] arguing that the purpose of the foundation "to research Alevism in a scientific manner, transmit it to young generations" would lead to support of a certain religious community (the Alevi community).[181] The Court of Appeals decided that the removal of the word "Alevi" would weaken the purpose of the foundation and it is not possible to say that this word, which conveys a fact in the society, expresses anything unlawful. As for the word "cem", since it refers to assemblies of Alevi worship, the Law on the Closure of Dervish Lodges was not applicable.[182] Lastly, the court held that the "*halk semahı*" is known as a cultural activity, hence legally speaking there was no problem.[183] It seems that, in order to facilitate the establishment of the foundation, a focus on the cultural dimensions of the foundation's purpose was chosen and the religious dimensions were disregarded or downplayed. *Cem* gathering or the *semah* were not considered manifestations of religion or belief in worship. The fact that the establishment of the foundation could not be justified as a right under freedom of religion or belief indicates, among other things, the vague and weak protection of the collective dimension of freedom of religion or belief.

In practice, the rule concerning the ban on the establishment of *vakıf* institutions with the purpose of supporting a certain religious community may have its exceptions. The Turkish Diyanet Foundation (Türkiye Diyanet Vakfi—TDV), which is a foundation under the Civil Code, was established in 1975 with the purpose of fostering knowledge of Islam, building mosques, and doing charitable work.[184] The purpose of the TDV has not been challenged by courts or administrative authorities. Taking into account that "fostering knowledge of Islam and building mosques" would benefit a certain community, namely Muslims, how is the purpose of the TDV reconciled with the prohibition found in Article 101(4) of the Turkish Criminal Code which stipulates that one cannot establish foundations that aim to support a certain race or community (religious community)?[185]

179 *Cem* rituals, religious practices performed by adherents of Alevi-Bektaşi, a belief system based on admiration for Ali, the fourth caliph after the prophet Muhammed.

180 *Semahs* can be described as a set of mystical and aesthetic body movements in rhythmic harmony.

181 Court of Appeals, 18th Chamber, E/1995/717, K/1995/1097, 31 January 1995.

182 Ibid.

183 Ibid.

184 With an amendment made in its endowment deed in 1993 this Vakıf re-oriented itself to a ministry to Muslims abroad. Türkiye Diyanet Vakfi [Turkish Diyanet Foundation], *Activity Report, 1995–1997* (Türkiye Diyanet Vakfi Publications, 1997).

185 Türkiye Diyanet Vakfi statute.

Even if members of belief groups manage to establish foundations, for small communities the management of a foundation proves to be burdensome financially and administratively. The reason for this is that managing a foundation requires legal and accounting know-how as well as financial resources.[186] These include detailed declarations related to finances and activities.[187] Foundations have to conduct internal auditing, or have it done through independent external financial auditors, but in both cases the auditors must have a certificate required by the VGM.[188] For small communities it might not be possible to have skilled persons who can acquire the required certificate for auditing and expensive to hire an external auditor. Taking into account the burdensome administrative requirements involved in managing foundations and the heavy risk of repercussions that may follow, it does not seem possible to manage a foundation without legal counsel and accounting support. These burdensome processes cast doubt on the suitability of foundations as a legal entity formula in the exercise of the collective dimension of freedom of religion or belief.

The oversight of the VGM also constitutes a significant shortcoming of the foundations formula as an alternative legal entity status for religious or belief communities. For years, VGM has been the state agency empowered to take control of foundations that allegedly were not being used in accordance with their original purpose or did not have a legally constituted board.[189] Hatemi points out that the VGM "feels obligated to open court cases" for the dissolution of foundations and the removal of the managers of foundations upon receipt of memoranda from security institutions.[190] The VGM, the central body dealing with foundations, can apply to the court against this approval.[191]

In conclusion, the suitability and adequacy as well as accessibility of the foundation formula needs to be questioned in the context of the enjoyment of the right to freedom of religion or belief and the right to property. The foundation provides an *indirect* arrangement for property ownership and the financing of related activities (place of worship, charitable activities, etc.). However, as it has been demonstrated above, registering property indirectly, in the name of a foundation provides a very weak protection in contrast to direct ownership.[192] While it may be possible to carry out some religious activities through foundations, even as such, the extensive supervision of the VGM gives rise to a situation where the foundation system for religious communities compromises autonomy and makes

186 In addition to the initial endowment, the running of a foundation also involves costs including financial fines in cases where foundations fail to fulfill all management tasks required by the VGM.

187 Vakıflar Yönetmeliği [Regulation on Foundations], Articles 34–38.

188 Ibid. In order to have the certificate by taking a test, which is provided by the VGM, one must be a certified accountant or have worked at the VGM as a lawyer or inspector for five years. Regulation on Foundations, Article 43.

189 Kaya, N. (2011) *The Right to Association of Groups That Advocate for the Rights of Minorities in Turkey*, Euro Mediterranean Human Rights Network, p. 37.

190 Hatemi, *supra* note 67, p. 811.

191 *Supra* note 151, Article 103 of the Turkish Civil Code.

192 The Council of Europe Venice Commission, *supra* note 15, para. 37.

them vulnerable to interference by the state, such as the confiscation of property. In addition, the management of foundations is a highly burdensome process not compatible with the facilitative approach states need to adopt in the protection of the right to freedom of religion or belief.

(b) Associations

The establishment of an association is another legal entity option that is available for members of belief communities. Still, the possibility for members of belief communities to establish ordinary associations with religious purposes is a relatively recent development. The Law on Associations that was adopted in 2004 in accordance with the 4th Harmonization Package in the context of the European Union Accession process omits the explicit prohibition on establishing associations based on religions or denominations that was found in the previous law.[193] The association formula, however, is not an option that is designed particularly as a legal entity type through which religious activity may be conducted or with particular reference to the nature and needs of religious communities in the exercise of their right to manifest their religion or belief together. An association is a private law legal person that is formed by real or legal persons for the objective of realizing a certain purpose by bringing together knowledge and efforts not contrary to law.[194] The current Civil Code and the Law on Associations do not explicitly bar members of religious communities from establishing associations with religious purposes. There is no explicit prohibition in the Turkish Civil Code analogous to that which applies to foundations in Article 101(4) of the Civil Code. The Turkish Civil Code stipulates that associations "contrary to law and morals may not be established".[195]

In the context of freedom of religion or belief, the association formula has been utilized as a step for the building of worship places; associations are, often, established for the purpose of constructing places of worship. The function of associations as supporters of the construction of worship places other than mosques may have been inspired by the common practice of establishing associations for the construction of mosques.[196] However, there appear to be serious limitations and ambiguities of this formula, which create a lack of clarity and foreseeability as to the application of law. The application of this law becomes particularly ambiguous

193 The previous Law on Associations No. 2908, O.G. No. 18184, 7 October 1983 was a remnant of the 1980 military coup. Article 5 of the said law contains a far-reaching restrictions clause which explicitly prohibits the establishment of associations "based on certain religions or denominations or for the purpose of acting on behalf of them".

194 Dernekler Kanunu [Law on Associations] No. 5253, 4 November 2004, R.G. No. 25649, 23 November 2004, Article 2. Article 56 of the Turkish Civil Code.

195 Turkish Civil Code, Article 56.

196 It is common practice to establish associations with the purpose of building mosques, including the collection of money for the funding of the constructions and the project management of the construction. There are numerous examples of "Cami Yaptırma Derneği" (Association for the Building of a Mosque) in Turkey.

in relation to places of worship. The association option has been used by a number of belief communities, such as the Alevi, the Protestant churches and Jehovah's Witnesses.[197] Members of the Protestant community welcomed the possibility of establishing associations since it seems to have opened a route to acquiring a *certain* legal entity status as well as providing a first step for the establishment of places of worship.[198]

On the other hand, while the association formula may open the way for carrying out certain activities and thus meet some of the associative needs of these long-established belief communities, it is not designed as a form of religious institution or a legal entity status for a belief community. The association formula does not seem suitable for the organizational and institutional set-up of churches such as the Orthodox Patriarchate and the Armenian Patriarchate, or the Chief Rabbinate. The reason for this is they are not individuals coming together to accomplish a certain goal, which is the rationale of the ordinary association. They are leaderships of assumed communities, the members of which change all the time—yet the "assumed" community, *per se*, remains. In addition, in light of the ambiguity of the nature of their legal entity status, it is likely that they could not establish an association in any case. It has been observed that some of the churches and communities may not consider it proper to register as ordinary "associations", on a par with and under the same regulations and conditions as, for example, fitness clubs and automobile associations.[199]

There are a number of features of the Law on Associations and its Regulation that raise questions on the level of protection given to the right to association as well as the right to manifest religion or belief. These questions give rise to increased interference by the state in the associative activities of belief communities who opt for the association possibility. The number of real or legal persons that are needed for the establishment of an association is seven and must increase to 15 by the end of the first year of the life of an association.[200] The minimum number of founding members ranges between two and five in European countries.[201] This number may be a restrictive element that is incompatible with Articles 18 and 22 of the ICCPR and Article 9 in the light of Article 11 of the ECHR. The incompatibility becomes more evident when one considers belief communities that are very small and whose members may not wish to disclose their religious affiliation due to fear of discrimination and repression.

The required manner of operation for associations is highly burdensome; *inter alia*, associations have to keep six different books and three others for taxation and

197 See, for example, a report by The Association of Protestant Churches, Yildirim, M. and U. Şahin (2010) "'A Threat' or Under Threat? Legal and Social Problems of Protestants in Turkey", Istanbul: Anadolu Ofset.

198 Ibid., p. 5.

199 The Council of Europe Venice Commission, *supra* note 15, para. 43.

200 Article 2. The number must increase to 15 within the first year.

201 TÜSEV (2010) *Türkiye'de Derneklerin Örgütlenme Özgürlüğü Önündeki Engeller* [Obstacles Before the Right to Freedom of Association of Associations in Turkey], Istanbul: TÜSEV, p. 19.

financial auditing purposes,[202] the books must be kept in Turkish,[203] and the books must be approved by the City Directorate of Associations or the notary.[204] The manner in which general assemblies are made are regulated in detail and a copy of the general conclusions must be sent to the highest administrative authority in the city.[205] Associations must provide the civilian authority with a written statement on their national and international activities, personnel, financial situation, property etc. on a yearly basis, then these are audited by the city governorship or the Interior Ministry.[206] Receiving donations or aid from outside of Turkey is closely monitored by the state through the requirement of a notification of civilian administration before the receipt of the aid.[207] This process is burdensome on minority associations, including religious groups, which have scarce resources, including human and financial resources as well as necessary know-how.[208] The European Commission Progress report also notes that some of the requirements are subject to controls that do not observe proportionality.[209]

Despite the absence of an explicit prohibition of establishment of associations with a religious intent, the general requirement that the establishment of associations must be in accordance with the law may be problematic. It is particularly problematic when combined with the particular interpretation of the principle of *laiklik* since it creates a lack of precision and foreseeability of whether associations with religious purposes can be established and if they are established, whether their activities may be found illegal at some point. An example of this was demonstrated in 2005, when Jehovah's Witnesses tried to set up an association with "religious, informational and charitable" purposes.[210] The authorities rejected this on the ground that it was against Article 24 of the Constitution.[211]

202 Article 32 of the Regulation.
203 Article 33 of the Regulation.
204 Article 36 of the Regulation; such approvals also give rise to high costs.
205 Articles 13, 14, 15, 16, 17 of the Regulation.
206 Article 83 and 84 of the Regulation.
207 Article 21 of the Law on Foundations and Articles 18, 19 and 20 of the Regulation. The notification must be accompanied by protocols and other documents exchanged between the association and the aiding organization.
208 A relatively recent report examining the right to association demonstrates that the burdensome financial and auditing requirements constitute a significant problem for associations established by members of various minority groups. Kaya, *supra* note 189.
209 European Commission Turkey Progress Report 2010.
210 Interview with a representative of the JW community, April 2012.
211 Article 24 of the Turkish Constitution regulates freedom of religion. The first three paragraphs are on the nature of this freedom, while the last two set down certain restrictions, namely that: "(4) Education and instruction in religion and ethics shall be conducted under state supervision and control. Instruction in religious culture and moral education shall be compulsory in the curricula of primary and secondary schools. Other religious education and instruction shall be subject to the individual's own desire, and in the case of minors, to the request of their legal representatives. (5) No one shall be allowed to exploit or abuse religion or religious feelings, or things held sacred by religion, in any manner whatsoever, for the purpose of personal or political influence, or for even partially basing the fundamental, social, economic, political, and legal order of the state on religious tenets."

However a first instance court decided that the stated purpose was not in breach of Article 24, and rejected the claim to close the association.[212]

The nature of religious activity that can be carried out within the legal structure of an association and in its premises is not clear. This was demonstrated in a case against a private person, E.L.D., in relation to alleged church activity in the Word of Life (Hayat Sözü Derneği—HSD) premises.[213] Allegedly, she had admitted that the premises were used as a "house church" to the policeman who came to the association premises for investigation.[214] During the trial E.L.D. contended that she did not say that she was engaged in "house church activity" and that her activities were in line with the purposes of the Association that were found in its statute, namely, "to meet the needs of believers affiliated with the Christian Protestant faith".[215] The case was dismissed because the defendant denied the allegation that the premises were used as a "house church".[216] Even though the premises were not officially assigned or recognized as a place of worship, some of the activities, apparently, seemed similar to activities that one might expect to see in a church. In addition, it must be noted that a number of Protestant associations have been served notifications and in some cases they have been fined for using their respective association buildings for worship purposes.[217] Yet, an association may be established to build a place of worship, but the practice of worship in the building may lead to the closure of the association since the designation of such a place as a place of worship requires a different process.

The nature of supervision of associations through the Directorate of Associations under the Ministry of Interior weakens the suitability of this option for belief communities by increasing the vulnerability of belief communities against unjustified state interference and diminishing the autonomy of belief communities. The case of an Alevi association, Association for the Construction of Çankaya Cemevi (Çankaya Cemevi Yaptırma Derneği, CCYD hereafter), illustrates this point. The CCYD, which referred to its worship place *cem* house[218] as a place of worship in its statute, has been the subject of a legal dispute.[219] The Ministry of Interior asked the Directorate of Associations to request the Alevi Association to remove the reference to *cem* house as a place of worship.[220] The request was based on an opinion of the Presidency of Religious Affairs, which asserts that Muslims worship in mosques, thus ruling out the possibility of the recognition of the *cem* house as a place of worship. The case raises issues on the interference in the internal affairs,

212 Bakırköy 9th Peace Court, K2010/225, 24 May 2010.
213 Ibid.
214 Ibid.
215 Ibid.
216 Ibid.
217 Interview with Umut Şahin, General Secretary of the Association of Protestant Churches, February 2011.
218 Alevi community commonly worship in *cemevi* rather than mosques.
219 Decision of the Ankara 16th Peace Court, 5 October 2011.
220 Yildirim, M. (2011) "TURKEY: The Right to Have Places of Worship – A Trapped Right". Available: http://www.forum18.org/Archive.php?article_id=1549 [Accessed 16 January 2015].

not least the building and maintenance of places of worship in accordance with the particular dogma of the belief community and the neutrality of the state. The case has been decided in favor of the association by the court's rejection of the request for closure,[221] yet in contrast, considering the same case and overturning its decision, the Court of Appeals referred to Law No. 677 saying that it closes *tekke* and *zaviye* but allows the existence of mosques and *mesjid* and thus decided that the statute of the association is contrary to law, although Law No. 677 does not refer to *cem* houses.[222] The Court of Appeals also recalled the status of Law No. 677 and said that none of its provisions may be interpreted in a way to be understood to be incompatible with the provisions of the Constitution.[223] The court interprets Law. No. 677 to mean that no Islamic place of worship other than a mosque or *mesjid* may be established.[224] It does not consider the *cem* house as an equivalent of *tekke* or *zaviye*. The High Court of Appeals also recalled no provision of Law No. 677, which seeks to protect secularism, contrary to the Turkish Constitution. The reasoning also recalls that the Diyanet is tasked with the management of places of worship and mosques and *mesjid* may be opened with the permission of the Diyanet.[225] Thus it is inferred from the permission to operate mosques and *mesjid* that no Islamic place of worship other than these may be lawful. Thus reference to an "unlawful" place of worship leads the Court of Appeals to conclude that the statute of the association is contrary to law and therefore necessitates the dissolution of the association by a court decision.[226] Interestingly, while numerous previous administrative or judicial decisions relied on the Diyanet Opinion, in this reasoning the Court of Appeals does not refer to the Diyanet Opinion to the effect that Muslims worship in mosques. The reason for this may be to strive for a reasoning that is based on legislation instead of a theological opinion.

There are significant flaws in the construction of the reasoning by the Court of Appeals. The question of whether *cem* houses and *tekke* and *zaviye* are identical or not is not considered. If they had concluded that *cem* houses are identical to *tekke*, it would not be possible to allow their existence without amending Law No. 677. The court, however, concludes that only "mosques and *mesjid*" are allowed; this conclusion is based on the reference in Law No. 677 that allows mosques and *mesjid* to remain where *tekke* and *zaviye* are used for these purposes. In addition, the Diyanet is given the mandate to operate only mosques and *mesjid*. Since *cem* houses are not considered as *tekke*, these are not prohibited as such. This is also

221 *Supra* note 219.

222 *Radikal*, "Yargıtay Cemevine Kapıyı Kapattı" [Court of Appeals Closes the Door to Cemevi], 25 July 2012.

223 Ibid.

224 Court of Appeals 7th Chamber of the Civil Division, E/2012/262 and K/2012/3351, 10 May 2012.

225 Article 35 of Law No. 633 Diyanet İşleri Başkanlığı'nın Kuruluşu ve Görevleri Hakkında Kanun [The Establishment and Mandate of the Presidency of Religious Affairs], 22 June 1965.

226 Article 89 of the Civil Code stipulates that when the purpose of an association becomes contrary to law and morals a court will decide its dissolution.

evident in the fact that there are hundreds of *cem* houses operating in the country and they are not closed or considered illegal.[227] Thus their existence is not contrary to law. The fact that the Diyanet is given the task to administer mosques and *mesjid* does not necessarily mean that no other Islamic places of worship are allowed. Indeed, it only means that if there are Islamic places of worship other than mosques or *mesjid*, the Diyanet does not have a mandate to operate them. Therefore the decision to consider the reference to *cem* house as a place of worship is not based on law.

The reasoning does not include any reference to the right to freedom of religion or belief, nor does it consider the consequences of the denial of the recognition of the *cem* houses as places of worship for the association or the Alevi community.

The association option has also been used to a limited extent by the traditional non-Muslim communities that existed in Turkey before the Republic was established, yet not without concern. Members of the Greek Orthodox community have established the RUMVADER association for the purpose of coordinating the support for the community foundations dedicated to meet the needs of the Greek Orthodox community.[228] Some members have stated that there is a certain hesitation on the part of the community to join the association as members based on a fear that there will be government intrusion in their activities.[229]

Consequently, the association does not provide a means for religious or belief groups to acquire legal personality, as such. Overall, however, the association formula appears as a useful *auxiliary* legal entity option that *members* of religious communities may avail themselves of. Nonetheless, the burdensome bureaucratic processes it involves, the strict oversight of public authorities, the unclarity of acts that can be performed under the association structure appear as elements that diminish the effectiveness of this formula.

6.5 Assessment of the Compatibility of Turkey's Legislation and Practice with International Law

The purpose of this chapter has been to review Turkish legislation and practice on the right of belief communities to acquire legal personality and make an evaluation of their compatibility with Turkey's international law obligations. International standards related to legal personality of belief communities have

227 According to official figures there are 937 *cem* houses: (2013) "CHP'li Aygün, Bilgi Edinme Yasası kapsamında Türkiye'deki cemevlerinin sayısal profilini ortaya çıkardı" [CHP's Aygün Used Freedom of Information Law to Find out Cemevis' Quantitative Profile in Turkey], T24.

228 Interview with a member of the executive board of the RUMVADER, 12 March 2011.

229 Ibid.

been reviewed in Chapter 3 in detail; below is a succinct recollection of the essential framework within which an assessment of the Turkish case will be made.

The right to acquire legal personality is an integral part of the effective protection of the right to freedom of religion or belief linked to the rights to association, judicial protection and property. Article 9 of the ECHR and Article 18 of the ICCPR guarantee believers the right to manifest their religion or belief either alone or in community with others. As the ECtHR held: "religious communities traditionally and universally exist in the form of organized structures".[230] Therefore the organizational aspects of religious community activities are inseparable from Article 9. The ECtHR also observed the significance of ensuring the collective dimension of freedom of religion or belief saying: "Were the organizational life of the [religious] community not protected by Article 9 of the Convention, all other aspects of the individual's freedom of religion would become vulnerable".[231] Many acts representing the organizational life of belief communities are listed by the HRCttee as protected acts under the right to manifest religion or belief, such as, *inter alia*, worship including ritual and ceremonial acts, the building of places of worship, the display of symbols, and the observance of holidays and days of rest, the freedom to choose their religious leaders, priests and teachers, the freedom to establish seminaries and the freedom to distribute religious texts or publications.[232] In the case of *Metropolitan Church of Bessarabia and Others v. Moldova* it was observed that not being recognized, the Church could not operate, its priests could not conduct divine service, its members could not meet to practice their religion and, not having legal personality, that it was not entitled to judicial protection of its assets.[233]

As demonstrated in Chapter 3, more often than not, in domestic legal systems, legal personality is a crucial pre-condition for many activities that belief communities engage in in the manifestation of their religion or belief, as well as a way of direct exercise of rights by belief communities. Therefore, practically speaking, there is a positive obligation on the part of states to create an adequate legal framework for acquiring legal personality. This positive obligation was recognized explicitly in the ECtHR's jurisprudence: "there is a positive obligation incumbent on the State to put in place a system of recognition which facilitates the acquisition of legal personality by religious communities".[234] This must be coupled with the absence of arbitrary and undue interference by the state in this process.

230 *Hasan and Chaush v Bulgaria*, 26 October 2000, European Court of Human Rights, No. 30985/96, para. 62.

231 Ibid.

232 Human Rights Committee, General Comment 22, Article 18, UN Doc. HRI/GEN/1/Rev.1 at 35 (1994), para.4.

233 *Metropolitan Church of Besserabia v. Moldova*, 13 December 2001, European Court of Human Rights, No. 45701/99, para. 105.

234 *Magyar Kereszteny Mennonita Egyhaz and Others v. Hungary*, 8 April 2014, European Court of Human Rights, Nos. 70945/11, 23611/12, 26998/12, 41150/12, 41155/12, 41463/12, 41553/12, 54977/12 and 56581/12, para. 90.

The European Court has also relied on the right to association. The ECtHR held in the case of *Hasan and Chaush v. Bulgaria* that,

> Where the organization of the religious community is at issue, Article 9 of the Convention must be interpreted in the light of Article 11, which safeguards the associated life against unjustified State interference. Seen in this perspective, the believers' right to freedom of religion encompasses the expectation that the community will be allowed to function peacefully, free from arbitrary State intervention.[235]

The refusal by state authorities to grant legal entity status to an association of individuals amounts to an interference with the right to freedom of association.[236] This is also applicable to religious communities. The Guidelines prepared by the Office for Democratic Institutions and Human Rights and the Venice Commission, although not legally binding, state that restrictions on the right to legal personality for the religious communities are "inconsistent with both the right to association and freedom of religion or belief".[237]

The denial of legal personality results in the impossibility for belief communities to access courts with direct legal capacity and benefit from judicial protection. The ECtHR addressed this problem eloquently by observing that

> one of the means of exercising the right to manifest one's religion, especially for a religious community, in its collective dimension, is the possibility of ensuring judicial protection of the community, its members and its assets, so that Article 9 must be seen not only in the light of Article 11, but also in the light of Article 6.[238]

Therefore, the denial of legal entity status may result in an infringement of Article 6(1) of the European Convention. Similarly, the denial of legal personality or capacity to own renders the right to property meaningless for belief communities since they cannot legally establish a link between the community, as a legal person, and the property in question.

The inhibition in the Turkish legal system that denies belief communities the right to acquire legal personality, as such, results in the infringement of a number of human rights. The denial by Turkey to allow belief communities to acquire legal personality results in the impossibility for belief communities to *directly* exercise certain key aspects of their right to freedom of religion or belief, particularly in its collective dimension. This leads to an interference in the right to manifest their freedom of religion or belief in conjunction with the right to association. A

235 *Hasan and Chaush v Bulgaria*, *supra* note 230, para. 62.
236 *Sidiropulous v. Greece*, 10 July 1998, European Court of Human Rights, No. 26695/95.
237 OSCE-Venice Commission *Guidelines for the Review of Legislation Pertaining to Religion or Belief*, *supra* note 3.
238 *Metropolitan Church of Besserabia v. Moldova*, *supra* note 233, para. 118.

number of examples of recognition of legal personality of belief groups or their representatives in some court cases have been presented above, yet they fail to provide an adequate legal framework. Since belief communities cannot acquire legal personality, they cannot exercise certain key aspects of the right to freedom of religion or belief *directly* and *effectively*. This means that a belief community cannot for example directly purchase or own a place of worship or even open a bank account.

In order to acquire a limited form of legal personality, members of belief communities must establish foundations or associations which provide only indirect access to the enjoyment of fundamental rights. This formula allows some of their members to establish foundations or associations and, indeed, may be instrumental in meeting certain needs related to worship, practice and teaching. However, these will not be exercised directly by the belief community as such, i.e. the community will not be the owner of a place of worship.

It has been demonstrated above that the foundations formula and the association formula involve a significant degree of state supervision and interference as well as risk of discrimination based on religion. These formulas only allow the foundation or association to exercise the right to property, not the belief community itself. Also, it has been explained in the relevant sections above that the requirements for the maintenance and operation of foundations and associations have been and still are subject to various legislative and administrative measures that entail a high risk of arbitrary and unjust interference by the state. Hence foundations and associations run a high risk of losing control over property. An appropriate legal entity status particularly drawn up for belief communities must protect the right of belief communities to own property without undue state interference. Moreover, the right to freedom of religion or belief is rarely considered by the Turkish judiciary in the assessment of cases pertaining to associations and foundations even though there are significant implications for freedom of religion or belief.

The Venice Commission's Opinion does not consider the availability of alternative legal entity status as an adequate formula:

> The fact that leaders and members of a religious community can use alternative forms of organizing their religious life different from establishing an association with legal personality does not change the legal situation. The mere fact that the religious community concerned may have certain alternatives available to compensate for the interference resulting from State measures, while it may be relevant in the assessment of proportionality, cannot lead to the conclusion that there was no State interference with the internal organization of the community concerned.[239]

Indeed, the association and foundation formulas may be seen as, only, auxiliary options for religious or belief communities and not as substitutes for an adequate form of legal entity status necessary for the exercise of the collective dimension of freedom of religion or belief.

239 The Council of Europe Venice Commission, *supra* note 15, para. 55.

The general obstacle before acquisition of legal personality as belief communities and the limitations of existing associative possibilities in the Turkish legal framework constitute interference in the right to manifest one's religion or belief in community with others. The question then is whether such interference may be justified under international provisions protecting freedom of religion or belief. This assessment is bound to be a hypothetical one since the Turkish government is not in a position to present its arguments for this interference.

The ECtHR holds that states are entitled to verify whether a movement or an association "carries on, ostensible in pursuit of religious aims, activities which are harmful to the population or public safety".[240] Hence supervision or monitoring of activities of legal entities established by belief groups may not be deemed incompatible with the protection of the right to freedom of religion or belief. Nevertheless, a general ban on or denial of acquisition of legal personality by belief groups as such seems incompatible with the protection of the right to freedom of religion or belief and the right to association,[241] particularly when many peaceful religious groups are subject to infringement on a number of rights as it has been observed in this chapter. Indeed it is expected that communities of believers should be ready to "practice their faith within the constitutional framework of their states".[242]

On the other hand, Turkey may argue that the denial is justified considering that such association based on religious affiliation may pose a threat to secularism and public order. Indeed, it may be reasonable to foresee a situation where groups of believers organize themselves under a legal entity which is strictly opposed to the secular nature of the state or which seeks the creation of divisions in the country based on religious affiliation. In such a case Turkey would not be *unguarded*, since it is possible to restrict the right to manifest religion or belief and the right to association by law, in pursuit of the protection of public order or the rights and freedom of others in a democratic society in a manner compatible with respective restriction clauses found in relevant provisions. The purpose of the international provisions on the right to manifest religion or belief is to protect the rights of the individuals rather than the protection of state interests. In cases where state interests mandate the restriction of fundamental human rights these must be in strict compliance with the relevant restriction clauses enshrined in the ECHR and ICCPR. A categorical denial of the right to acquire legal personality, particularly when considering the effect such denial has on the rights to freedom of religion or belief, right to association, right to judicial protection and right to property, seems not proportional to the aim that might be pursued. Therefore, such denial is not in harmony with the protection scheme of the international provisions on freedom of religion or belief.

240 *Maunussakis and Others v. Greece*, 13 December 2001, European Court of Human Rights, No. 45701/99, para. 40; *Stankov and the United Macedonian Organization Ilinden v. Bulgaria*, Nos. 29221/95 and 29225/95 para. 84.
241 This view is also expressed by the Council of Europe Venice Commission, *supra* note 15, para. 65.
242 The OSCE Vienna Concluding Document, Article 16.3.

The formulation of a legal entity status for belief communities that takes into account the nature of belief communities and their activities will bring Turkey closer to complying with international human rights obligations. In this regard, the Venice Commission recommended that Turkey provides a legal framework that would allow the non-Muslim religious communities adequate access to court and the right themselves to hold property, without having to do this through the foundation model.[243] Surely this recommendation is valid for any belief community, Muslim and non-Muslim.

6.6 Toward the Formulation of a Legal Entity Status for Belief Communities

The OSCE-Venice Commission guidelines for the assessment of legislation pertaining to religious freedom are applicable for the creation of such a category. Hence if/when Turkey drafts legislation on legal entity status of religious or belief communities these principles should be followed:

> In general, out of deference for the values of freedom of religion or belief, laws governing access to legal personality should be structured in ways that are facilitative of freedom of religion or belief; at a minimum, access to the basic rights associated with legal personality—for example, opening a bank account, renting or acquiring property for a place of worship or for other religious uses, entering into contracts, and the right to sue and be sued—should be available without excessive difficulty.[244]

The possibility and need to establish *supra* bodies with functions such as coordination or oversight of legal entities formed by belief communities, as well as the nature of such bodies, are questions that must be addressed when creating an adequate legal framework for the protection of the collective dimension of freedom of religion or belief. A report prepared by a group of members of the Armenian Apostolic community states the purpose of the recognition of legal personality for minorities:

> The purpose is to ensure that the assets of the community are protected through central coordination, planning and inspection, that the fate of institutions are not left alone to the goodwill of independent foundation management, the prevention of waste of resources, and that these are used appropriately in accordance with their purposes.[245]

243 The Council of Europe Venice Commission, *supra* note 15, para. 71.

244 OSCE-Venice Commission *Guidelines for the Review of Legislation Pertaining to Religion or Belief*, *supra* note 3.

245 Döşemeciyan, K., M. Bebiroğlu, Y. Özuzun (2011) *Non-Muslim Minorities Report.* Available: http://hyetert.blogspot.com/2011/02/musluman-olmayan-azinliklar-raporu-2011.html [Accessed 16 January 2015].

A draft law proposal prepared by Prof. Hüseyin Hatemi foresees the establishment of certain religious *supra* bodies with certain functions that may create coordination with community foundations.[246] Accordingly, the *supra* bodies include the Istanbul Orthodox Patriarchate, Istanbul Armenian Orthodox Patriarchate, Rabbinate of Turkey and the Syriac Deputy Patriarchate of Turkey.[247]

Whether *supra* bodies will be of a religious nature appears as an immediate question waiting to be resolved. If religious communities formed religious institutions it would be reasonable to expect that the *supra* bodies that might be established would be also of a religious nature. Yet, considering the non-Muslim minorities in Turkey which are also ethnic minorities, in particular, Greeks, Armenians and Jews, they also have a non-religious dimension to their associative activities. These may include hospitals, schools, old-people's homes etc. which have evolved to gradually exclude their religious ethos. Community foundations that benefit such community endeavors may well prefer to be organized under a non-religious *supra* body. Yet, historically the religious heads of their communities have also been the heads of these institutions. In fact, as it has been discussed in Chapter 5, the Lausanne Treaty refers to the minority beneficiaries as non-Muslims and not as ethnic groups. This issue remains an unresolved matter and has been increasingly discussed among the so-called Lausanne minorities. A solution that permits the establishment of non-religious *supra* bodies that may have oversight and coordination functions over community foundations and which provide resources for activities that are not of a strictly religious nature seems reasonable. Similarly, a legal framework that permits the establishment of *supra* religious bodies, such as those in Hatemi's proposal above, that may assume an oversight role over community foundations or other institutions would be reasonable and necessary. It must be added immediately that it may not always be easy to draw the line between the work of the religious community and the work of the non-religious community. Dialogue within these communities will determine the course that will be taken. What is clear, however, is that the *supra* body and its nature are questions that must be tackled in the process of creating an adequate legal framework.

In sum, the impossibility of acquiring legal personality, as such, undermines the protection of the right to freedom of religion or belief in Turkey by significantly weakening the rights to associate, assemble, own, worship, establish places of worship and schools and thus also train clergy, which constitute vital components of the right to freedom of religion or belief. It denies belief communities the right to access to court which is the *sine qua non* for effective remedy for all rights violations. It also weakens the position of belief communities vis-à-vis the state by

246 Hatemi, *supra* note 67, p. 812.

247 As for Turkish citizens who are affiliated with the Catholic denomination, Hatemi's proposal includes the establishment through a special law of a Union of Foundations of the Catholic Community. For Protestant Community Foundations, the related *supra* body will be the State Ministry responsible for the Religious Public Services unless a Union of Protestant Community Foundations. Hatemi, *supra* note 67, pp. 815–817.

depriving them of a legally recognized status. These manifestations would include actions, *inter alia*, electing/appointing leaders, employing religious personnel, establishing and maintaining worship places, training clergy, including the establishment of relevant schools for this purpose, engaging in charitable work, collecting donations etc.[248] From Turkey's perspective the acquisition of legal personality by belief communities, as such, appears to be incompatible with Turkey's unique circumstances. Yet, a substantiated justification is not presented for this categorical ban. The latter results in the vulnerability of belief communities as they cannot benefit from the empowering and enabling function of legal personality. As a result, over the course of decades religious or belief communities have been subjected to discriminatory and unlawful treatment which has led to the loss of community property. What is lost is not only property but important resources that could have been used to sustain the community life, culture and religious practice.

Legal entity formulas that are available for belief communities in Turkey provide inadequate protection of the associative rights of members of belief communities that are protected by the right to freedom of religion, belief and the right to association in international human rights law.[249] They provide a certain indirect legal personality, yet fall short of providing vital elements of effective and direct legal personality; the existing models do not allow for direct ownership by religious or belief communities. Also, they do not provide for direct representation of religious communities, this particularly in the exercise of the right to access courts. Instead belief groups are obliged to own property or represent themselves in courts through an indirect institution. Such an approach fails to take into account the direct connection to the property and its use by communities. On the contrary, the existing forms of legal entity impose structures upon belief communities that are not compatible with their nature.

The available legal personality formulas then are further weakened by the fact that these indirect institutions are under the supervision of the General Directorate of Associations and the General Directorate of Foundations respectively. The extensive control of these institutions is further politicized by their direct relationship to the Prime Minister's Office and the Ministry of Interior respectively, thus making belief communities that benefit from these models vulnerable to internal and international political conjecture.

The quasi recognition of a certain legal personality by some court decisions and the conjectural decisions of some of the courts related to foundations and associations constitute clear signs of lack of a clear and predictable law and uniform application of it. In addition, since the association and foundation entities are not designed as religious institutions, as such, belief communities that opt for them always run the risk of trespassing outside the legal frameworks when they act like religious communities. Unclear rules constitute the source of lack of effective exercise and protection of the right to freedom of religion or belief in its collective dimension and the accompanying discriminatory and unsystematic administrative and judicial

248 Article 6 of the 1981 Declaration.
249 ICCPR, Articles 18 and 22, ECHR, Article 9 and 11.

practice. The failure to provide an adequate legal standard inevitably results in an extensive sphere of discretion that is created for those who apply the law, both courts and administrative authorities. Such lack of clarity and unpredictability are far from fulfilling the requirement that restrictions ought to be prescribed by law as stipulated in the restrictions' clauses of Article 18 of the ICCPR and Article 9 of the ECHR. The lack of clarity results in practice that is far from uniform and often discriminatory.

The right to acquire legal personality has not been viewed as a right protected within the scope of the right to freedom of religion or belief. Instead it is viewed on the axis of secularism, national security and interests where national and international political context appear to remain important factors. Turkey's improvement of the foundation and association formulas has been limited and to a great extent dependent on the European Union accession process. In order to ensure the protection of the right to acquire legal personality the adoption of a rights based approach that views the issue primarily as a right that Turkey has an obligation to protect is vital.

In order to comply with international human rights obligations Turkey must create an adequate and suitable legal entity status for belief groups in order to enable and empower them to effectively enjoy the right to manifest freedom of religion or belief in worship, teaching, practice and observance. The formulation of such a legal entity status must be informed by the nature of belief groups, their acts, their needs, and must include the participation of diverse belief groups in the drafting of this status and be compatible with the implications of international human rights provisions. The challenge in this process will be to seek a balance between facilitating the enjoyment of the right to freedom of religion/belief by belief communities and pursuing the legitimate aim of guaranteeing that the actions of these groups do not present any danger for a democratic society.

7 The Right of Religious or Belief Communities in Turkey to Freedom in their Internal Affairs

7.1 Introduction

As has been discussed in Chapter 4, the right of religious or belief communities to freedom in their internal affairs can be an expansive right depending on the dogma and traditions of individual religions or beliefs. Accordingly, here, the purpose is not to present an exhaustive review of issues that may be raised while considering freedom in the internal affairs. This would indeed be an impossible task because of the potentially countless forms of manifestations in worship, teaching, practice and observance that are also matters of internal affairs.[1] Instead, the focus will be on four key rights that raise issues pertaining to the protection of freedom in the internal affairs in Turkey: the right to establish places of worship, the right to teach religion or belief in places suitable for this purpose, the right to elect and appoint leaders and finally the right to observe days of rest and holidays. Deliberation on these components of the collective dimension of freedom of religion or belief will provide a comprehensive review of the extent of protection—or rather the lack of protection—conferred to the freedom in the internal affairs of belief groups in Turkey. The discussion and analysis will be based primarily on the consideration of applicable national legislation. Although this study has sought to include jurisprudence in relevant issues, it will be seen that numerous issues that are addressed have not become the subject of legal dispute. Therefore, in order to understand the manner in which legislation has been applied, and *rules of practice* where there is no directly applicable legislation, I have sought to include administrative practice and the input of belief communities through in-depth interviews.

7.2 Freedom in Internal Affairs

7.2.1 The Right to Worship or Assemble in Connection with a Religion or Belief, and to Establish and Maintain Places for these Purposes

The protection of the right to worship or assemble in connection with a religion or belief and to establish and maintain places of worship in Turkey serves as a

1 Here I do not follow the full framework used in Chapter 4 due to space limitations.

good illustration of the nature of *de jure* and *de facto* restrictions; this combination of restrictions presents a contrast to what appears to be a general recognition of the right to freedom to worship. There are 85,413 mosques in Turkey,[2] yet they may be only administered by the Diyanet İşleri Başkanlığı (the Presidency of Religious Affairs; hereafter, the Diyanet) which means that a group of Muslims may not establish and maintain their own mosque if they wished to remain outside the Diyanet structure. The Alevi[3] may establish cultural associations where they assemble for worship, yet these are categorically denied the status of a place of worship based on the Diyanet's view that "Muslims worship in mosques".[4] While relatively newer religious groups, like Protestants and Jehovah's Witnesses, are generally tolerated by public authorities when they assemble and worship in premises they consider places of worship, successful applications to acquire place of worship status have been rare.[5] Tolerance implies allowing the existence of these worship places as well as the gathering for worship and not pursuing prosecution; however, tolerance does not confer any rights. The Latin Catholic community continues to lose church property—which has been in its possession over the past centuries—as a result of not having legal personality and thus not being able to prove ownership of church property.[6] The Syriac community is still waiting for its application for a place of worship to be processed. The application was submitted in 2010 for a church building for their community which has grown in numbers as a result of immigration from their traditional homeland in south-east Turkey.[7] These are only some of the indicators of the problems that are encountered in the exercise of the right to establish and maintain places of worship in Turkey. The fact that all communities experience legal problems in the exercise of the right to establish places of worship shows that there is a systematic problem that is not limited to a handful of special situations. As duly noted in the European Union 2015 Progress Report on Turkey, in regards to religious freedom there is "a need

2 This is a 2013 figure and is taken from the statistics of the Presidency of Religious Affairs' website, http://www.diyanet.gov.tr/tr/kategori/istatistikler/136 [Accessed 16 January 2015].

3 The Alevi are a Muslim minority which combines Shi'ism with Sufism. For more on the Alevi identity, see Shankland, D. (1998) *The Alevis in Turkey: The Emergence of a Secular Islamic Tradition*, London and New York: Routledge; and Olsson, T., E. Ozdalga and C. Raudvere (eds.) (1998) *Alevi Identity: Cultural, Religious and Social Perspectives*, London and New York: Routledge.

4 Opinion of the Diyanet, A Communication (No. 1773), sent by the Diyanet to the Interior Ministry on 17 December 2004.

5 See p. 208.

6 Interview with the representative of the Latin Catholic Church in Turkey Mr. Rinaldo Marmara, date 16 November 2012. An example is the Santa Maria Church in İzmir; since the church does not have legal personality, it is not able to own property. Thus all the property of the church has been transferred to the Treasury. *İzmirport* (2013) "Hz. İsa'ya Baba İsmini Sordu" (He Asked Jesus His Father's Name), 28 June 2013.

7 Interview with the Chair of the Virgin Mary Chaldean Church Foundation on 25 June 2013.

to amend and implement the legal framework in line with ECtHR rulings, Council of Europe recommendations and EU standards".[8]

Here we will examine the protection of the right to establish and maintain places of worship in the national legal system by looking at three key areas where restrictions persist. These restrictions will be assessed in light of international law standards identified in Chapter 4. The purpose is to both identify the inconsistencies between Turkish legislation and practice and international standards, as well as determine whether and how the standard of international review may be improved. Following a presentation of generally applicable legislation, the assessment will look at the following: (a) Planning regulations, (b) Permission of public authority, (c) Legal personality.

Though not explicitly stated, the general protection of the right to worship or assemble in connection with religion or belief and to establish and maintain places for these purposes is found in Article 24 of the Turkish Constitution:

> Everyone has the right to freedom of conscience, religious belief and conviction.
>
> Acts of worship, religious services, and ceremonies shall be conducted freely, provided that they do not violate the provisions of Article 14.
>
> No one shall be compelled to worship, or to participate in religious ceremonies and rites, to reveal religious beliefs and convictions, or be blamed or accused because of his religious beliefs and convictions.[9]

Here the emphasis is on "acts of worship" and "religious services and ceremonies", in addition to an explicit protection against coercion to worship. On the other hand, acts inextricably linked to worship, such as establishing and maintaining places of worship are not included. Thus the substantive scope of the right to worship is established and shaped through legislation and regulations, decisions of public authorities as well as jurisprudence.

There are a number of legislative regulations that are applicable to the establishment and maintenance of places of worship. In this context, an important

8 European Commission Turkey 2015 Report, 10 November 2015. Available: http://ec.europa.eu/enlargement/pdf/key_documents/2015/20151110_report_turkey.pdf [Accessed 1 May 2016], p. 63.

9 Article 24 of the Turkish Constitution, paras 1, 2, 3. Article 14 reads:

> None of the rights and freedoms embodied in the Constitution shall be exercised with the aim of violating the indivisible integrity of the state with its territory and nation, and endangering the existence of the democratic and secular order of the Turkish Republic based upon human rights.
>
> No provision of this Constitution shall be interpreted in a manner that enables the State or individuals to destroy the fundamental rights and freedoms embodied in the Constitution or to stage an activity with the aim of restricting them more extensively than stated in the Constitution.
>
> The sanctions to be applied against those who perpetrate these activities in conflict with these provisions shall be determined by law.

legislative change has been introduced by the AKP government in 2003 in relation to the harmonization packages for the European Union accession process which opened the way for the establishment of places of worship other than mosques.[10] Prior to this legislative amendment, only mosques and *mesjid* could be established. Through this amendment the word "mosque" in the Public Works Law was changed to "place of worship".[11] While the phrase "place of worship" implies a neutral and broad scope of protection, in practice this term has been interpreted narrowly to encompass mosques and *mesjid*, churches and synagogues. As will be briefly explained below, the *cem* houses, where significant groups of the Alevi community worship, have not been understood by the authorities to be protected under Article 9 of the Public Works Law since they have not been recognized as places of worship. The implications of this significant change in legislation cannot be emphasized enough for religious or belief groups that worship in places of worship other than mosques and *mesjid*, in particular Christians and Jews. For example, in 2002, the places of worship of 23 congregations of Turkish Christians were declared to be in violation of municipal building laws and notice was given that these would be shut down if worship acts continued in these premises.[12]

Practice and outcomes, however, demonstrate that the right to establish places of worship fails to be effectively protected in Turkey. The legislative change brought by reforms to harmonize Turkish legislation with EU standards in the field of freedom of religion or belief has not been supported by facilitative regulations, interpretation and practice. Since the legislative change of 2003, less than a handful of non-Muslim places of worship—churches and synagogues—have gained place of worship status,[13] and *cem* houses continue to be denied recognition as places of worship.[14]

10 İmar Kanunu (Public Works Law), Law No. 3194, 3 May 1985, R.G. No. 18749, 9 May 1985, Additional Provision 2 (amending Article 9), 15 July 2003. Additional Provision 2 reads:

> In the development of zoning plans, the required places of worship shall be designated taking into account the conditions of the planned districts and regions and their future needs. Provided that the permission of the highest civilian administrator is obtained and the zoning legislation is respected, places of worship can be built in the provinces, sub-provinces and towns. Places of worship cannot be allocated for other purposes in violation of the zoning legislation.

11 Ibid., Article 9.

12 Report of the UN Special Rapporteur, UN Doc. A/57/274 (2002), paras 52, 53 (Turkey).

13 Şar Aşmayim Sinagogue in Kemerburgaz, Istanbul (2006) and the Istanbul Protestant Church (2006) in Altıntepe.

14 Even the most recent Alevi opening does not go as far as recognizing the *cem* houses as places of worship on a par with mosques, churches and synagogues. Instead a new status "belief center" is proposed by the government, which is categorically refused by the Alevi community. *Cumhuriyet*, "Alevi Açılımına Maddi Bakış" [A Material Look to the Alevi Opening], 27 June 2013. See also Subaşı, N. (2010) *Alevi Çalıştayları Nihai Raporu* [Final Report on the Alevi Workshops], Ankara: Devlet Bakanlığı.

Nevertheless, in practice, religious or belief groups continue to assemble and worship in premises that are not legally recognized as places of worship. While assembly for worship in these premises is not generally interfered with by public authorities, it is important to note that there are financial, legal and social consequences of non-recognition. Financially, recognized places of worship enjoy exemptions from certain taxes, for instance, property tax, electricity and water tax. Belief communities whose buildings do not have a place of worship status cannot benefit from these exemptions, and therefore are faced with increased financial burdens. In addition, legal and social recognition is highly important as it confers certain legitimacy on and acceptance of religious or belief groups, both in the eyes of the public authorities and society in general. This is particularly important for groups that may be new and/or that are seen as marginal groups. Not having a status of worship place, believers who assemble in their place of worship run the risk of interference by public authorities for worship in premises that are not recognized by public authorities as places of worship. More fundamentally, however, the persistent denial of granting of place of worship status—despite formal equality and general protection of freedom of religion or belief—undermines justice and continues to nurture the deeply entrenched inequalities. This gives rise to violations of the right to manifest religion or belief in worship and discrimination. Therefore the importance of changing the paradigm in which this right is exercised—from tolerance to respect, fulfilment and promotion of the right to freedom of religion or belief—cannot be overemphasized.[15]

(a) Suitability of Planning Regulations

For a long time local planning regulations have constituted an important and common constraining factor on the right to establish and maintain places of worship. Authorization and permission for places of worship constitute a key sphere where decisions of public authorities lead to serious constraints. The right to establish places of worship is partly regulated by the Zoning Law (ZL) which stipulates that:

> In the development of zoning plans, the required places of worship shall be designated, taking into account the conditions of the planned districts and regions and their future needs. Provided that the permission of the highest

15 By becoming parties to international treaties, states assume obligations and duties under international law to respect, to protect and to fulfill human rights. Briefly, the obligation to respect means that states must refrain from interfering with or curtailing the enjoyment of human rights. The obligation to protect requires states to protect individuals and groups against human rights abuses. The obligation to fulfill entails positive action by states to facilitate the enjoyment of basic human rights. For further reading, see the General Comment of the Human Rights Committee on General Comment No. 31: The Nature of the General Legal Obligation Imposed on States Parties to the Covenant, 29 March 2004, HRI/GEN/1/Rev.9 (Vol. I), p. 241.

> civilian administrator is obtained and the zoning legislation is respected, places of worship can be built in the provinces, sub-provinces and towns. Places for worship cannot be allocated for other purposes in violation of the zoning legislation.[16]

Municipalities are to plan for worship places as a part of their work for city planning.[17] Non-Muslim minorities who have applied to municipalities for the designation of places of worship report that municipalities tend to designate only mosques in the city plans.[18] Outcomes are consistent with this claim; none of the 22 worship halls of the Jehovah's Witnesses are recognized as places of worship and in relation to the applications made by the Jehovah's Witnesses for each, the response has been that "there is no religious premises designated in our city plan other than the existing mosques".[19] Protestants have similar experiences; in response to more than 20 applications, only one of the church communities was successful in gaining a place of worship status for the church building they had been using.[20] The experiences of Protestants and Jehovah's Witnesses are important indicators of the state of the right to establish places of worship in Turkey because these groups are relatively new and in need of acquiring new places of worship. Since municipalities do not take into account the needs or requests of these communities in city planning the communities are left with premises which they use for worship purposes yet lack place of worship status. Were the municipalities to take into account the needs or requests of the people in their areas who worship in places other than mosques, they could designate suitable places and the problem could be easily resolved. The reasons underlying this practice must be the subject of further study.

In addition to zoning plans, until 2013 local municipalities drafted regulations that lay down the standards pertaining to structure and construction that are required of places of worship. It should be remembered that these regulations were relevant only for worship places other than mosques since the latter must be built in conformity with the standards determined by the Diyanet.[21] The

16 Additional Provision 2, *supra* note 10.

17 Regulation Annex 2.

18 Umut Şahin, APC, Representative of Jehovah's Witnesses, 4 January 2013.

19 Ibid., email correspondence with Ahmet Yorulmaz. This response is usually given as a written statement.

20 *Supra* note 18, interview with Umut Şahin.

21 Izmir Greater City Municipality Public Works Regulation, Article 84, revised on 12 April 2013, no longer available online. See also the Report of the UN Special Rapporteur following his Turkey visit A/55/280/Add.1, para. 160 (country visit to Turkey):

> 160. The following recommendations are made to the Turkish authorities with respect to the Christian, Greek Orthodox and Armenian minorities: [...] (d) The Government should guarantee minorities the right to establish and maintain their own places of worship, and should allow them to build such facilities in places where new communities have taken root. Any limitations in this respect, for example urban development regulations, should be consistent with international

Regulations outlined fairly strict standards which did not seem to take into account the diverse nature, needs and financial capabilities of religious or belief groups. For example, according to the Izmir Greater City Municipality Regulation, a place of worship, in a new planning sector, cannot be built on a zoning parcel that is smaller than 2,500 square meters.[22] The suitability of standards pertaining to the structure of the places of worship and the nature and needs and indeed the dogma of belief groups pertaining to their places of worship are also relevant for the effective protection of this right. Often belief communities are small in number and they neither need such a large premises nor do they have the financial resources to buy such sizable land.[23] The Jehovah's Witnesses observed that the criteria established by the municipalities are designed for mosques and are not suitable for their meeting halls.[24]

Again, until 2013, there was no guideline as to the nature of the criteria for a place of worship in an area of the city which has not been newly opened for development. This meant that when a religious or belief group sought to establish a new place of worship in an already developed area there was no standard which could serve as a basis for the application process and which public authorities could refer to when processing such applications. In the absence of any guidelines, it has been difficult to ensure due process and avoid arbitrary decisions.

The experience of the Protestant community in Turkey is a vivid illustration of the power relations that seem to take over the process, compromising a clearly defined due process. In a typical application process members of the community apply to the municipality for the recognition of their existing premises as a place of worship, or where that is not possible, a request is made to the municipality to be shown a place where a place of worship may be built.[25] A typical response stipulates that the existing premises do not comply with the Regulation—in the absence of criteria for already developed areas—and there is no available plot which may be used for the construction of a new place of worship other than a mosque.[26] The procedural complexities, in addition to vagueness, compel the applicants to always rely on the good will of the public authorities, thus strengthening the status of public authorities in this power relation vis-à-vis the religious group. This explanation given by a Protestant for

jurisprudence (see General Comment of the Human Rights Committee), and this means that any non-conforming regulations should be repealed or revised.

22 Ibid.

23 *Supra* note 18, interview with Umut Şahin.

24 *Supra* note 19, interview with Ahmet Yorulmaz.

25 Yıldırım, M. and U. Şahin (2010) *"A Threat" or Under Threat? Legal and Social Problems of Protestants in Turkey*, Istanbul: Association of Protestant Churches, pp. 32–35.

26 Ibid. Three places of worship of the Jehovah's Witnesses have been closed following similar process and in regards to two of the ensuing court cases, having exhausted domestic remedies, applications to the ECtHR have been made. *Supra* note 19, interview with Ahmet Yorulmaz.

unsuccessful applications is typical and reflects the multi-dimensional nature of the problem:

> Local administrations, and in particular municipal governments, concerned with losing votes because people see them as involved in opening churches or letting churches be opened, respond negatively to requests for places of worship. This behavior reveals the depth of the problem and the need for a multi-pronged solution.[27]

A report published by the Association of Protestant Churches in 2010 underlines that local municipalities have occasionally sought the opinion of the Diyanet in the process of dealing with their applications for a place of worship.[28] It is not clear how systematically public authorities include the Diyanet in processes dealing with applications for places of worship other than mosques and *mesjid*. It is difficult to see the purpose and the legal basis for consulting the Diyanet. The opinions of the Diyanet do not have a binding nature; however, the inclusion of a certain religious authority or institution in the decision-making process of a public authority raises serious questions, not least in regards to the principle of neutrality. It is not possible to reconcile the practice of consulting with a particular religious authority or religious institution while processing decisions pertaining to places of worship with international law obligations.[29]

The ineffectiveness of the protection of the right to establish places of worship other than mosques leaves minority religious communities powerless and vulnerable. As a result, communities remain in their premises—without a place of worship status—where the group of believers are only tolerated to continue to worship and assemble. Clearly, such a situation stands in contrast with one where a group of believers—empowered as right holders—follow clear and appropriate guidelines and a due process which they can foresee and that, if followed, will lead to a positive outcome. While these groups are generally tolerated, without a place of worship status the risk of interference is ever present. Closure of premises and court cases are not non-existent. Numerous cases are ongoing as a result of closure by public authorities of premises used for worship purposes, churches and meeting halls, without place of worship status.[30] More recently, Jehovah's Witnesses have taken their case to the ECtHR where Turkey has been found in violation of Article 9.[31]

27 Association of Protestant Churches—Committee for Religious Freedom and Legal Affairs, *supra* note 25, p. 37.
28 Association of Protestant Churches—Committee for Religious Freedom and Legal Affairs, *supra* note 25.
29 The OSCE/ODIHR, OSCE and Venice Commission *Guidelines for Review of Legislation Pertaining to Religion or Belief.* Available: http://www.osce.org/odihr/13993 [Accessed 16 January 2015], p. 17.
30 *Supra* note 18, interview with Umut Şahin.
31 *Yehova'nın Şahitlerini Destekleme Derneği and Others v. Turkey and Yehova'nın Şahitlerini Destekleme Derneği v. Turkey*, 24 May 2016, European Court of Human Rights, App. Nos. 36915/10 and 8606/13 respectively.

The municipal regulations pertaining to places of worship have been annulled together with the relevant provision of two regulations published by the Ministry of Environment and Urbanization.[32] Accordingly the only rules pertaining to the construction of places of worship other than mosques no longer deal with the size of the plot of land or the structure of the building. This arrangement is valid as of 2013, and therefore there is as yet no information about its application.

(b) The Approval of the Public Authority

Under the Zoning Law, in order to acquire a place of worship status, the "approval of the highest civilian administrator" is also necessary.[33] The criteria which are taken into account in the assessment of applications for approval are, however, not explicitly stipulated. Therefore, religious or belief groups applying to the relevant public authorities do not have access to clear and foreseeable criteria for their application or which can be challenged in court.

The court cases concerning the approval of places of worship are scarce in number. Since most applications of Protestants and Jehovah's Witnesses to the municipalities for the designation of places of worship have not been accommodated, these applications have not come to the stage of being considered by the "highest civilian public authority".[34] It has been reported that two applications, Diyarbakır Protestant Church and Van Protestant Church, are pending with the respective public authorities.[35] These have not yet been the subject of any court proceedings.

The court cases concerning places of worship and the approval of public authorities have so far been related to Alevi worship places, *cem* houses, where the relevant Governorships have denied approval.[36] In regards to the rejection of applications for the recognition of *cem* houses by civilian authorities two reasons stand out: the Diyanet opinion and Law No. 677 concerning the closure of *tekke* and *zaviye*.

A Communication (No. 1773), sent by the Diyanet to the Interior Ministry on 17 December 2004, states that:

> It is not possible to consider *cemevi* and other places as places of worship because Alevism, which is a sub-group within Islam, cannot have a place of

32 Mekansal Planlar Yapım Yönetmeliği [Regulation on the Construction of Residential Plans], R.G. No. 29030, 14 June 2014 and amendments to the Planlı Alanlar TİP İmar Yönetmeliği [Regulation on the Reconstruction of Planned Spaces], R.G. No. 18916, 2 November 1985.

33 İmar Kanunu (Public Works Law), *supra* note 10.

34 In practice, as noted above, there have been two successful applications for designation of places of worship. These obtained both designation of place of worship by the respective municipalities and the approval of relevant public authorities.

35 Email correspondence with the representative of the Association of Protestant Churches on 23 July 2013, on file with the author.

36 See for example the case of the Çankaya Cemevi Yaptırma Derneği below.

worship other than mosques or *mesjid* that are common places of worship within Islam.[37]

The Alevi have criticized the Diyanet for issuing an Opinion on Alevism and the public authorities for taking this opinion into account in their decisions concerning the Alevi.[38]

The second objection centers on the Law on the Obstruction of Dervish Lodges (*Tekke*) and Shrines (*Türbe*) and the Abolition of the Position of Caretakers of Shrines and Certain Titles (hereafter "Law No. 677") which was the basis for the nationwide closure of the *tekke*,[39] in 1925.[40] It is helpful here to briefly consider this law in order to help the outside observer to understand the sensitivity around it as well as its function. Law No. 677 has a special legal status; as a reform law that aims to protect secularism, under the Turkish Constitution, it cannot be understood to be contrary to the Constitution.[41] The justification for the law states that firstly, there is a contradiction between the fundamental understanding of the state and the *tekke*, and secondly that the Turkish Republic, which is on the way to becoming a stable state, cannot tolerate these kind of "medieval incidents and institutions".[42] Article 1 of Law No. 677 declares the closure of all *tekke* and *zaviye* and *türbe* which have been traditional places of worship or centers of religious activity for various Islamic

37 A Communication (No. 1773), sent by the Diyanet to the Interior Ministry on 17 December 2004. For example, in an application for the opening of a *cem* house at the Turkish Grand National Assembly (Türkiye Büyük Millet Meclisi, TBMM) where there is currently only *mesjid* found, the Presidency of the TBMM rejected the application with reference to the Diyanet Opinion on *cem* houses. See *Milliyet*, "Meclis'te Cemevi Talebine Ret" [Refusal to Cemevi Request at the Assembly], 9 July 2012.

38 See for example, EnSonHaberler, "Çamuroğlu: Diyanet Alevilik Üzerinden Fetva Veremez", 12 July 2012. Available: http://www.ensonhaber.com/camuroglu-diyanet-alevilik-uzerine-fetva-veremez-2012-07-12.html [Accessed 16 January 2015].

39 *Tekke* are places where sufi thought, understanding and discipline are studied, deepened and presented to the people. Kara, M. (1999) *Din Hayat Sanat Açısından Tekkeler ve Zaviyeler* [Dervish Lodges from the Perspective of Religion, Life, Art], Istanbul: Dergah Publications, p. 43.

40 Tekke ve Zaviyeler ile Türbelerin Seddine ve Türbedarlar ile Bazı Unvanların Men ve İlgasına Dair Kanun [Law on the Closure of the Dervish Lodges and Shrines] Law No. 677, 30 November 1925.

41 Article 174 of the Turkish Constitution.

42 The resurgence in the Eastern part of Turkey led by Sheikh Said, seemingly against the secular reforms, seems to have played a major role in the decision for the closure of the *tekke*. Kara, *supra* note 39, p. 267. The author is quoting from a book written by a foreign observer. The great secularization reforms of 1924 related to the ulema and not the dervish. It became clear however that the most risky resistance against the reforms were going to come from the dervish and not the ulema. The ulema, who used to utilize state authority for a long time, were not inclined to rise up against the state. The dervish on the other hand were used to independence and resistance. They took advantage of the people's trust and loyalty.

traditions, including the Alevi tradition.[43] The law is not a neutral law in the sense of closing places of worship generally; instead it names the types of places of worship it abolishes.[44]

Law No. 677 has been, at times, critical in relation to the non-recognition of *cem* houses as places of worship. In a case related to the construction of a *cem* house, the Çankaya Cemevi Yaptırma Derneği (Cankaya Cem House Building Association, hereafter ÇCYD) has been prosecuted for describing the *cem* house as a place of worship in its statutes. Following the refusal by the ÇCYD of the request from the Interior Ministry to remove the references to *cem* house as a place of worship from its statutes,[45] the Governorship initiated a court case via the Ankara Prosecutor's Office to close the ÇCYD down.[46] The first degree court relied on Article 9 of the ECHR and held that the right to freedom of religion or belief includes the right to establish places of worship. The first degree court did not consider the *cem* houses as *tekke* or *zaviye*—which could not be opened according to Law No. 677.[47] The, highly technical, explanation for this was that the *tekke* and *zaviye* were places which housed the sheik or dervish and that the *cem* houses do not have such a function.[48] It, however, held that the rituals in the *cem* houses may indeed be prohibited by Law No. 677, but these needed to be assessed in light of contemporary legal norms. The court held that taking into account Article 9 of the ECHR and the principle of secularism in the Turkish Constitution the state cannot determine what constitutes "worship or a place of worship" and found that the establishment of *cem* houses was not contrary to the ECHR or the Turkish Civil Code,[49] and the Law on Associations.[50] In conclusion, there was no need to dissolve the association because of the reference to *cem* house as a place of worship in its statutes.

In contrast, the Court of Appeals overturned the decision of the first instance court and referred to Law No. 677 saying that it closes *tekke* and *zaviye* but allows

43 The Memoirs of Hamdullah Suphi, a member of Parliament who openly opposed the closure of the *türbe* (shrines), testify that Mustafa Kemal viewed the closure of *türbe* as the elimination of a certain mentality and perhaps also as a temporary measure with a view to open them again in ten years' time. Kara, *supra* note 39, p. 280.

44 In the following decades many shrines and dervish lodges were opened as museums. For example the Galata Mevlevihane was closed with Law No. 677; however, it was opened as the Divan Literature Museum in 1975 and as the Galata Mevlevihane Museum in 2011. Similarly, the Hacı Bektaş Veli Lodge, which continues to be very important for the Alevi Bektashi community, was closed with Law No. 677 and opened as a museum in 1964. While the status of museum has contributed to the preservation of these buildings, it has cut the ties of the communities with the buildings and made it impossible to use these buildings for worship purposes.

45 The Directorate for Associations of the Ministry of Interior sent a letter to the Ankara Governorship, referring to this Diyanet opinion of 30 March 2005 Letter No. 1277.

46 Ankara 16th Peace Court, E/2010/492, 4 October 2011.

47 Ibid.

48 Ibid.

49 Türk Medeni Kanunu [Turkish Civil Code] No. 4721, 22 November 2001.

50 Dernekler Kanunu [Law on Associations] No. 5231, 17 July 2004.

the existence of mosques and *mesjid*.[51] It is important to note that Law No. 677 does not refer to *cem* houses. The Court of Appeals also recalled the status of Law No. 677 and said that none of its provisions may be interpreted in a way as to be incompatible with the provisions of the Constitution.[52] It went on to argue that Law No. 677 excludes the establishment of any Islamic place of worship other than mosques or *mesjid*.[53] Interestingly, the reasoning does not consider whether the *cem* house is equivalent to *tekke* or *zaviye*, but instead, proceeds with the assumption that Law No. 677 only allows mosques and *mesjids*.

The reasoning also recalls that the Diyanet is tasked with the management of places of worship and that these may be opened with the permission of the Diyanet.[54] Thus it infers from this permission to operate mosques and *mesjid* that no Islamic place of worship other than these may be lawful. Therefore based on the reference to an "unlawful" place of worship in the association's statute the Court of Appeals concludes that the statute of the association is contrary to law and therefore necessitates the dissolution of the association by a court decision.[55]

Interestingly, while numerous previous administrative or judicial decisions relied on the Diyanet opinion, in this reasoning the Court of Appeals does not refer to the Diyanet opinion which states that Muslims worship in mosques.[56] The reason for this may be to strive for a reasoning that is based on legislation instead of a theological opinion, thus, perhaps, taking into account public criticism generated by taking into account opinion of the Diyanet in the decisions of public authorities.

There are significant flaws in the reasoning by the Court of Appeals. It did not consider the question of whether *cem* houses and *tekke* and *zaviye* are identical or not. If it had concluded that *cem* houses are identical to *tekke*, for example, it should not be possible to allow the *de facto* existence of *cem* houses without amending Law No. 677. Instead, it concluded that only "mosques and *mesjid*" are allowed and this is based on the reference in Law No. 677 to allowing mosques and *mesjid* to remain where *tekke* and *zaviye* are used for these purposes. In addition, under its law, the Diyanet is given the mandate to operate only mosques and *mesjid*. Since *cem* houses are not considered as *tekke* these are not prohibited as such. This is also evident in the fact that there are hundreds of *cem* houses operating in the country and they are not closed or considered illegal.[57] Hence their

51 *Radikal*, "Yargıtay Cemevine Kapıyı Kapattı" [The Court of Appeals Closed the Door on Cem Houses], 25 July 2012.

52 Ibid.

53 7th Chamber of the Civil Division of the Court of Appeals, E/2012/262, K/2012/3351, 10 May 2012.

54 In accordance with Article 35 of the Diyanet İşleri Başkanlığı Kuruluş ve Görevleri Hakkında Kanun (Law on the Establishment and Mandate of the Presidency of Religious Affairs) Law No. 633, 22 June 1965, Official Gazette No. 12038, 2 July 1965.

55 Article 89 of the Civil Code stipulates that when the purpose of an association becomes contrary to law and morals a court will decide for its dissolution. Medeni Kanun (Civil Code), Law No. 4721, 22 November 2001, Official Gazette No. 24627, 8 December 2001.

56 For the Diyanet opinion see *supra* note 38.

57 See p. 217.

existence is not contrary to the domestic law. The fact that the Diyanet is given the task to administer mosques and *mesjid* does not necessarily mean that no other Islamic places of worship are allowed to exist. In fact, it would mean that if there are Islamic places of worship other than mosques or *mesjid*, the Diyanet does not have a mandate to operate them. Therefore the decision of the Court of Appeals that regards the reference to *cem* house as a place of worship in the association's statute as unlawful cannot be prescribed by law.

The reasoning of the Court of Appeals does not include any reference to the right to freedom of religion or belief, nor does it consider the consequences (proportionality) of the denial of the recognition of the *cem* houses as places of worship for the association or the Alevi community.

Paradoxically, despite the strong refusal to grant place of worship status to *cem* houses, according to the Office of the Prime Minister there are 598 *cem* houses in Turkey.[58] None of them has a place of worship status. This results in the impossibility for members of the Alevi community to avail themselves of the benefits granted to places of worship, as well as denying these Alevi houses of worship the social status and prestige other places of worship enjoy. Socially, having a legally recognized place of worship gives a religious community a high social standing and helps its followers not to be marginalized. The importance of the latter is increased in light of widespread intolerance in Turkish society towards members of other religions.[59]

Mosques and *mesjid* are subject to a different regulation based on the requirements of the Presidency of Religious Affairs.[60] Mosques must be opened with the permission of the Diyanet and are administered by the Diyanet.[61] In 1998, following political developments of "28 February",[62] an amendment was made to

58 Response of the Office of the Prime Minister to a communication of Member of Parliament Doc. No. B.02.0.004./954, 16 July 2012, see *Hürriyet*, Cemevi Sayısı 598 [Number of Cem Houses 598], 27 July 2012, Available: http://www.hurriyet.com.tr/gundem/21077587.asp [Accessed 16 January 2015].

59 Çarkoğlu, A. and E. Kalaycıoğlu (2009) *Türkiye'de Dindarlık: Uluslararası bir Karşılaştırma* [Religiosity in Turkey: An International Comparison] Istanbul: Sabancı University Publications.

60 İmar Kanunu [Public Works Law], *supra* note 10.

61 Medeni Kanun [Civil Code], *supra* note 55.

62 National Security Memorandum on the Measures that Need to be Taken Against Actions Contrary to the Regime and Reactionary Movements. Articles 13 and 9 of National Security Council Decision No. 406, 28 February 1997. The role played by the military in the making of this memorandum is considered a soft intervention or as popularly named a "post-modern coup" by the military into the political system. Through this intervention, the Prime Minister Necmettin Erbakan was removed from his position, without dissolving the parliament. The memorandum started a process called the 28 February Process where measures were taken to protect secularism. Other measures include, eight years' compulsory primary education, closure of Islamic sects, and closure of illegal Quran courses. Generally on this period see Bayramoğlu, A. (2007) *28 Şubat: Bir Müdahalenin Güncesi* [February 28: The Diary of an Intervention], Istanbul: İletişim Publications; and for the text of the Memorandum and its implications, see Günay, N. (2001) "Implementing the 'February 28'

the Law on the Diyanet to the effect that the administration of any mosque built by real or legal persons, opened for worship whether with or without permission, must be transferred to the Diyanet.[63] Thus mosques built by private citizens were nationalized according to a report by the Mazlum-Der.[64] Indeed, the Cadastral Law stipulates that buildings that are used for public service will be registered under the name of public institutions, and mosques and cemeteries are listed as buildings used to provide "public services".[65] Names of other places of worship, such as churches, synagogues or *cem* houses are not mentioned. This reflects a preferential view of mosques as the only places of worship that provide public services.

The perspective of viewing certain manifestations of religion or belief solely as enjoyable through public religious services raises questions when assessing compatibility of national legislation in the light of international standards. The practical outcome of this perspective and ensuing legislative arrangement is that it is not possible to establish a mosque and appoint religious personnel outside of the Diyanet structure. Members of religious communities may collect funds toward the construction of mosques and have them built but they cannot own them even through associations. Such regulation singles out the Diyanet as the sole subject of the exercise of the right to establish places of worship and appoint religious leaders in the context of Sunni-Muslim practice. While there may be demands to establish and maintain mosques outside of the Diyanet structure these demands have not, yet, been subject to court cases; instead, negotiations with political leaders have been the processes of engagement by religious minorities.

(c) Acquisition of Legal Personality

Apart from the status of the premises as a place of worship, the question of the linkage between legal personality of a belief community and ownership of a place of worship also becomes an important factor for the protection of the right to establish and maintain places of worship. The fact that in Turkey no belief community may acquire legal personality, as such,[66] negatively affects the enjoyment

Recommendations: A Scorecard", Research Notes No. 10, Washington Institute for Near East Policy, May, in particular p. 14. For the an overview of the 28 February period and the absence of a space of negotiations and mediations between society and state on unavoidable disagreements related to such public policies see An-Naim, A.A. (2008) *Islam and the Secular State: Negotiating the Future of Shari'a*, Harvard: Harvard University Press, pp. 206–215.

63 Mazlum-Der (2010) *Türkiye'de Dini Ayrımcılık Raporu* [Report on Religious Discrimination in Turkey], Istanbul: Mazlum-Der Publications, p. 214.

64 Ibid.

65 Article 16 (A) of Kadastro Kanunu [Cadastral Law], Law No. 3402, 21 June 1987, Official Gazette No. 19512, 9 July 1987.

66 The Venice Commission recommended that Turkey provides a legal framework that would allow the non-Muslim religious communities, as such, adequate access to court and the right themselves to hold property, without having to do this through the foundation model. "Opinion on the Legal Status of Religious Communities in Turkey and the Right

of, and creates a gap in, the effective protection of the right to establish and maintain places of worship in Turkey. Groups of believers cannot own a place of worship as a composite body through an adequate form of legal personality. The association and foundation formulas[67] only create an indirect form of legal entity status which is substantially different than the community as such having direct ownership. The far-reaching supervision involved in the foundation and association formulas may also place the places of worship at risk as changes in legislation and/or practice may create conditions that allow the state to confiscate the buildings or exercise control over repairs etc.[68] The strategic importance of legal personality in the process pertaining to the establishment, maintenance and ownership of places of worship illustrates the nature of vulnerability of belief communities that is created by the denial of legal personality to them. An appalling example is the Latin Catholic Church in Turkey; lacking legal personality of any kind,[69] the community can neither own property, nor seek judicial review of cases where it has lost possession of property as a result of not having legal personality. So far, the Latin Catholic community has not sought legal remedies and instead seeks to find a political solution to the problem through negotiations between Turkish authorities and the Holy See.[70]

Legally speaking, gathering for worship in a building that is not legally recognized as such, or calling it a *cem* house, church or a similar name may result in prosecution. A number of church buildings that had links to legal associations have been formally warned by local police that worship in their buildings is

of the Orthodox Patriarchate of Istanbul to Use the Adjective 'Ecumenical'", Venice Commission, Opinion No. 535/2009, 15 March 2010, para. 71.

67 An association is a private law legal person that is formed by real or legal persons for the objective of realizing a certain purpose by bringing together their knowledge and efforts and that is not contrary to law. Dernekler Kanunu [Law on Associations] No. 5253, 4 November 2004, Official Gazette No. 25649, 23 November 2004, Article 2. Article 56 of the Turkish Civil Code. While the association formula may open the way for carrying out certain activities and thus meet some of the associative needs of these long-established belief communities it is not designed as a form of religious institution or a legal entity status for a belief community. The association formula does not seem suitable for the organizational and institutional set-up of churches such as the Orthodox Patriarchate and the Armenian Patriarchate, or the Chief Rabbinate. A foundation is an endowment the income of which is dedicated to a certain purpose, yet, Article 101(4) of the Turkish Civil Code, prohibits the establishment of a foundation "contrary to the characteristics of the Republic as defined by the Constitution, Constitutional rules, laws, morals, national integrity and national interest, or with the aim of supporting a distinctive race or community". See more in Chapter 6.

68 For historical experiences see Kurban, D. and K. Hatemi (2009) *Bir Yabancılaştırma Hikayesi: Türkiye'de Gayrimüslim Vakıf ve Taşınmaz Mülkiyet Sorunu* [A Story of Alienation: The Problem of non-Muslim Minorities' Problems Pertaining to Foundations and Unmoveable Property], Istanbul: TESEV Publications.

69 *Supra* note 6, interview with Rinaldo Marmara.

70 In the New Constitution drafting process the main request of the Catholic community from the Constitutional Reconciliation Commission has been the recognition of the Catholic Church as a legal person. *Milliyet Daily*, "Yeni Anayasa Çalışmaları Devam Ediyor" [Work on New Constitution Continues], 16 April 2012.

unlawful.[71] The reason given is that the buildings are not legally recognized as places of worship and therefore they cannot be used for worship purposes. The government has also shown "goodwill" toward the so-called Lausanne minorities allowing them to assemble for worship in churches that have historic significance for them, such as the Ahtamar Church in Van for the Armenian Apostolic community,[72] and the Sumela Monastery for the Greek Orthodox community.[73] While these may be considered as gestures of tolerance toward assemblies for worship and non-Muslim minorities, it is important to remember that these actions do not go as far as conferring rights and fall short of solving the problems concerning the right to establish places of worship.

As outlined above, in Turkey there is indeed a general recognition of the right to assemble for worship and establish and maintain places of worship in the Constitution and it is regulated through applicable legislation. Processes pertaining to building places of worship and acquiring place of worship status ostensibly appear neutral; however, as the input from minority religious groups demonstrates, the process does not appear to be designed for worship places other than mosques. This is also evident in the outcomes: the number of successful applications for place of worship status—other than mosques—is scarce. It is difficult to see the justification for this practice. The results of these restrictions—the non-recognition as a place of worship—are numerous; *inter alia*, the risk of interference and inability to benefit from advantages stemming from the recognition as a place of worship. That which should be a routine procedure, recognition of place of worship, seems nearly impossible to obtain. Such restrictions and refusals, rather, must be exceptional, must be justified, and proportionate to the aim pursued and necessary in a democratic society.

In conclusion, it follows from the above account that the right to establish and maintain places of worship is restricted in a number of ways which, often, cumulatively create obstacles to the effective enjoyment of this right. It is in the processes involving the municipalities and the governorship where this right is denied. Inflexible planning regulations are, more often than not, suitable to the nature and demands of belief groups in Turkey. The process involving municipalities appears arbitrary. The process involving the approval of the Governorships lacks transparency and foreseeable criteria. The rejection of the Alevi *cem* houses as places of worship by the public authorities, Governorships, involves an assessment of the legitimacy of a place of worship. The fundamental problem of lack of legal personality demonstrates the inter-dependency of the various components of the right to freedom of religion or belief. Not having legal personality, religious communities cannot enjoy the right to own property and seek judicial protection.

71 *Supra* note 18, interview with Umut Şahin.

72 The Armenian Apostolic community is allowed to hold worship mass once a year at the Akdamar church. The first service was held on 19 September 2010. *Haberiniz*, "Ermeniler Akdamar Ayini için Van'a Akın Ediyor" [Armenians Flooding to Van for Akdamar Mass], 9 July 2011.

73 *Sabah*, "Sümela Manastırı'danki Ayin için Hazırlıklar Başladı" [Preparations Underway for Mass to be Held in Sumela Monastery], 2 August 2012.

The importance of clear, foreseeable and adequate and suitable procedures as well as facilitative administrative processes are clearly illustrated in the Turkish case; indeed it is not an exaggeration to say that the right to establish places of worship is a "trapped right". The Turkish case also shows that international compliance control mechanisms need to exercise strict scrutiny when assessing restrictions on the right to establish places of worship. The wide margin of appreciation given to states and the accommodation of the planning regulations will not contribute to upholding the right to establish places of worship domestically in accordance with international human rights law. Thus, subtle forms of discrimination will remain veiled. It is the task of review mechanisms to unveil the less obvious ways of discrimination such as through ostensibly neutral planning regulations and city plans.

7.2.2 The Right to Teach a Religion or Belief in Places Suitable for these Purposes

As has been discussed in Chapter 4, the right to manifest religion or belief in teaching and more specifically the right "to teach" religion or belief "in places suitable" for these purposes is a vital component of the right to freedom of religion or belief. Though both individuals as well as collectivities exercise this right, it is important to note that for the religious or belief group this right plays a key role in the preservation, development and transmission of religious dogma, tradition and identity. Manifestation in teaching may take diverse forms, *inter alia*, the right to teach one's own group about the fundamentals of the faith, the right to teach others about one's faith with a view to proselytize, to teach with the purpose of training clergy, to open schools, as well as extending to engage in acts necessary to fulfill the aforementioned, such as establishing schools for religious instruction and publishing and disseminating relevant materials. Here, the assessment will be restricted to the protection of this right as it is manifested in teaching for the purpose of educating one's congregation and formal teaching aimed at training religious leaders and personnel since these two forms are crucial for the protection of the collective identity of a religious or belief group.

Currently, teaching of religion in Turkey is a highly regulated and a significantly restricted issue. In addition, outcomes indicate serious inequalities in the accessibility of this right for diverse religious or belief communities. There is no legislative framework for establishing schools by religious or belief communities with the purpose of educating their followers in their religion or belief. Similarly, schools or seminaries may not be established to train religious personnel. As a result, no faith based school may be established by any religious or belief community. These limitations stand in striking contrast to the state's involvement in and facilitation of teaching religion, solely Islamic and based on the *Hanafi* tradition. National education curricula, which must be adhered to by all schools, instates compulsory Islamic religious instruction through the Religious Culture and Ethics lessons. Programs of theological faculties in public universities are designed to teach only Islam and as far as training of religious personnel is concerned only accommodate the needs of the Sunni-Muslim community. While the Sunni-Muslim community has the possibility of benefiting from state funded and provided religious instruction services, still, they cannot exercise the right to manifest religion or belief by actively establishing schools or providing formal education to their followers or train religious personnel. Muslim minorities within the majority Muslim population and non-Muslim communities are not able to train religious personnel and teach their followers their religion or belief freely, neither does the state provide any religious training services aimed at meeting the needs of these communities.

It is useful to note and underscore the following regarding the meanings attributed to "religion", "theology" and "Islam" in the context of relevant national legal instruments. References in the Turkish Constitution and legislation pertaining to education to "religion" *usually* are taken to mean Islam by public authorities, and Islam is understood in accordance with the teachings on "true Islam" of the Diyanet.[74] Theological education and theology faculties in universities categorically deal with "Islamic theology". While it is not possible to go into depth about the use of these terms and their implications for the protection of freedom of religion or belief, it is important to know that references to these terms in legislation do not necessarily comprise neutral meanings—such as "religion" referring to all religions or "theology" referring to theology of all religions—and that there is a need to establish what meaning is attributed to each term.

Legislation pertaining to the Turkish national education system and its implications to the right to manifest religion or belief in teaching cannot be adequately understood without highlighting the emergence of this system as a reaction to the fragmented and religion based or influenced education system of the Ottoman Empire. Historically, teaching of religion and training of religious personnel was viewed as an activity carried out within the realm of religious communities. Together with the numerous reforms following the establishment of the Republic of Turkey, the fragmented and old education system was abolished and a new unified national education system was created through Law No. 430 on the Unification of Education in 1924, which also had the purpose of redefining the role of religion in education.[75] The Law on the Unification of Education enjoys special protection as a Reform Law and it cannot be interpreted in a way where it is deemed unconstitutional.[76] Consequently, the *Madrasah*, that had been the religious schools of the Ottoman era, were abolished, and in the sphere of religious education, the new law foresaw the establishment of vocational theological schools and theology faculties in universities.[77]

Not surprisingly, policies on religious instruction have been, and continue to be, important means of shaping society for all political parties. Between the years 1927–1949, no religious instruction was permitted in schools and only in 1949 did the Ministry of Education allow a course on religion in 4th and 5th grades of

74 See Gözaydın, İ. (2009) *Diyanet: Türkiye'de Dinin Tanzimi* [The Diyanet: Arrangement of Religion in Turkey], Istanbul: İletişim Publications.

75 Law No. 430 of 3 March 1340 (1924) on the Unification of the Educational System.

76 Turkish Constitution, Article 174.

77 Ibid. The Law on the Unification of the Education System foresaw the transfer of the madrasa to the Ministry of Education which closed them shortly after via an administrative decision.

primary school.[78] The course was optional, depending upon a written request from parents, and it was taught outside the regular school hours. Together with the passage to multi-party democracy, a new government (the Demokrat Parti) was established in 1956 and the openness of this party led to the introduction of a religion course into secondary schools, with the possibility of exemption.[79] Finally, following the military coup in 1980, the "Religious Culture and Knowledge of Ethics" course became obligatory for all secondary level schools thus constitutionally securing the status of the religion course in all schools, public and private.[80] The restrictions on the right to manifest religion or belief in teaching are inevitably and intricately linked to the contextual state-religion relations reflected in the national education policy with its unique goals and sensitivities. The latter has been inadequately guided by human rights obligations. The account above only begins to demonstrate the various political considerations affecting the nature and extent of protection of the right to manifest religion or belief in teaching.

The Turkish Civil Code grants the right to "determine the religious education of the child" to the mother and father.[81] Moreover, any contract that would restrict the rights of the mother and father in this respect is considered null and void.[82] "Determine", however, does not necessarily amount to the right to raise children in line with one's religious or philosophical beliefs. Indeed, Turkey has placed a reservation on Article 2 of Protocol 1 of the ECHR which protects the right to education and recognizes that states will respect the right of parents and legal guardians to raise their children in line with their religious or philosophical convictions.[83] Turkey's reservation states that Article 2 of Protocol 1 of the European Convention shall not violate the provisions of Law No. 430 on the Unification of Education.[84]

Under the general framework of the secular education system, teaching of religion or belief in Turkey may be carried out only under state supervision according to the Turkish Constitution.[85] There is no legal framework for the formal teaching of religion or belief outside of state supervision. There exists no school that would provide a formal degree, similar to, for example, the public vocational theological schools or theology faculties where instruction is based on Islam as interpreted by state institutions. State holds monopoly over religious education in primary, middle and high schools. Under the Law on Private Educational Institutions

78 Adanalı, H. (2001) *Religious Education in Schools*, Ankara: Ankara University.
79 Ibid.
80 There are various explanations for the gradual integration of religious education in the curriculum of public schools between the years 1949–1982. These explanations include the need to provide the public with sound religious knowledge; the impact of the Second World War, which made the need for religion and morality more sensible; the threat of communism; the erosion of traditional and moral values; and, finally, the threat of terrorism which claimed approximately 20 lives per day before the military coup of 1980.
81 Turkish Civil Code, Article 341.
82 Ibid.
83 Article 2 of Protocol 1 of the European Convention on Human Rights.
84 CoE, Treaty Office records.
85 Turkish Constitution, Article 24.

"education institutions identical or similar to ones that provide religious education cannot be opened".[86] Hence, the practice has been that religious/belief groups teach their religion or belief, *inter alia*, in their places of worship, receive formal education outside the country or establish associations or foundations for the purpose of research and teaching through which teaching may be possible. Yet, these cannot provide degrees comparable to those provided in schools within the Ministry of Education system.

Thus, for individuals or groups who cannot or, prefer not to make use of the public religious training or instruction opportunities, the right to manifest religion or belief in teaching continues to be a categorically denied right. Non-Muslim groups and non-Sunni Islamic groups and, indeed, some Sunni-Muslim groups that would wish to provide religious education outside the public education system, suffer the consequences. In an effort to provide for the needs of the communities and transmit religious dogma, in particular with respect to children and youths, religious instruction often takes place in the communities' places of worship, albeit without formal accreditation. The view that "beyond the official school system, there is no restriction on private religious instruction"[87] fails to represent the actual situation. The constitutional provision stating that "other religious instruction may be carried out under state supervision" may be interpreted in a narrow fashion to mean "other formal religious instruction" or broadly to mean "any other religious instruction". There have been cases where it has been broadly interpreted. For example, in 2002 Protestant congregations were served notifications that "religious instruction could only be carried out under state supervision".[88] The nature of the acts of teaching religion by these congregations was to teach their own congregants and those who were interested in visiting their churches, which did not have a legal place of worship status. The, less than certain and clear, respect for the right to teach one's religion to one's members leads to fear within religious communities that such teaching may be interfered with by the public authorities.[89] This adds to the vulnerability of religious or belief communities. In order to avoid conflict, there are cases where summer camps or courses that in reality aim to teach children in religion are named "vacation camps" or "clubs" in order avoid potential problems.[90]

86 Özel Öğretim Kurumları Kanunu [Law on Private Educational Institutions] No. 5580, 8 February 2007.
87 Öktem, E. and M. Uzun (2010) "IACL: National Report on the Republic of Turkey", in *IACL National Reports*, International Centre for Law and Religion, p. 713.
88 Interview with the General Secretary of the Association of Protestant Churches Umut Şahin, January 2013.
89 For example, the Alevi groups meeting in homes, for many years, had a "watchmen" who would watch the outside of homes where the Alevi would worship and teach their religion, fearing that the authorities or a non-Alevi would notice their activity.
90 Representatives of a number of religious communities interviewed throughout the course of this book have referred to the challenges to organize camps or courses for teaching the youth about their religion and the feeling of being compelled to "name" it something else like "vacation camp", "club" or "cultural seminar". To ensure

In fact, the existing arrangement "leads" individuals or groups to be the *recipients* of the public services pertaining to teaching of religion. Compulsory Religious Culture and Knowledge of Ethics classes are available for all, but only benefit certain groups of Muslims and indeed interfere in the right to have a religion or belief of many students and the right of parents to raise their children in line with their religious or philosophical beliefs.[91] Middle and high school education with Islamic emphasis is available for Muslims,[92] optional lessons on the Quran and the Life of the Prophet Mohammed became available in public schools in the 2012–2013 school year.[93] It is important to note here that the public religious instruction in schools is criticized for being fundamentally based on Sunni Islam and for excluding other Islamic traditions, *inter alia*, the Alevi tradition.[94] Religion classes are available at the so-called officially recognized Lausanne non-Muslim minority schools under the supervision of the Ministry of Education.[95]

Quran courses are available outside of school curricula only through programs administered by the Presidency of Religious Affairs.[96] This arrangement also contains numerous restrictions. Apart from the Presidency of Religious Affairs, no real or legal persons, including foundations and associations may open such courses.[97] There are Sunni-Muslims who often complain that two hours per week cannot be

confidentiality the names of these representatives and their respective communities will not be disclosed here.

91 For a comprehensive evaluation of these lessons, including their diverse societal demands, see a Report by Reform in Education Initiative, "Din ve Eğitim", February 2011, Sabancı University. Available: http://erg.sabanciuniv.edu/sites/erg.sabanciuniv.edu/files/DinVeEgitim.pdf [Accessed 16 January 2015]. Gözaydın, İ. (2009) "Türkiye'de Din Kültürü ve Ahlak Bilgisi ders kitaplarına insan hakları merceğiyle bir bakış" [A Human Rights Perspective on the Books of the Religious Culture and Knowledge of Ethics Course Books in Turkey], in G. Tüzün, (Der.), *Ders kitaplarında insan hakları ıı tarama sonuçları* [Results of the Human Rights Screening of School Books], İstanbul: Tarih Vakfı, pp. 167–193.

92 The İmam and Preachers High Schools are established according to Article 4 of the Act of Unification of Education and Article 32 of Basic Law of National Education No. 1739 and they serve both as vocational schools and preparatory schools for higher education. On these vocational theological middle and high-schools (Imam Hatip) and their function and growth, see Mardin, Ş. (2001) *Religion, Society, and Modernity in Turkey*, Syracusa University Press, pp. 26–298; Elügür, B. (2014) *The Mobilization of Political Islam in Turkey*, Istanbul: Başkent University Press, pp. 85–135; Bozan, İ. (2007) *Devlet ile Toplum Arasında bir Okul: İmam Hatip Liseleri...bir Kurum: Diyanet İşleri Başkanlığı* [Between State and Society], Istanbul: TESEV.

93 *Milliyet*, "Kur'an-ı Kerim, liselerde seçmeli ders olarak okutulacak" [The Quran will be an Optional Course in High Schools], 5 September 2012.

94 European Commission, Turkey Progress Report, 2011.

95 Kaya, N. (2009) *Unutmak mı asimilasyon mu? Türkiye'nin Eğitim Sisteminde Azınlıklar* [Forgotten or Assimilated? Minorities in Turkey's Education System], Istanbul: Minority Rights Group.

96 Öktem and Uzun, *supra* note 87.

97 Diyanet İşleri Başkanlığı Kur'an Kursları ile Öğrenci ve Yurt ve Pansiyon Yönetmeliği [The Presidency of Religious Affairs Regulation on the Quran Courses and Student and Dormitories] Devlet Bakanlığı ve Başbakan Yardımcılığından, Yayımlandığı Resmi Gazete Tarihi: 3 March 2000, Article 7. Article 8 stipulates that only children who have

enough to meet the "need for religion".[98] It is reported that the age limit for taking part in the Quran courses constitutes an interference considering the early age *hafiz* (individuals who memorize the Quran) training needs to start.[99] Adults may apply for evening courses on the Quran.[100] In these courses all materials must be found "appropriate" by the Diyanet.[101] Training on the Quran in mosques is subject to the approval of the administrative authority,[102] which is indicative of the powers of the public authorities which includes approval of basic religious services.

As noted above, only the Diyanet may organize Quran courses. Numerous associations that have opened Quran courses have been sanctioned on the basis of operating private courses unlawfully.[103] According to Mazlum-Der, an Islamic human rights organization, even legitimate dormitories connected to legal Quran courses may be closed "upon rumors [concerning] actions against Atatürk's principles and reforms, actions towards dividing the indivisible unity of the country with its nation, as well as racism".[104] In a case dealing with a child activity center where children were taught the Quran, the *namaz* ritual, as well as religious songs, the Court of Appeals dealt with the case on the basis of using the center for purposes other than the permissible activities found in its statute.[105] The right to freedom of religion or belief has not been considered in the judicial assessment. In 2013, these rules were relaxed with the annulment of Article 263 of the Turkish Criminal Code, which prescribes imprisonment of individuals who open education institutions that are contrary to law and has been used as the basis for closing unauthorized Quran courses.[106] No new regulation was put in place, however, leaving this sphere in ambiguity.

In short, the right to teach religion or belief to a religious or belief group's followers is not ensured and highly restricted—arguably a denied right. This remains in stark contrast to the extent of funding and institutional support given to the state imposed and supplied religious instruction based on the majority's religious tradition.

The inability to train religious personnel remains at the forefront of the various issues raised by the obstacles before the right to teach religion or belief. A number of religious communities, such as the Caferi, Jewish and some Christian

completed primary school may take part in the Quran Courses. And according to Article 16 these courses start in the first week of October and end in the last week of May.

98 Adanalı, *supra* note 78.

99 Mazlum-Der, *supra* note 63, p. 216.

100 Article 32(a).

101 Article 26.

102 Article 33.

103 Court of Appeals Criminal 9th Chamber, E/1980/4847 and K/1980/4952, 12 December 1980. Court of Appeals Criminal 4th Chamber, E/2000/6756 and K/2000/6043, 27 September 2000.

104 Mazlum-Der, *supra* note 64, p. 217.

105 Court of Appeals 4th Criminal Chamber, E2003/8828 and K2004/10232, 19 October 2004.

106 Yıldırım, M. (2013) *Monitoring Report on the Right to Freedom of Religion or Belief*, January–June 2013, Istanbul: Norwegian Helsinki Committee, p. 30.

communities, send potential candidates for religious instruction abroad. Certain Christian communities, on the other hand, have been demanding a solution to the problem of training clergy in formal theological schools, including universities, in Turkey. The Armenian Apostolic Church is anxious to train more priests and, in 2006, asked the Ministry of Education to allow the establishment of a state university faculty on Christian theology which also includes instruction by the Patriarchate.[107] In the meantime, Armenian Apostolics continue to seek religious training abroad.[108] In an effort, perhaps, to solve the problems concerning higher education for Christian religious personnel, for some time the government has been considering the possibility of opening a suitable department in the existing faculties of theology which teach Islamic theology. Nevertheless, no substantive step or outcome appears in sight. The Department of The Cultural Studies of World Religions established in 1999 in Istanbul University, proposed as an alternative to the Halki Seminary, was closed in 2011 because the Higher Education Council had failed to allocate faculty and student quotas.[109] Still, the Greek Patriarchate, in pursuit of a solution through the public education system, insists on the re-opening of the Halki seminary.[110] As a result of the obstacles to establishing appropriate educational institutions, many religious communities must send their candidates for teachers or leaders abroad for religious training. This alternative, naturally, has many disadvantages, like the financial burden on the communities and the reluctance of candidates to return to Turkey after training abroad.[111]

As far as the so-called Lausanne minorities are concerned, as in many other aspects of freedom of religion or belief, the right to teach religion is viewed through the "reciprocity" lens by the government,[112] where formulas are developed by the state in a way to ensure similar solutions for the Turkish minority in Greece.[113] For example, throughout the Republic, religious communities have been denied the right of formal private teaching based on their religious traditions; nevertheless, the Greek Orthodox Halki Seminary (vocational middle school) continued to train religious personnel until 1971 when it was closed as a result of tensions in relations with Greece. This has significantly undermined rights

107 *Hürriyet*, "Mutafyan: Hıristiyan İlahiyat Fakültesi açılsın" [Mutafyan: A Christian Theological Faculty Should Open], 20 April 2002. Available: http://webarsiv.hurriyet.com.tr/2002/04/20/114928.asp [Accessed 16 January 2015].

108 Interview with a member of the Spiritual Council of the Armenian Apostolic Church, 30 July 2014.

109 *Milliyet*, "Ruhban Okulu'nun alternatifi kapandı" [The Alternative of the Seminary has been Closed], 1 October 2012.

110 The seminary was closed in 1971 after the Patriarchate, in order to avoid being administered by the state, chose not to comply with a state requirement to nationalize.

111 Kaya A. and Ö. Genç (2011) *Belief Groups in Turkey: A New Framework for Problems and Demands*, Istanbul: Alevi Vakıfları Federasyonu, p. 22.

112 On the principle of reciprocity see Chapter 5 of this book.

113 For a number of formulas that have not been carried out see, *Radikal*, Betül Kotan, "38 Yıllık bir Yılan Hikâyesi: Heybeliada Ruhban Okulu" [Long Tale of 38 Years: the Halki Seminary], 10 April 2009.

protected, among others, by the Lausanne Treaty.[114] While the use of the reciprocity principle by Turkey does not change the crux of the issue as a human right, the reciprocity perspective embraced by the state does add another dimension that cannot be ignored when seeking corrective action by the Turkish state.

The teaching of religion in higher education is subject to the significant bureaucratic control and financial burden applicable to establishing universities in Turkey. Considering the limited financial resources of minority religious communities, the suspicion entrenched in the state apparatus against them, the establishment of a private university where theological education can be provided does not present itself as a real option. Public and Foundation (private, non-profit) Universities in Turkey are established through a decision of the Cabinet and all university education must be carried out under state supervision.[115] The Turkish higher education system has a centralized structure and, whether public or private, all universities must be founded through the adoption of law.[116] The Council of Higher Education supervises universities and their programs must be regularly accredited. The establishment of new faculties need to be approved by the Council of Higher Education.[117]

Islamic religious groups have been able to establish Islamic theology faculties through foundation universities.[118] There is, however, no example of a non-Sunni or non-Muslim private university that has an appropriate theological program. Despite the absence of a ban on establishing a theological faculty through a foundation university, the difficulties and complexities of the bureaucratic process and needs in terms of, not least, the financial[119] and human resources make it very difficult, if not impossible, for most religious groups to establish private theological faculties.[120] Most public universities have an Islamic theological faculty. The first private Islamic theological faculty was established within Fatih University in 2010 with the decision of the Cabinet.[121] In 2014 the Islamic Research Center under the 29 Mayıs University, owned by the Diyanet Foundation, applied to establish the first International Islamic University.[122]

114 For a thorough account of the closing process and following developments see Macar, E. and M.A. Gökaçtı (2005) *Heybeliada Ruhban Okulu'nun Geleceğine ilişkin Tartışmalar ve Öneriler* [Discussion and Recommendations Pertaining to the Future of the Heybeliada Theological Seminary], Istanbul: TESEV.

115 Turkish Constitution, Article 130.

116 The Higher Education Law No. 2547. There were no private universities in Turkey until 1984 and private universities may only be established by non-profit foundations.

117 Ibid.

118 Fatih University is known to be affiliated with the Gülen movement.

119 A minimum of 15 million TL (approximately 7 million Euros) is required for the establishment of a foundation that will have the purpose of establishing a university.

120 Telephone interview with Ali Gül from Ehl-i Beyt İnanc Derneği, 17 December 2012.

121 See Fatih University website. Available: http://ilahiyat.fatih.edu.tr/ [Accessed 17 December 2014].

122 *Hürriyet*, "Diyanet'ten İslam Üniversitesi" [Islamic University from the Diyanet], 1 October 2014.

The assessment of the protection of a human right should include the assessment of indications of the outcomes expected as a result of the protection of the right in question; the non-existence of any higher education institution that provides education in minority religions demonstrates that necessary structural and process related changes are yet to take place. This situation, when viewed in contrast to the institutional and financial state support evident in the existence of Islamic theological faculties established in public universities must have implications for the assessment of the effectiveness of protection of the right to freedom of religion or belief in Turkey. Human rights compliance control mechanisms have yet to find a way to address these kind of inequalities. In adjudication the questions asked concern whether there is an interference in the right to manifest religion or belief; however there may be situations where the exercise of a right is possible in theory, but not possible in practice. While state support of certain religions or religious groups is not usually seen as amounting to interference in the right to freedom of religion or belief of other groups, as is evident in the Turkish case it creates a substantial inequality, particularly when combined with restrictions in the exercise of the right to manifest one's religion or belief in teaching.

Teaching of religion or belief is a fundamental component of the right to freedom of thought, conscience, religion or belief. It is expressed explicitly in the core international religious freedom provisions. Everyone has the right to manifest religion or belief, alone or in community with others in worship, *teaching*, observance or practice.[123] As noted earlier, the Turkish Constitution does not explicitly protect the right to manifest one's religion or belief in teaching.[124] Instead, it *regulates* education and instruction in religion and makes it subject to state strict supervision and control:

> Education and instruction in religion and ethics shall be conducted under state supervision and control. Instruction in religious culture and moral education shall be compulsory in the curricula of primary and secondary schools. Other religious education and instruction shall be subject to the individual's own desire, and in the case of minors, to the request of their legal representatives.[125]

"Other religious instruction" that is under state supervision and control is restricted to formal schooling in the *Hanafi* Islamic tradition since only the latter is provided in the theological faculties. In middle and high school level, there are the state-run *Imam Hatip* schools, which are vocational schools for raising *imams* and *hatips*,[126] and, these, too, provide teaching based on the *Hanafi* Islamic tradition. It is not possible to establish similar vocational schools for other faiths.

123 Article 9 of the ECHR, Article 18 of the ICCPR.
124 See Chapter 5.
125 Article 24(3).
126 *İmams* and *hatips* are Islamic religious leader and Quran reader respectively.

The lack of an adequate legal framework which would allow religious communities to establish schools, both to teach their followers and to train religious personnel, makes the protection of the right to manifest religion or belief in teaching highly ineffective in Turkey. The failure to solve this problem has a direct consequence on the ability to preserve the identity of communities. The inability to transmit dogma and traditions to new generations and to train religious leaders and teachers is weakened as a result. The restrictions on the right to manifest religion or belief in teaching and the enormous state financial and institutional funding provided for the state trained religious personnel—following the *Hanafi* Islamic tradition, together contribute to deepening of inequalities.

The lack of a provision in Turkish legislation for the training of religious leaders compels religious or belief groups to improvise solutions for their communities. The Caferi, who are close to the Shia tradition of Islam, send their clergy to Iran and Iraq for theological education in Shia Islamic tradition.[127] Some of the clergy have received adequate education and training to teach others; however, it is not possible for them to establish a school, therefore all training must take place in the mosque, where one cannot receive a formal degree. Some religious communities have established associations with the purpose of research and education of their religion; often training here takes place through seminars.[128] None of these institutions may provide formal degrees comparable to those offered by the state institutions.

7.2.3 The Right to Train, Appoint, Elect or Designate by Succession Appropriate Leaders Called by the Requirements and Standards of any Religion or Belief

While the right to train and the right to appoint religious leaders are inter-related, not least because they are in many ways dependent on each other, the right to train leaders and the right to appoint, elect or designate by succession appropriate leaders need to be assessed separately. The former is subject to legislation on education and the latter is regulated based on other laws and, often, by administrative decisions in Turkey. Here our analysis will focus on the right to appoint, elect or designate by succession appropriate leaders called by the requirements and standards of any religion or belief since issues pertaining to training of religious leaders have been addressed in the previous section.

Appointment of religious leaders and their proper functioning as foreseen in respective religious traditions are vitally important for the healthy life of any religious or belief community. While the role of religious leaders in various religious traditions may vary, their role in giving a vision to the community as well as management of religious functions are common to most traditions. Generally

127 *Aksiyon*, “Ankara’da Erbain Hazırlığı” [Erbain Preparations in Ankara], 11 January 2011.

128 *Inter alia*, the Caferi have established *Caferilik İnancını Tanıtma Araştırma ve Eğitim Derneği* [Association for Promoting of and Research and Training in Caferi Faith], *CEM Vakfi Alevi-Islam Din Hizmetleri Başkanlığı*, Alevi Araştırma Merkezi, Hasat Kilise Hizmetleri Derneği.

speaking, the leadership organization in itself is in fact an expression of their beliefs, deeply rooted in their understanding or interpretation of sacred texts or traditions.[129] This is also true for the titles used by religious leaders. Therefore any interference in this sphere must be rigorously assessed with reference to international human rights standards.

Current legislation and administrative practice in Turkey applicable to the right to appoint, elect and designate religious leaders is far from uniform, clear and foreseeable. There is no general legislative regulation pertaining to the organization of internal affairs of religious or belief communities. Legislation and administrative practice differ based on certain categories of religious leadership: the Presidency of Religious Affairs, religious leaders of the so-called Lausanne religious minorities that are recognized by the Turkish government as protected by the Lausanne Treaty (Jewish, Armenian Apostolic and Greek Orthodox), Muslim communities organized outside the Diyanet framework and non-Muslim religious communities outside the Lausanne framework. Since this book focuses on the protection of freedom of religion or belief for groups that seek to exercise the right to freedom of religion or belief outside the Diyanet structure, legal issues pertaining to the appointment of leaders within the Diyanet structure will be briefly described.

The lack of general regulation on the appointment of religious leaders may give the impression that there is complete freedom in the sphere of electing religious leaders; however, as it will be shown below, with regard to selected communities there is a significant degree of interference, at times amounting to obstruction. In contrast to the absence of general rules in this sphere, Law No. 677 is explicitly and directly applicable to the prohibition of the use of *certain* Islamic religious leadership titles.[130] The law is not a neutral law prohibiting the use of all religious titles. Christian and Jewish titles or religious titles found in the Sunni-Islamic tradition are not mentioned in the law. Other Muslim religious leaders within the Diyanet structure, namely the *imam* and *mufti*, are subject to the legislation governing the Diyanet and public servants.[131] Moreover, the three so-called Lausanne religious minorities are subject to an unclear administrative process over which they have little control.

Following Turkey's independence war and the establishment of the Republic in 1923, a certain political sensitivity prevailed and this had direct impact on the appointment of religious leaders of certain religious communities. For example in

129 Minnerath, R. (2004) "The Right to Autonomy in Religious Affairs", in T. Lindholm, W.C. Durham and B.G. Tahzib-Lie (eds.), *Facilitating Freedom of Religion or Belief: A Deskbook*, Dordrecht: Martinus Nijhoff, p. 291.

130 Tekke ve Zaviyelerin Kapatılmasına İlişkin Kanun [Closure of Dervish Monasteries and Tombs, the Abolition of the Office of Keeper of Tombs and the Abolition and Prohibition of Certain Titles] Act No. 677 of 30 November 1341 (1925).

131 Law No. 633 Diyanet İşleri Başkanlığı'nın Kuruluşu ve Görevleri Hakkında Kanun [Law on the Establishment and Duties of the Presidency of Religious Affairs and the Addition of Four Temporary Provisions to This Law], 26 April 1976 and Devlet Memurları Kanunu [Law on Public Servants] No. 657, 14 July 1965, Resmi Gazete [Official Gazette] (R.G.), 23 July 1965, No. 12056.

1933, the Syriac Patriarchate in Mardin could no longer resist the subtle and open pressure of the state and moved to Syria "temporarily" when the community considered the move necessary.[132] The Alevi-Bektashi center—*dergah*—was moved to Albania following the closure of *tekke* and *zaviye* in 1925. Similarly, in 1925 Konstantinos, who had been elected the Greek Patriarch, was sent by the public authorities to Thessaloniki in Greece. When Greece took the matter to the League of Nations claiming that this act violated the Lausanne Treaty, Turkey threatened to close and send the Patriarchate out of Turkey, Greece withdrew its complaint and the matter was closed by presenting the situation as if Konstantinos had resigned on his own accord.[133]

Since this book deals with the assessment of the right to manifest religion or belief outside the Diyanet structure we will not examine the leadership appointment process in this public body in depth. It is important to note, however, that the religious leadership scheme within the Diyanet structure is highly regulated. The Prime Minister appoints the Head of the institution.[134] Officially, he does not represent the Muslim community; he represents the Diyanet.[135] The Muslim population that worships in the mosques run by the Diyanet is not involved in the appointment of the *imam*, the *mufti* and the Head of the Diyanet. There have been calls to review and change the selection methods to allow participation of the community in the process.[136] These have not, yet, produced any results.

State interference is most evident in the appointment of religious leadership of three non-Muslim religious communities—the Jewish, the Greek Orthodox and the Armenian Apostolic. It will be remembered that Turkey recognizes solely these communities as religious communities subject to the minority protection scheme of the 1923 Lausanne Treaty.[137] The Lausanne Treaty protects the right to freedom of religion or belief and the right of non-Muslims to run their religious institutions freely; however, it does not specify a certain procedure for the election of religious leaders, implicitly leaving this to the communities to decide for themselves in accordance with their traditions.[138] As will be shown below, the process of selecting leaders for these three communities takes place in the state apparatus' administrative or executive section lacking precise, accessible and foreseeable rules.

According to the Ministry of Interior, Directorate of the Minority Issues Evaluation Section, for example, in the appointment of the Armenian Patriarchate, a certain legal framework exists.

> The affairs and transactions related to minorities are carried out in accordance with Articles 37–45 of the Lausanne Treaty, affairs and transactions

132 *Taraf*, Hür, A., "Mezopotamya'nın Kadim Halkı Süryaniler" [The Ancient People of Mesopotamia-Syriacs], 14 December 2008.

133 Ibid.

134 Ibid.

135 Article 3 of Law No. 6002.

136 Gözaydın, *supra* note 74.

137 See p. 126.

138 Articles 38–44.

concerning our Armenian citizens are carried out in accordance with the ancient precedents and customs of the community.[139]

This statement, however, raises a number of questions. Who determines what ancient customs are, the state or the community? How is the content of these ancient customs and precedents determined? If it is the community's rules or customs, do they have the right to modify them? What rules will apply if there is a disagreement between the state and the community or within the community on the substance of these rules? The validity of Regulations pertaining to the administration of the *millets* in the Ottoman Empire is far from clear.[140] While the state administration does not provide a definitive answer on the nature of the validity of these Regulations, its practice indicates that certain elements of the Ottoman practice are continued. The lack of certainty and foreseeability in this context results in a situation where the state is ultimately the sole actor who determines the applicable legal rules. Hence the minorities in question remain dependent on the public authorities to determine applicable rules. The dependence of minority communities on the decisions of public authorities strengthens the weak position of these communities *vis-à-vis* the state.

Notwithstanding the legal vacuum concerning the election of the religious leaders, since the establishment of the Turkish Republic, the Jewish, Greek Orthodox and Armenian Apostolic communities have applied for state permission when electing or appointing their religious leaders. By doing this, the practice established during the Ottoman period has been maintained to a certain degree. Without a legal basis the election process, however, becomes ultimately outside of the control of the religious communities themselves. The main reason for this is that the process of application for state permission in order to elect or appoint the religious leader is not required by any law, yet, *de facto* required by what may be called an *established practice.*

The account of a typical process of election leaders of these three communities will be useful to understand the interferences in the right to appoint, elect or designate religious leaders. The elections of the Chief Rabbi and the two Patriarchs do not follow a pre-determined procedure. Whenever a need for the election of a religious leader arises, permission for that particular election must be obtained and the permission is not valid for any subsequent election. The procedure is defined throughout the process, with changes in criteria as well as reciprocal negotiations; "each election is different".[141] The draft of the election regulation is prepared by the religious communities; this includes the criteria for candidates and term of service. However, the Ministry of Interior may advise changes, or declare

139 Email response to information request from Ministry of Interior, 27 August 2010.

140 See more on these Regulations in Chapter 5. The Turkish judiciary's reliance on these texts also varies. See Chapter 6.

141 Interview with the representative of the Jewish community who wished to remain anonymous, November 2010.

certain provisions incompatible with existing regulations—whether or not this is in the regulations.[142]

It is very important to note that the communities, in preparing election regulations to submit to the Turkish authorities, are strongly guided by what they think may be acceptable to the state, in the light of their previous experiences.[143] This is particularly reflected in the criteria for who may be chosen as the leader.[144] Apart from insisting that all members of leadership bodies are Turkish citizens, presently, the government does not generally interfere in the appointments below the level of the head of the religious community. In effect the citizenship criteria functions as a restriction on the eligibility of spiritual leaders from outside of Turkey and strengthens the state's position against the religious communities and provides a means of facilitating or restricting the right to freedom of religion or belief. For example, in the past the Turkish state has terminated the citizenship of Silifke and Alaşehir metropolits,[145] or recently, allowed the citizenship applications of non-Turkish clergy.[146] Generally speaking, the religious leader must be a Turkish citizen, at least 40 years of age, have certain religious training, and be trustworthy in the eyes of the Turkish government.[147] The last condition was a condition required by the Turkish state in all previous elections. However, in the 2009 elections the Istanbul Governorship informed the Election Committee of the Jewish community that this provision must be changed to stipulate that the Chief Rabbi must "have a good reputation in the eyes of the state and society".[148] Again this change in the requirement does not have a legal basis or precise and foreseeable criteria, it depends on the discretion of public authorities.

The experience of the Armenian Apostolic community has been the most recent and vivid illustration that interference in the appointment of leadership is far reaching and effects the functioning of the community. Following the health-related seclusion of the Patriarch elected for life, the question of a successor became an important one for the healthy functioning of the community's religious affairs.[149] The rules or lack of rules concerning appointment of leaders for the Armenian Apostolic community are far from clear. According to the public authorities the Armenian Patriarchate seems to be subject to an 1863

142 Ibid.
143 Ibid.
144 Ibid.
145 This is characterized as a move in 1960, following the Cyprus crises, to increase pressure on the Patriarchate. Macar, E. (2012) *Cumhuriyet Döneminde İstanbul Rum Patrikhanesi* [Istanbul Greek Patriarchate in the Republican Period], Istanbul: İletişim Publications, p. 203, quoting from *Cumhuriyet* newspaper of 21 April 1964.
146 *Hürriyet*, "Patrik Adaylarına Vatandaşlık Kapıda" [Possible Citizenship Candidates for the Patriarchates], 22 July 2010.
147 *Supra* note 141, interview with the representative of the Jewish community.
148 Ibid.
149 Yıldırım, M. and O. Oering (2010) "Turkey: Why State Interference in the Election of Chief Rabbi, Greek Orthodox and Armenian Patriarchs?", Oslo: F18News. Available: http://www.forum18.org/archive.php?article_id=1477 [Accessed 16 January 2015].

Regulation,[150] concluded between the Ottoman administration and the Patriarchate. A new regulation annulling this has not been drafted since the establishment of the modern Turkish Republic, and there are differing views among lawyers as to whether or not the 1863 Regulation is still valid. Also, if it were valid, the extent to which the 1863 Regulation is included in the established practice of appointing religious leaders is not certain. This Regulation does not specify a course of action in the case of serious illness of the Patriarch since it only makes provision for the course of action to be taken in the case of death or resignation from office.[151]

Two different factions in the Armenian Apostolic community approached the government separately; one asked the government to allow the selection of a Co-Patriarch, believing that a new Patriarch may only be chosen upon the death of the previous Patriarch,[152] the other, the Council of Armenians in Turkey, asked for the election to be allowed to select a new Patriarch.[153] Eventually, the Interior Ministry wrote to the community *via* the Istanbul Governor's Office, rejecting both the proposals presented from within the Armenian community, arguing that Church regulations did not envisage the possibility of electing a new Patriarch while the incumbent is still alive or a Co-Patriarch.[154] The Interior Ministry determined that only a Patriarchal Vicar-General (*Patrik Genel Vekili*), could be elected to lead the community until the current Patriarch dies.[155] The government justified its decision to refuse the election of a Co-Patriarch by stating that such a position is not foreseen in the existing Regulations—interestingly, nor is the appointment of a Patriarchal Vicar-General. Bebiroğlu observes that such a position has not existed within the Armenian Orthodox Church since 1709 and it is not in their tradition.[156] The government thus assumed the role of regulator and imposed a solution to the problem that was not asked for by the community. The Spiritual Council of the Armenian Apostolic Church elected an Archbishop to the newly created post of Vicar-General.[157] Thus, not only did the community not select its leader freely, it was not even able to determine the title of their religious leader.

Interaction between public authorities and the religious communities varies, however. For example, when the current Chief Rabbi was elected in December 2002, the office of Chief Rabbi was decided *by the community* to be for a seven-year term, not a lifetime appointment as it had been previously.[158] This was acceptable to the government. Taking a step that broke with established practice, in 2004 Patriarch Bartholomew had named several foreign citizens to membership

150 Bebiroğlu, M. (2010) "Eş Patrik Seçimi ve Son Gelişmeler" [Election of a Co-Patriarch and Latest Developments], *Hyetert*. Available: http://www.hyetert.com/yazi3.asp?s=3&Id=681&DilId=1 [Accessed 16 January 2015].

151 Regulation on the Armenian Community.

152 Yıldırım and Oering, *supra* note 149.

153 Bebiroğlu, *supra* note 150.

154 Ibid.

155 Ibid.

156 Ibid.

157 Ibid.

158 *Supra* note 141, interview with the representative of the Jewish community.

of the Holy Synod, without consulting the government.[159] Amid an outcry by Turkish nationalists, who called for the Patriarch to be expelled from the country, Prime Minister Erdoğan indicated that this was an internal issue for the Church. After years of urging on the part of the Patriarchate and apparently as a result of the August 2009 meeting between Bartholomew and Erdoğan, the government finally agreed that foreign bishops of dioceses under the Ecumenical Patriarchate could apply for Turkish citizenship. Patriarch Bartholomew immediately wrote to the bishops urging them to do so, pointing out that when the election of his successor takes place, "they will have the right to elect and to be elected".[160]

The title used by the leaders of the so-called Lausanne religious communities has also been interfered with by public authorities. When the Chief Rabbi Haleva's term expired in late 2009, the government refused to allow an election (by direct vote of members of the Jewish community throughout Turkey) to take place, unless the post title was changed from "Chief Rabbi of Turkey" to "Chief Rabbi of Turkish Jews".[161] Following the finalization of the election criteria the government permitted an election to the post of Chief Rabbi of Turkish Jews, which Haleva won in May 2010.[162] The Turkish authorities do not officially recognize the title "Ecumenical Patriarch", and instead insist on the title "Fener Rum Patriği" (Patriarch of Fener), limiting the geographical jurisdiction of the Patriarch,[163] whereas the Patriarchate considers itself "ecumenical".[164] The Turkish Court of Cassation has made a legal proclamation on the ecumenical title of the Patriarchate saying, "the Patriarchate is an institution which bears only religious powers as the church of the Greek minority in Turkey", and that "there is no legal basis for the claim that the Patriarchate is ecumenical".[165] The Armenian Patriarchate also has jurisdiction outside Turkey, over the tiny Armenian community on the Greek island of Crete.[166] The Turkish government—as with the Ecumenical Patriarchate—rejects the terminology used by the Armenian Apostolic Church itself for its Patriarch, namely, "Patriarch of Constantinople". Instead, the state refers to him as *Ermeni Patrik* (Armenian Patriarch). The government also tries to reject the Ecumenical Patriarch's wider jurisdiction or authority over Orthodox communities outside the country—including direct jurisdiction over dioceses in eastern Greece.[167]

159 Yıldırım and Oering, *supra* note 149.
160 Ibid.
161 *The Jewish Chronicle*, "Turkish Authorities Stall Rabbi Election", 4 March 2012. Available: http://www.thejc.com/node/29072 [Accessed 30 December 2014].
162 Yıldırım and Oering, *supra* note 149.
163 Fener is the name of the district of Istanbul in which the Patriarchate is located.
164 This title has been used by the Patriarch in Constantinople since the 6th century, and was continued after the city came under Ottoman rule in 1453.
165 Court of Cassation, 2005/10694, judgment of 2007, 4th Penal Chamber.
166 See the official website of the Armenian Patriarchate, *The Armenian Patriarchate of Constantinopolis*, http://www.armenianchurch-ed.net/our-church/patriarchate-of-constantinople [Accessed 1 December 2014].
167 Yıldırım and Oering, *supra* note 149.

In contrast, the practice concerning the small Armenian Protestant community stands out as the exception to the high level of interference in the election of leaders of the so-called Lausanne minorities; they do not experience any interference in the election and appointment process of their religious leaders. Religious groups that are not interfered with in the appointment of spiritual leaders include the Latin Catholics, expatriated communities of the Anglican Church and the German Evangelical congregation. Turkish Protestants, Jehovah's Witnesses and the Bahai also have freely appointed their leaders. This practice reflects the special significance of the Jewish, Greek Orthodox and Armenian Apostolic communities that triggers rigorous oversight and interference by the state. The different rules and practice concerning the appointment of leaders of religious groups demonstrate that interference is deemed necessary at varying degrees by the state.

For the so-called Lausanne communities the seal of approval following the complicated process of election of the religious leader appears to retain certain significance in a number of ways. For instance, this process confers the head of the religious community a status, as such, that creates a *de facto* state recognition of him as the representative of the community and ensures no other self-appointed person may claim such a position.[168] Secondly, arguably, the possible consequences of not applying for permission forces religious communities to follow the *imposed* practice. It is highly unlikely that any of these three ethnic or religious minority groups would challenge this established practice, wanting to avoid the conflict this might create. The possible consequences of not applying for permission might include non-recognition of the religious leader by the state for the purpose of representing their ethnic or religious community and withholding the permission to wear religious clothing in places outside of places of worship. The latter permission is given to one clergy of each religious community by a decision of the Committee of Ministers.[169] The diverse issues and interests to consider and the delicate balance that the so-called Lausanne minorities have to seek in the process of appointing their religious leaders illustrates the need for effective protection of the right to appoint leaders.

In contrast to a lack of regulation concerning the religious leadership of non-Muslim communities, there is a specific legislation that prohibits the use of certain religious titles as well as the exercise of corresponding capacities regarding certain Islamic traditions. Law No. 677 has important implications for religious leadership of certain Islamic communities.[170] According to the Constitution, Law. No. 677 is considered part of the reform laws category, laws that seek to protect *laiklik* and therefore no constitutional provision may be understood or interpreted in a way to render Law No. 677 unconstitutional.[171] Article 1 declares the closure of all *tekke*

168 *Supra* note 143, interview with the representative of the Jewish community.
169 Article 1, Bazı Kisvelerin Giyilemeyeceğine Dair Kanun [Law Related to Prohibition on Wearing Certain Garments] No. 2596, 3 December 1934, R.G. No. 2879, 13121934.
170 Article 174 of the Turkish Constitution.
171 Ibid.

and *zaviye* and *türbe* and explicitly prohibits the use of a variety of Islamic and superstitious titles:

> In all tarikats, the use of titles and attributes like Sheikh, Dervish, Mürit [Disciple], Dedelik [Elder], sayyid [descendant of Prophet Mohammed], Çelebi [a title for a leader of dervish order], Babalık [Father], Emirate, Naiplik [Regency], Khaliphat, sorcery, breathers on sick people for healing, fortune-telling and soothsaying, and nüshacılık [writing prayers] for the purpose of *murada kavuşturmak*, and the exercise of these services and the wearing of garments for them is prohibited.[172]

The same Article foresees a prison sentence, not less than three months, and a monetary fine, not less than 50 Turkish Lira.

These prohibited titles are commonly used to refer to historical religious figures as well as religious leaders of today, yet this explicit prohibition is seldom applied. It has been reported that, in the past, in the practice of Alevi community "when the *dede* administered the *cem*", there was "warning and threat" but no sanctions.[173] As far as the judicial process is concerned, in a case concerning the act of fortune telling, also prohibited by Law No. 677, the Court of Appeals held that the purpose of Law No. 677 was "to protect the society from superstition and protect the people from abuse that these might cause".[174] Other elements necessary to establish this crime were to be known as a person who is engaged in these acts and routine and regular engagement.[175] On the other hand, reading the Quran and writing a prayer for a person that is ill with the purpose of wishing that he/she gets well is not considered "breathing or *nüshacılık*".[176] Since such *abuse* could not be established in the case—the fortune telling appeared to be a form of entertainment and the person did not do this activity as a source of income—the person in question was acquitted.[177]

A village imam was convicted for violating Law No. 677, Article 1(2) for "making *muska*—written charm—and engaging in *üfürükçülük*—breathing on sick people in order to cure them" and thus profiting from or taking advantage of the village community.[178] In another case a person was convicted for breathing on

172 Article 1 of the Turkish Constitution.

173 Interview with lawyer Hasan Gülşan who has extensively worked on Alevi cases, March 2013.

174 The General Council of the Court of Appeals E/1955/9 and K/1955/17, 6 July 1955.

175 Ibid.

176 Ibid.

177 Ibid.

178 The General Council of Court of Appeals E/1983/7–403 and K/1984/243, 25 June 1984. In another case a fortune teller was accused of both "fortune telling" and "theft" as he took the money from the person whose fortune he was telling. Both crimes were treated separately and he was convicted of both fortune telling and theft. E1997/1438 and K1997/1358, 3 February 1997. Where fortune telling is not a subject of complaint and only a matter of entertainment between consenting persons Law. No. 677, Article 1(2) may not be applicable.

persons for the purpose of breaking a spell; however, whether there was profit or not was not considered.[179] Yet, "profiting or benefiting" was considered an indispensable element for the crime of "breathing and writing prayers" as well as the fact that the person in question is "known by the title of breather".[180] On the other hand, a Court of Appeals held that a person charged with using the title "caliph" and engaging in acts that a caliph would engage in, like gathering people around him to form a *tarikat* (Islamic brotherhood, literal meaning *the way*), should be found guilty of violating Law No. 677, Article 1(2).[181]

Interestingly, it appears that individuals who are Alevi *dede* or *mürşid* have not been convicted for violating Law No. 677 despite the widespread existence of this office, albeit informally.[182] Ersal, in his study on the Veli Baba Sultan Dervish Lodge (Veli Baba Sultan Dergahı), describes a very lively religious community where religious leaders use some of the titles that are prohibited in Article 1 of Law No. 677.[183] They do not use the Dervish Lodge, except for religious visits, but continue their religious activities in homes with various religious leaders, *dede* or *mürşid*, actively administering religious services and rituals. The application of the relevant legal provisions seems to be inconsistent. Ersal observes that there was a position of Watchman in times of "prohibition" who would watch for the gendarmerie while the people and their leaders would hold religious services in homes, but they say this position no longer exists.[184] An Alevi customary jurisdiction decision was—albeit indirectly—the subject of a court decision; an Alevi complained of "defamation" because within the Alevi customary judicial system the *dede* and other members of the group declared him "düşkün"[185] and expelled him from the community because of adultery.[186] The court decided the case on the basis of "defamation" and did not review the case on the use of the *dede* title nor on the customary legal system involved.

The account above illustrates the differing and fragmented *de jure* and *de facto* rules that are applicable to the right to elect and appoint leaders for religious communities in Turkey. Now, we will turn to examine the compatibility of key

179 Court of Appeals 7th Criminal Chamber, E/1976/3580, K/1976/3580, 20 April 1976

180 Ibid.

181 Court of Appeals 7th Criminal Chamber, E/2003/12950 and K/2003/05182, 31 May 2005. However the objection of the prosecutor on procedural grounds was found admissible hence the case was dismissed.

182 A review of Court of Appeals cases did not lead to any cases where the use of the *dede* or *mürşit* titles was the subject matter of a case. This was also confirmed by several Alevi lawyers who were interviewed. *Inter alia*, by Hasan Gülşan, March 2013 and Namık Sofuoğlu, September 2013.

183 Ersal, M. (2009) *Alevi İnanç Dede Ocakları Üzerine bir Örneklem: Veli Baba Sultan Ocağı* [A Study on the Alevi Belief Dede Houses: Veli Baba Sultan House], Ankara: Alevi-Bektaşi Kültür Enstitüsü Publications.

184 Ibid., p. 89.

185 Meaning "fallen".

186 *Gazetevatan*, "Alevi Hukuk Yargıdan Döndü" [Alevi Customary Law Annulled by the Judiciary], 7 July 2010.

elements of these practices with standards established by international law, freedom of religion or belief in its collective dimension.

Both the UN and ECHR protection schemes attribute strong protection to the right to appoint leaders for religious groups which demonstrates a conception of the right to freedom of religion or belief that recognizes the importance of this component of the collective dimension for both groups of believers. The HRCttee has not considered a communication on this issue; however, in its General Comment on Article 18, it held that the right to freedom of religion or belief includes the protection of "acts integral to the conduct by religious groups of their basic affairs, such as the freedom to choose their religious leaders, priests and teachers".[187] Whenever states decide to interfere with these "internal" aspects of organization of a religious group, they also interfere with its "autonomy" of the group in question.

The ECtHR has noted in a number of cases, that the personality of the religious leaders is of importance to the members of the religious community and that participation in the organizational life of the community is a manifestation of one's religion, protected by Article 9 of the Convention.[188] The Strasbourg organs attribute strong protection to the international organization of religious communities, and remarkably not necessarily based on the high status of the right to association in the ECHR system, as an issue falling under Article 9 as interpreted in the light of Article 11.[189]

The requirement for state permission or regulation involved in the process of election and appointment of religious leaders raises issues with regard to the right of religious communities to be free in their internal affairs, particularly one as critical as the right to appoint their own leader in accordance with their own doctrines and traditions. The effect of requirements or in fact, in some cases, prohibition, must be felt at varying degrees in individual religious communities. Yet, it is not difficult to imagine that these regulations or prohibitions would amount to interference in the right to manifest religion or belief in its collective dimension. Such interference must be justified in accordance with international law provisions; prescribed by law, pursuing a legitimate aim to protect public order, health and rights and freedoms of others and is necessary in a democratic society. In the cases of the so-called Lausanne minorities, it is hard to find the legal basis for the current practice which seems to be based on "established practice" yet lacks foreseeability and precision. The incompatibility of the practice with the requirement that any restriction must be prescribed by law is also evident in the fact that every election is and has been different. Interestingly, these claims have not been the subject of any legal dispute in the domestic jurisdiction, therefore we do not have information on how the judiciary would adjudicate these cases.

Moreover, the fact that each and every election is arbitrarily treated differently puts the religious communities in a highly vulnerable position. The main reason

187 General Comment 22 of the HRC on Article 18 of the ICCPR, para. 4.

188 *Hasan and Chaush v Bulgaria*, 26 October 2000, European Court of Human Rights, No. 30985/96.

189 Ibid., para 62.

for this is that the government's arbitrary decisions are affected by factors which these religious communities cannot expect or control. The lack of an adequate legal framework that is compatible with international human rights law may be an indication of mistrust of these minorities. At the core of the changing nature of administrative practice may be that the Turkish state views relations with these three communities as strongly linked to foreign policy matters—not as a matter of the freedom of religion or belief of its citizens.[190] As it has been illustrated in Chapter 6, for decades these communities have been subject to the changing relationships between Turkey and other countries.

Active interference by Turkey into the right of religious leaders to use of the title that they consider appropriate in accordance with their religion or belief would constitute an interference with religious freedom. Indeed, it is difficult to see why and when any state would need to interfere in the usage of a title by any religious groups. This implausibility was also observed by the Venice Commission in relation to the obstacles before the use of the title "ecumenical" by the Greek Orthodox Patriarch. The Venice Commission Opinion held that "only in exceptional cases it may be justified to deny to a religion the right to choose and use a certain name".[191] In addition, the opinion notes that it is not possible to see how any of the requirements listed in Article 9 paragraph 2 would possibly be applicable in such a case, as neither public safety nor public order nor any of the other concerns can be affected at all by the Patriarchate using its ancient title of "ecumenical".[192] The Council of Europe's Venice Commission urged Turkey to recognize the right of the Patriarchate to use the title "ecumenical".[193]

The same arguments could be relevant for the ban on the use of certain titles by Law No. 677. The implications of the application of Law No. 677 for the right to manifest religion or belief in the internal organization of a religious community and in particular the use of certain titles and the appointment of religious leader needs to be further explored. As it has been shown above, for an act to be punishable under Law No. 677, an "advantage" by the use of the title and performance of function was considered necessary by the judiciary, depending on the individual circumstances of the case. Where "taking advantage" would amount to, for example, interference

190 Bali, R. (2004) *Devletin Yahudileri ve "Öteki Yahudiler"* (State's Jews and "Other Jews"), Istanbul: İletişim Publications.

191 The Venice Commission also held that

> an explicit prohibition to use a certain name which forms part of the identity of a religion usually is an interference with and possibly a violation of the rights under Article 9, the use of a different name in the correspondence or at official events etc. may—depending on the particular circumstances—be a mere political question, not a legal issue under the Convention. However, such a policy of "re-naming", first being a matter of political correctness, may reach the level of an interference when it is combined with other measures discriminating the religious group on grounds that are not in line with the ECHR and in particular with Article 14.

Supra note 29.

192 The OSCE/ODIHR, OSCE and Venice Commission Guidelines for Review of Legislation Pertaining to Religion or Belief, *supra* note 29, para. 93.

193 *Supra* note 67.

in the rights of others or public order or health, state interference could be justified. In order to ensure the right to appoint leaders and use titles in accordance with a religion or belief, legislation could be drafted differently, rather than a categorical ban on the use of certain titles. In fact, certain provisions of civil or criminal code could already be applicable to provide protection against abuses of the use of the title.

7.2.4 The Right to Observe Days of Rest and to Celebrate Holidays and Ceremonies in Accordance with the Precepts of One's Religion or Belief

The right to observe days of rest and celebrate holidays and ceremonies in accordance with the precepts of one's religion or belief may be a right with a broad scope depending on the content of the dogma and tradition in question. As it has been observed in Chapter 4, in addition to, for example, having a right to take holidays from work, manifestations pertaining to diverse forms of ceremonies in accordance with the religion or belief in question are also within the scope of this right. Here our focus will be limited to the right to take days off from work in order to be able to observe a day of rest or celebrate and observe holidays and ceremonies.

Days that are special in a particular religion or belief are also days when believers generally gather together for, *inter alia*, worship, celebration and special ceremonies. Participation in these events or ceremonies is important for the preservation and transmission of dogma and identity. Therefore whether believers are free from work to gather becomes a crucial precondition of whether such worship can take place or not. On the other hand, accommodation for the needs of various religious communities in this sphere requires macro level arrangements by states and raises diverse policy issues. The religious holidays of the Alevi, Bahai, Christians, Jews are not set aside as national holidays, neither do they have a right to take these days off from work or school. The Alevi community in Turkey has expressed demands for the recognition of the Ashura Day as a national holiday,[194] yet without any results.

In the public and private sectors, accommodation for "time off" to observe religious holidays remains in the sphere of administrative decision processes that lack a legal basis that is apparent to employers and employees. In recent years, there have been reports that at public universities Christian and Jewish faculty have been allowed administrative leave on Jewish and Christian holidays, provided that these days are deducted from their annual leaves.[195] Whether Muslims are allowed to take time off to participate in the customary Friday prayers and daily *namaz* is dependent on the employers' discretion; there is no obligation on the part of the employers to accommodate such requests.[196] Some employees wishing to take time off to perform their daily prayers have been reportedly threatened with dismissal from their jobs and applicants have been asked in job interviews whether

194 *Takvim*, Aşure'ye Resmi Tatil [Official Holiday for Ashura], 1 April 2011.
195 Interview with faculty member who preferred to remain anonymous, January 2013.
196 Mazlum-Der Human Rights Report 2011. Available: http://istanbul.mazlumder.org/webimage/turkiye_raporu_24tem.pdf [Accessed 1 December 2014].

they perform *namaz* or not, and those who did were not employed.[197] On the other hand, it has also been reported that at a university the deans of faculties were given directives by the rector not to schedule lectures at the time of Friday prayers.[198] When such accommodation is wholly left to the discretion of the authorities without any legal basis it may be difficult to establish a non-discriminatory and consistent practice.

Official religious holidays in Turkey include the Islamic—Ramadan and Sacrifice—Holidays.[199] Sunday is the weekly holiday, and, in contrast to many Muslim countries, Friday is not a day of rest in Turkey.[200] Individuals affiliated with religions or beliefs that celebrate holidays other than or, in addition to these, the officially recognized Ramadan and Sacrifice holidays, must use their annual leave days in order to be able to observe their days of rest or holidays. A right to take time off from work to observe periods of prayer at particular times of the day and to observe a religious holiday is not legally recognized.

Neither public nor private employers are legally required to make *reasonable accommodation* for employees' religious observances. Rules concerning taking time off from work for times of prayer or observing religious holidays are determined explicitly or implicitly by private companies through company culture and image, professional chambers and the legislation that affects the intersection of public and private. Labour Law protects against religious discrimination.[201] But anti-discrimination legislation in Turkey is weak and existing legal remedies are rarely accessible.[202] The possibility to effectively benefit from the available legal

197 *Yeni Akit*, 29 September 2011, "Fabrikada Namaz Yasağı"; such cases are rarely prosecuted.

198 *Bianet*, "YTÜ Rektörü: Cumaları Namaz Saatine Ders Koymayın Dedim" [Rector of Yıldız Teknik Üniversitesi: I told them not to schedule lessons at the time of Friday prayers], 16 January 2015. Available: http://www.bianet.org/bianet/egitim/143601-ytu-rektoru-cumalari-namaz-saatine-ders-koymayin-dedim [Accessed 16 January 2015].

199 Ulusal Bayram ve Genel Tatiller Hakkında Kanun [Law on National Holidays and General Vacations], Law No. 2429 17 March 1981, R.G. 17282, 19 March 1981, Article 2(B).

200 The change of weekly holiday from Friday to Sunday has been introduced as one of the Reforms of the modern Turkish Republic. Law No. 2739 Ulusal Bayram ve Genel Tatiller Hakkında Kanun [Law on National Holidays and General Holidays], Article 3, 27 May 1935.

201 Other prohibited grounds are language, race, gender, political opinion, philosophical beliefs, religion and denomination and similar grounds: Article 5 of Labor Law, 22 May 2033 İş Kanunu [Labor Law] No. 4857, R.G. 0/06/2003 No. 25134. For an analysis of protection against discrimination based on religion in Turkish Labor Law, see Sural, N. (2009) "Islamic Outfits in the Workplace in Turkey, a Muslim Majority Country", *Comparative Labour Law and Policy Journal*, Spring, pp. 569–596.

202 Following democratization steps taken in 2009 the Turkish government has promised to adopt a comprehensive anti-discrimination law that would also establish a Council on Combatting Discrimination and Equality with the capacity to receive complaints. The relevant draft law has been pending at the Turkish Grand National Assembly and no steps have been taken since 2010. At the time of finalizing this book, December 2016, the government has still not adopted a comprehensive anti-discrimination legislation.

protection against religious discrimination is significantly diminished by the lack of information among employees, and the difficulty of proving that the discrimination was based on religion. There is also a general powerlessness felt by those affected, e.g. religious minorities, women and students, in light of the power dynamics involved in the available complaint procedures.

Recognition of special holidays or days of rest and ceremonies in accordance with the precepts of one's religion or belief in Turkey seems to be at the periphery of the right to freedom of religion or belief. So far, there have not been any court cases dealing with the right to observe periods of prayer at particular times during the day or the refusal to permit individuals to take time off to observe religious holidays. This may be an indication of the fact that the right to freedom of religion or belief is not understood in a way to include a right for the recognition of special religious holidays or days of rest or days for special ceremonies. Or, perhaps, it indicates that believers have internalized this lack of accommodation and do not have hope that legal remedies will lead to satisfactory results. Hypothetically, if non-accommodation for observance of special days of rest or religious holidays were the subject of court cases, in light of high courts' decisions that intensely rely on the principle of *laiklik*, we may expect that the denial of such requests will be accepted by courts on grounds of "having a politically and religiously neutral workplace".[203]

It is useful to recall international standards for the right to observe days of rest and celebrate holidays in accordance with one's religion or belief. The core religious freedom provisions do not include an explicit reference to this right. Yet, the HRCttee's GC 22 explicitly refers to "the observance of holidays and days of rest" as a form of manifestation protected as such under Article 18.[204] In country visits, the UN Special Rapporteur has noted accommodations for religious holidays with satisfaction whenever such legislative steps were taken.[205] On the other hand, as has been demonstrated in Chapter 4, the jurisprudence of the Strasbourg organs concerning claims pertaining to requests for time off from work for daily prayers does not attribute a positive obligation on the part of states to accommodate times of prayer or days of rest.[206]

As far as international standard setting is concerned, indeed, a positive obligation to grant believers time off from work, either to observe their days of rest or to participate in religious ceremonies, is far from established. Perhaps, accommodations made for individuals or groups who wish to take days off in order to

203 Sural, N. (2009) "Islamic Outfits in the Workplace in Turkey, a Muslim Majority Country", Comparative Labour Law and Policy Journal, Spring, pp. 569–596.

204 Human Rights Committee, General Comment 22 on Article 18 of the ICCPR, para. 4.

205 E/CN.4/2002/73/Add.1, paras 29–32 and 125 (country visit to Argentina), para. 125 and E/CN.4/1996/95/Add.1, paras 48–49 (country visit to Pakistan), para. 49.

206 Concerning the case of a Muslim teacher whose request to take time off from work in order to attend Friday prayers was refused, the European Commission held that, since he had taken the position accepting the conditions of the employment there was no violation of Article 9. *X. v. United Kingdom*, 12 March 1981, European Commission on Human Rights (Admissibility), No. 8160/78.

participate in holidays or special days set aside for special ceremonies or recognition of holidays of religious minorities are seen more as "steps or measures that could be encouraged" in multi-cultural societies, less so as a right that creates positive obligations for states and that can be enforced. Indeed, this right remains at the periphery of the right to freedom of religion or belief as it is protected in international law.

The legislation and practice in Turkey does not protect a right to take time off from work to observe days of rest or to participate in religious ceremonies, worship or celebrations. In this respect, Turkey's stance appears to be consistent with the weak international protection afforded to this right.

Indeed the Turkish case is a useful example of how less than clear standard setting at the international level may lead or contribute to weak and ineffective compliance review at the domestic level. Key factors contributing to this situation are the lack of clear obligations of states, including the scope and nature of obligations, and the seemingly inconsistent standard setting at the universal and regional level. Whereas in compliance review at the UN level states are expected to respect the right to observe days of rest or holidays in accordance with religion or belief, Strasbourg organs have clearly tended not to deduce positive obligations for states to protect the same right.

In conclusion, key components of the right to freedom in the internal affairs of religious or belief groups examined above illustrate the harsh restrictions on the right to freedom of religion or belief in its collective dimension in Turkey. Despite a general protection of freedom of religion of belief in the Turkish legislation and occasional legislative improvements, *results or outcomes* show that there is a serious failure to effectively protect the right to freedom of religion or belief in Turkey. This calls to mind the assertion—which has been made in the racial discrimination context—that there might be a need for paradigmatic change, otherwise "the system merely swallows the small improvement one has made and everything remains the same".[207]

In numerous cases pertaining to the right to freedom of religion or belief, the judiciary tends to not see the religious freedom issues, as such; instead it deals with the claims with reference to legislative provisions that deal with other fields of law, such as Public Works Law or Civil Code or the principle of secularism. Alternatively, it could be argued that the provisions that are chosen by the judiciary in the construction of the reasoning are aimed at producing a certain outcome: to overlook the implications of the right to freedom of religion or belief.

In the exercise of the right to establish places of worship it is possible to identify a pattern of wide discretion left to public authorities in the determination and application of regulations and plans that are instrumental in the effective protection of this right. The right to manifest religion or belief in teaching is by far the most restricted right with the state holding a tight monopoly in the field of religious education. The inconsistent and arbitrary practice pertaining to the election

207 Delgado, R. and J. Stefancic (2012) *Critical Race Theory: An Introduction*, New York: NYU Press, p. 57.

and appointment of religious leaders indicates that despite strong international protection of the right to freedom in the internal organization of religious communities Turkey chooses not to take corrective action. Finally, the right to observe days of rest and to celebrate holidays and ceremonies in accordance with the precepts of one's religion or belief remains at the periphery of the right to freedom of religion or belief at the national level as it is the case at the international level. Whether a component of freedom of religion or belief enjoys a robust international protection or not is not the only factor determining Turkey's performance on the issue. However, it determines the standard that can be advocated for at the national level as well as the nature of legal remedies that religious or belief groups can seek.

8 Conclusion

Silence speaks loudest.

The subject of this book is the collective dimension of freedom of religion or belief in international human rights law. The purpose of the book has been to explore the notion of the collective dimension of freedom of religion or belief with a view to seeking ways to improve the protection of the right to freedom of religion or belief in international law.

To this end, in Chapters 2 to 4 the book has sought to explore the substantive scope of the collective dimension and the manner in which it has been interpreted by relevant international law adjudicators and to identify to what extent—if any—the international standard of compliance review may be improved when dealing with national protection systems. A comprehensive theory of the collective dimension of freedom of religion or belief in international law has not been developed so far in legal doctrine and it is hoped that a substantial contribution of this book is that which it makes to our understanding of the notion of the collective dimension. International human rights standards applicable to the protection of the rights to acquire legal personality and to freedom in the internal affairs of religious or belief communities have been examined in order to understand the nature of protection and identify challenges and ways of moving forward.

Chapters 5 to 7 of the book have critically assessed the protection of the collective dimension of freedom of religion or belief in Turkey based on the standards identified in Chapters 2 to 4. The case study on Turkey is valuable and useful in, not least, two ways: first, the study provides a comprehensive, albeit not exhaustive, normative assessment on the protection of freedom of religion or belief in Turkey, thus making a contribution to the academic literature, and secondly, the case study helps to identify gaps in international standards of review.

As far as legal sources are concerned, the discussions in Chapters 2 to 4 have been based primarily on the ICCPR and the jurisprudence of the HRCttee and the ECHR, and the jurisprudence of the Strasbourg organs. When relevant, other sources of a soft law nature have also been relied upon, such as the work of the UN Special Rapporteur and, to a lesser extent, the relevant OSCE guidelines. This deliberate comparative approach has enabled the study, on the one hand, to draw from global and regional systems when seeking to understand the notion of the collective dimension of freedom of religion or belief, and, on the other hand, to identify and critically assess similarities and differences in the approaches of these protection schemes.

A central assumption of this book has been that the international protection of the collective dimension of the right to freedom of religion or belief would provide a solid normative basis and protection for the claims pertaining to the right to freedom of religion or belief that have a collective nature. Throughout the study this assumption has been tested in concrete cases that have been addressed, principally, based on the standards established by human rights instruments and the respective jurisprudence of the HRCttee and the European bodies. It would seem that the central assumption of the book presents itself as an ideal to strive for, instead of an already established matter. It appears that the limited scope and nature of obligations, the unwillingness to address the collective nature of claims as well as to tackle broad-scale, often repressive, policies and legislation behind restrictions, and, as far as the European context is concerned, the wide margin of discretion granted to states remain as challenges that must be overcome in order to advance the effectiveness of the protection that is already enshrined in the relevant religious freedom provisions. Notwithstanding these shortcomings, the normative basis of the collective dimension both at the global and European regional levels create a potentially comprehensive basis for the normative protection of acts and diverse forms of collectivities involved in the exercise of the collective dimension of freedom of religion or belief as discussed in Chapter 2.

Important assumptions with regard to the Turkish case have been that a better understanding of the international obligations pertaining to the right to freedom of religion or belief in its collective dimension and improved international review mechanisms are necessary to improve the protection of freedom of religion or belief in its collective dimension in Turkey. Yet, it appears that a "better understanding" and "good international review mechanisms" would not necessarily result in the effective protection of this right. A particularly good test of this pertains to the restrictions on the claims of religious or belief communities and individuals belonging to the communities pertaining to legal personality and the rights to establish associations and foundations. With regard to the latter rights, international positive obligations are clearly defined and strong. These obligations are apparent to the Turkish judiciary as they allude to them in numerous cases, yet the *willingness* to apply these standards ensuring the obligations appears to be the key factor that is missing. This does not, however, mean that "better understanding" and "good international review mechanisms" are of no use. On the contrary, these hold important functions in pointing to the standard that must be strived for and lay the foundations for legal claims brought by those who wish to exercise the right to freedom of religion or belief in its collective dimension.

In Chapter 2 we began by exploring the notion of the collective dimension of freedom of religion or belief with a view to examining its legal basis and determining its scope, nature of obligations, as well as boundaries. While the book has demonstrated the importance of the collective dimension of freedom of religion or belief for both various forms of groups of believers and individuals, it has also become clear that we do not yet have a coherent and well-developed theory of "the collective dimension of freedom of religion or belief". The latter term is viewed with suspicion at times, particularly when it is perceived to mean "the right of a religion or belief"; "on the axis of individual and collective rights, a hierarchically supreme right that leads to unjustifiable restrictions on the rights and freedoms of others"; or even "a particular constitutional arrangement defining strong entanglement of state with a certain religion". Or, often, it is given a limited recognition as solely the rights of religious institutions. It has been an aim of the book to distinguish the scope of the right as well as the subject—the who—of the right in order to better understand its scope and boundaries. This study does not constitute an exhaustive theory of the collective dimension of freedom of religion or belief; yet, by exploring questions pertaining to the substantive content of the right, the study has shown that the collective dimension of freedom of religion or belief is not solely limited to "the rights of religious institutions", that it protects all acts/manifestations of freedom of religion or belief that have a collective dimension. The study has also demonstrated that the collectivities as rights holders may vary, including natural groups, religious or belief groups that have acquired legal personality, and individuals who come together to exercise an act informally. The key for international adjudication appears to be the ability to see and the willingness to address the collective nature of claims pertaining to the collective dimension of freedom of religion or belief cases. This remains a challenge. Indeed, a greater understanding, recognition and enforcement of the scope of the collective dimension of freedom of religion or belief will significantly contribute to advancing the protection of freedom of religion or belief through international law.

Despite their limitations, international human rights norms pertaining to freedom of religion or belief potentially provide a solid substantive basis for the right to acquire an adequate form of legal personality for belief groups. The key *enabling* and *empowering* role of legal personality in the protection of the collective dimension of freedom of religion or belief has been illustrated in Chapters 3 and 6. The recognition of the right to acquire legal personality as an essential component of the collective dimension of freedom of religion or belief may be further strengthened with the substantive focus by international review mechanisms. This study has shown that this inquiry, however, should not be limited to the question of the mere availability of a legal personality option for belief groups; instead it should be qualified by exploring the directness of the linkage between the belief groups and legal entity in question as well as the acts that become possible once legal entity status is obtained. Moreover, the adequacy and suitability of existing models of legal entity status for belief communities' enjoyment of the right to manifest religion or belief in worship, teaching, observance and practice, the accessibility of the legal entity status and state supervision involved must be critically examined. As the Turkish case has shown, the mere existence and availability of certain legal entity formulas does not sufficiently amount to fulfilling the positive obligation to provide legal personality for belief groups to exercise the right to freedom of religion or belief in its collective dimension. The potential of rigorous and probing application of the restriction clauses has become evident in the review and analysis of particularly the relevant case law pertaining to legal personality matters. This potential must be realized by adjudicators by taking on a more *active* role. Evaluation of the grounds for including probing, scrutiny, requesting and relying on statistical information as well as asking for comparative information from states that can help identify patterns of discrimination may be some ways of being active.

Focus on the collective nature of acts and diverse forms of collectivities has also led to a broader view of the meaning of the freedom in the "internal affairs"—autonomy—of religious or belief communities, as opposed to understanding internal affairs solely with reference to "internal organization". As it has been illustrated in Chapter 4, autonomy can be an expansive issue depending on the dogma of the belief group in question. A comprehensive, yet not exhaustive, review of various forms of manifestations, *inter alia*, the right to establish places of worship, to train and appoint clergy, to teach religion or belief and to observe days of rest has revealed that international protection varies, not least, in terms of the identification of positive obligations as well as the assessment of restriction clauses as they are applied to these rights. The notion of autonomy needs to be utilized as an interpretive tool in the adjudication of claims pertaining to the collective dimension, beyond cases where solely internal organization matters are addressed. In addition to the generally recognized forms of the aforementioned manifestations, in Chapter 4 I have also argued that a right to use religious law can also be deduced from the provisions protecting the right to manifest religion or belief in practice.

The comparative approach adopted in the study has aimed to demonstrate the similarities and differences in the standard setting by the Strasbourg organs and the HRCttee in their respective jurisprudence on the right to freedom of religion or belief. The comparative review in this study confirms the finding of Paul Taylor that the European Court has shown an evident willingness to allow states a wide discretion through broad interpretation of limitation clauses, distinct from the more consistent approach taken by the HRCttee.[1] The ECtHR has interpreted the scope of manifestations of religion or belief in a narrow fashion and has relied on other rights, such as the right to freedom of association and right to fair trial (right to judicial protection), when assessing claims that at the same time raise issues pertaining to freedom of religion or belief and other human rights. While this may be reflective of the conception of the scope of the right to freedom of religion or belief of the European Court, on a positive note, since the jurisprudence of the ECtHR is solid and coherent on these rights this practice has resulted in stronger protection of the right to manifest religion or belief. In contrast, the HRCttee has demonstrated a consistent and coherent conception of freedom of religion or belief, embracing a broad conception of manifestations as outlined in General Comment 22 and did not feel the need to rely on other rights, such as the right to association, when claims pertaining to associative rights of religious/belief

1 Taylor, P.M. (2005) *Freedom of Religion: UN and European Human Rights Law and Practice*, Cambridge: Cambridge University Press, pp. 343 and 350.

groups were addressed. Notably, states have not been granted a margin of appreciation when the HRCttee has assessed justification of restrictions on the right to manifest religion or belief, including the collective dimension where sensitive state-religion relations have added complicating dimensions. It is interesting that considering that the HRCttee deals with diverse arrangements of state-religion relations it would seem that this exposure has not led to granting a wide margin of appreciation where it is not possible to identify a "common global standard"; instead the international scrutiny remained the same regardless of whether the latter existed or not. It might be argued that it is precisely this exposure to global variations of forms of manifestations and diverse state-religion arrangements that led the HRCttee both to appreciate different forms of manifestations as well as consistently to apply the restrictions clause. It should be borne in mind, however, that so far the ECtHR has had to deal with more and more complex questions involving balancing of interests based on freedom of religion or belief than the HRCttee.

The Turkish case study has illustrated that, often, restrictions on freedom of religion or belief in its collective dimension involve underlying factors deeply rooted in certain state-religion relation constructions as well as certain sensitivities—in the Turkish case, nationalism and minority issues. These are considered "given" or "legitimate" grounds for restrictions by national authorities, including the judiciary. Unfortunately, these grounds for restrictions are rarely assessed with scrutiny at the domestic level as the analysis of relevant jurisprudence has shown. Yet, when states are given a margin of appreciation in such cases, indeed, international review suffers and victims suffer as a result. Therefore, for effective international review, it is vital to bring out the potential within relevant restriction provisions and exercise rigorous examination of the latter.

The, at times, distinct conceptions of the HRCttee and the Strasbourg organs on the scope of the right to freedom of religion or belief and the nature of ensuing obligations appear as a factor weakening the standard of international review. It is important to maintain universal human rights standards without differences in the substantive content of the right to freedom of religion or belief.

Overall, the Turkish case study has illustrated the need to change the paradigm in which the right to freedom of religion or belief in its collective dimension is exercised; from tolerance to respect, fulfill and promote the right to freedom of religion or belief. The substantial need to urgently improve the understanding of the scope of freedom of religion or belief in its collective dimension in Turkey and corresponding standard setting and implementation has become evident throughout the study. International obligations pertaining to the collective dimension of freedom of religion or belief are not effectively utilized in standard setting and adjudication, despite significant human rights consequences for all groups of believers, including non-believers.

In Turkey, the right to freedom of religion or belief has a narrow scope; the strongest protection appears to be afforded to the protection against coercion to believe or worship in a particular way—yet this does not extend to the recognition of the right to conscientious objection to military service, a passive recognition of the right to worship, not effectively extending to related acts, and a significant degree of regulation of other aspects of the right to manifest religion or belief. The collective dimension of freedom of religion or belief is highly restricted, arguably, precisely because of the collective nature of the rights it protects. While Turkey appears distant to the protection of the exercise of the collective dimension, at the same time, it assumes *selected* roles with implications on the collective dimension where the Turkish state functions as the provider of public religious services. This arrangement often leaves the state as the sole holder of control—monopoly—over certain forms of manifestation. Certain elements of the collective dimension that groups of believers would together exercise are taken over by the state which functions as, *inter alia*, a public service provider, facilitator and funder. Moreover, in the process of providing these "services" the relevant state institutions function as shapers of religious dogma and tradition. This state involvement presents itself in varying degrees. For example, with absolute monopoly over the management of mosques and Islamic religious instruction through Quran courses; the legal framework does not allow any private acts in these spheres, including Muslims and non-Muslims. On the other hand, there exists the possibility, albeit highly restricted, for the selection of religious leaders and establishment of places of worship. Yet, the case-study has shown that the processes that religious or belief groups engage in while exercising these rights leave a large sphere of discretion to the public authorities, far from ensuring a legal framework that effectively protects these rights. The outcomes may be taken as indications of patterns of discrimination in the exercise of these rights. Teaching of religion stands out by far as the most restricted component of the collective dimension of the right to freedom of religion or belief. The extent of obstruction of this right becomes particularly grave when viewed in contrast to the state's engagement in teaching of religion based on the Sunni-Muslim tradition. Indeed, the collective dimension of freedom of religion or belief in Turkey has a narrow scope that delivers few possibilities for religious or belief groups.

In contrast to a general commitment to the protection of freedom of religion or belief, the lack of a coherent and solid basis for freedom of religion or belief in its collective dimension becomes strikingly concrete in relation to specific components of this right. Legislation pertaining to various components of the collective dimension of freedom of religion or belief is dispersed in different laws, such as the Cadastral Law, Public Works Law, or Civil Code. While such fragmentation is not necessarily a hindrance to the protection of freedom of religion or belief, the fact that when considering claims, the public authorities, including the judiciary, rarely consider the issues raised in relation to freedom of religion or belief, presents a significant setback. In this context silence about the right to freedom of religion or belief speaks loudest. This lack of consideration is also reflective of the conception pertaining to freedom of religion or belief. Such conception appears to fail to draw connections with concrete cases of freedom of religion or belief, albeit not formulated with a direct link to freedom of religion or belief, with the general protection of freedom of religion or belief in the Constitution and international instruments to which Turkey is a party. Indeed, the lack of utilization of the Turkish Constitutional provisions and international norms pertaining to the right to freedom of religion or belief by the Turkish judiciary is particularly striking. Thus, claims brought by stakeholders end up being situated as weak claims in the constructions of reasoning where numerous aspects of freedom of religion or belief are perceived as merely "acts" that are in contradiction to secularism or national security and not acts that are protected under various freedom of religion or belief provisions. Arguably, such normative terms actually disguise "state interest" which appears to be the underlying interest in applied restrictions.

Strikingly, the study has shown that the judiciary often fails to consider the right to freedom of religion or belief as protected in international law in its assessment of cases that directly raise questions pertaining to this right. The reason for this silence is unclear and there could be numerous explanations. The general findings pertaining to the Turkish judiciary, which indicate that it is influenced by a perception of "threat and danger",[2] and that "political climate" is important in the judiciary, are certainly compatible with and explain the findings concerning the Turkish case-study, particularly in Chapter 6. Yet, taking into account the historical and political context that this book has sought to provide along with the legal issues it has explored, it is possible to foresee that were the judiciary to apply and interpret freedom of religion or belief in line with international standards, it is likely that ensuing decisions would be politically controversial given the underlying sensitivities behind the restrictions in the first place. Thus, in order for substantial improvement of the right to freedom of religion or belief in its collective dimension in Turkey, an exceptionally independent and willing judiciary that is ready to understand and address freedom of religion or belief in assessing relevant claims, as such, and public authorities who are willing to enforce ensuing decisions are indispensable. Alternatively, broad changes in the political context in the long run may make it possible to change the approach of the judiciary and other public authorities to issues concerning freedom of religion or belief in its collective dimension.

In the Turkish context, the denial of legal personality to religious or belief groups, as such, stands out as a key issue that presents itself as a challenge to the Turkish conception of the right to freedom of religion or belief in its collective dimension. The implications of this denial and the inadequacy of alternative formulas, in the form of associations and foundations, have been illustrated in Chapter 6. The notion that legal personality of religious or belief communities is categorically incompatible with Turkey's *laik* (secular) nation(-alist) state model must be informed by and harmonized with a new conception of freedom of religion or belief that respects the elements of the latter as established by international law instruments. International review mechanisms and national and international human rights bodies are compelled to seek corrective action on the part of the state so that the positive obligation on the part of states to create an adequate form of legal personality may be realized in Turkey.

Chapter 7, which focuses on four key components of freedom in the internal affairs, *inter alia*, establishing places of worship, freedom to teach, observing days

2 Sancar, M. (2009) *Adalet Bazen Es Geçiliyor* [Justice is Sometimes Overlooked], Istanbul: TESEV, pp. 142 and 143.

of rest and holidays in accordance with religion or belief, has presented the complexities involved in the protection of the right to freedom of religion or belief in its collective dimension in Turkey. Again, despite a general constitutional commitment to the protection of freedom of religion or belief, the concrete cases that were examined indicate the importance of scrutiny of administrative processes and the outcomes. The right to establish places of worship and the right to appoint religious leaders, indeed, appear to be "lost in administration" through the wide discretion granted to public authorities and what ostensibly seem like neutral criteria. Any meaningful assessment of the state of the right to freedom of religion or belief ought to include an assessment of outcomes. Statistical information on to what extent diverse religious or belief groups can exercise rights needs to be included in the assessment. The importance of this has become evident in the Turkish case study, in particular with reference to the right to establish places of worship and teach religion or belief.

What does the future hold for the protection of the collective dimension of freedom of religion or belief in Turkey? It would seem that a willingness to better understand the implications of Turkey's human rights obligations under international law as well as to implement them with courage could substantially improve the standard of protection of the right to freedom of religion or belief. A coherent and well-founded conception and an ensuing legislative and administrative practice upholding international standards seems difficult to achieve as long as rightful claims pertaining to the enjoyment of the latter are viewed incompatible with, *inter alia*, the dominant understanding of nation-state and *laiklik* (secularism). The assumption that Turkey's particularities mandate a public interest to strictly regulate public manifestations of religion or belief control needs to be challenged. In this process, the main actor of change is the government which is also the primary actor responsible for Turkey's human rights obligations. The continuing process of change in Turkey, an upcoming new Constitution for Turkey, engagement of civil society institutions in the change as well as global and regional international mechanisms involved in the review of Turkey's implementation of international law hold significant opportunities for influencing change to bring the protection of the right to freedom of religion or belief closer to adhere to international law standards. If human rights law is not made an active part of the process of change, in terms of setting the standard and being given due consideration in drafting and applying legislation, it will have very limited transformative power in Turkey. Human rights standards are to play the role of "conscience"[3]—saying what ought to be—while it is the "will" of the decision makers that is key to change. In the process of eradication of the conditions that result in a failed system of protection, human rights law can contribute significantly, although surely it cannot by itself provide the cure. In this context, the state's role in religion is in need of being re-formulated—it must continuously evolve—by embracing impartiality and neutrality, ensuring pluralism and respecting equal rights and equal

3 Therefore it is of extreme importance that internationally upheld standards are coherent.

access to rights, respecting the right to freedom in the internal affairs of religious or belief groups as it has been broadly described here.

One of the aims of this study has been to explore and identify ways in which the standard of international review could be improved based on the Turkish case study and the latter has shown some areas in which improvements can be sought. At least three areas for possible improvement may be identified. First, the little and selective attention given to the right to freedom of religion or belief in the assessment of claims pertaining to the latter should lead international adjudicators not to rely on the national authorities, including the judiciary, to review and assess the application of restrictions clauses with utmost scrutiny. They should show more restraint in relying on the margin of appreciation of national authorities. This assessment must include focus on administrative processes and outcomes. Secondly, it appears that a coherent and precise approach to the scope and nature of obligations pertaining to the collective dimension would be a factor that could strengthen domestic protection efforts while at the same time further improving international standard setting. Finally, international mechanisms tasked with international review of domestic protection schemes would be more effective if they sought to improve their capacities to increase their ability to address and tackle general repressive legislation and practices and establish means for follow-up and implementation. The Turkish case has demonstrated that many issues do not become the subject of court cases, thus compliance control mechanisms other than those dealing with individual complaints gain greater importance in the cases of countries where the situation is similar to Turkey.

Regarding the limitations of this book, the fact that a number of possible sources could not be included needs to be stated. It would be useful to underscore again that originally this study aimed to include the decision-making processes of public authorities—who implement relevant laws and regulation—in the context of the themes explored in this book. However the reluctance on the part of public authorities to participate in the study made this impossible. A better understanding of the criteria employed by public authorities through the information presented by the latter would have made the identification of gaps and problems as well as patterns in the protection of the collective dimension more complete. The inclusion of statistical analysis pertaining to affected groups would also have contributed to depicting a fuller picture as well as illustrating diverse dimensions of processes and outcomes in the enjoyment of the rights explored. While such statistical analysis is lacking, effort has been made to include the perspectives of affected groups through in-depth interviews with the representatives of religious or belief groups.

As far as future research is concerned, an in-depth and multi-disciplinary examination of the effects of financial or other state support to certain religions or certain religious institutions on the protection and enjoyment of the right to freedom of religion or belief would be beneficial. What elements are necessary for such support to raise issues pertaining to impartiality and neutrality and prohibition of discrimination in relation to the right to freedom of religion or belief would surely contribute to our understanding of the latter. A study on the decision-making processes of public authorities related to the exercise of the collective dimension of freedom of religion or belief would contribute to our understanding of the protection of freedom of religion or belief. Studies involving statistical data pertaining to outcomes of the exercise of freedom of religion or belief by various religious or belief groups in Turkey would make comparative assessments possible.

This study has shown the importance of the collective dimension of freedom of religion or belief for the protection of the right to freedom of religion or belief as well as the shortcomings, such as the lack of a coherent approach to recognize the collective nature of claims at the global and regional levels of human rights protection schemes, the lack of positive obligations as well as, at times, a tendency to accommodate state restrictions of international law jurisprudence in the protection of this right. It has also highlighted the implications of historically evolved state-religion relations on the protection of the collective dimension of freedom of religion or belief and the normative demands created by the latter. These implications constitute a challenge to international law adjudicators. They are tasked with presenting effective ways of engagement to advance the protection of the right to freedom of religion or belief.

Moreover, this book has shown the paradoxical state of affairs concerning the protection of freedom of religion or belief in Turkey, in particular in its collective dimension. On the one hand, the general protection of freedom of religion or belief as a constitutional right exists, yet, on the other hand, there is a lack of effective protection of basic components of the right in practice. A willingness to incorporate a coherent understanding of the right to freedom of religion or belief in legislation and practice will greatly contribute to advancing the protection of the right to freedom of religion or belief in Turkey. Such an understanding, which may constitute the cornerstone of standard, may lead to harmonizing the understandings of national interest, *laiklik* and nationalism, which have been and continue to be the underlying reasons for many restrictions with human rights standards. While Turkey's involvement in religion does not change the crux of the issues pertaining to the extensive interferences in the manifestations of religion, it surely adds new complicating dimensions that cannot be ignored.

Bibliography

Monographs and Articles

Adanalı, H. (2001) *Religious Education in Schools*, Ankara: Ankara University.

Adıvar, H.E. (2009) *Türkiye'de Şark-Garp ve Amerikan Tesirleri* [East–West and American Influences in Turkey], Istanbul: Can Publications.

Akandji-Kombe, J.F. (2007) *Positive Obligations under the European Convention on Human Rights, Human Rights Handbooks No.7*, Council of Europe.

Akgündüz, A. (1996) *Islam Hukukunda ve Osmanlı Tatbikatında Vakıf Müessesesi* [The Institution of Foundations in Islamic Law and Ottoman Practice], Istanbul: İstanbul Üniversitesi Publications.

An-Naim, A.A. (2000) "Islam and Human Rights: Beyond the Universality Debate", *ASIL Annual Meeting Proceedings*, Washington: ASIL.

An-Naim, A.A. (2008) *Islam and the Secular State: Negotiating the Future of Shari'a*, Harvard: Harvard University Press.

Arai-Takahashi, Y. (2002) *The Margin of Appreciation Doctrine and the Principle of Proportionality in the Jurisprudence of the European Court of Human Rights*, Leiden: Intersentia.

Asad, T. (2003) *Formations of the Secular: Christianity, Islam, Modernity*, San Fransisco: Stanford University Press.

Aslan, Z. (2002) "Temel Hak ve Özgürlüklerin Sınırlanması: Anayasa'nın 13. Maddesi Üzerine Bazı Düşünceler" [The Restriction of Fundamental Rights and Freedoms: Some Thoughts on Article 13 of the Constitution], *Anayasa Yargısı*, No.19.

Bakar, D. (2002) "Uygulamadan Ayrımcılık Örnekleri" [Practical Examples of Discrimination], in *Ulusal, Ulusalüstü ve Uluslararası Hukukta Azınlık Hakları* [Minority Rights under National, Supra-National and International Law], Istanbul: Istanbul Bar Association Publications.

Bali, R. (2004) *Devletin Yahudileri ve "Öteki Yahudiler"* [State's Jews and "Other Jews"], Istanbul: İletişim Publications.

Baer, G. (1997) "The Waqf as a Prop for the Social System (Sixteenth–Twentieth Centuries)", *Islamic Law and Society* 4.

Barnes, R.J. (1987) *An Introduction to Religious Foundations in the Ottoman Empire*, Leiden: Brill.

Başlar, K. (2004) "Uluslararası Antlaşmaların Onaylanması, Üstünlüğü ve Anayasal Denetimi Üzerine" [On the Ratification and Superiority of International Treaties], *Milletlerarası Hukuk ve Milletlerarası Özel Hukuk Bülteni*, Prof. Dr. Sevin Toluner'e Armağan, 24(1–2).

Bayramoğlu, A. (2007) *28 Şubat: Bir Müdahalenin Güncesi* [February 28: The Diary of an Intervention], Istanbul: İletişim Publications.

Bebiroğlu, M. (2008) *Osmanlı Devletinde Gayrimüslim Nizamnameleri* [Regulations of non-Muslim Communities Under the Ottoman State], Istanbul: Adam.

Berry, S.E. (2012) "A Tale of Two Instruments", *Netherlands Quarterly of Human Rights*, 30(1).

Bossuyt, M.J. (1987) *Guide to the "Travaux Préparatoires" of the International Covenant on Civil and Political Rights*, Leiden: Martinus Nijhoff Publishers.

Boyle, K. (2004) "Human Rights, Religion and Democracy: The Refah Party Case", *Essex Human Rights Review*, 1(1): 1–16.

Boyle, K. (2007) "Freedom of Religion in International Law", in J. Rehman and S. Breau (eds.), *Religion, Human Rights and International Law: A Critical Examination of Islamic State Practices*, Leiden and Boston: Martinus Nijhoff Publishers.

Boyle, K. and J. Sheen (eds.) (1997) *Freedom of Religion and Belief: A World Report*, London: Routledge.

Bozan, İ. (2007) *Devlet ile Toplum Arasında bir Okul: İmam Hatip Liseleri...bir Kurum: Diyanet İşleri Başkanlığı* [Between State and Society], Istanbul: TESEV Publications.

Bozkurt, G. (1998) *Azınlık İmtiyazları Kapitülasyonlardan Tek Hukuk Sistemine Geçiş* [The Transition from Minority Privileges Capitulations to a Unified Legal System], Ankara: Atatürk Kültür, Dil ve Tarih Yüksek Kurumu.

Brems, E. (2003) "The Approach of the European Court of Human Rights to Religion", in J.C. Mohr (ed.), *Die Rechtsstellung des Menschen im Völkerrecht*, Tübingen: Mohr.

Brown, D. (2007) "A Destruction of Muslim Identity: Ontario's Decision to Stop Shari'a Based Arbitration", *North Carolina Journal of International Law and Commercial Regulation*, Spring.

Broyde, M.J. (1996) "Forming Religious Communities and Respecting Dissenter's Rights", in J. Witte, Jr. and Johan D. van der Vyver (eds.), *Religious Human Rights in Global Perspective: Religious Perspectives*, Leiden: Martinus Nijhoff.

Buergenthal, T. (1995) *International Human Rights in a Nutshell*, 2nd. edn, Minnesota: West Publishing Co.

Buergenthal, T. (2001) "The U.N. Human Rights Committee", in J.A. Frowein and R. Wolfrum (eds.), *Max Planck Yearbook of United Nations Law*, Vol. 5, Dordrecht: Kluwer.

Çağlar, B. (1994) "Türkiye'de Laikliğin Büyük Problemi" [The Great Problem of Secularism in Turkey], *Cogito* 1, Summer.

Çakır, R. and İ. Bozan (2005) *Sivil, Şeffaf ve Demokratik bir Diyanet İşleri Başkanlığı Mümkün mü?* [A Civil, Transparent and Democratic Presidency of Religious Affairs-Possible?], Istanbul: TESEV Publications.

Can, O. (2002) "Anayasa Değişiklikleri ve Düşünceyi Açıklama Özgürlüğü" [Constitutional Amendments and the Freedom to Express Thoughts], *Anayasa Yargısı*, 19.

Can, O. (2014) "Vicdani Red ve Anayasa" [Consciencious Objection and the Constitution], in O. Çınar and C. Üsterci (eds.), *Çarklardaki Kum: Vicdani Red* [Sand in the Wheels: Conscientious Objection], Istanbul: İletişim.

Care, J.C. (2006) "Between a Rock and a Hard Place", in A. Whiting and C. Evans (eds.), *Mixed Blessings: Laws, Religions and Women's Rights in the Asia-Pacific Region*, Leiden: Martinus Nijhoff.

Çarkoğlu, A. and E. Kalaycıoğlu (2009) *Türkiye'de Dindarlık: Uluslararası bir Karşılaştırma* [Religiosity in Turkey: An International Comparison], Istanbul: Sabancı University Publications.

Çavuşoğlu, N. (1994) *İnsan Hakları Avrupa Sözleşmesi ve Avrupa Topluluk Hukuku'nda Temel Hak ve Hürriyetler Üzerine* [On Fundamental Rights and Freedoms in the European Convention on Human Rights and European Union Law], Ankara: Ankara Üniversitesi Siyasal Bilgiler Fakültesi İnsan Hakları Merkezi Yayınları.

Çetin, F. (2002) "Yerli Yabancılar" [Indigenous Aliens] in *Ulusal, Ulusalüstü ve Uluslararası Hukukta Azınlık Hakları* [Minority Rights in National, Supranational and International Law], Istanbul: İstanbul Bar Publications.

Chaib, S.Q. (2002) "Religious Accommodation in the Workplace: Improving the Legal Reasoning of the European Court of Human Rights", in K. Alidadi, M.C. Foblets, J. Vrielink (eds.), *A Test of Faith: Religious Diversity and Accommodation in the European Workplace*, Leiden: Ashgate.

Charlesworth, H. (1999) "The Challenges of Human Rights Law for Religious Traditions", in M.W. Janis and C. Evans (eds.), *Religion and International Law*, Leiden: Martinus Nijhoff.

Chinkin, C. (2001) "Cultural Relativism and International Law", in C. Howland, *Religious Fundamentalisms and the Human Rights of Women*, New York: Palgrave Macmillan.

Çizakça, M. (2000) *A History of Philanthropic Foundations*, Istanbul. Boğaziçi University Press.

Council of Europe (1993) *Freedom of Conscience*, Strasbourg: Council of Europe Publications.

Crause, K. and M. Scheinin (eds.) (2009) *International Protection of Human Rights: A Textbook*, Turku/Åbo: Åbo Akademi University Institute for Human Rights.

Cumper, P. (2003/2004) "Europe, Islam and Democracy: Balancing Religious and Secular Values", in *European Yearbook of Minority Issues*, Vol. 3, Leiden: Brill.

Danchin, P.G. and Lisa Forman (2002) "The Evolving Jurisprudence of the European Court of Human Rghts and the Protection of Religious Minorities", in Peter Danchin and Elizabeth A. Cole (eds.), *Protecting the Human Rights of Religious Minorities in Eastern Europe*, New York: Colombia University Press.

Dane, P. (2001) "The Varieties of Religious Autonomy", in G. Robbers (ed.), *Church Autonomy – A Comparative Survey*, Frankfurt: Peter Lang.

De Jong, C.D. (2000) *The Freedom of Thought Conscience and Religion or Belief in the United Nations (1946–1992)*, The Hague: Intersentia–Hart.

Delgado, R. and J. Stefancic (2001) *Critical Race Theory: An Introduction*, New York: NYU Press.

Demir, H.S. (2011) *Avrupa İnsan Hakları Mahkemesi Kararları Işığında Türkiye'de Din ve Vicdan Özgürlüğü* [Freedom of Religion and Conscience in Turkey in Light of the Decisions of the European Court of Human Rights], Ankara: Adalet.

Devroye, J. (2009) "The Case of D.H. and Others v. the Czech Republic", *North Western Journal of International Human Rights*, 7, Spring.

Dickson, B. (1995) "The United Nations and Freedom of Religion", 44 *International and Comparative Law Quarterly* 327.

Dinçkol, B. (1992) *1982 Anayasası Çerçevesinde ve Anayasa Mahkemesi Kararlarında Laiklik* [Secularism within the Framework of the 1982 Constitution and the Judgments of the Constitutional Court], Istanbul: Kazancı Kitap.

Dinçkol, B. (2002) "Türkiye'de Anayasal Düzen ve Laiklik", İstanbul Ticaret Üniversitesi Resmi İnternet Sitesi. Available: http://www.iticu.edu.tr/uploads/kutuphane/dergi/d1/M00007.pdf [Accessed 1 March 2015].

Dinstein, Y. (1992) "Freedom of Religion and the Protection of Religious Minorities", in Y. Dinstein and M. Tabory (eds.), *The Protection of Minorities and Human Rights*, Dordrecht: Martinus Nijhoff.

Distein, Y. (ed.) (1992) *The Protection of Minorities and Human Rights*, Dordrecht/London: Martinus Nijhoff.

Dröge, C. (2003) "Positive Verpflichtungen der Staaten in der Europaischen Menschenrechtskonvention" Summary in *Beitrage zum Auslandischen öffentlichen Recht und Völkerrecht*, Band 159, Max Planck Gesellschaft zur Förderung der Wissenschaften.

Durham Jr. W.C. (1996) "Perspectives on Religious Liberty: A Comparative Framework", in J.D. van der Vyder and J. Witte Junior (eds.), *Religious Human Rights in Global Perspective*, Dordrecht: Martinus Nijhoff.

Durham Jr. W.C. (1999) *Freedom of Religion or Belief: Laws Affecting the Structuring of Religious Communities*, ODIHR Background Paper 1999/4. Published by the Office for Democratic Institutions and Human Rights of the Organization for Security and Cooperation in Europe.

Durham Jr. W.C. (2001) "The Right to Autonomy in Religious Affairs", in G. Robbers (ed.), *Church Autonomy – A Comparative Survey*, Frankfurt: Peter Lang.

Durham Jr. W.C. (2004) "Religious Association Laws", in T. Lindholm, W.C. Durham Jr., B.G. Tahzib-Lie (eds.), *Facilitating Freedom of Religion or Belief: A Deskbook*, Dordrecht: Martinus Nijhoff.

Durham Jr. W.C. (2004) "Facilitating Freedom of Religion or Belief through Religious Association Laws", in T. Lindholm, W.C. Durham and B.G. Tahzib-Lie (eds.), *Facilitating Freedom of Religion or Belief: A Deskbook*, Dordrecht: Martinus Nijhoff.

Durham, W.C., N. Peterson and E. Sewell (2005) "Introduction to a Comparative Analysis of Religious Association Laws in Post-Communist Europe", in W.C. Durham and S. Ferrari (eds.), *Laws on Religion and the State in Post-Communist Europe*, Leuven: Peeters.

Dworkin, R. (1978) *Taking Rights Seriously*, Harvard: Harvard University Press.

Ekiz, S. (2007) "Avrupa İnsan Hakları Sözleşmesi Kapsamında Din ve İnanç Özgürlüğü" [Freedom of Religion and Belief under the European Convention on Human Rights], *(unpublished doctoral thesis)*, Dokuz Eylül University Institute of Social Science, Public Law.

Elügür, B. (2014) *The Mobilization of Political Islam in Turkey*, Cambridge: Cambridge University Press.

Ersal, M. (2009) *Alevi İnanç- Dede Ocakları Üzerine bir Örneklem: Veli Baba Sultan Ocağı* [A Study on the Alevi Belief Dede Houses: Veli Baba Sultan House], Ankara: Alevi-Bektaşi Kültür Enstitüsü Yayınları, 6.

Evans, C. (2001) *Freedom of Religion under the European Convention on Human Rights*, Oxford: Oxford University Press.

Evans, C. and C.A. Thomas (2006) "Church-State Relations in the European Court of Human Rights", *Brigham Young University Law Review*.

Evans, M.D. (1997) *Religious Liberty and International Law in Europe*, Cambridge: Cambridge University Press.

Evans, M.D. (2009) *Manual on the Wearing of Religious Symbols in Public Areas*, Strasbourg: Council of Europe.

Gadirov, J. (2007) "Freedom of Religion and Legal Pluralism", in M.L.P. Loenen and J.E. Goldschimidt (eds.), *Religious Pluralism and Human Rights in Europe: Where to Draw the Line?* Cambridge: Intersentia.

Gavison, R. and N. Perez (2008) "Days of Rest in Multicultural Societies: Private, Public, Separate?", in P. Cane, C. Evans and Z. Robinson (eds.), *Law and Religion in Theoretical and Historical Contexts*, Cambridge: Cambridge University Press.

Gerber, H. (1984) "The Waqf Institution in Early Ottoman Edirne", in G.R. Warburg and G.G. Gilbar (eds.), *Islamic Studies in Islamic Society: Contributions in Memory of Gabriel Baer*, Haifa: Haifa University Press.

Ghanea, N. (ed.) (2003) *The Challenge of Religious Discrimination at the Dawn of the New Millennium*, Leiden: Martinus Nijhoff.

Ghanea, N. (ed.) (2007) *Does God Believe in Human Rights?*, Dordrecht: Martinus Nijhoff.

Ghanea, N. (2011) "Religion and Human Rights: An Introduction", in J. Witte, Jr. and M.C. Green (eds.), *Religion, Equality, and Non-Discrimination*, Oxford: Oxford University Press.

Ghanea, N. and A. Xanthaki (eds.) (2005) *Minorities, Peoples and Self-Determination*, Dordrecht: Martinus Nijhoff.

Gözaydın, İ. (2009) "Türkiye'de Din Kültürü ve Ahlak Bilgisi ders kitaplarına insan hakları merceğiyle bir bakış", in G. Tüzün (Der.), *Ders kitaplarında insan hakları u tarama sonuçları içinde* [Results of the Human Rights Screening of School Books], Istanbul: Tarih Vakfi.

Gözaydın, İ. (2009) *Diyanet: Türkiye Cumhuriyeti'nde Dinin Tanzimi* [The Presidency of Religious Affairs: The Arrangement of Religion in the Turkish Republic], Istanbul: İletişim Publications.

Gözler, K. (2000) *Türk Anayasa Hukuku* [Turkish Constitutional Law], Ekin Kitapevi.

Gözler, K. (2001) "Anayasa Değişikliğinin Temel Hak ve Hürriyetler Bakımından Getirdikleri ve Götürdükleri" [Pros and Cons of the Constitutional Amendments on Fundamental Rights and Freedoms], *Ankara Barosu Dergisi*, 59, 4.

Gözler, K. (2010) "1982 Anayasası'na Göre Din Eğitim ve Öğretimi" [Religious Instruction and Teaching Under the 1982 Constitution], Prof. Dr. Tunçer Karamustafaoğlu'na Armağan, Ankara: Adalet Publications.

Gülmez, M. (2004) "Anayasa Değişikliği Sonrasında İnsan Hakları Sözleşmelerinin İç Hukuktaki Yeri ve Değeri" [The Place and Value of Human Rights Treaties After the Constitutional Amendment], *Türkiye Barolar Birliği Dergisi*, September–October.

Günay, N. (2001) "Implementing the 'February 28' Recommendations: A Scorecard", Research Notes No. 10, Washington Institute for Near East Policy.

Gunn, T.J. (1996) "Adjudicating Rights of Conscience under the European Convention on Human Rights", in J. van der Vyver and J. Witte (eds.), *Religious Human Rights in Global Perspective: Legal Perspectives*, Dordrecht: Martinus Nijhoff.

Gunn, T.J. (2003) "The Complexity of Religion and the Definition of 'Religion' in International Law", 16 *Harvard Human Rights Law Journal*.

Hammer, L.M. (2001) *The International Human Right to Freedom of Conscience: Some Suggestions for its Development and Application*, Surrey: Ashgate.

Hatemi, H. (1969) *Onceki ve Bugünkü Türk Hukuku'nda Vakıf Kurma Muamelesi* [Establishment of Foundations in the Old and Contemporary Turkish Law], Istanbul: İstanbul University Press.

Hatemi, H. (1979) *Medeni Hukuk Tüzelkişileri I* [Civil Law Legal Persons I], Istanbul: İstanbul University Press.

Hatemi, H. (2004) "Cemaat Vakıfları Konusunda Düşünceler" [Thoughts About Community Foundations], in *Özsunay Armağanı*, Istanbul: İstanbul University Press.

Henrard, K. (2012) "A Critical Appraisal of the Margin of Appreciation Let to States Pertaining to 'Church-State Relations' under the Jurisprudence of the European Court of Human Rights", in K. Alidadi, M.C. Foblets, J. Vrielink (eds.), *A Test of Faith? Religious Diversity and Accommodation in the European Workplace*, Surrey: Ashgate.

İnalcık, H. (2000) *Osmanlı'da Devlet Hukuk Adalet* [State, Law and Justice of the Ottoman], Eren.

International Council on Human Rights Policy (2009) *When Legal Worlds Overlap: Human Rights, State and Non-State Law*, Versoix: ICHRP.

İşeri, A. (1964) "Vakıflar" [Foundations], in *Ankara Üniversitesi Hukuk Fakültesi Dergisi*, 21, 1–4.

Kaboğlu, İ.Ö. (2002) *Özgürlükler Hukuku* [Law of Freedoms], Istanbul: İmge Kitapevi.

Kaboğlu, İ.Ö. (2005) *Ulusal, Ulusalüstü ve Uluslararası Hukukta Azınlık Hakları* [Minority Rights under National, Supra-National and International Law], Istanbul: Istanbul Bar Publications.

Kaboğlu, İ.Ö. (2009) *Anayasa Hukuku Dersleri* [Lessons on Constitutional Law], Istanbul: Legal.

Kalaycıoğlu, E. (2009) "Democracy, Islam and Secularism in Turkey", in N.J. Brown and E. Shahin (eds.), *The Struggle Over Democracy in the Middle East: Regional Politics and External Policies*, London: Routledge.

Kaptan, E. (2002) *Lozan Konferansı'nda Azınlıklar Sorunu* [The Question of Minorities in the Lausanne Conference], Istanbul: Harp Akademileri Press.

Kara, İ. (2008) *Cumhuriyet Türkiyesi'nde bir Mesele olarak İslam* [Islam as an Issue in the Turkish Republic], Istanbul: Dergah Publications.

Kara, M. (1999) *Din Hayat Sanat Açısından Tekkeler ve Zaviyeler* [Dervish Lodges from the Perspective of Religion, Life, Art], Istanbul: Dergah Publications.

Karaman, H. (1974) *Mukayeseli Islam Hukuku* [Comparative Islamic Law], Istanbul: İz Publications.

Kaya, A. and Ö. Genç (2011) *Türkiye'de İnanç Grupları: Sorunlara ve Taleplere Yönelik Yeni bir Çerçeve* [Belief Groups in Turkey: A New Framework for Problems and Demands], Istanbul: Alevi Vakıfları Federasyonu.

Lehnhof, L.S. (2002) "Freedom of Religious Association: The Right of Religious Organizations to Obtain Legal Entity Status under the European Convention", *Brigham Young University Law Review*, 2(16), 561–609.

Leigh, I. and A. Hambler (2014) "Religious Symbols, Conscience, and the Rights of Others", *Oxford Journal of Law and Religion*, 3.

Lerner, N. (1981) "Toward a Draft Declaration against Religious Intolerance and Discrimination", 11 *The Israel Yearbook on Human Rights.*

Lerner, N. (1982) "The Final Text of the UN Declaration against Intolerance and Discrimination Based on Religion or Belief", 12 *The Israel Yearbook on Human Rights.*

Lerner, N. (1997) "Religious Human Rights Under the United Nations", in J. van der Vyver and J. Witte Junior. (eds.), *Religious Human Rights in Global Perspective*, Dordrecht: Martinus Nijhoff.

Lerner, N. (2000) *Religion, Belief and International Human Rights*, Maryknoll, New York: Orbis.

Lerner, N. (2003) *Group Rights and Discrimination in International Law*, Dordrecht: Martinus Nijhoff.

Lev, Y. (2005) *Charity, Endowments and Charitable Institutions in the Medieval Islam*, Florida: University Press of Florida.

Liskofsky, S. (1980) "The United Nations Draft Declaration on the Elimination of All Forms of Religious Intolerance", UNESCO Doc. SS79/CONF.607/10, Annex V.

Macar, E. (2012) *Cumhuriyet Döneminde İstanbul Rum Patrikhanesi* [Istanbul Greek Patriarchate in the Republican Period], Istanbul: İletişim.

Manchini, S. (2010) "The Crucifix Rage: Supranational Constitutionalism Bumps Against the Counter-Majoritarian Difficulty", 6 *European Constitutional Law Review.*

Mardin, Ş. (2001) *Religion, Society, and Modernity in Turkey*, Syracuse University Press.

Mardin, Ş. (2007) *Türkiye'de Din ve Siyaset* [Religion and Politics in Turkey] 13th edn, Istanbul: İletişim.

Martínez-Torrón, J. and W. Cole Durham (2010) *Religion and the Secular State*, Provo: Bringham Young University.

Mayring, P. (2000) *Nitel Sosyal Araştırmaya Giriş* [Introduction to Qualitative Social Research], Adana: Baki Kitapevi.

Meray, S.L. (2003) *Lozan Barış Konferansı Tutanaklar Belgeler* [Lausanne Peace Conference Records Documents], Series 1, Vol. 1, Book 2, 2nd edn, Istanbul: YKY Publications.

Minnerath, M. (2004) "The Right to Autonomy in Religious Affairs", in T. Lindholm, W. C. Durham and B.G. Tahzib-Lie (eds.), *Facilitating Freedom of Religion or Belief: A Deskbook*, Leiden: Martinus Nijhoff.

Moon, G. and R. Allen (2000) "Substantive Rights and Equal Treatment in Respect of Religion and Belief: Towards a Better Understanding of the Rights, and Their Implications", 6 *European Human Rights Law Review* 580.

Mowbray, A.R. (2004) *The Development of Positive Obligations Under the European Convention on Human Rights by the European Court of Human Rights*, Oxford: Hart Publishing.

Nowak, M. (2004) *UN Covenant on Civil and Political Rights, CCPR Commentary*, 2nd revised edn, Antwerp/Oxford: N P Engel.

Olsson, T., E. Ozdalga and C. Raudvere (eds.) (1998) *Alevi Identity: Cultural, Religious and Social Perspectives*, London and New York: Routledge.

Öktem, A.E. (2002) *Uluslararası Hukukta İnanç Özgürlüğü* [Freedom of Religion or Belief in International Law], Ankara: Liberte.

Öktem, E. (2010) "Turkey", *Religion and the Secular State: National Report*, International Centre for Law and Religion Studies.

Oran, B. (2004) *Türkiye'de Azınlıklar: Kavramlar, Lozan, İç Mevzuat, İçtihat, Uygulama* [Minorities in Turkey: Concepts, Lausanne, Domestic Law, Case-Law, Practice], Istanbul: İletişim.

OSCE-Venice Commission (2004) *Guidelines for Review of Legislation Pertaining to Religion or Belief*, OSCE ODIHR.

Özenç, B. (2006) *Avrupa İnsan Hakları Sözleşmesi ve İnanç Özgürlüğü* [The European Court of Human Rights and Freedom of Religion or Belief], Istanbul: Kitap.

Öztürk, N. (2003) *Azınlık Vakıfları* [Minority Foundations], Istanbul: Altınküre.

Podoprigora, R. (2004) "Freedom of Religion and Belief and Discretionary State Approval of Religious Activity", in T. Lindholm, W.C. Durham and B.G. Tahzib-Lie (eds.), *Facilitating Freedom of Religion or Belief: A Deskbook*, Leiden: Martinus Nijhoff.

Reyna, Y. and E. Zonana (2003) *Son Yasal Düzenlemelere Göre Cemaat Vakıfları* [Community Foundation under Recent Legal Changes], Istanbul: Gözlem Publications.

Rivers, J. (2008) *Defamation of Religions and Human Rights*, Aachen: Missio.

Robbers, G. (ed.) (1996) *State and Church in the European Union*, Nomos.

Şahbaz, İ. (2004) "Avrupa İnsan Hakları Sözleşmesi'nin Türk Yargı Sistemindeki Yeri" [The Place of the European Convention on Human Rights in the Turkish Juridical System], *Türkiye Barolar Birliği Dergisi*, Eylül/Ekim 54.

Sancar, M. (2009) *Adalet Bazen Es Geçiliyor* [Justice is Sometimes Overlooked], Istanbul: TESEV.

Sancar, M. and E.Ü. Atılgan (2009) *Adalet biraz es geçiliyor: Demokratikleşme Sürecinde Hakimler ve Savcılar* [Justice is Somewhat Overlooked: Judges and Prosecutors in the Democratization Process], Istanbul: TESEV.

Scheinin, M. (1999) "Article 18", in G. Alfredsson and A. Eide (eds.), *The Universal Declaration of Human Rights, A Common Standard of Achievement*, The Hague: Martinus Nijhoff.

Scheinin, M. (2004) "How to Resolve Conflicts Between Individual and Collective Rights?", in M. Scheinin and R. Toivanen (eds.), *Rethinking Non-Discrimination and Minority Rights*, Institute for Human Rights, Åbo: Åbo Akademi University Publications.

Schokkenbroek, J. (1998) "The Basis, Nature and Application of the Margin of Appreciation Doctrine in the Case Law of the ECHR", 19 *Human Rights Law Journal.*

Scolnikov, A. (2011) *The Right to Religious Freedom in International Law: Between Group Rights and Individual Rights*, London: Routledge.

Seidman, I. (2006) *Interviewing as Qualitative Research: A Guide for Researchers in Education and Social Sciences*, New York: Teachers College Press.

Şenel, Ş. and Z. Tuyan (2009) "1926–1967 Yılları Arasında Türkiye Cumhuriyeti'nde Kurulan Tesisler (Vakıflar)" [Institutions (Foundations) Established in the Turkish Republic Between the Years 1926–1967], *Akademik Bakış* (IBT), 3(5), Winter.

Shaheen, S.A. (2007) "Religious Pluralism, Human Rights and Muslim Citizenship in Europe: Some Preliminary Reflections on an Evolving Methodology for Consensus", in M.L.P. Loenen and J.E. Goldschmidt (eds.), *Religious Pluralism and Human Rights in Europe: Where to Draw the Line?* Cambridge: Intersentia.

Shankland, D. (1998) *The Alevis in Turkey: The Emergence of a Secular Islamic Tradition*, London and New York: Routledge.

Şimşir, B.N. (1990) *Lozan Telgrafları (1922–1923)* [Lausanne Telegrams (1922–1923)], Ankara: Türk Tarih Kurumu Publications.

Şimşir, B.N. (2003) "Lozan'a Göre Azınlıklar", *80. Yılında 2003 Penceresinden Lozan Sempozyumu* [On its Symposium on 80th Anniversary of Lausanne—from the Window of 2003], Ankara: Türk Tarih Kurumu Publications XVI. Series No. 100.

Sullivan, D.J. (1988) "Advancing the Freedom of Religion or Belief through the UN Declaration on the Elimination of Religious Intolerance and Discrimination", *American Journal of International Law*, 88.

Sullivan, D.J. (1992) "Gender Equality and Religious Freedom: Toward a Framework for Conflict Resolution", 24 *NYUJ International Law & Politics.*

Sullivan, W.F. (2005) *The Impossibility of Religious Freedom*, Boston: Princeton University Press.

Sural, N. (2009) "Islamic Outfits in the Workplace in Turkey, a Muslim Majority Country", *Comparative Labour Law and Policy Journal*, Spring: 569.

Tahzib, B.G. (1996) *Freedom of Religion Freedom of Religion or Belief: Ensuring Effective International Legal Protection*, Dordrecht: Martinus Nijhoff.

Tanör, B. (1991) *Türkiye'nin İnsan Hakları Sorunu* [Turkey's Human Rights Problem], Istanbul: BDS.

Tanör, B. (2000) "İnanç ve Din Özgürlüğü" [Freedom of Belief and Religion], in G. Alpkaya and Others (eds.), *İnsan Hakları* [Human Rights], Istanbul: YKY.

Tanör, B. and N. Yüzbaşıoğlu (2005) *1982 Anayasasına Göre Türk Anayasa Hukuku* [Turkish Constitutional Law According to the 1982 Constitution], Istanbul: YKY Publications.

Tanyu, H. (2006) *Yehova Şahitleri* [Jehovah's Witnesses], Elips Kitap.

Taylor, P.M. (2005) *Freedom of Religion: UN and European Human Rights Law and Practice*, Cambridge: Cambridge University Press.

Temperman, J. (2007) "25th Anniversary Commemoration of the Adoption of the 1981 UN Declaration on the Elimination of Intolerance and Discrimination based on Religion or Belief: a Report", *Religion and Human Rights* 2.

Temperman, J. (2010) *State-Religion Relationships and Human Rights Law: Towards a Right to Religiously Neutral Governance*, Leiden: Martinus Nijhoff.

Thornberry, P. (1991) *International Law and the Protection of Minorities*, Oxford: Clarendon Press.

Uitz, R. (2007) *Freedom of Religion*, Belgium: Council of Europe Publishing.

Ulusoy, A. (2004) *Kamu Hizmeti İncelemeleri* [Study on Public Service], Ülke Kitapları.

Van Dijk, P., F. von Hoof, A. van Rijn and L. Zwaak (2006) *Theory and Practice of the European Convention on Human Rights*, The Hague: Intersentia.

Ven, J.A. van der (2008) "Religious Rights for Minorities in a Policy of Recognition", 3 *Religion and Human Rights*, 155.

Viljanen, J. (2003) *The European Court of Human Rights as a Developer of the General Doctrines of Human Rights Law: A Study of the Limitations Clauses of the European Convention of Human Rights*, Tampere: Tampereen Yliopisto.

Villaroman, N.G. (2012) "The Right to Establish and Maintain Places of Worship: The Development of Its Normative Content under International Human Rights Law", in S. Ferrari and S. Pastorelli (eds.), *Religion in Public Spaces*, Leiden: Ashgate.

Vural, H.S. (2013) *Türkiye'de Din Özgürlüğüne İlişkin Anayasal Güvence* [Constitutional Protection of Freedom of Religion in Turkey], Ankara: Seçkin Publications.

Yildirim, M. (2010) "Conscientious Objection to Military Service: International Human Rights Law and the Case of Turkey", *Religion and Human Rights*, 5.

Yildirim, M. (2012) "Religion in the Public and Private Turkish Workplace: the Approach of the Turkish Judiciary", in M.C. Foblets, K. Alidadi and J. Vrielink (eds.), *A Test of Faith? Religious Diversity and Accommodation in the European Workplace*, Surrey: Routledge.

Yildirim, M. (2013) "The Return of Property to Community Foundations in Turkey: The Restitution Decree", *European Yearbook of Minority Issues*, 9.

Yildirim, M. (2013) *Monitoring Report on the Right to Freedom of Religion or Belief*, January–June 2013, Istanbul: Norwegian Helsinki Committee.

Yildirim, M. and U. Şahin (2010) *"A Threat" or Under Threat? Legal and Social Problems of Protestants in Turkey*, Istanbul: Association of Protestant Churches.

Wiener, M. (2007) "The Mandate of the Special Rapporteur on Freedom of Religion or Belief: Institutional, Procedural and Substantive Legal Issues", 2 *Religion and Human Rights*, 3.

Zürcher, E.J. (2003) *Modernleşen Türkiye'nin Tarihi* [History of Turkey in the Modernization Process], Istanbul: İletişim Publications.

International Instruments

1923 Treaty of Peace with Turkey Signed at Lausanne, 24 July 1923, The Treaties of Peace 1919–1923, Vol. II (New York: Carnegie Endowment for International Peace, 1924.)

1948 Universal Declaration of Human Rights, G.A. Res. 217A, UN doc. A/810, 10 December 1948, 217 A (III).

1950 European Convention on Human Rights, Convention for the Protection of Human Rights and Fundamental Freedoms, as amended by Protocol No. 11, Rome, 4 November 1950, UNTS 213:222.

1966 International Covenant on Civil and Political Rights, G.A. Res. 2200A (XXI), 21 UN GAOR Supp. (No. 16), p. 52, UN Doc. A/6316 (1966), 999 UNTS 171.

1966 Optional Protocol to the International Covenant on Civil and Political Rights, G.A. Res. 2200A (XXI), 21 UN GAOR Supp. (No. 16) at 59, UN Doc. A/6316(1966), 999 UNTS 302.

1966 International Covenant on Economic, Social and Cultural Rights, 16 December 1966, United Nations, Treaty Series, Vol. 993, 3.

1969 United Nations, Vienna Convention on the Law of Treaties, 23 May 1969, United Nations, Treaty Series, Vol. 1155, 331.

1981 Declaration on the Elimination of Religious Intolerance and Discrimination, GA Res. 36/55, 36 UN GAOR Supp. (No. 51), p. 171, UN Doc. A/36/51, 1981.

1989 Concluding Document of the Vienna Meeting of Representatives of the Participating States of the Conference on Security and Cooperation in Europe, adopted on 17 January 1989.

1989 UN General Assembly, Convention on the Rights of the Child, 20 November 1989, United Nations, Treaty Series, Vol. 1577, 3.

1996 Council of Europe, European Social Charter (Revised), 3 May 1996, ETS 163.

1998 Protocol 11 to the European Convention for the Protection of Human Rights and Fundamental Freedoms, restructuring the control machinery established thereby, entry into force 1 November 1998.

Case Law of International Courts and Treaty Bodies

European Court of Human Rights

97 Members of the Gladani Congregation of Jehovah's Witnesses v. Georgia, 2007, No. 71101/01.

Ahmet Sadik v. Greece, 7 October 2002, No. 50776/99 and 52912/99.

Asatruarfelagid v. Iceland, 7 July 2011, Nos. 22897/08.

Belgian Linguistics v. Belgium, 23 July 1968, Nos. 1474/62, 1677/62, 1691/62, 1769/63, 1994/63 and 2126/64.

Buscarini and Others v. San Marino, 18 February 1999, No. 24645/94.

Canea Catholic Church v. Greece, 16 December 1997, No. 25528/94.

Cârmuirea Spirituală a Musulmanilor din Republica Moldova v. Moldova, 14 June 2005, App. No. 12282/02.

Cha'are Shalom Ve Tsedek v. France, 27 July 2000, No. 27417/95.

Dahlab v. Switzerland, 15 February 2001, No. 42393/98.

Darby v Sweden, 23 October 1990, No. 11581/85.

DH and Others v. Czech Republic (Grand Chamber), 13 November 2007, No. 57325/00.

Dubowska and Skup v. Poland, Nos. 33490/96 and 34055/96 (1997) DR89, 156.

Efstratiou v. Greece, 18 December 1996, No. 24095/94.

Fener Rum Lisesi Vakfi v. Turkey, 9 January 2007, No. 34478/97.

Fernandez Martinez v. Spain, 12 June 2014, No. 56030/07.

Feti Demirtas v. Turkey, 17 January 2012, No. 5260/07.

Golder v. United Kingdom, 21 February 1975, No. 4451/70.

Hasan and Chaush v. Bulgaria, 26 October 2000, No. 30985/96.

Hasan and Eylem Zengin v. Turkey, 9 October 2007, No. 1448/04.

Hoogendijk v. the Netherlands (Admissibility), 6 January 2005, No. 58641/00.

Kokkinakis v. Greece, 25 May 1993, No. 14307/88.

Lautsi v. Italy (Grand Chamber), 18 March 2011, No. 30814/06.

Leyla Sahin v. Turkey (Grand Chamber), 10 October 2005, No. 44774/98.

Manoussakis v Greece, 29 August 1996, No. 18748/91.

Maunussakis and Others v. Greece, 13 December 2001, No. 45701/99.

Metropolitan Church of Bessarabia and Others v. Moldova, 13 December 2001, No. 45701/99.

Obst v. Germany, 23 September 2012, No. 425/03.

Otto Preminger Institut v. Austria, 1994, No. 295-A.

Petrovic v. Austria, 27 March 1998, No. 20458/92.

Refah Partisi (the Welfare Party) and Others v. Turkey, Grand Chamber, 13 February 2003, Nos. 41340/98, 41342/98, 41343/98 and 41344/98.

Religionsgemeinschaft Der Zeugen Jehovas and Others v. Austria, 31 July 2008, No. 40825/98.

Schüth v. Germany, 23 September 2010, No. 1620/03.

Sidiropoulos v. Greece, 10 July 1998, No. 1594/1614.

Sidiropulous v. Greece, 10 July 1998, No. 26695/95.

Siebenhaar v. Germany, 3 February 2011, No. 18136/02.

Sinan Isik v. Turkey, 2 February 2010, No. 21924/05.

Stankov and the United Macedonian Organization Ilinden v. Bulgaria, 2 October 2001, Nos. 29221/95 and 29225/95.

Supreme Holy Council of the Muslim Community v. Bulgaria, 16 December 2004, No. 39023/97.

Svya Mychaylivska Parafiya v. Ukraine, 17 June 2007, No. 77703/01.

Svyato-Mychalivska Parafiya v. Ukraine, 14 June 2007, No. 77703/01.

The Christian Federation of Jehovah's Witnesses in France v. France (Admissibility), 6 November 2001, No. 53430/99.

The Moscow Branch of Salvation Army v. Russia, 5 October 2006, No. 72881/01.

The Sunday Times v. United Kingdom, 26 April 1979, No. 6538/74.

Yedikule Sırp Pırgiç Ermeni Hastanesi Vakfi v. Turkey, 16 December 2008, No. 50147/99.

European Commission on Human Rights

A.R.M. Chappell v. United Kingdom, 1987 (Admissibility) No. 12587/86, 53 DR 241, December 1987, p. 246.

C. v. United Kingdom, 1983, No. 10358/83.

Campbell and Cosans v. United Kingdom, 25 February 1982, Nos. 7511/76, 7743/76.

Church of X v. United Kingdom., 1968 (Admissibility), No. 3798/68, 13 Y.B. Eur. Conv. on H.R. 306, 1968.

Iglesia Bautista El Salvador and Ortega Moratilla v. Spain, 1992 (Admissibility), No. 17522/90, 72 DR 256, December 1992.

Omkarananda and the Divine Light Zentrum v. Switzerland, 1981 (Admissibility), No. 8118/77, 25 DR 105, 1981.

Scientology Kirche Deutschland v. Germany, 1997 (Admissibility), No. 34614/97.

X and the Church of Scientology v. Sweden, 1979, No. 7805/77, 16.

X. v. United Kingdom, No. 8160/78, 22 Eur. Commission H.R. Dec. & Rep. 27, 33 (1981)

Case law of Turkish Courts

Anayasa Mahkemesi [Constitutional Court], 07.03.1989, E/1989/1 and K/1989/12, AMKD No. 12 (1991), 133–165.

Anayasa Mahkemesi [Constitutional Court], 25 October 1983, E2/1983 and K2/1983, AMKD, No. 20, 364.

Anayasa Mahkemesi [Constitutional Court], E/22/2008, K/82/2010, 17 June 2010, R.G. No. 27812, 11 January 2011.

Anayasa Mahkemesi [Constitutional Court], E/1970/53, K/1971/76, 21 October 1971, Anayasa Mahkemesi Kararları Dergisi [Journal of Judgments of the Constitutional Court] (AMKD) No. 10, 52–79.

Ankara 31st Asliye Hukuk Mahkemesi [Civil Court of First Instance], E/819/2000, K/370/2001, 12 June 2000.

Asliye Sulh Mahkemesi [Civil Court of Peace] Edirne 1st, E/1998/469, K/1998/715, 22 December 1998.

Asliye Sulh Mahkemesi [Civil Court of Peace] Edirne 2nd, E/2000/277, K/2002/304, 30 May 2002.

Asliye Sulh Mahkemesi [Civil Court of Peace], Ankara 16th, E/2010/492, 4 October 2011.

Asliye Hukuk Mahkemesi [Civil Court of First Instance], Case No. 2010/225, 24 May 2010.

Danıştay [Council of State], 8th Chamber, 28 December 2007, E/2006/4107, K/2007/481, 29 February 2008, E/2007/679, K/2008/1461.

Danıştay [Council of State], 8th Chamber, E/2006/4107, K/2007/481, 28 December 2007, E/2007/679, K/2008/1461, 29 February 2008.

Yargıtay [Court of Appeals] 4th Chamber of the Criminal Division, E/2000/6756, K/2000/6043, 27 September 2000.

Yargıtay [Court of Appeals] 9th Chamber of the Criminal Division, E/1980/4847, K/1980/4952, 12 December 1980.

Yargıtay [Court of Appeals] 2nd Chamber, E/4449, K/4399, 6 July 1971.

Yargıtay [Court of Appeals] 7th Chamber, E/2012/262, K/2012/3351, 10 May 2012.

Yargıtay [Court of Appeals] 7th Criminal Chamber, E/2003/12950, K/2003/05182, 31 May 2005.

Yargıtay [Court of Appeals] 8th Chamber, E/2008/3743, K/2009/773, 12 February 2009.

Yargıtay [Court of Appeals], 18th Chamber, E/9599/2001, K/10706/2001, 4 January 2002.

Yargıtay [Court of Appeals], 18th Circuit, E/3402/2000, K/5989/2000, 29 May 2000.

Yargıtay [Court of Appeals], 18th Circuit, E/1995/717, K/1995/1097, 31 January 1995.

Yargıtay [Court of Appeals], 4th Chamber, E/2005/10694, K/2007/5603.

Yargıtay [Court of Appeals], 7th Chamber of the Civil Division, E/2012/262, K/2012/3351, 10 May 2012.

Yargıtay [Court of Appeals], 7th Criminal Circuit, E/1976/3580, K/1976/3580, 20 April 1976.

Yargıtay [Court of Appeals], E/2002/4282, K/2002/5693, 17 December 2002.

Yargıtay [Court of Appeals], 2nd Chamber, 4449E, 4399K, 6 July 1971.

Yargıtay Genel Kurulu [The General Council of High Court of Appeals], E/1983/7–403, K/1984/243, 25 June 1984.

Yargıtay Genel Kurulu [The General Council of the High Court of Appeals], E/1955/9, K/1955/17, 6 June 1955.

Yargıtay Hukuk Genel Kurulu [General Legal Council of the Court of Appeals], E/971/2–8420, K/974/505, 8 May 1974.

The Human Rights Committee

Lubicon Lake Band v. Canada, Communication No. 167/1984, UN Doc. Supp. No. 40 (A/45/40) at 1 (1990)

M.A.B., W.A.T. and J.-A.Y.T. v. Canada, Communication No. 570/1993, UN Doc. CCPR/C/50/D/570/1993 (1994)

Malakhovsky, S. and Alexander Pikul v. Belarus, Comm. No. 1207/2003 (Views of 26 July 2005).

Sister Immaculate Joseph and the 80 Teaching Sisters of the Holy Cross of the Third Order of Saint Francis in Menzingen of Sri Lanka v. Sri Lanka, Comm. No. 1249/2004 (Views of 21 October 2005).

Waldman, Arieh Hollis v. Canada, Communication No. 694/1996 (views of 3 November 1999) (2000) 7(2) IHRR 368.

Westerman, Paul v. The Netherlands, Communication No. 682/1996 (views of 3 November 1999) (2000) 7(2) IHRR 363.

Decisions and Documents of International Organizations

United Nations

Human Rights Committee

UN Doc. HRI/GEN/1/Rev.1 at 35 (1994), General Comment No. 22 of the Human Rights Committee on Article 18.

HRCttee General Comment 32 on Article 14, UN Doc. CCPR/C/GC/32, 23 August 2007.

HRCttee General Comment 31 on *The Nature of the General Obligation Imposed by the States Parties to the Covenant*, UN Doc. CCPR/C/21/Rev.1/Add.13, 2004.

HRCttee General Comment No. 34, UN Doc. CCPR/C/GC/34/CRP.2 (2010), para. 48.

HRCttee General Comment No. 16 on Article 17 (Right to Privacy), UN Doc. HRI/GEN/1/Rev.1 at 21 (1994).

HRCttee, General Comment 27, UN Doc. CCPR/C/21/Rev.1/Add.9, 2 November 1999.

HRCttee, 50th Session, *Concluding Observations: Costa Rica*, UN Doc. CCPR/C/79/Add.31.

HRCttee, *Concluding Observations: Uzbekistan*, UN Doc. CCPR/C/UZB/CO/3, 7 April 2010.

HRCttee, *Concluding Observations: Jordan*, UN Doc. CCPR/C/79/Add.35, para. 10.

HRCttee, *Concluding Observations: Iran*, UN Doc. CCPR/C/79/Add.25, para. 16.

HRCttee, *Concluding Observations: Mongolia*, UN Doc. CCPR/C/MNG/CO/5, 2 May 2011.

HRCttee, *Concluding Observations of the Human Rights Committee: Iran*, UN Doc. CCPR/C/79/Add.25.

HRCttee, *Concluding Observations Islamic Republic of Iran*, 3 August 1993, CCPR/C/79/Add.25.

HRCttee, *Concluding Observations: the Republic of Moldova*, 5 August 2002, CCPR/CO/75/MDA.

HRCtee, *Concluding Observations: Bulgaria*, 19 August 2011, CCPR/C/BGR/CO/3.

UN Special Rapporteur

Report of the Special Rapporteur on Freedom of Religion or Belief, UN Doc. A/67/303, 13 August 2012.

Report of the UN Special Rapporteur on Freedom of Religion or Belief, UN Doc. A/HRC/10/8/Add.1, 16 February 2009

Report of the Special Rapporteur on Freedom of Religion or Belief, Mission to Paraguay, UN Doc. A/HRC/19/60/Add.1.

Report of the UN Special Rapporteur following his Turkey visit A/55/280/Add.1, para. 160, 11 August 2000.

Report of the UN Special Rapporteur, UN Doc. A/57/274, 2002.

Digest of the Special Rapporteur on freedom of religion or belief, http://www.ohchr.org/EN/Issues/FreedomReligion/Pages/Standards.aspx [Accessed 11 November 2014].

Report of the UN Special Rapporteur on Freedom of Religion or Belief, UN Doc. A/HRCTTEE/10/8/Add.3, 26 January 2009.

Report of the UN Special Rapporteur on Freedom of Religion or Belief, UN Doc. A/HRC/6/5, 20 July 2007.

Report of the Special Rapporteur on Freedom of Religion or Belief, Asma Jahangir, and the Special Rapporteur on contemporary forms of racism, racial discrimination, xenophobia and related intolerance, Doudou Diène, UN Doc. A/HR/2/3, 20 September 2006.

Report of the UN Special Rapporteur on Freedom of Religion or Belief, A/HRC/16/53/Add.1, 14 February 2011.

Report of the UN Special Rapporteur on Freedom of Religion or Belief, UN Doc. A/HRC/19/60, 22 December 2011.

SR Report on Communications to Governments, UN Doc. HRC/4/21/Add.1, 8 March 2007.

Other

Krishnaswami, Arcot (1960) "Study of Discrimination in the Matter of Religious Rights and Practices", UN Doc. E/CN.4/Sub.2/200/Rev.1, UN Sales No. 60. XIV.2.

Benito, E.O. (1989) *Elimination of All Forms of Intolerance and Discrimination Based on Religion or Belief*, Human Rights Study Series No. 2, UN Sales No. E. 89. XIV.3, Geneva: United Nations Centre for Human Rights.

OSCE Human Dimension Commitments (2005) Vol. 1: Thematic Compilation, Warsaw: OSCE/ODIHR, 2nd ed.

OSCE/ODIHR (2004) *OSCE and Venice Commission Guidelines for Review of Legislation Pertaining to Religion or Belief.*

Submission to the Sub-Commission on Prevention of Discrimination and Protection of Minorities (1949) "Definition and Classification of Minorities", UN Doc. E/CN.4/Sub.2/85.

Toledo Guiding Principles on Teaching about Religions and Beliefs in Public Schools (2007) ODIHR Advisory Council of Experts on Freedom of Religion and Belief.

Venice Commission (2010) "Opinion on the Legal Status of Religious Communities in Turkey and the Right of the Orthodox Patriarchate of Istanbul to Use the Adjective 'Ecumenical'", Venice Commission, Opinion no. 535/2009, 15 March.

National Legal Material

Turkey

Aslında Vakıf Olan Tarihi ve Mimari Kıymeti Haiz Eski Eserlerin Vakıflar Umum Müdürlüğüne Devrine Dair Kanun [Law on the Transfer of Works that Have Historical and Architectural Value that are Actually Vakıfs to the General Directorate of Foundations], No. 7044, 10 September 1957.

www.ingramcontent.com/pod-product-compliance
Ingram Content Group UK Ltd.
Pitfield, Milton Keynes, MK11 3LW, UK
UKHW010956180926
475701UK00004B/392
* 9 7 8 0 3 6 7 5 9 5 4 3 2 *